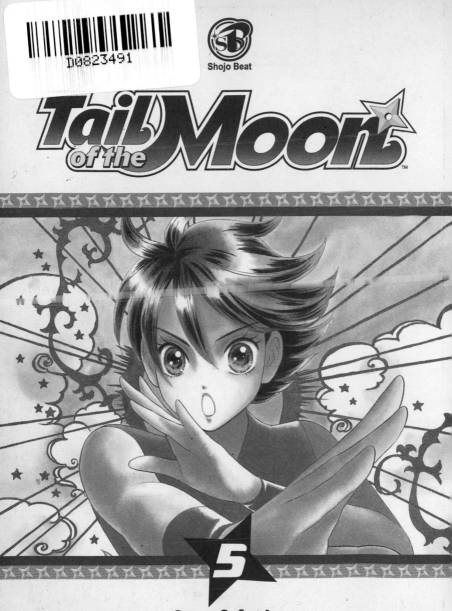

SB
Shojo Beat

Tail of the Moon
of the

5

Story & Art by
Rinko Ueda

Volume 5

CONTENTS

Story Thus Far...

It is the Era of the Warring States. Usagi is a failure as a ninja, but she is a skilled herbalist. She is working hard to qualify as a ninja so she can be the bride of Hattori Hanzo (aka "Shimo no Hanzo").

Usagi is living in Hamamatsu as Lord Ieyasu Tokugawa's herbalist. She is told that she may return to Iga once she succeeds in creating the elixir of eternal youth, so she heads for a mountain with Goemon and the others to meet a hermit who knows the recipe. There they meet the hermit, and after much trouble they are given the elixir. However, Yukimaru throws it into the fire! The hermit then teaches them that such an elixir should not exist, and tells them what eternal life truly is.

Usagi is given permission to return to Iga at last—and not only does Hanzo come to pick her up, but he even hugs her!! This leads him to tell her that she has gained too much weight. After they return to Iga, a mysterious woman suddenly appears...

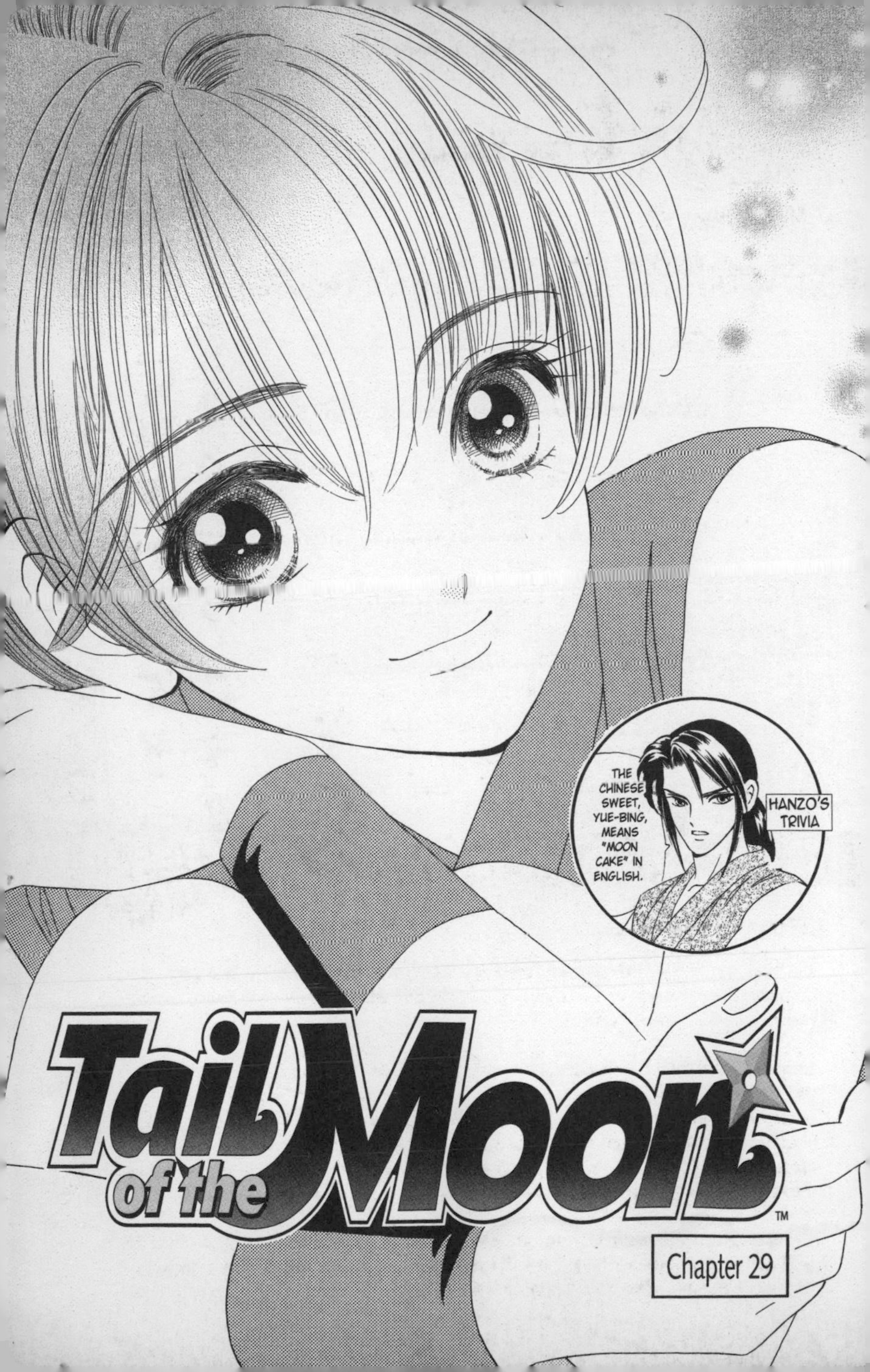

HANZO'S TRIVIA
THE CHINESE SWEET, YUE-BING, MEANS "MOON CAKE" IN ENGLISH.
Tail of the Moon™
Chapter 29

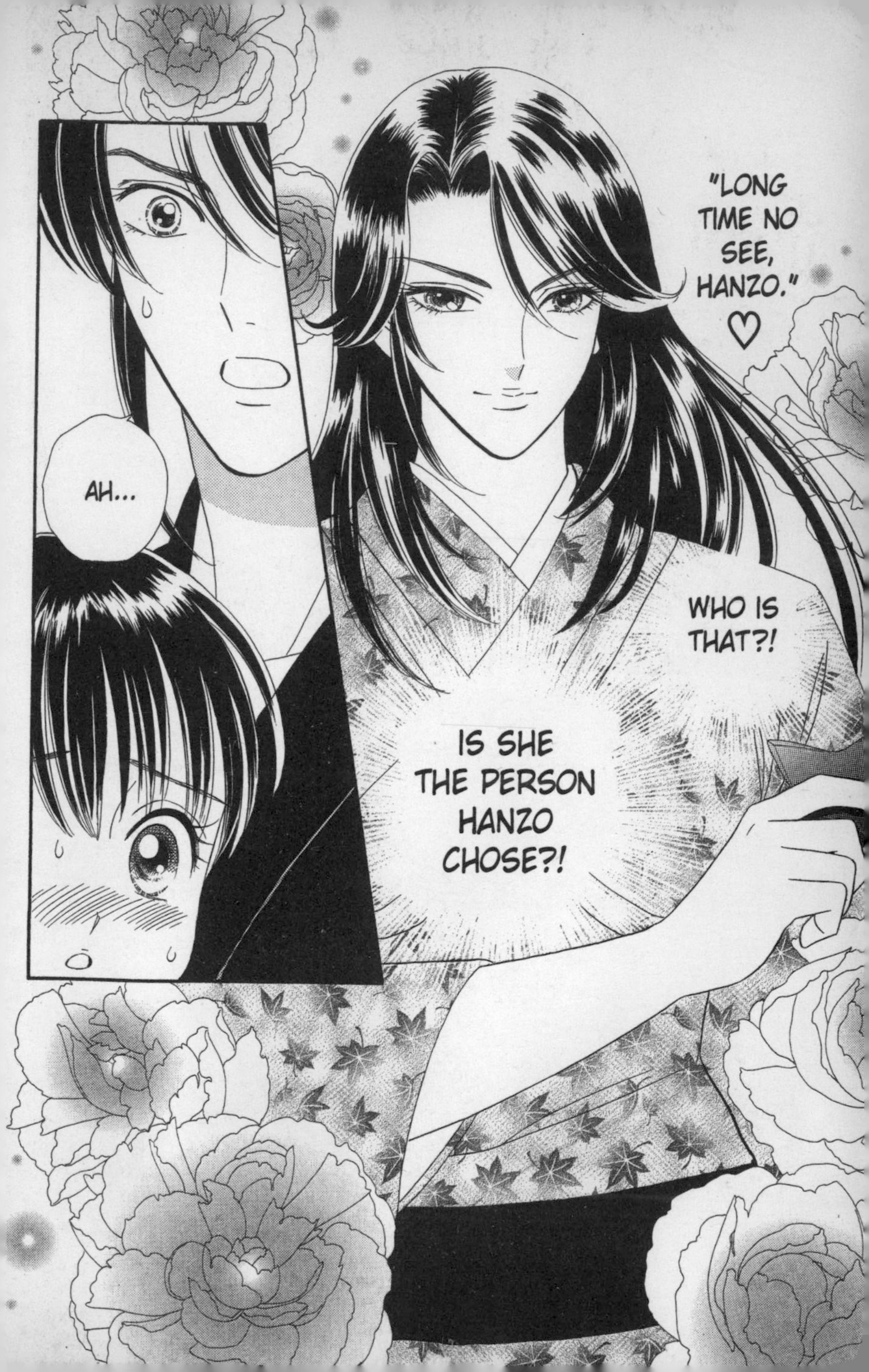
"LONG TIME NO SEE, HANZO." ♡
WHO IS THAT?!
IS SHE THE PERSON HANZO CHOSE?!
AH...

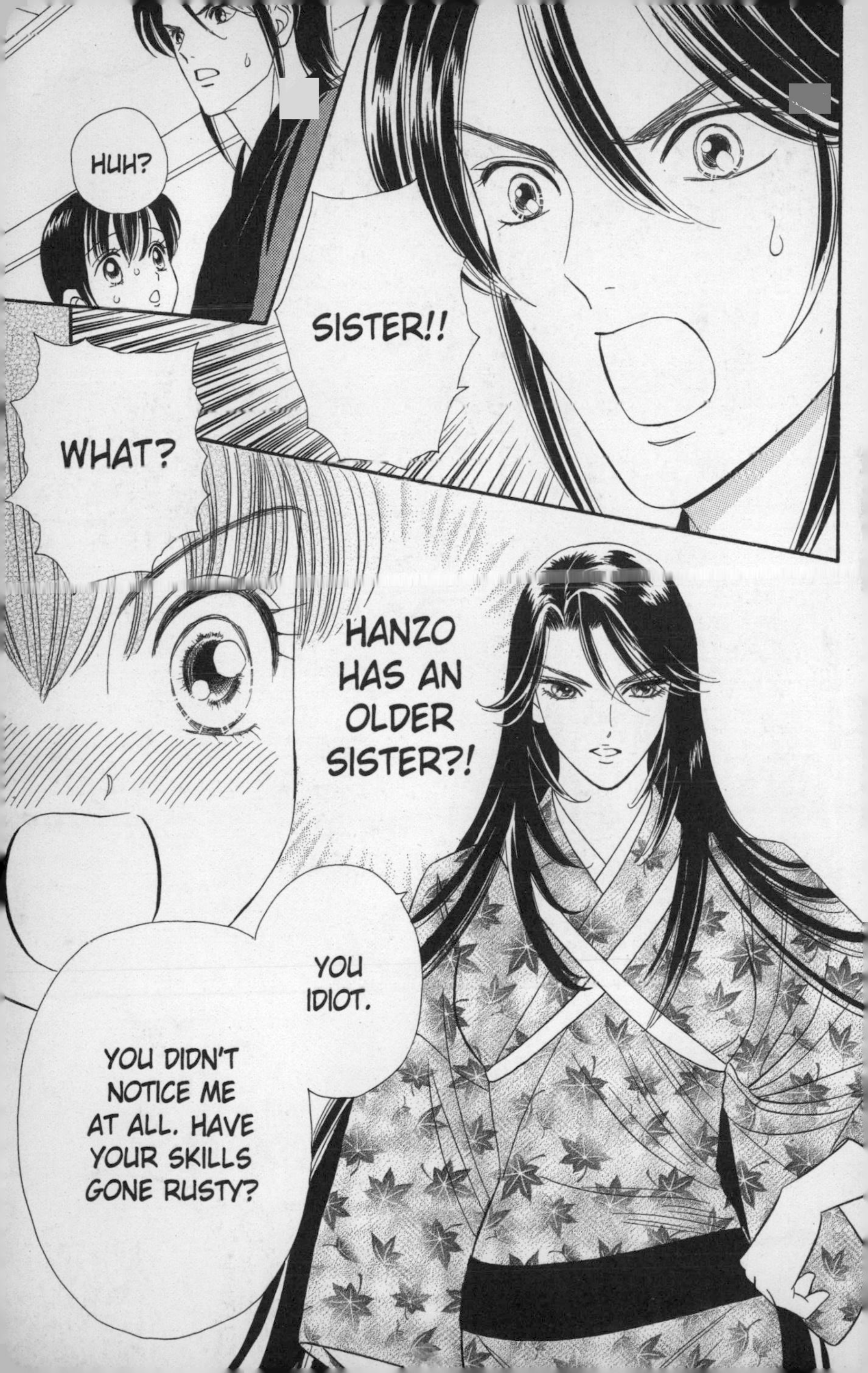
SISTER!!
HUH?
WHAT?
HANZO HAS AN OLDER SISTER?!
YOU IDIOT.
YOU DIDN'T NOTICE ME AT ALL. HAVE YOUR SKILLS GONE RUSTY?

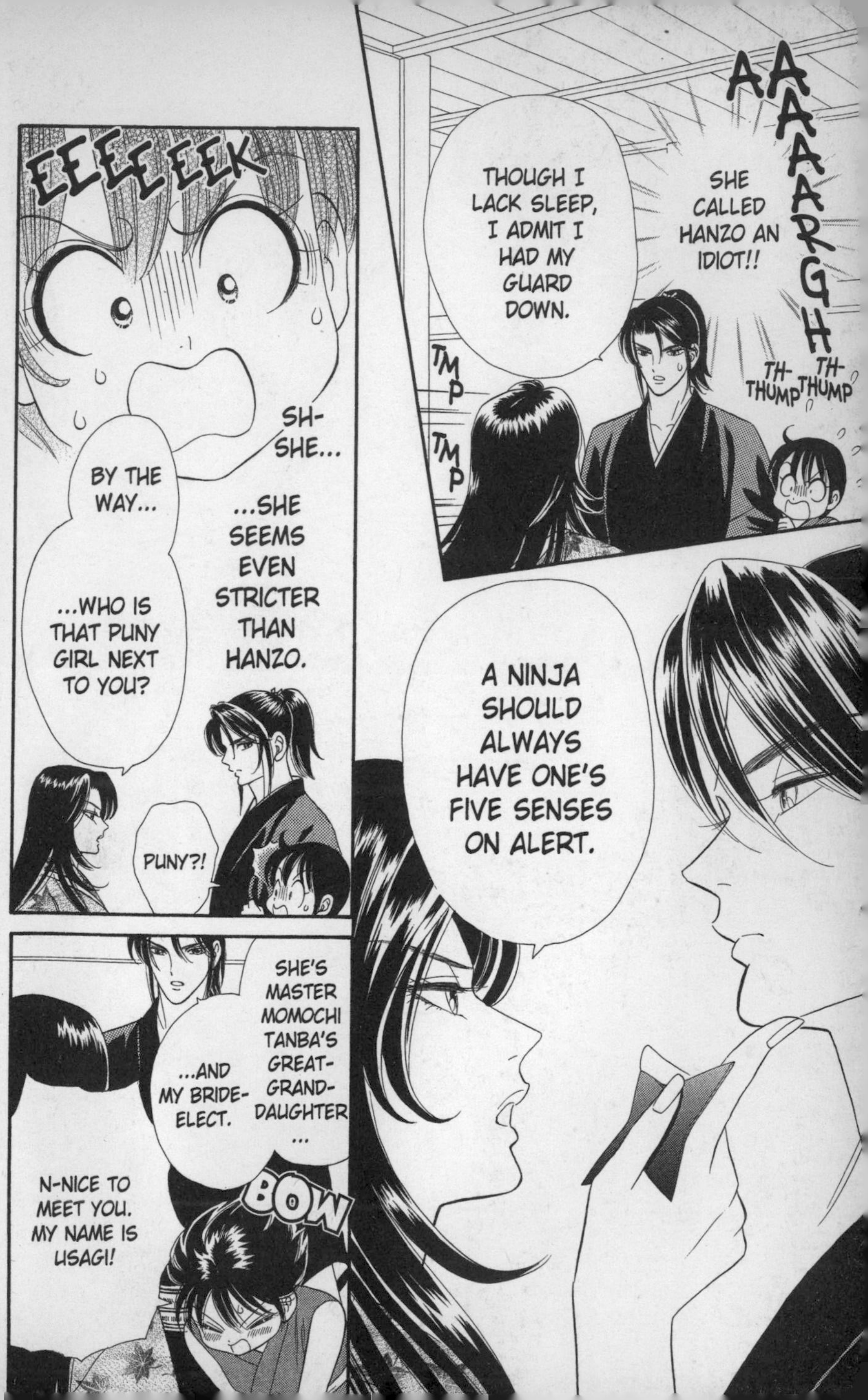

AAAAAARGH
SHE CALLED HANZO AN IDIOT!!
THOUGH I LACK SLEEP, I ADMIT I HAD MY GUARD DOWN.
TH-THUMP TH-THUMP
TMP TMP
A NINJA SHOULD ALWAYS HAVE ONE'S FIVE SENSES ON ALERT.
EEEEEEK
SH-SHE...
...SHE SEEMS EVEN STRICTER THAN HANZO.
BY THE WAY...
...WHO IS THAT PUNY GIRL NEXT TO YOU?
PUNY?!
SHE'S MASTER MOMOCHI TANBA'S GREAT-GRAND-DAUGHTER...
...AND MY BRIDE-ELECT.
BOW
N-NICE TO MEET YOU. MY NAME IS USAGI!

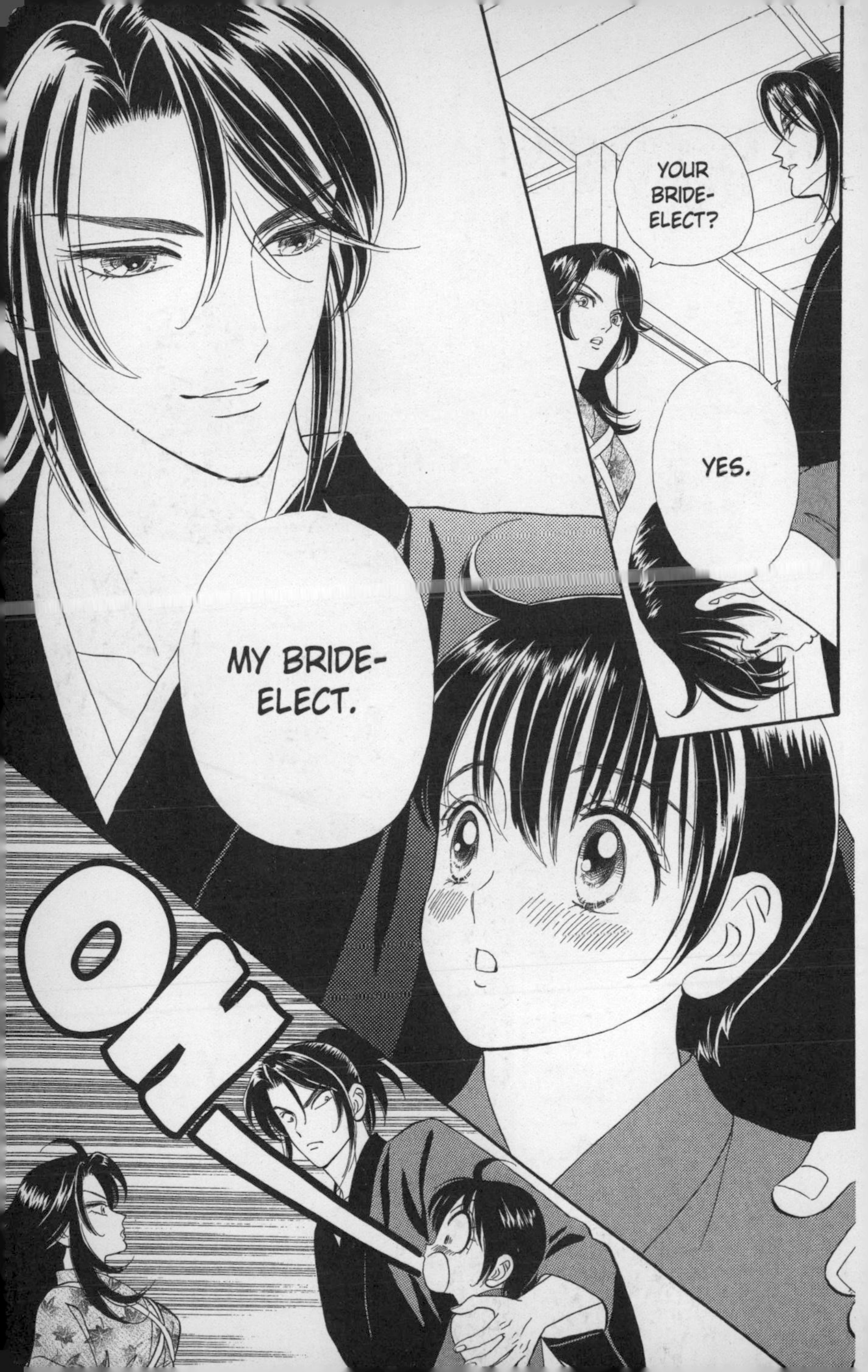
YOUR BRIDE-ELECT?
YES.
MY BRIDE-ELECT.
OH

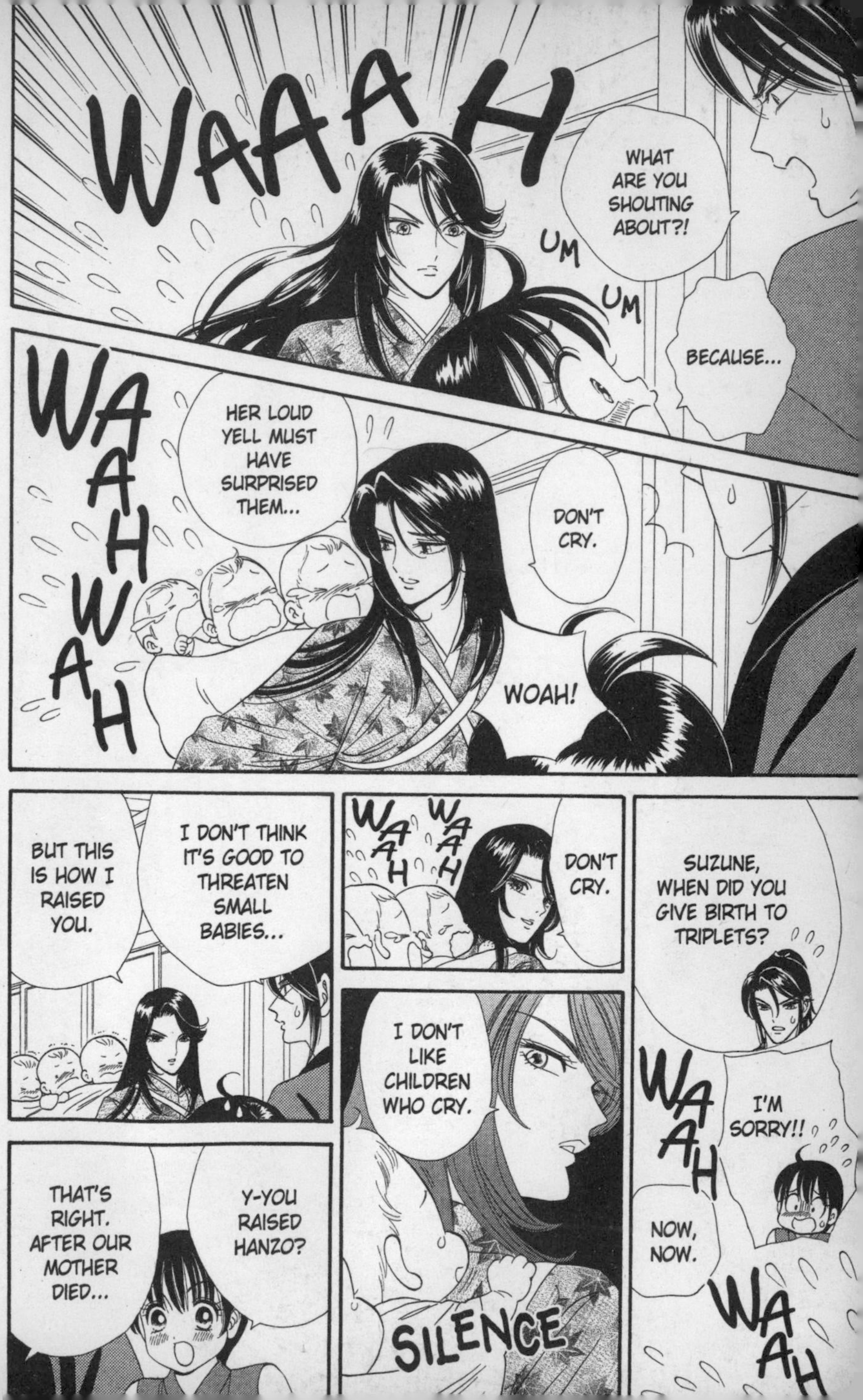
WAAAH
WHAT ARE YOU SHOUTING ABOUT?!
UM
UM
BECAUSE...
DON'T CRY.
HER LOUD YELL MUST HAVE SURPRISED THEM...
WOAH!
WAAHWAAH
SUZUNE, WHEN DID YOU GIVE BIRTH TO TRIPLETS?
WAAH
I'M SORRY!!
NOW, NOW.
WAAH
WAAH
WAAH
DON'T CRY.
I DON'T LIKE CHILDREN WHO CRY.
SILENCE
I DON'T THINK IT'S GOOD TO THREATEN SMALL BABIES...
BUT THIS IS HOW I RAISED YOU.
Y-YOU RAISED HANZO?
THAT'S RIGHT. AFTER OUR MOTHER DIED...

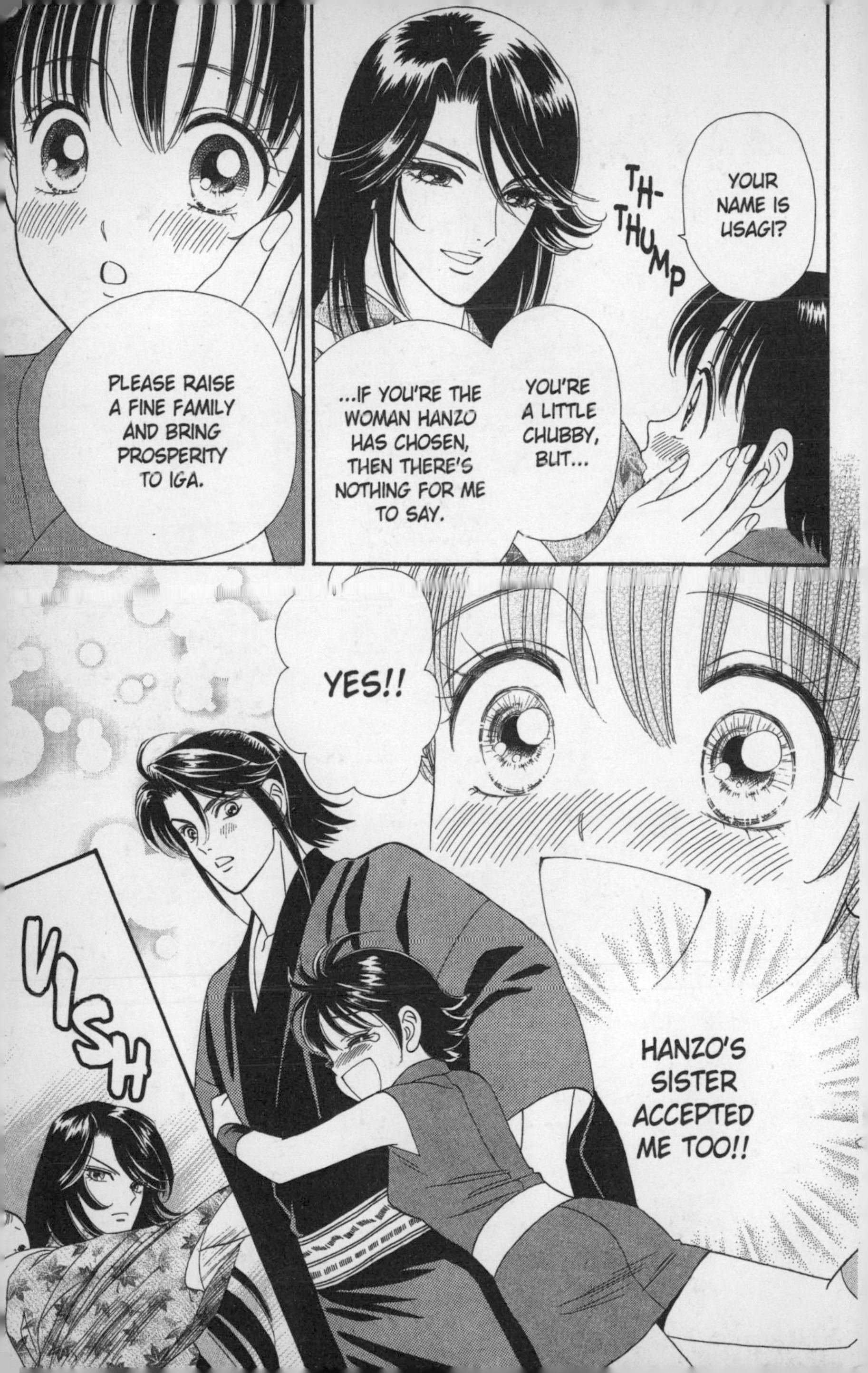
YOUR NAME IS USAGI?
TH-THUMP
YOU'RE A LITTLE CHUBBY, BUT...
...IF YOU'RE THE WOMAN HANZO HAS CHOSEN, THEN THERE'S NOTHING FOR ME TO SAY.
PLEASE RAISE A FINE FAMILY AND BRING PROSPERITY TO IGA.
YES!!
HANZO'S SISTER ACCEPTED ME TOO!!
VISH

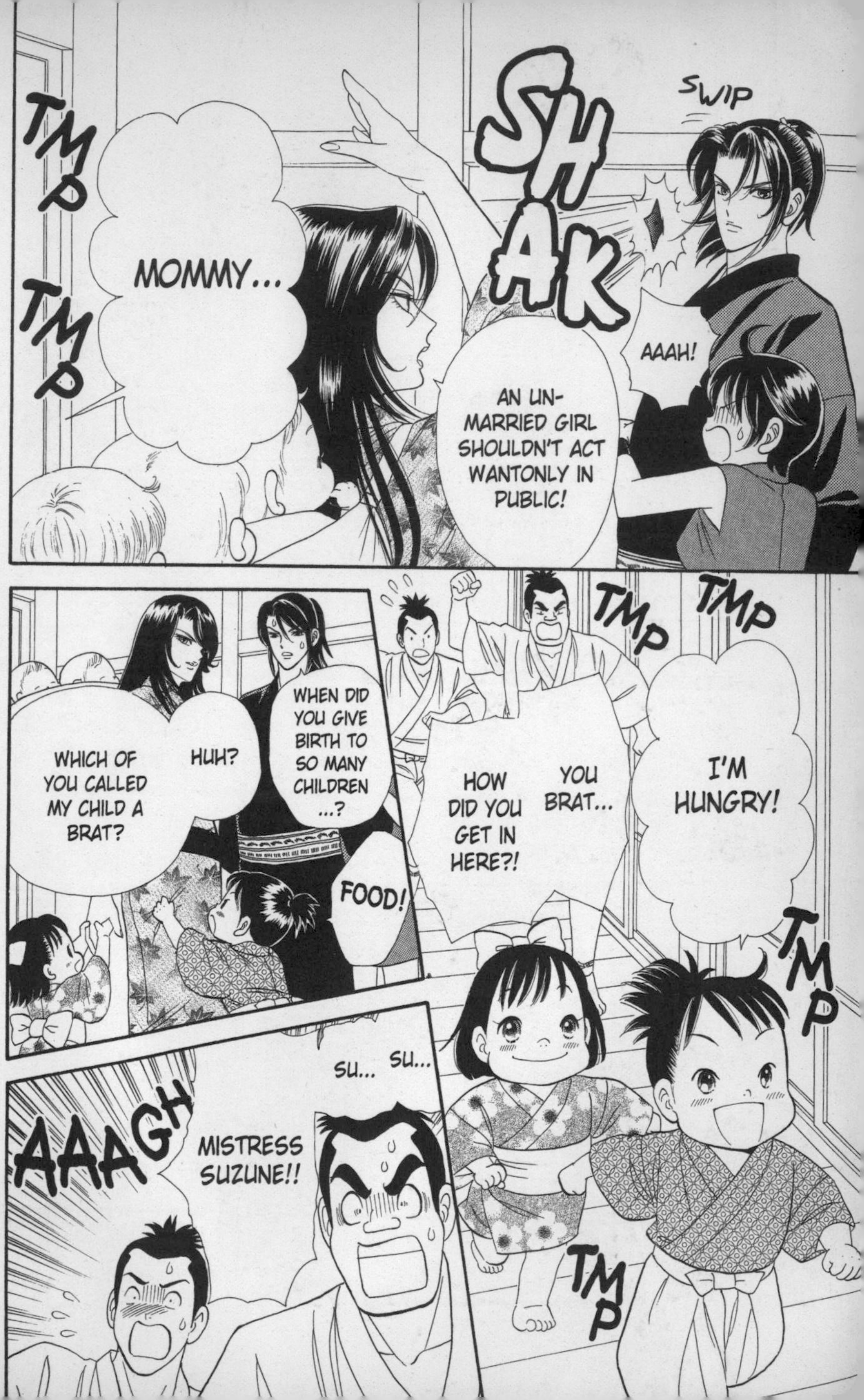
SWIP
SHAK
AAAH!
AN UN-MARRIED GIRL SHOULDN'T ACT WANTONLY IN PUBLIC!
MOMMY...
TMP
TMP
TMP
TMP
I'M HUNGRY!
YOU BRAT...
HOW DID YOU GET IN HERE?!
TMP
WHEN DID YOU GIVE BIRTH TO SO MANY CHILDREN ...?
HUH?
WHICH OF YOU CALLED MY CHILD A BRAT?
FOOD!
SU... SU...
MISTRESS SUZUNE!!
AAAGH
TMP

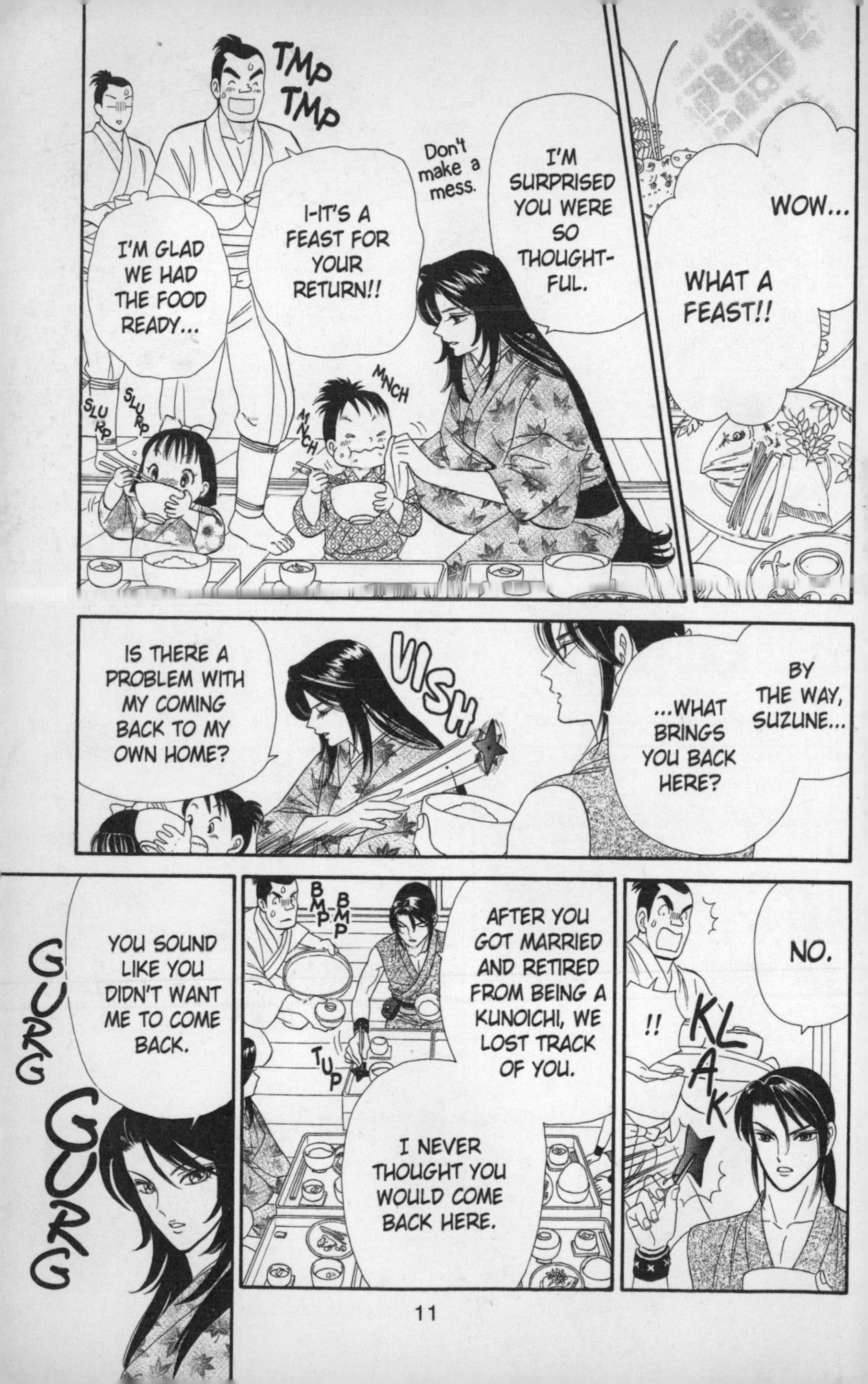
WOW...
WHAT A FEAST!!
I'M SURPRISED YOU WERE SO THOUGHTFUL.
Don't make a mess.
TMP TMP
I-IT'S A FEAST FOR YOUR RETURN!!
I'M GLAD WE HAD THE FOOD READY...
MNCH MNCH
SLURP SLURP
BY THE WAY, SUZUNE...
...WHAT BRINGS YOU BACK HERE?
VISH
IS THERE A PROBLEM WITH MY COMING BACK TO MY OWN HOME?
NO.
!!
KLAK
AFTER YOU GOT MARRIED AND RETIRED FROM BEING A KUNOICHI, WE LOST TRACK OF YOU.
BMP BMP
TUP
I NEVER THOUGHT YOU WOULD COME BACK HERE.
YOU SOUND LIKE YOU DIDN'T WANT ME TO COME BACK.
GURG GURG

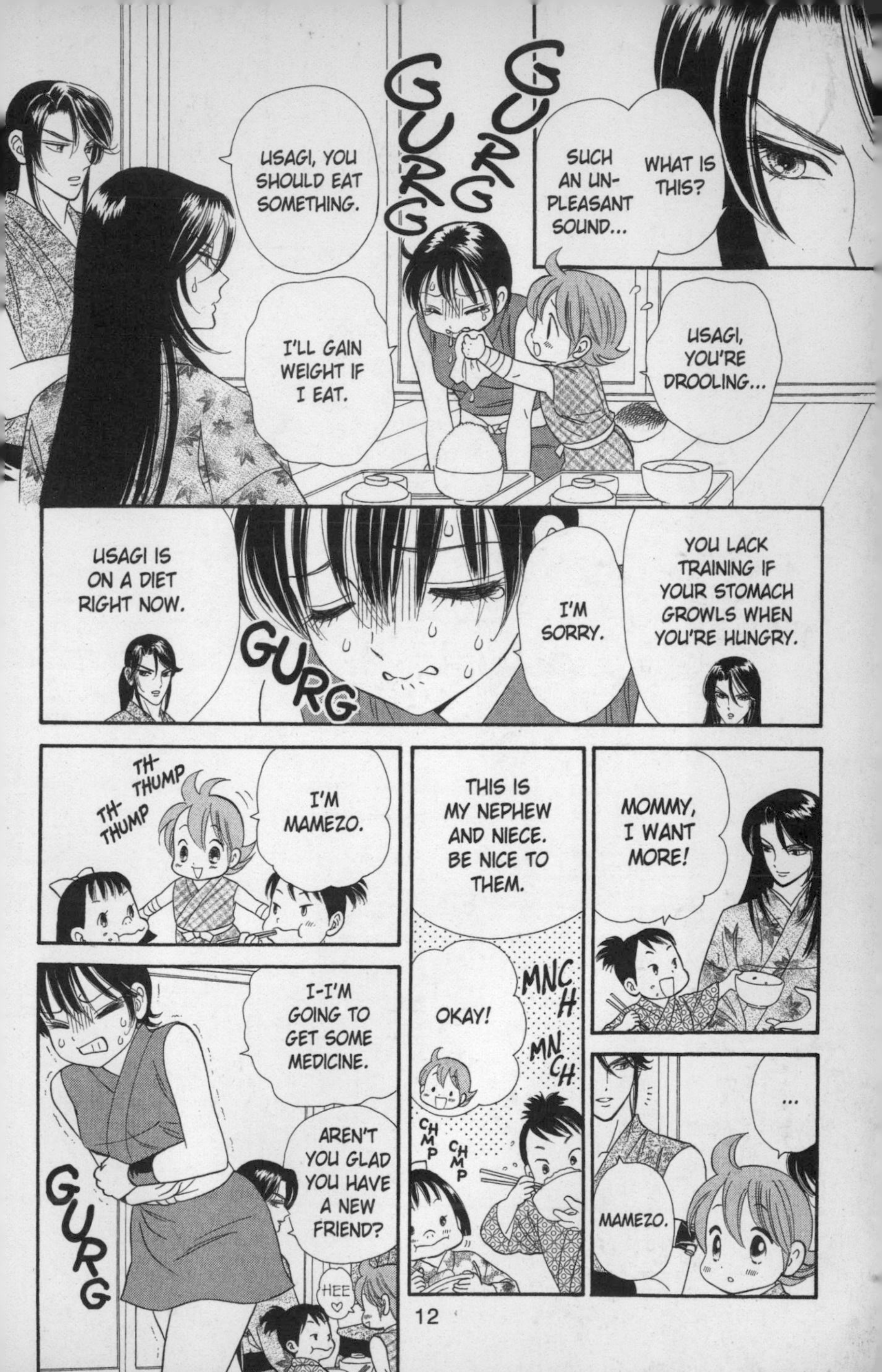
WHAT IS THIS?
SUCH AN UN-PLEASANT SOUND...
GURG
GURG
USAGI, YOU'RE DROOLING...
USAGI, YOU SHOULD EAT SOMETHING.
I'LL GAIN WEIGHT IF I EAT.
YOU LACK TRAINING IF YOUR STOMACH GROWLS WHEN YOU'RE HUNGRY.
I'M SORRY.
GURG
USAGI IS ON A DIET RIGHT NOW.
MOMMY, I WANT MORE!
...
MAMEZO.
THIS IS MY NEPHEW AND NIECE. BE NICE TO THEM.
MNCH
MNCH
OKAY!
CHMP
CHMP
I'M MAMEZO.
TH-THUMP
TH-THUMP
I-I'M GOING TO GET SOME MEDICINE.
AREN'T YOU GLAD YOU HAVE A NEW FRIEND?
HEE
GURG

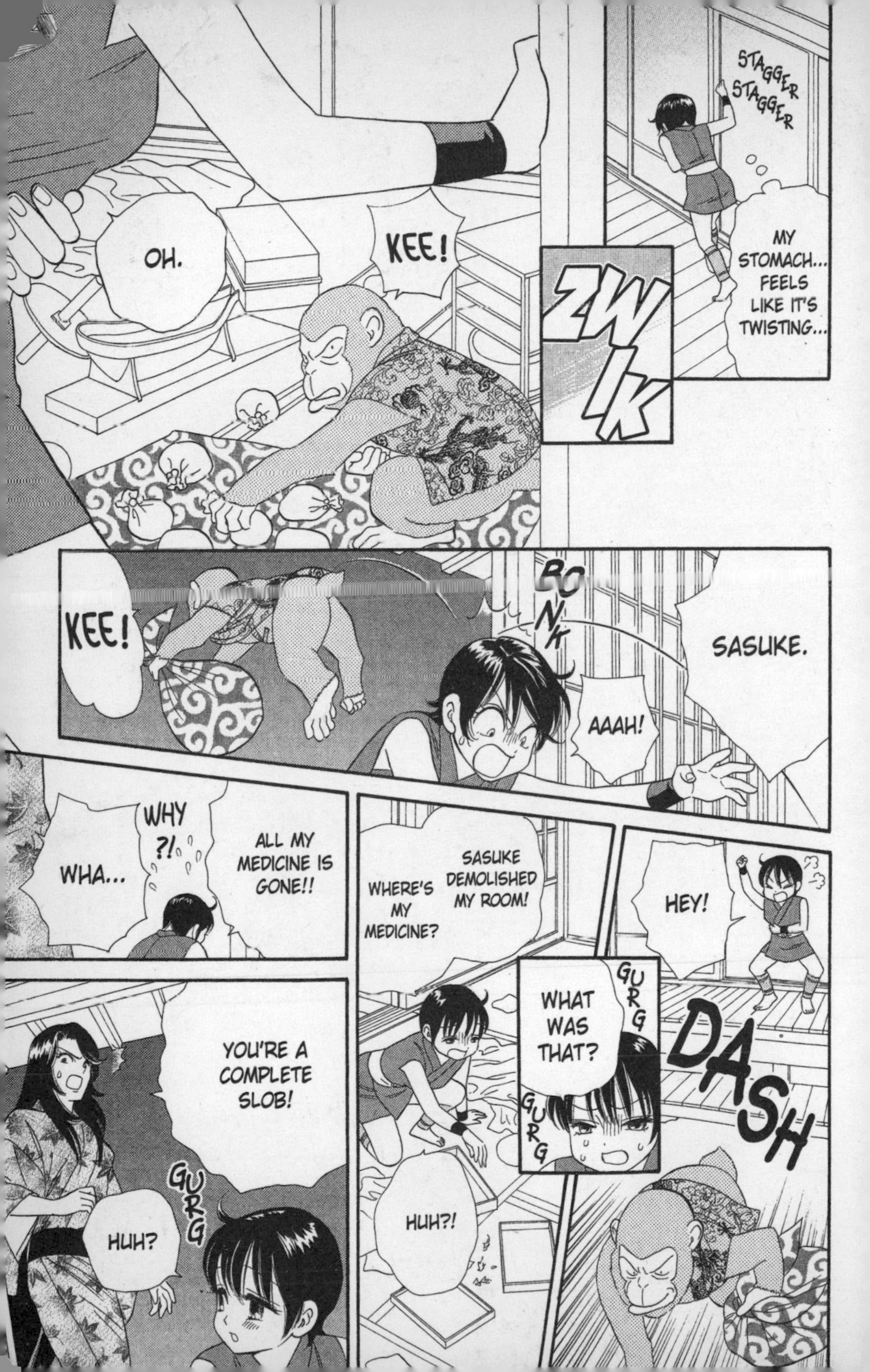
STAGGER STAGGER
MY STOMACH... FEELS LIKE IT'S TWISTING...
ZWIK
KEE!
OH.
SASUKE.
AAAH!
BONK
KEE!
HEY!
DASH
WHAT WAS THAT?
GURG GURG
SASUKE DEMOLISHED MY ROOM!
WHERE'S MY MEDICINE?
HUH?!
ALL MY MEDICINE IS GONE!!
WHY ?!
WHA...
YOU'RE A COMPLETE SLOB!
GURG
HUH?

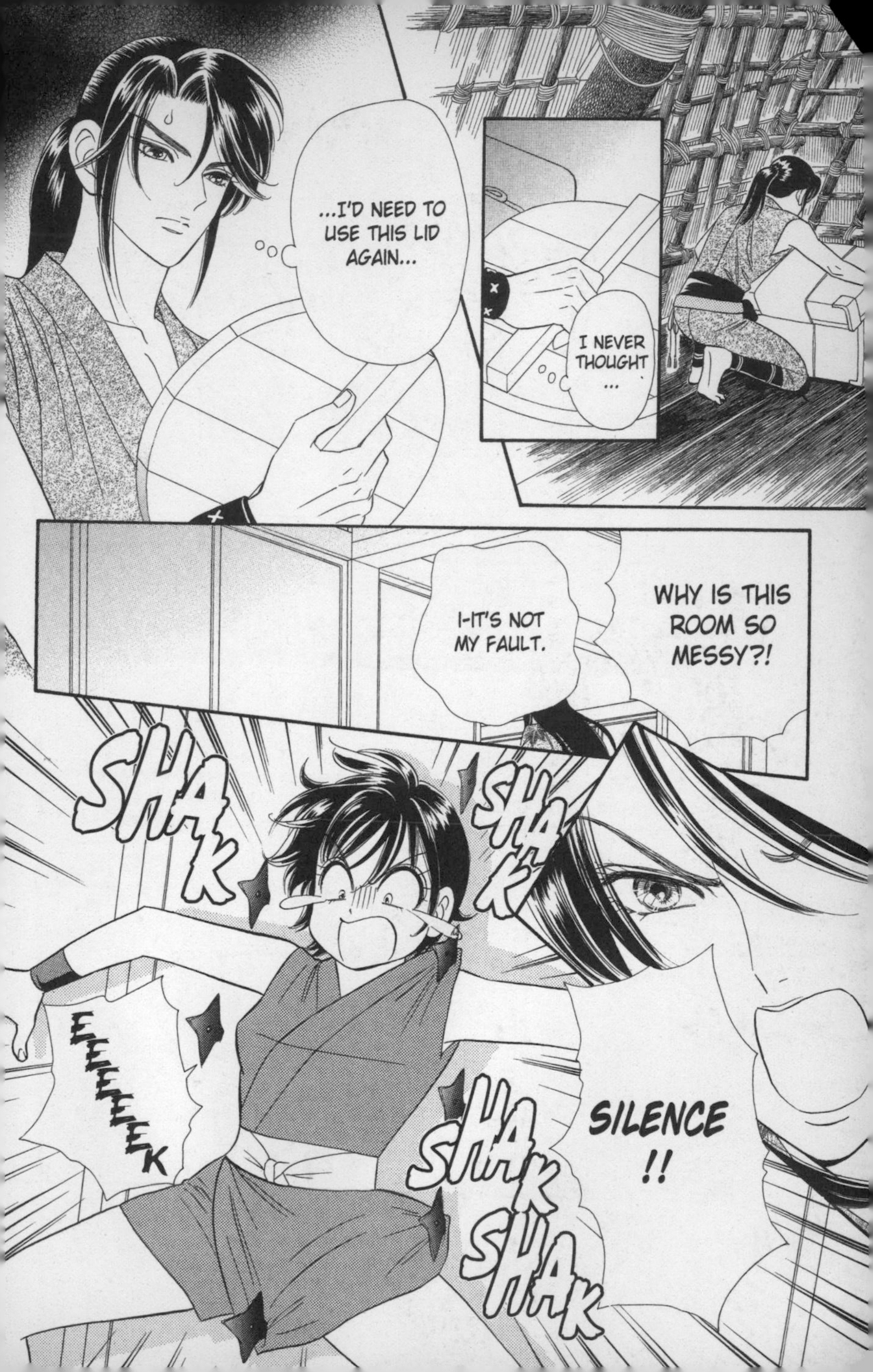
I NEVER THOUGHT ...
...I'D NEED TO USE THIS LID AGAIN...
WHY IS THIS ROOM SO MESSY?!
I-IT'S NOT MY FAULT.
SHAK
SILENCE !!
SHAK SHAK
SHAK
EEEEEEEK
SHAK

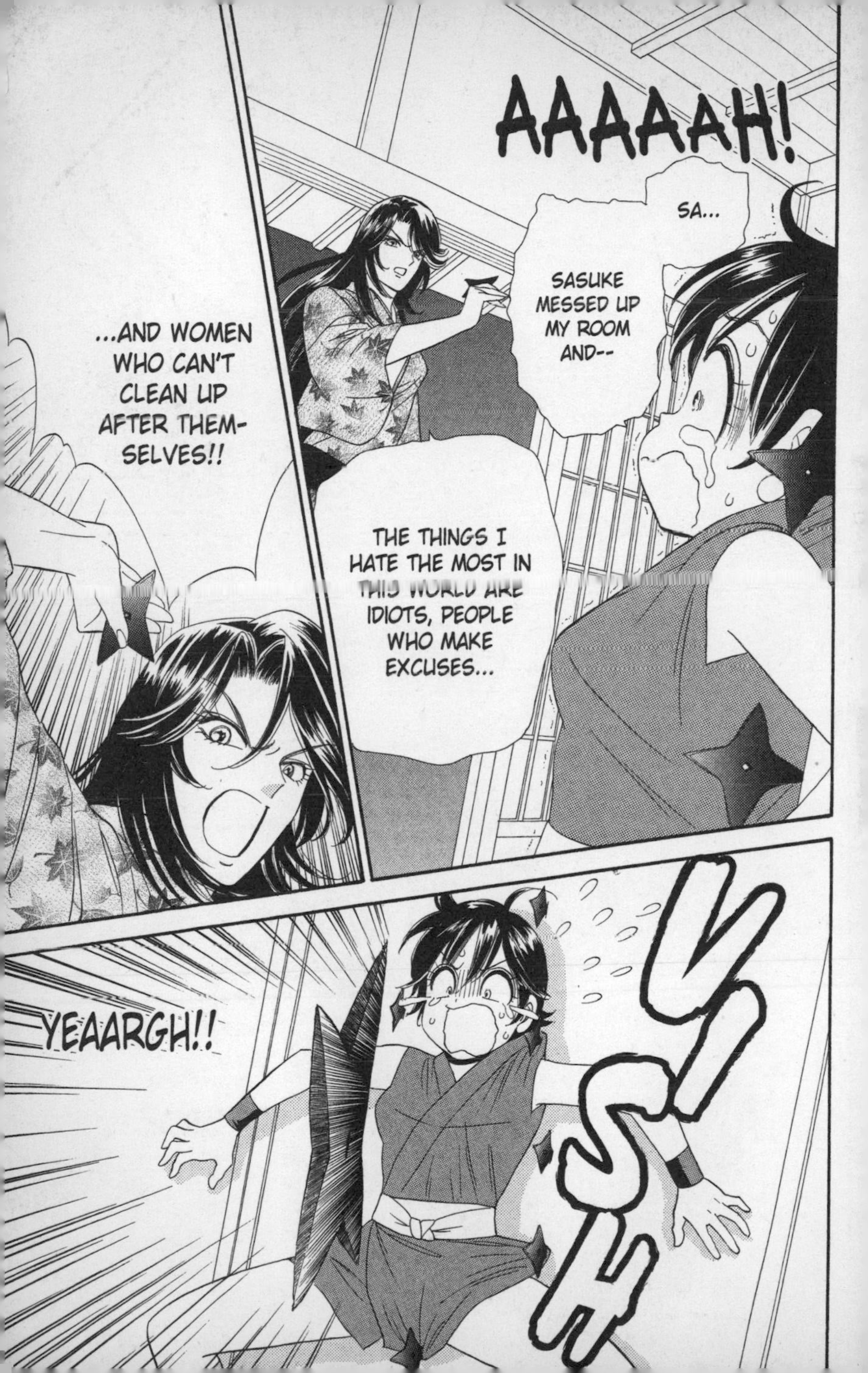
AAAAAH!
SA...
SASUKE MESSED UP MY ROOM AND--
THE THINGS I HATE THE MOST IN THIS WORLD ARE IDIOTS, PEOPLE WHO MAKE EXCUSES...
...AND WOMEN WHO CAN'T CLEAN UP AFTER THEMSELVES!!
YEAARGH!!

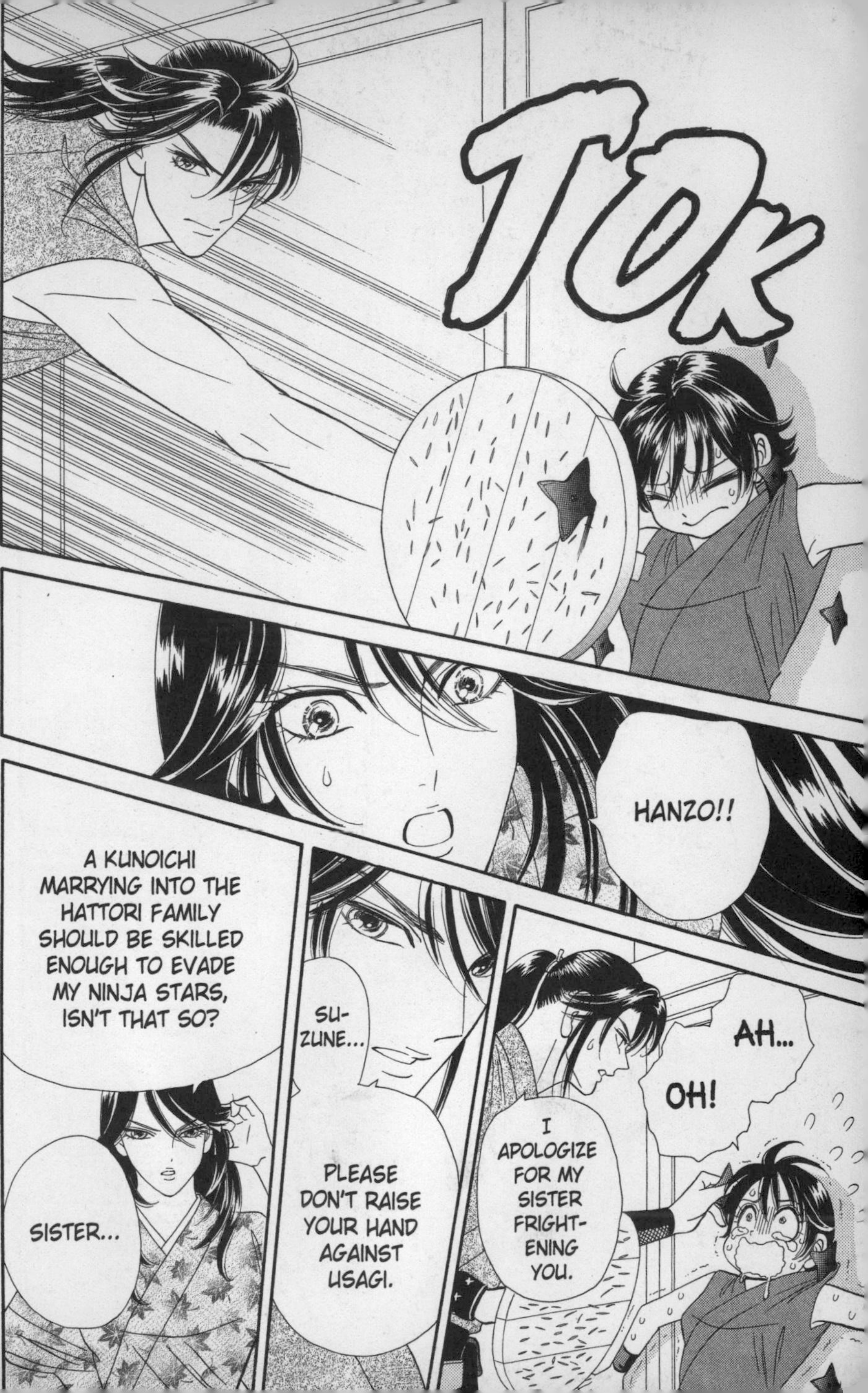
TOK
HANZO!!
AH... OH!
I APOLOGIZE FOR MY SISTER FRIGHT-ENING YOU.
SU-ZUNE...
PLEASE DON'T RAISE YOUR HAND AGAINST USAGI.
A KUNOICHI MARRYING INTO THE HATTORI FAMILY SHOULD BE SKILLED ENOUGH TO EVADE MY NINJA STARS, ISN'T THAT SO?
SISTER...

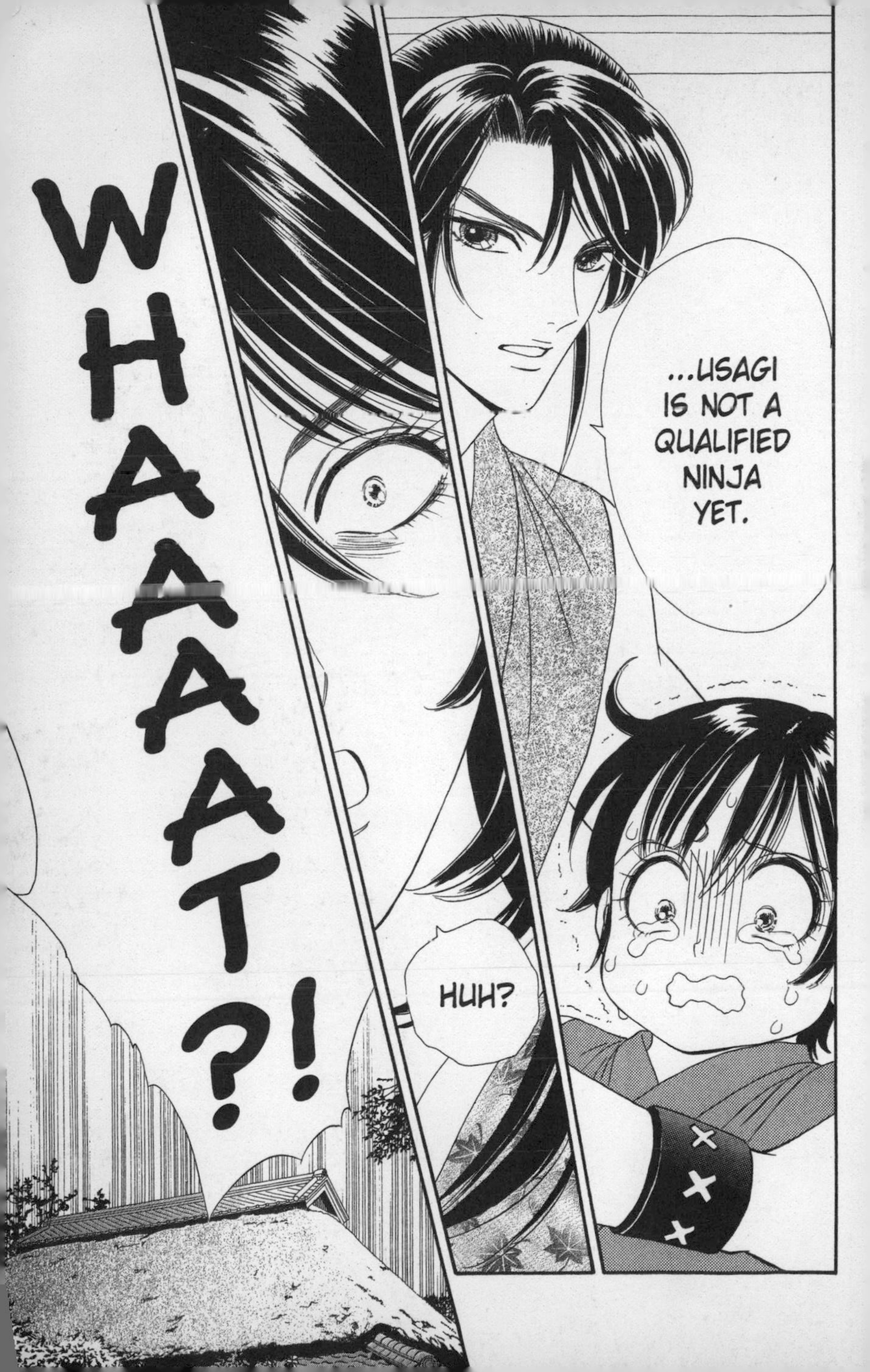
...USAGI IS NOT A QUALIFIED NINJA YET.
HUH?
WHAAAAT?!

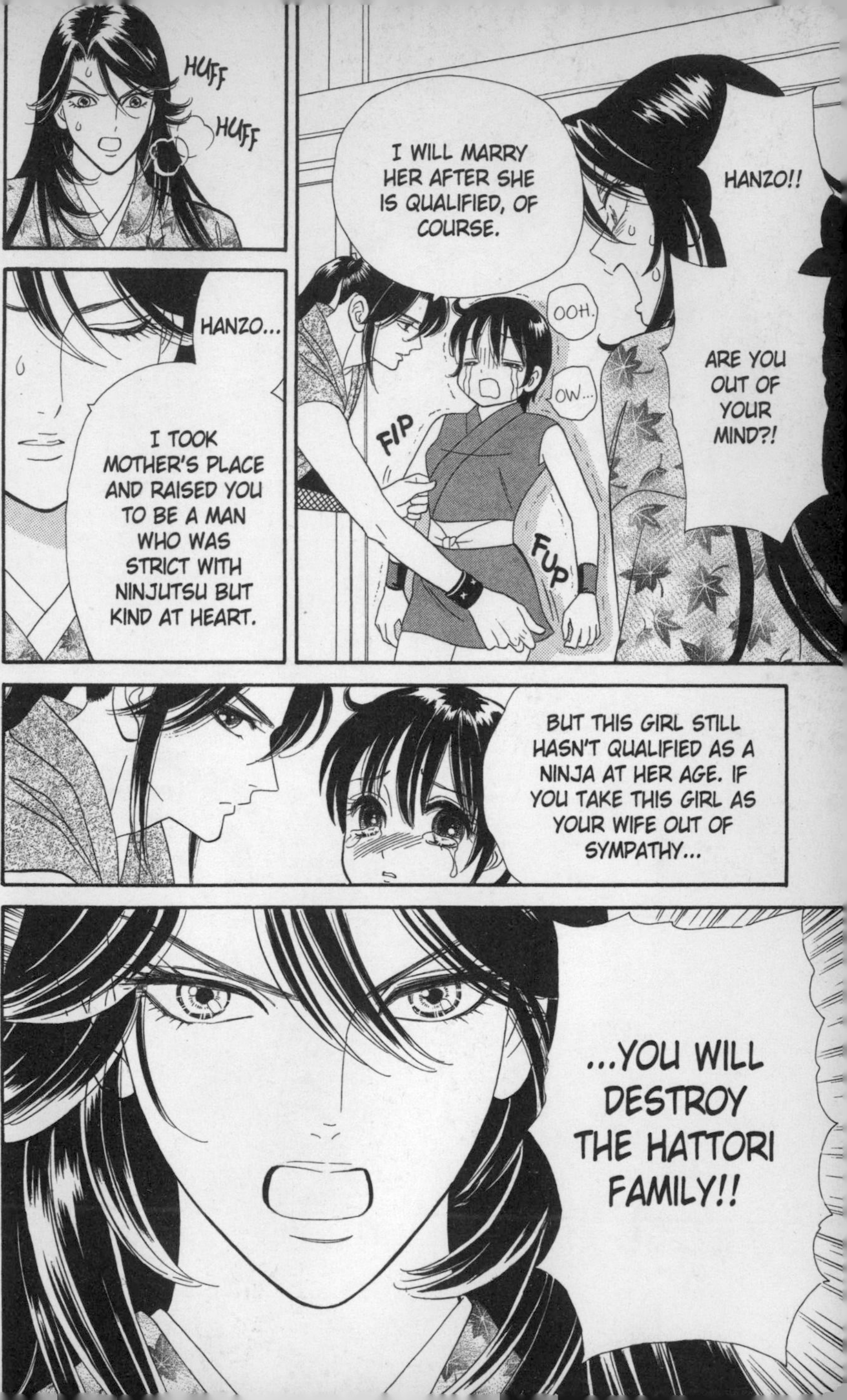
I WILL MARRY HER AFTER SHE IS QUALIFIED, OF COURSE.
HANZO!!
ARE YOU OUT OF YOUR MIND?!
OOH.
OW...
FIP
FUP
HUFF
HUFF
HANZO...
I TOOK MOTHER'S PLACE AND RAISED YOU TO BE A MAN WHO WAS STRICT WITH NINJUTSU BUT KIND AT HEART.
BUT THIS GIRL STILL HASN'T QUALIFIED AS A NINJA AT HER AGE. IF YOU TAKE THIS GIRL AS YOUR WIFE OUT OF SYMPATHY...
...YOU WILL DESTROY THE HATTORI FAMILY!!

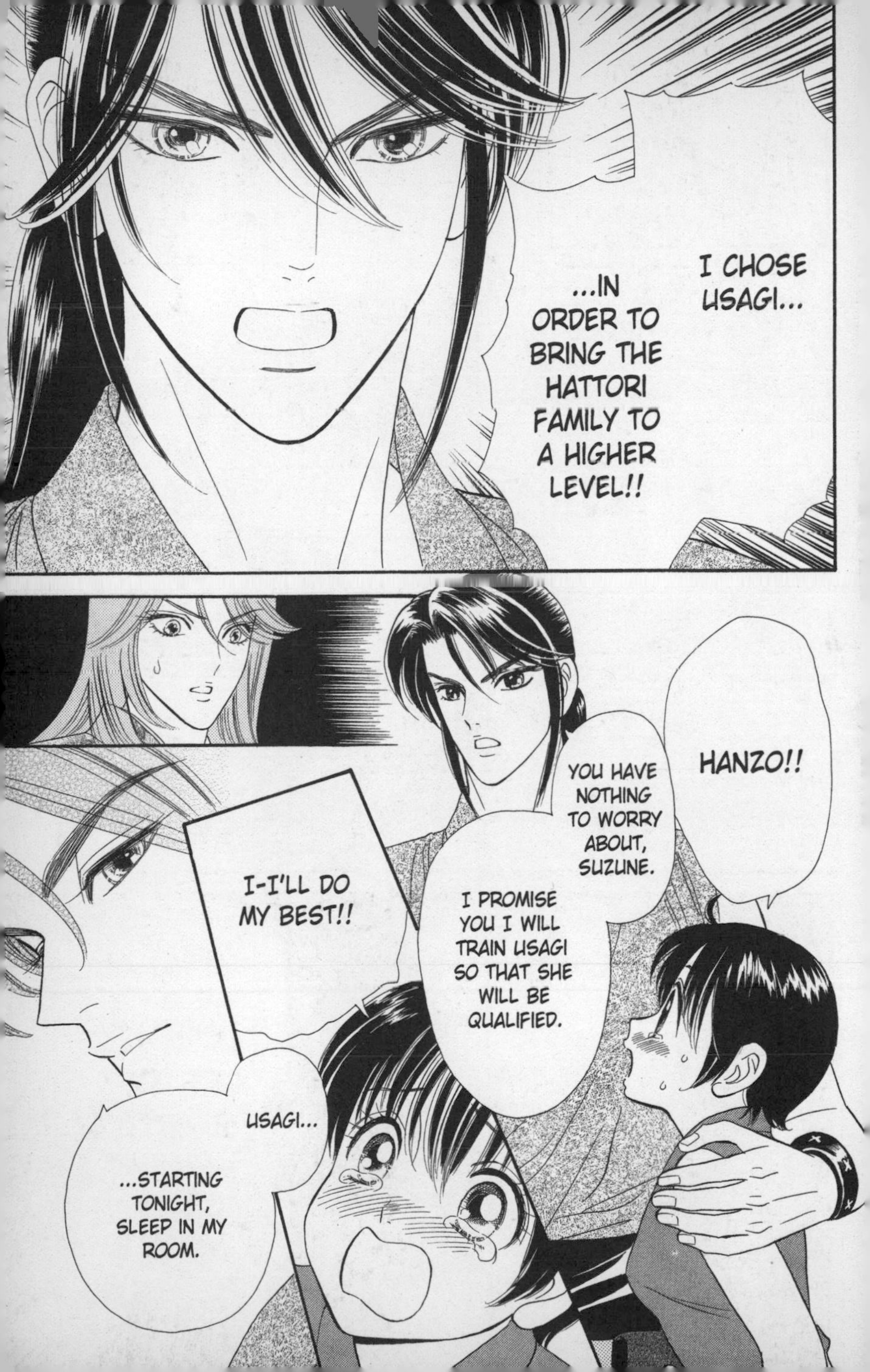
I CHOSE USAGI...
...IN ORDER TO BRING THE HATTORI FAMILY TO A HIGHER LEVEL!!
HANZO!!
YOU HAVE NOTHING TO WORRY ABOUT, SUZUNE.
I PROMISE YOU I WILL TRAIN USAGI SO THAT SHE WILL BE QUALIFIED.
I-I'LL DO MY BEST!!
USAGI...
...STARTING TONIGHT, SLEEP IN MY ROOM.

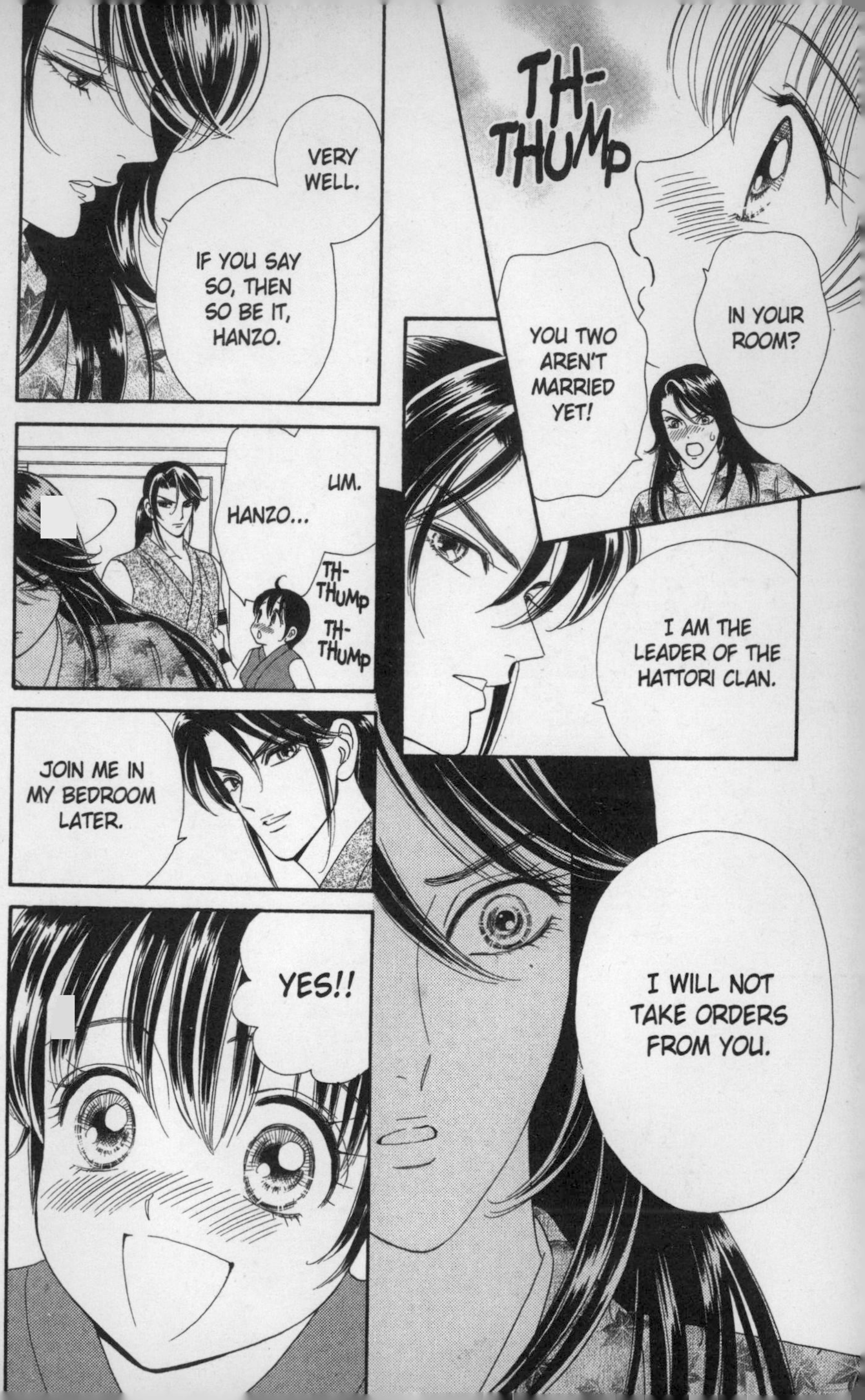
TH-THUMP
IN YOUR ROOM?
YOU TWO AREN'T MARRIED YET!
I AM THE LEADER OF THE HATTORI CLAN.
I WILL NOT TAKE ORDERS FROM YOU.
VERY WELL.
IF YOU SAY SO, THEN SO BE IT, HANZO.
UM.
HANZO...
TH-THUMP
TH-THUMP
JOIN ME IN MY BEDROOM LATER.
YES!!

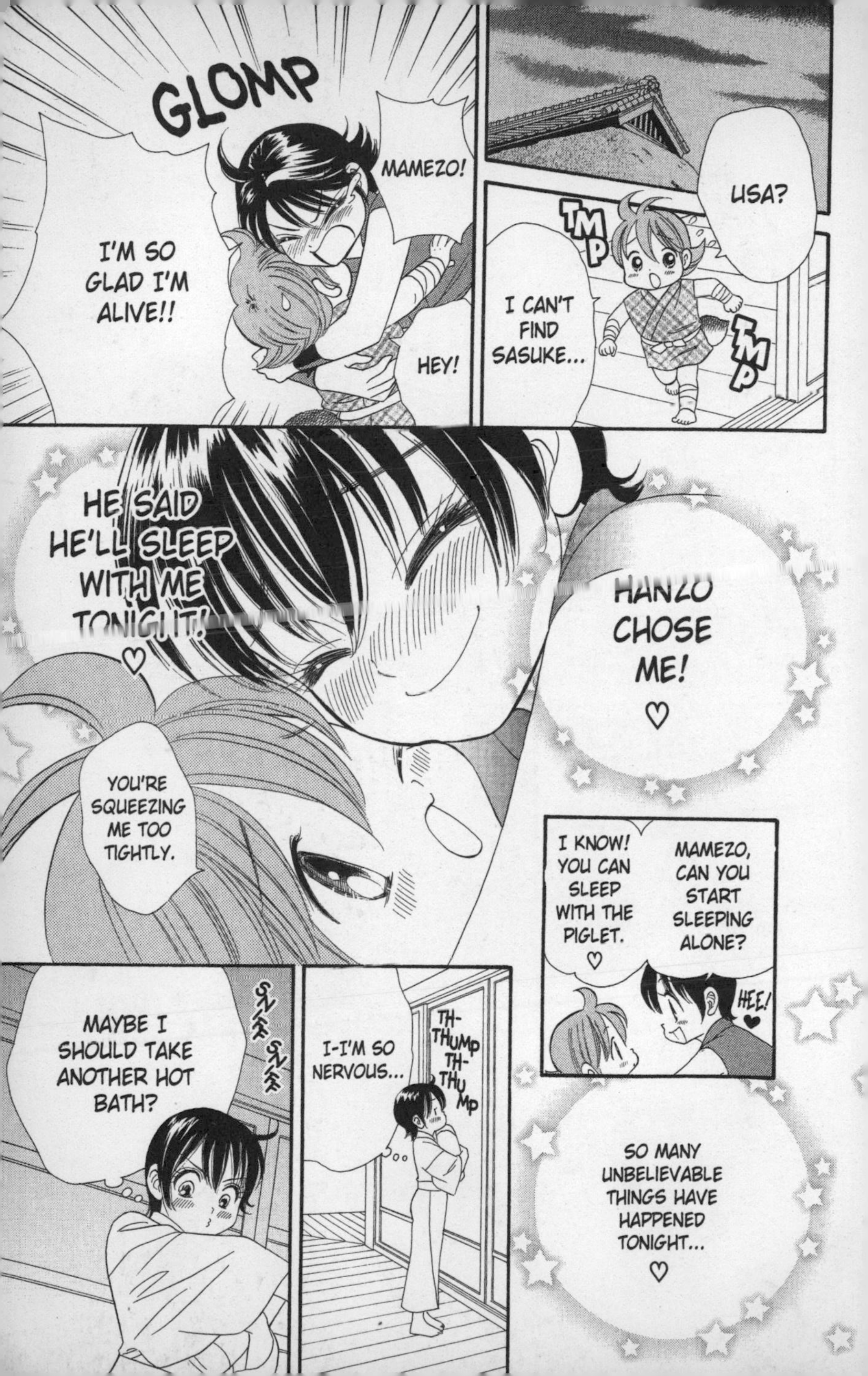
USA?
TMP
I CAN'T FIND SASUKE...
TMP
GLOMP
MAMEZO!
HEY!
I'M SO GLAD I'M ALIVE!!
HANZO CHOSE ME! ♡
HE SAID HE'LL SLEEP WITH ME TONIGHT! ♡
YOU'RE SQUEEZING ME TOO TIGHTLY.
MAMEZO, CAN YOU START SLEEPING ALONE?
I KNOW! YOU CAN SLEEP WITH THE PIGLET. ♡
HEE! ♥
SO MANY UNBELIEVABLE THINGS HAVE HAPPENED TONIGHT... ♡
TH-THUMP TH-THUMP
I-I'M SO NERVOUS...
SNIFF SNIFF
MAYBE I SHOULD TAKE ANOTHER HOT BATH?

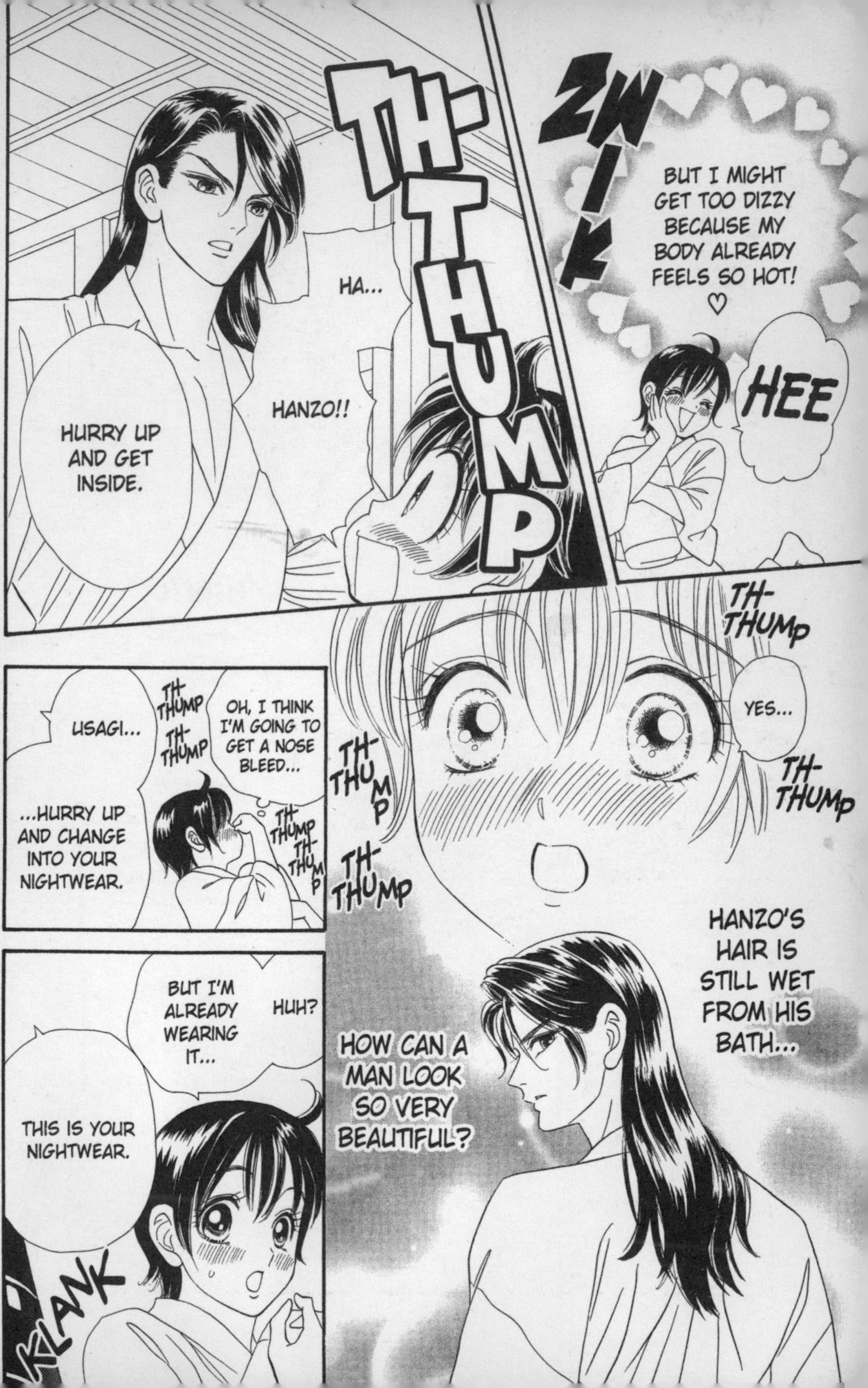
ZWIIK
BUT I MIGHT GET TOO DIZZY BECAUSE MY BODY ALREADY FEELS SO HOT! ♡
HEE
TH-THUMP
HA...
HANZO!!
HURRY UP AND GET INSIDE.
TH-THUMP
YES...
TH-THUMP
TH-THUMP
TH-THUMP
HANZO'S HAIR IS STILL WET FROM HIS BATH...
HOW CAN A MAN LOOK SO VERY BEAUTIFUL?
OH, I THINK I'M GOING TO GET A NOSE BLEED...
TH-THUMP
USAGI...
TH-THUMP
...HURRY UP AND CHANGE INTO YOUR NIGHTWEAR.
TH-THUMP
TH-THUMP
HUH?
BUT I'M ALREADY WEARING IT...
THIS IS YOUR NIGHTWEAR.
KLANK

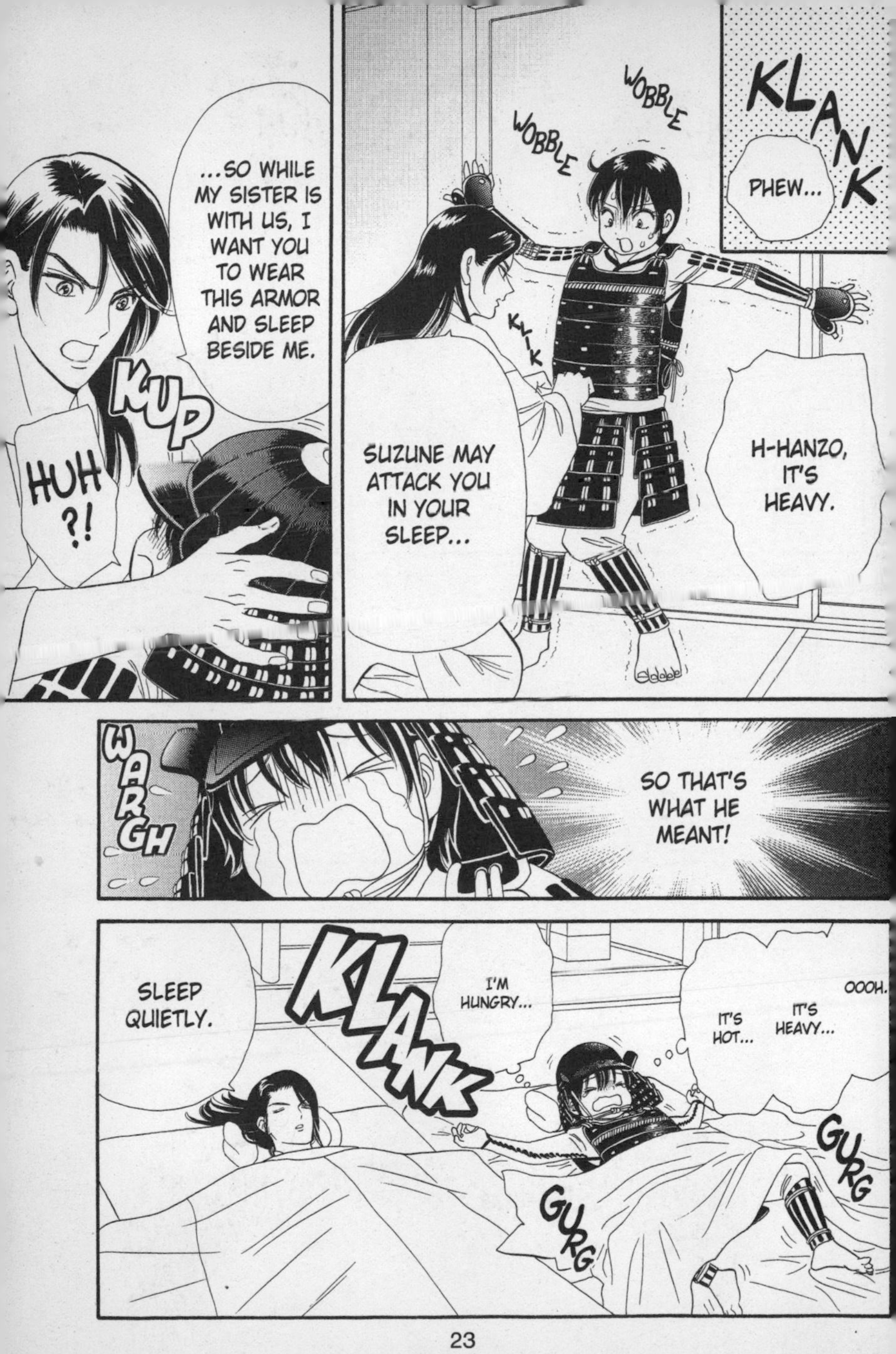
KLANK
PHEW...
WOBBLE
WOBBLE
H-HANZO, IT'S HEAVY.
KVIK
SUZUNE MAY ATTACK YOU IN YOUR SLEEP...
...SO WHILE MY SISTER IS WITH US, I WANT YOU TO WEAR THIS ARMOR AND SLEEP BESIDE ME.
KUP
HUH ?!
SO THAT'S WHAT HE MEANT!
WARGH
OOOH.
IT'S HEAVY...
IT'S HOT...
GURG
GURG
I'M HUNGRY...
KLANK
SLEEP QUIETLY.

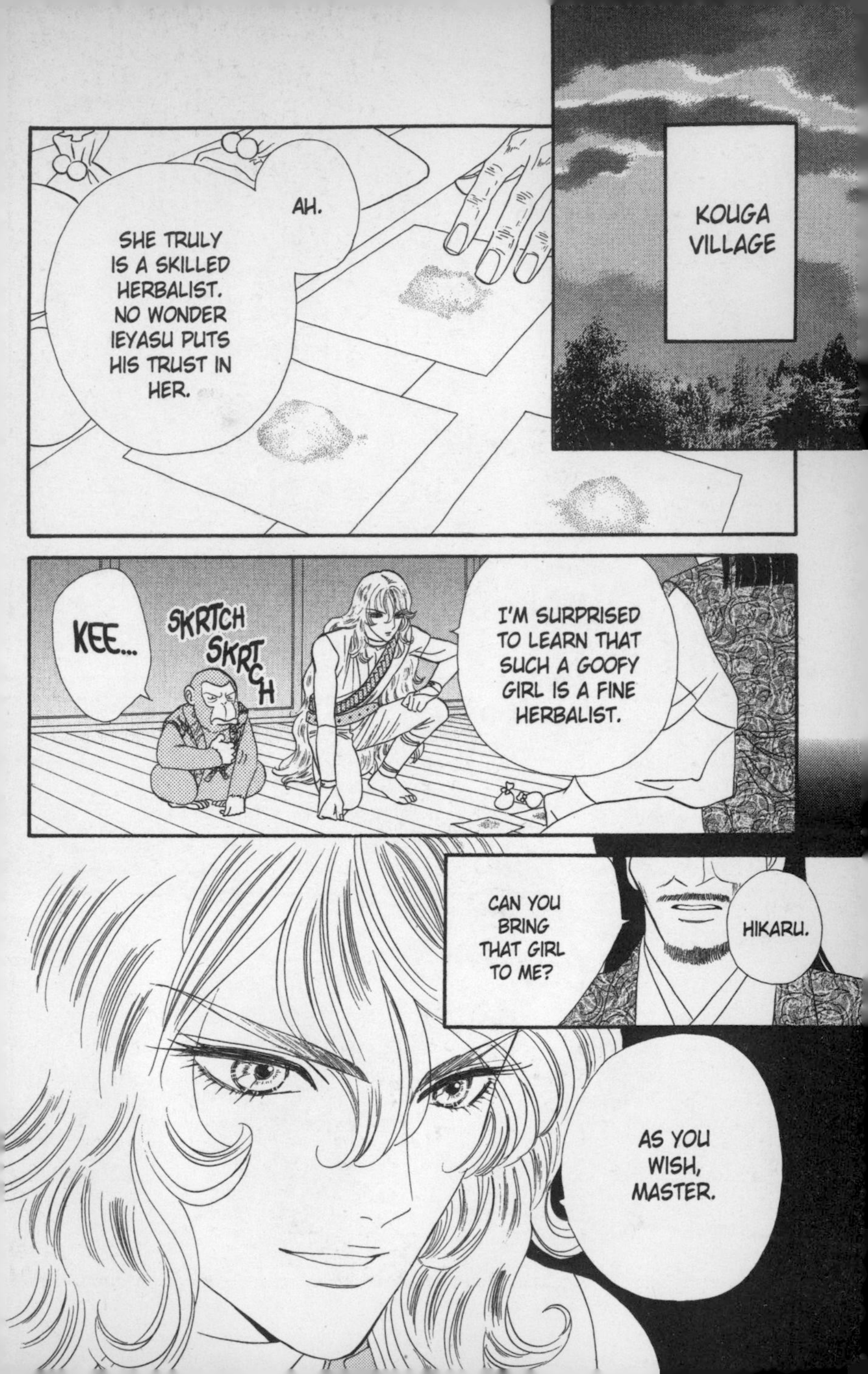
KOUGA VILLAGE
AH.
SHE TRULY IS A SKILLED HERBALIST. NO WONDER IEYASU PUTS HIS TRUST IN HER.
I'M SURPRISED TO LEARN THAT SUCH A GOOFY GIRL IS A FINE HERBALIST.
SKRTCH SKRTCH
KEE...
HIKARU.
CAN YOU BRING THAT GIRL TO ME?
AS YOU WISH, MASTER.

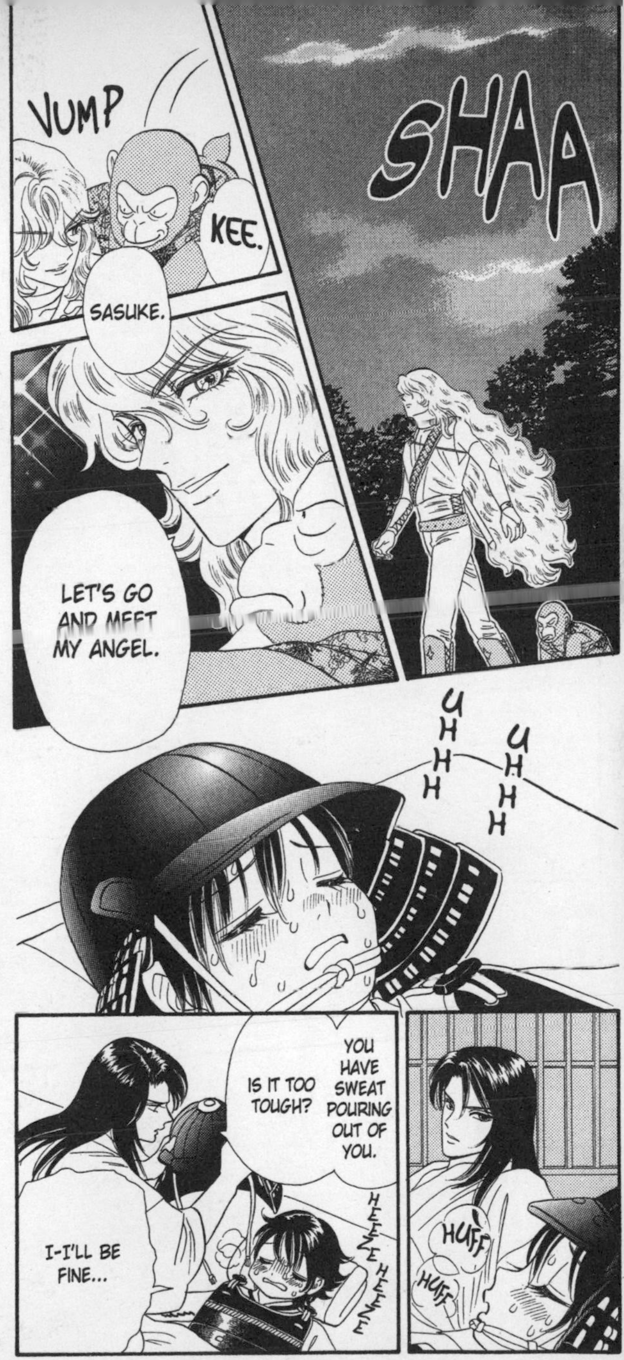
SHAA
VUMP
KEE.
SASUKE.
LET'S GO AND MEET MY ANGEL.
UHHH UHHH
HUFF HUFF
YOU HAVE SWEAT POURING OUT OF YOU.
IS IT TOO TOUGH?
I-I'LL BE FINE...
HEEZE HEEZE

Hello, it's Ue-Rin! ♪ We're now up to volume 5 of *The Tail of the Moon*...

It's due to everyone who is reading this manga right now that I am able to continue creating this happy-go-lucky manga!! I read 100% of the letters I receive. I gather my energy and inspiration from them.

Thank you...

I'd like to continue writing about my trip to Kouga here in this volume, so please look forward to it! ♪

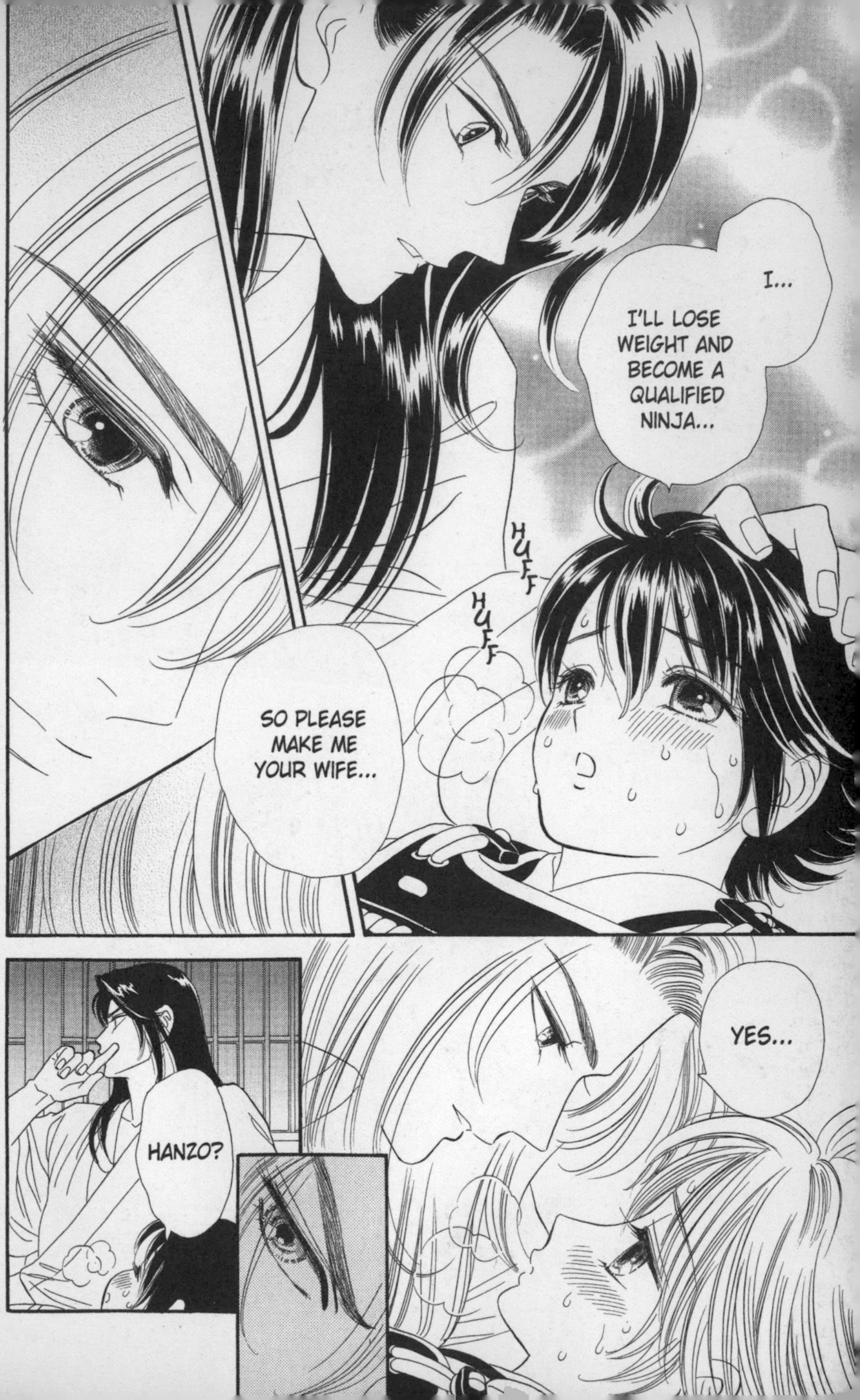
I...
I'LL LOSE WEIGHT AND BECOME A QUALIFIED NINJA...
HUFF
HUFF
SO PLEASE MAKE ME YOUR WIFE...
YES...
HANZO?

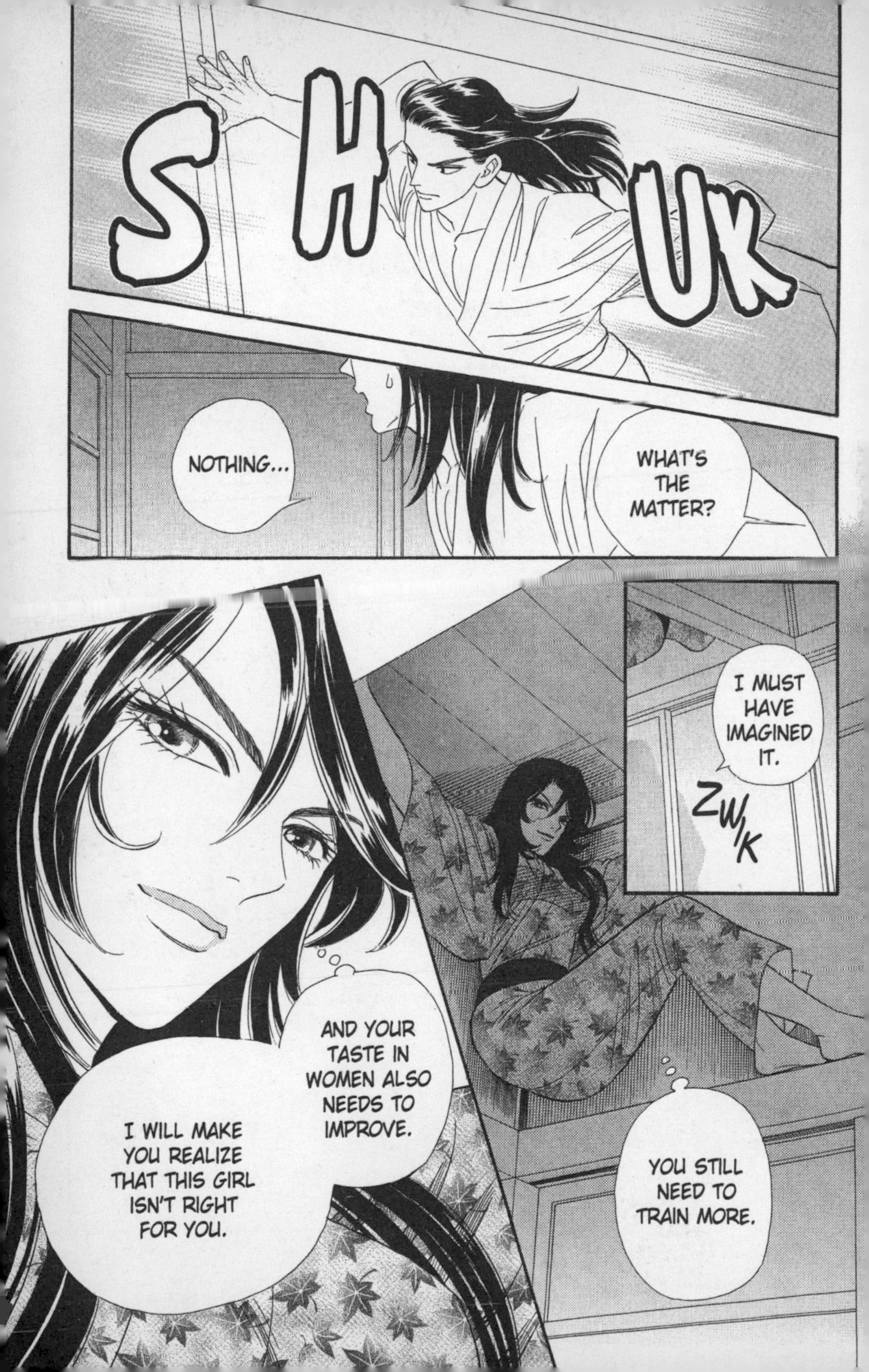
SHUK
WHAT'S THE MATTER?
NOTHING...
I MUST HAVE IMAGINED IT.
ZWIK
YOU STILL NEED TO TRAIN MORE.
AND YOUR TASTE IN WOMEN ALSO NEEDS TO IMPROVE.
I WILL MAKE YOU REALIZE THAT THIS GIRL ISN'T RIGHT FOR YOU.

TAIL OF THE MOON EXTRA: TODAY'S MISSION

"I WANT TO SEE HANZO IN A WHITE LAB COAT!"

-SHIMODA MICHIKO, KANAGAWA PREFECTURE

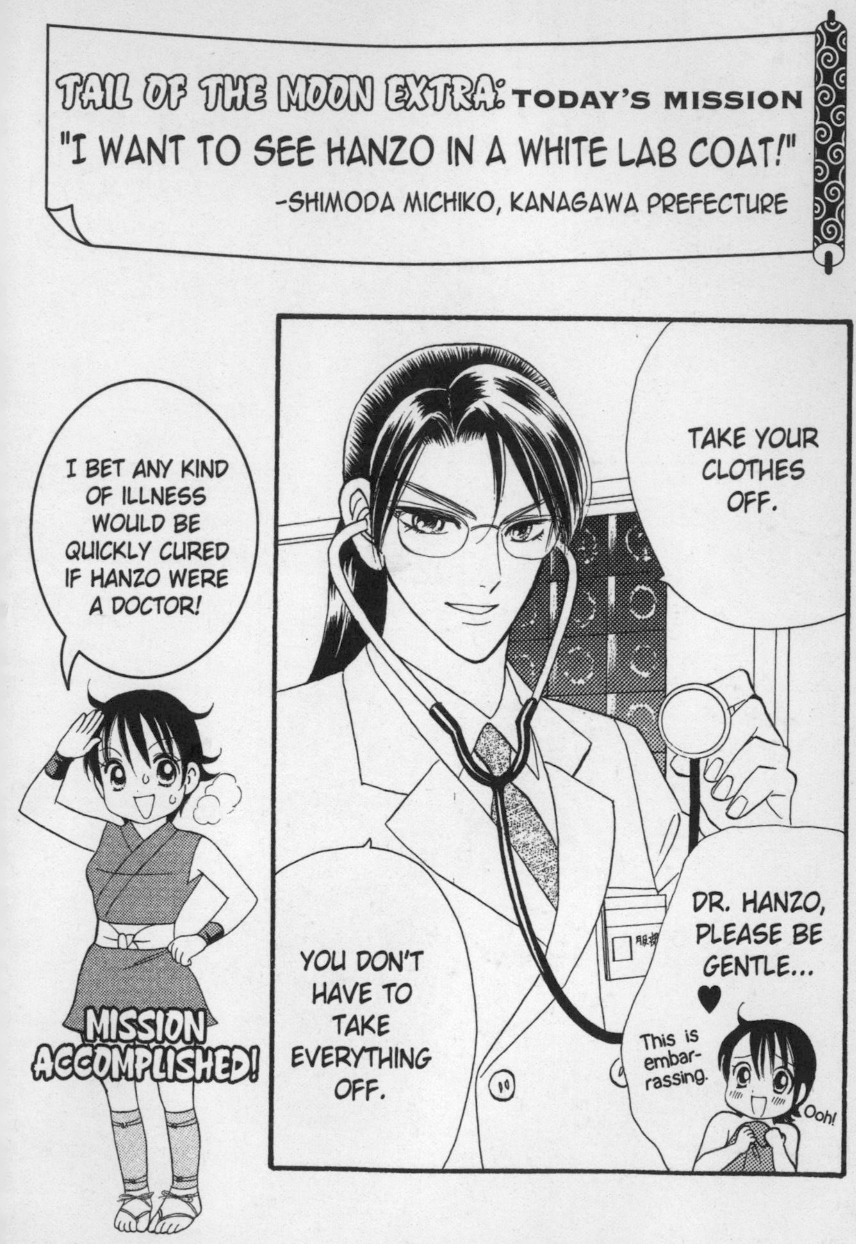
TAKE YOUR CLOTHES OFF.
DR. HANZO, PLEASE BE GENTLE...
This is embarrassing.
Ooh!
YOU DON'T HAVE TO TAKE EVERYTHING OFF.
I BET ANY KIND OF ILLNESS WOULD BE QUICKLY CURED IF HANZO WERE A DOCTOR!
MISSION ACCOMPLISHED!

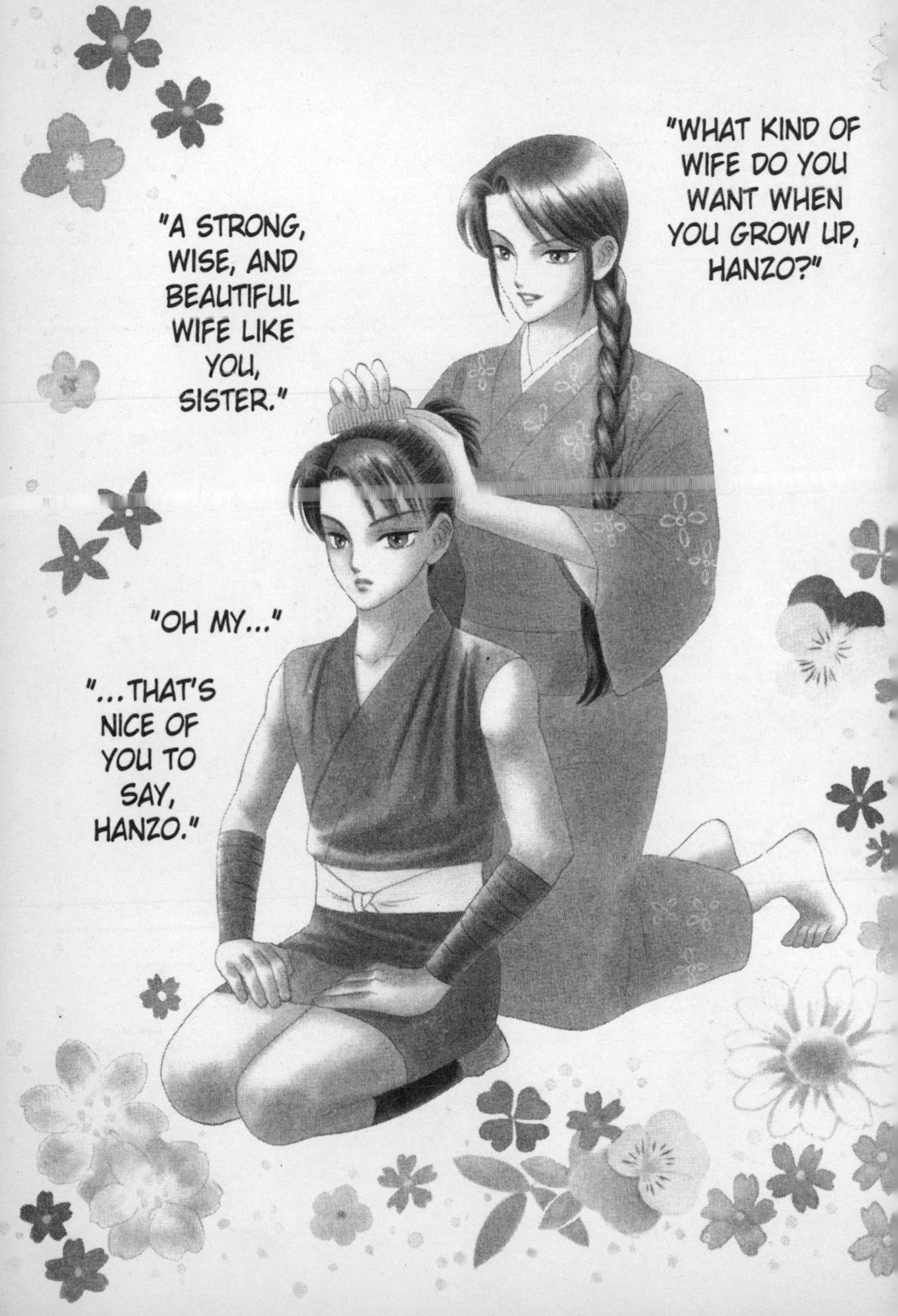
"WHAT KIND OF WIFE DO YOU WANT WHEN YOU GROW UP, HANZO?"
"A STRONG, WISE, AND BEAUTIFUL WIFE LIKE YOU, SISTER."
"OH MY..."
"...THAT'S NICE OF YOU TO SAY, HANZO."

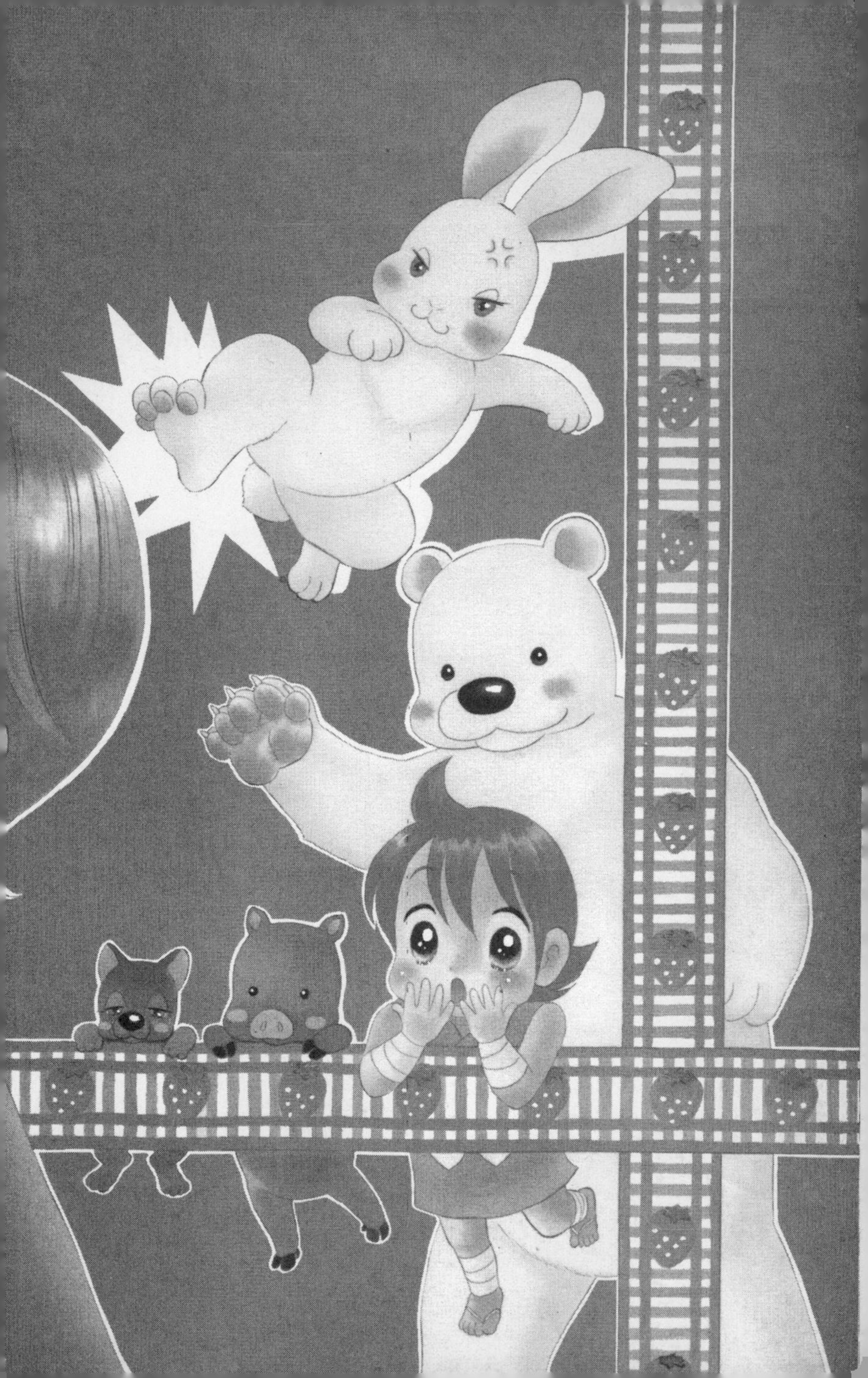

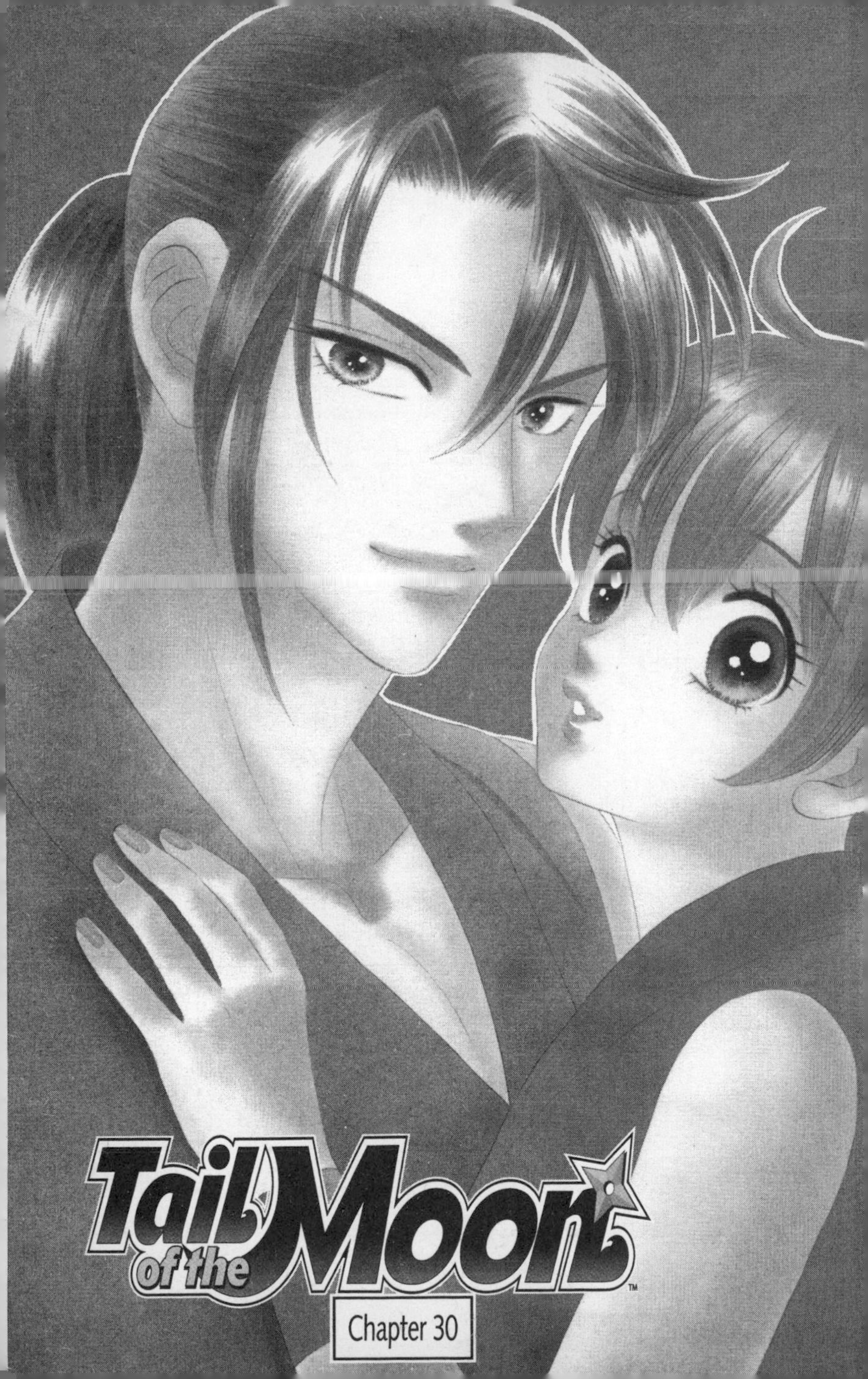
Tail of the Moon™
Chapter 30

TAIL OF THE MOON EXTRA: TODAY'S MISSION

"I WANT TO SEE IGA'S BEAUTIFUL MEN AS PIRATES!"

-JOHNNY HANZO LOVE, HOKKAIDO

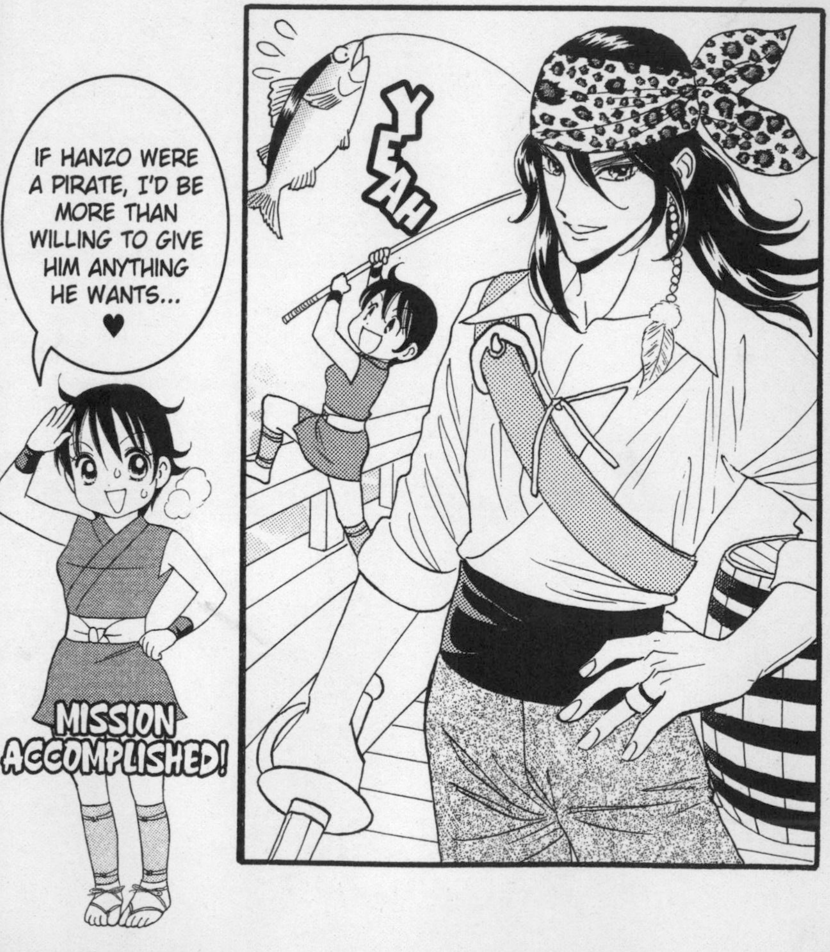
YEAH
IF HANZO WERE A PIRATE, I'D BE MORE THAN WILLING TO GIVE HIM ANYTHING HE WANTS... ♥
MISSION ACCOMPLISHED!

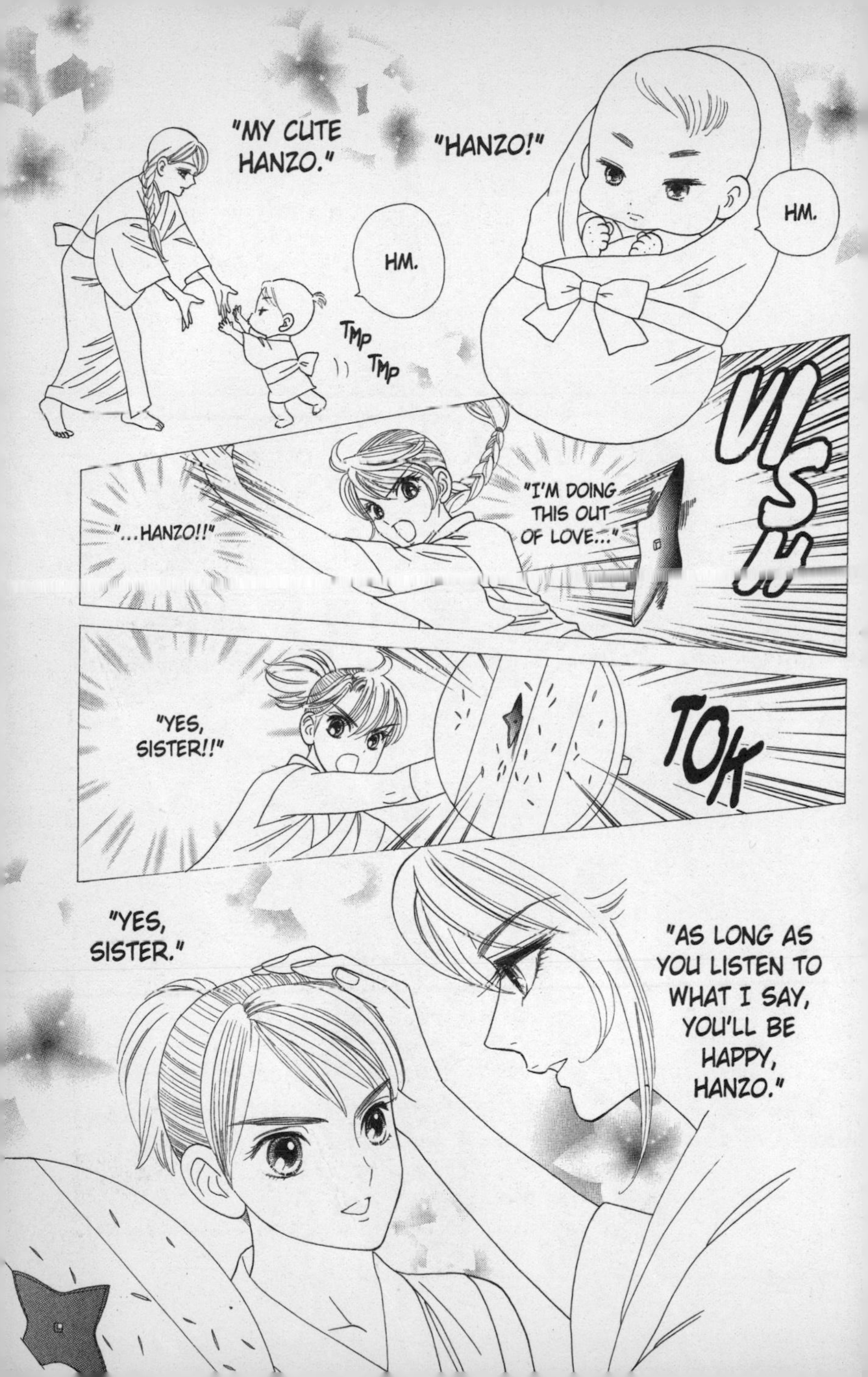
"HANZO!"
HM.
"MY CUTE HANZO."
HM.
TMP TMP
VISH
"I'M DOING THIS OUT OF LOVE..."
"...HANZO!!"
TOK
"YES, SISTER!!"
"AS LONG AS YOU LISTEN TO WHAT I SAY, YOU'LL BE HAPPY, HANZO."
"YES, SISTER."

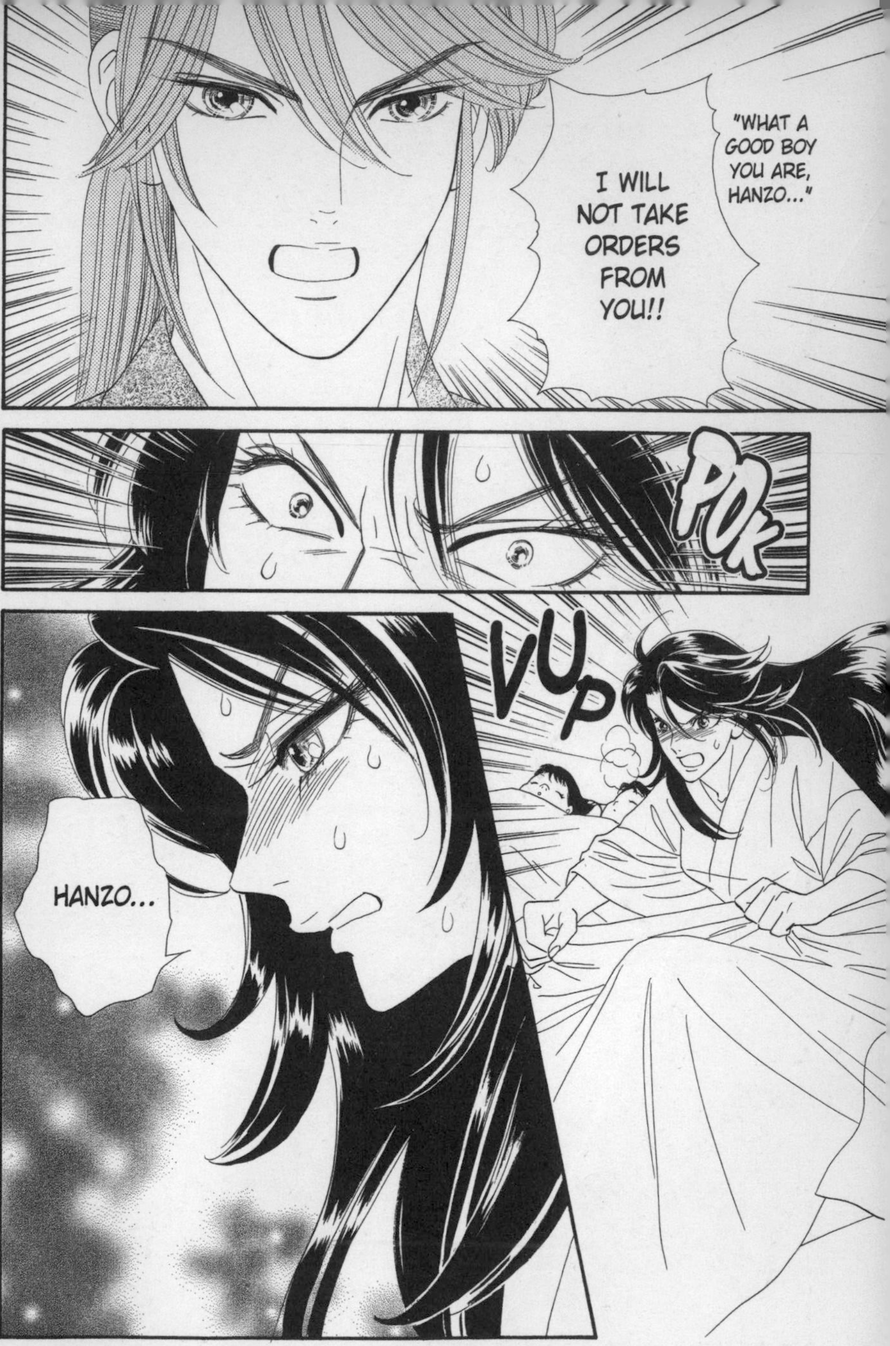
"WHAT A GOOD BOY YOU ARE, HANZO..."
I WILL NOT TAKE ORDERS FROM YOU!!
POK
VUP
HANZO...

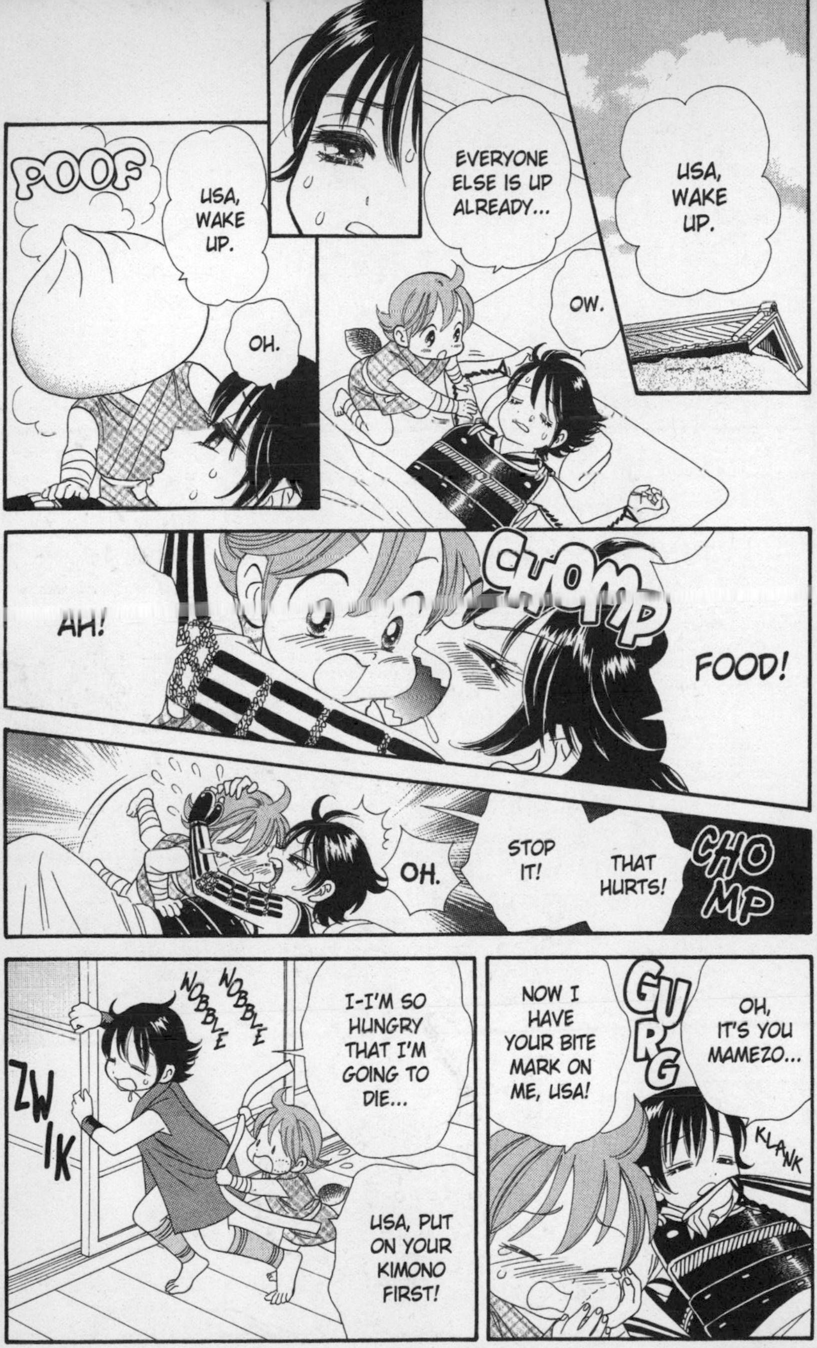
USA, WAKE UP.
EVERYONE ELSE IS UP ALREADY...
OW.
USA, WAKE UP.
POOF
OH.
FOOD!
CHOMP
AH!
CHOMP
THAT HURTS!
STOP IT!
OH.
OH, IT'S YOU MAMEZO...
GURG
NOW I HAVE YOUR BITE MARK ON ME, USA!
KLANK
I-I'M SO HUNGRY THAT I'M GOING TO DIE...
WOBBLE
WOBBLE
ZWIK
USA, PUT ON YOUR KIMONO FIRST!

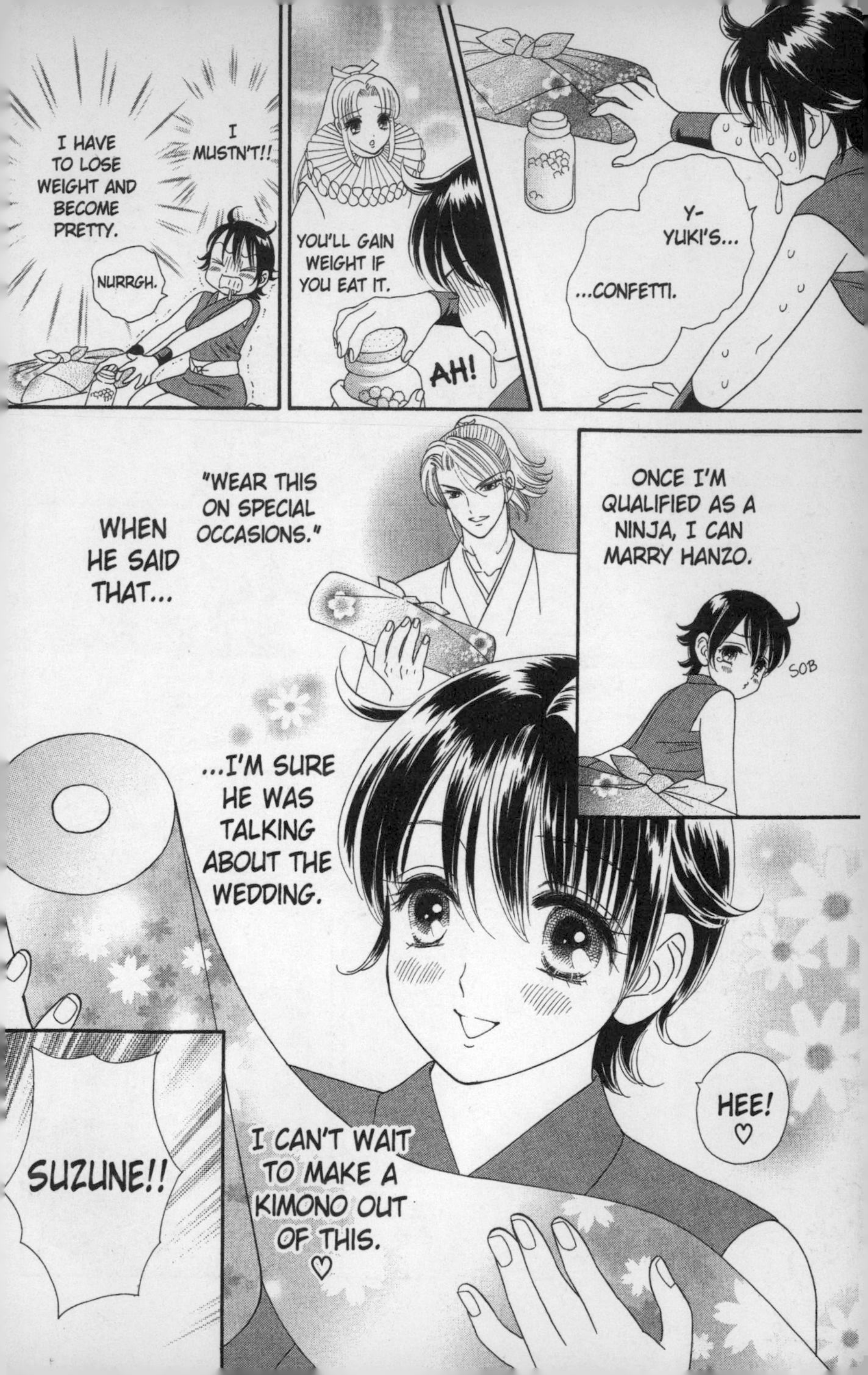
Y-
YUKI'S...
...CONFETTI.
YOU'LL GAIN WEIGHT IF YOU EAT IT.
AH!
I MUSTN'T!!
I HAVE TO LOSE WEIGHT AND BECOME PRETTY.
NURRGH.
ONCE I'M QUALIFIED AS A NINJA, I CAN MARRY HANZO.
SOB
"WEAR THIS ON SPECIAL OCCASIONS."
WHEN HE SAID THAT...
...I'M SURE HE WAS TALKING ABOUT THE WEDDING.
HEE! ♡
I CAN'T WAIT TO MAKE A KIMONO OUT OF THIS. ♡
SUZUNE!!

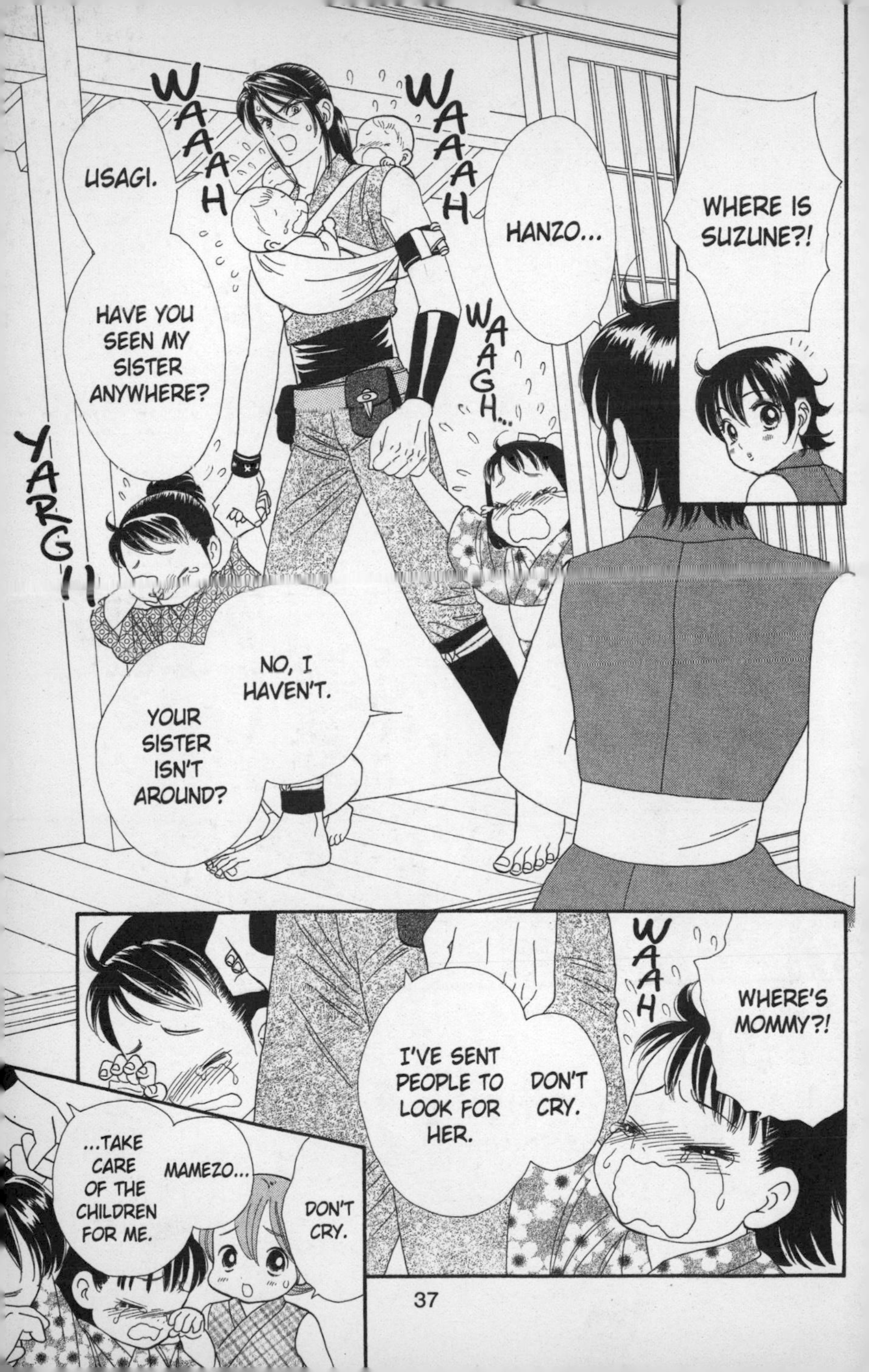
WHERE IS SUZUNE?!
WAAAAH
HANZO...
WAAAH
USAGI.
HAVE YOU SEEN MY SISTER ANYWHERE?
WAAGH...
YARG!!
NO, I HAVEN'T.
YOUR SISTER ISN'T AROUND?
WAAH
WHERE'S MOMMY?!
DON'T CRY.
I'VE SENT PEOPLE TO LOOK FOR HER.
DON'T CRY.
MAMEZO...
...TAKE CARE OF THE CHILDREN FOR ME.

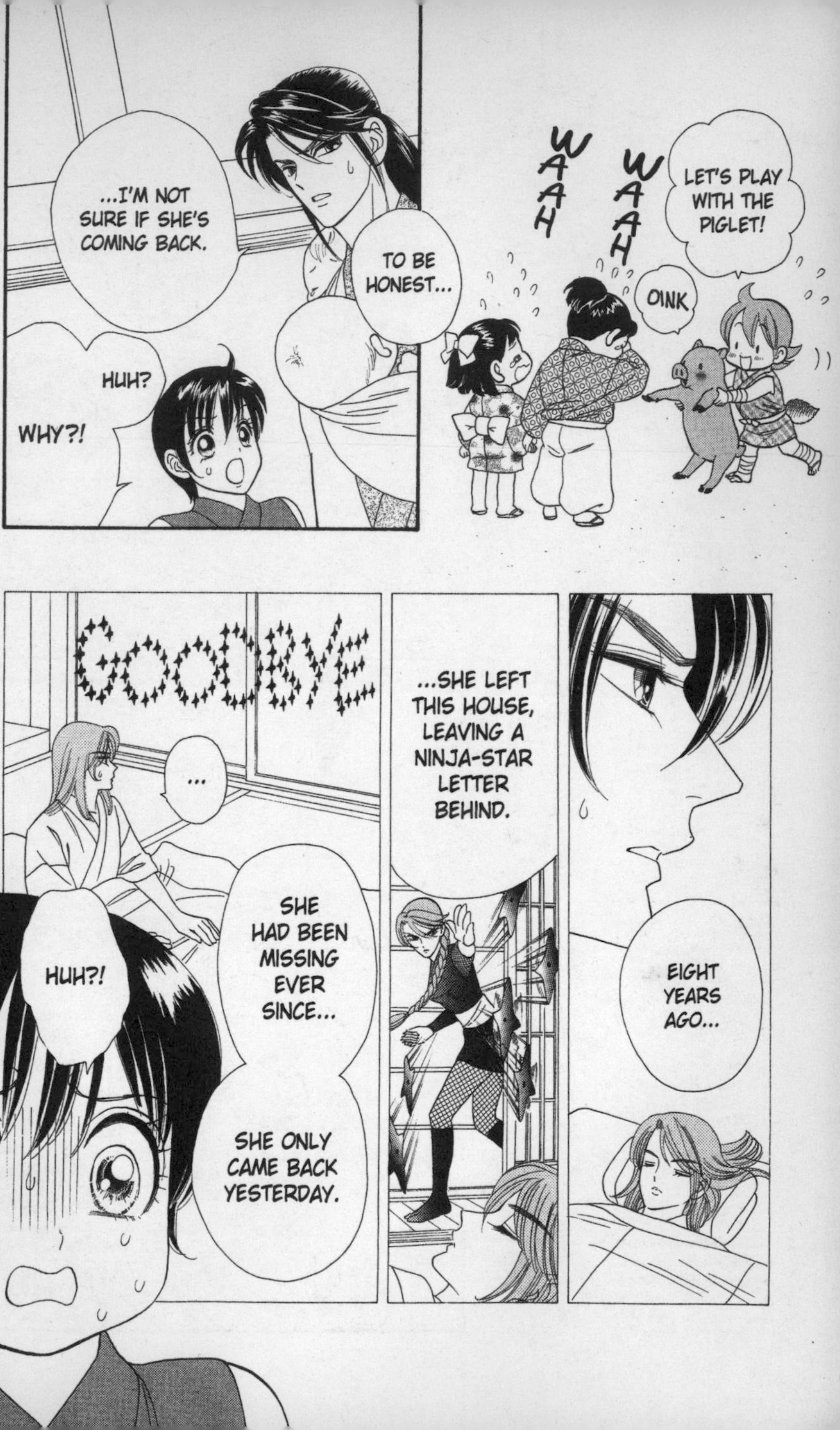
LET'S PLAY WITH THE PIGLET!
WAAH
WAAH
OINK
TO BE HONEST...
...I'M NOT SURE IF SHE'S COMING BACK.
HUH?
WHY?!
EIGHT YEARS AGO...
...SHE LEFT THIS HOUSE, LEAVING A NINJA-STAR LETTER BEHIND.
GOODBYE
...
SHE HAD BEEN MISSING EVER SINCE...
SHE ONLY CAME BACK YESTERDAY.
HUH?!

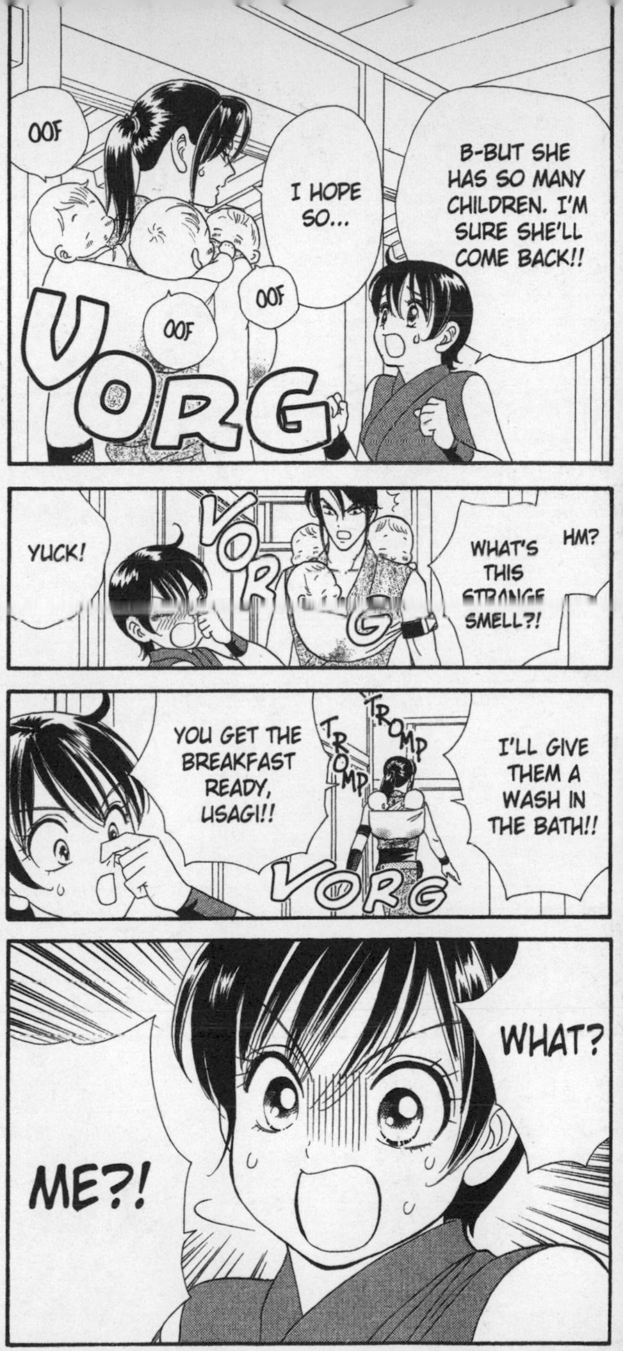
B-BUT SHE HAS SO MANY CHILDREN. I'M SURE SHE'LL COME BACK!!
I HOPE SO...
OOF
OOF
OOF
VORG
HM?
WHAT'S THIS STRANGE SMELL?!
VORG
YUCK!
I'LL GIVE THEM A WASH IN THE BATH!!
TROMP
TROMP
YOU GET THE BREAKFAST READY, USAGI!!
VORG
WHAT?
ME?!

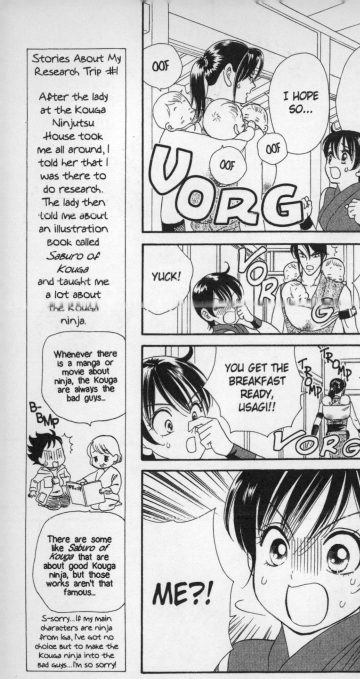

Stories About My Research Trip #1

After the lady at the Kouga Ninjutsu House took me all around, I told her that I was there to do research. The lady then told me about an illustration book called *Saburo of Kouga* and taught me a lot about the Kouga ninja.

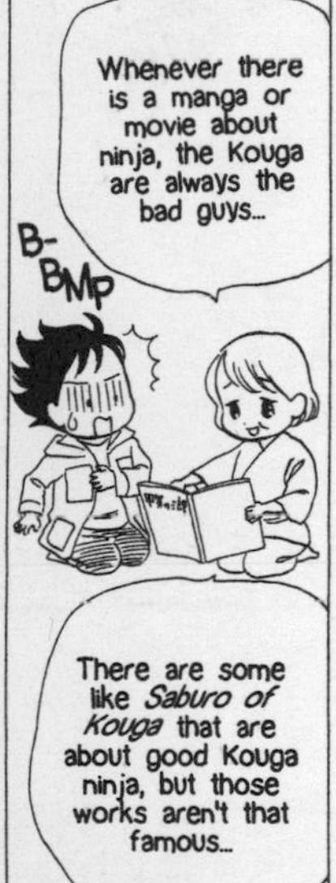
Whenever there is a manga or movie about ninja, the Kouga are always the bad guys...
B-BMP
There are some like *Saburo of Kouga* that are about good Kouga ninja, but those works aren't that famous...

S-sorry...If my main characters are ninja from Iga, I've got no choice but to make the Kouga ninja into the bad guys...I'm so sorry!

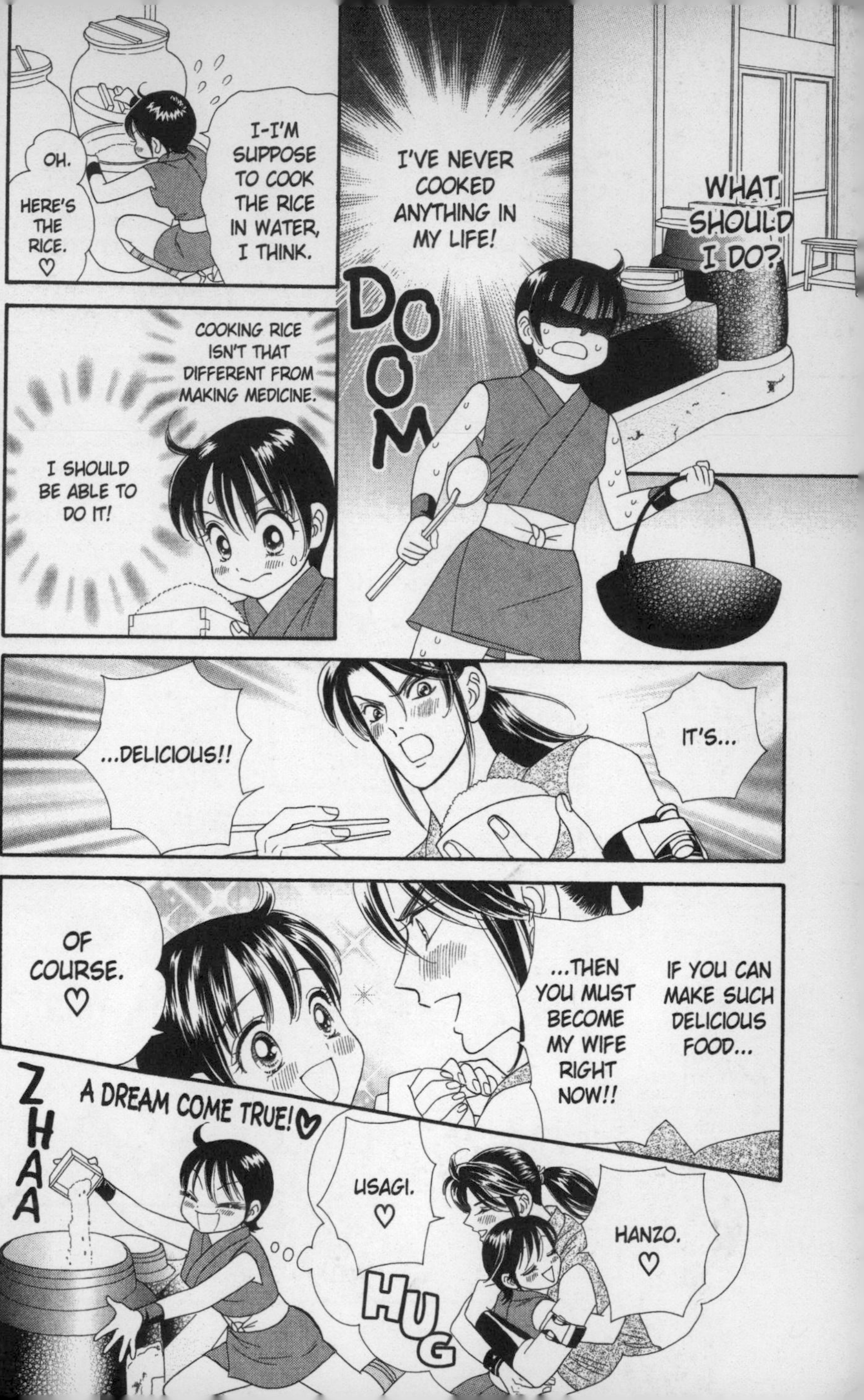
WHAT SHOULD I DO?
I'VE NEVER COOKED ANYTHING IN MY LIFE!
DOOM
I-I'M SUPPOSE TO COOK THE RICE IN WATER, I THINK.
OH.
HERE'S THE RICE. ♡
COOKING RICE ISN'T THAT DIFFERENT FROM MAKING MEDICINE.
I SHOULD BE ABLE TO DO IT!
IT'S...
...DELICIOUS!!
IF YOU CAN MAKE SUCH DELICIOUS FOOD...
...THEN YOU MUST BECOME MY WIFE RIGHT NOW!!
OF COURSE. ♡
HANZO. ♡
HUG
USAGI. ♡
A DREAM COME TRUE! ♡
ZHAA

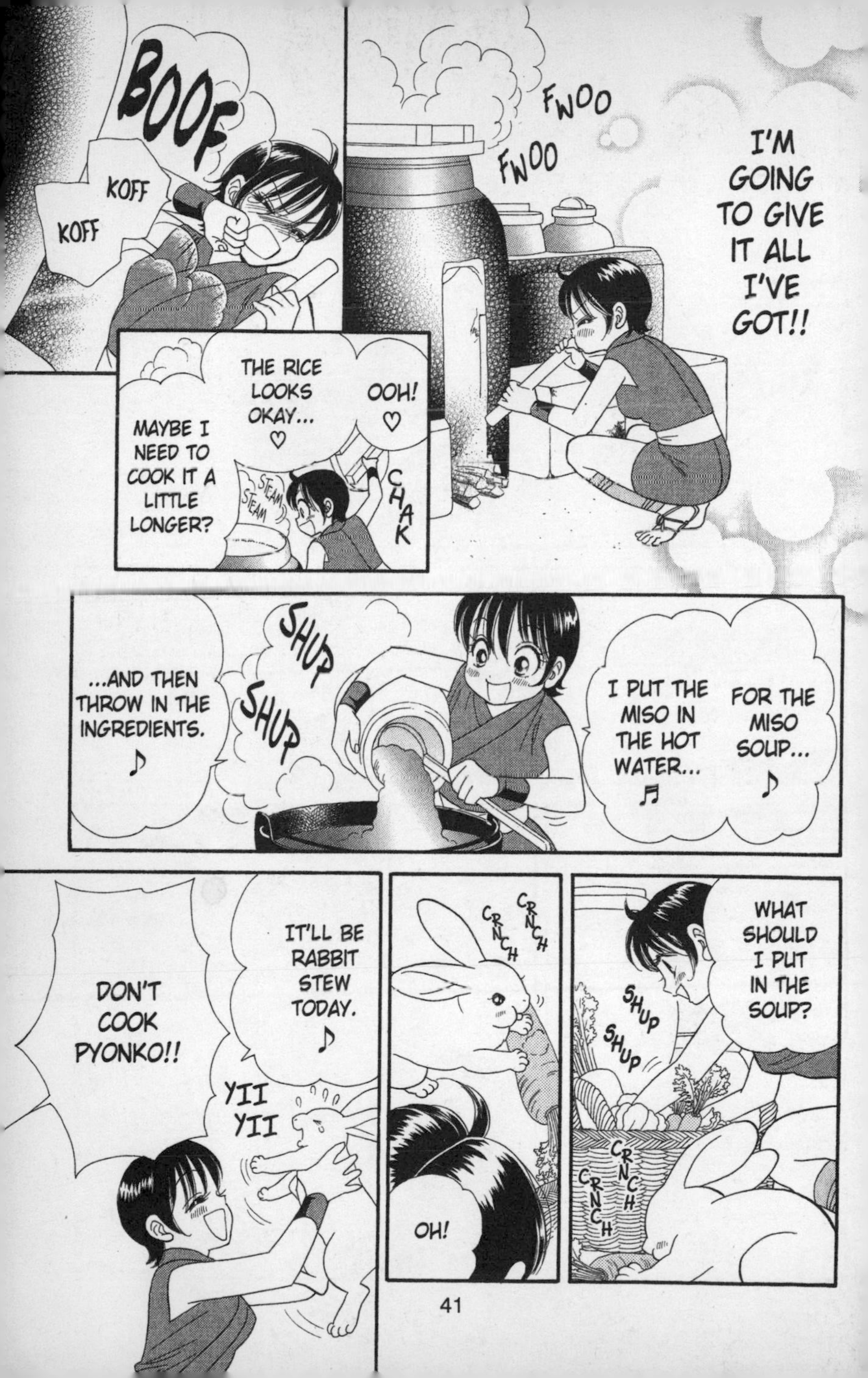
FWOO
FWOO
I'M GOING TO GIVE IT ALL I'VE GOT!!
BOOF
KOFF
KOFF
OOH! ♡
THE RICE LOOKS OKAY... ♡
MAYBE I NEED TO COOK IT A LITTLE LONGER?
CHAK
STEAM
STEAM
FOR THE MISO SOUP... ♪
I PUT THE MISO IN THE HOT WATER... ♬
SHUP
SHUP
...AND THEN THROW IN THE INGREDIENTS. ♪
WHAT SHOULD I PUT IN THE SOUP?
SHUP
SHUP
CRNCH
CRNCH
CRNCH
CRNCH
OH!
IT'LL BE RABBIT STEW TODAY. ♪
DON'T COOK PYONKO!!
YII
YII

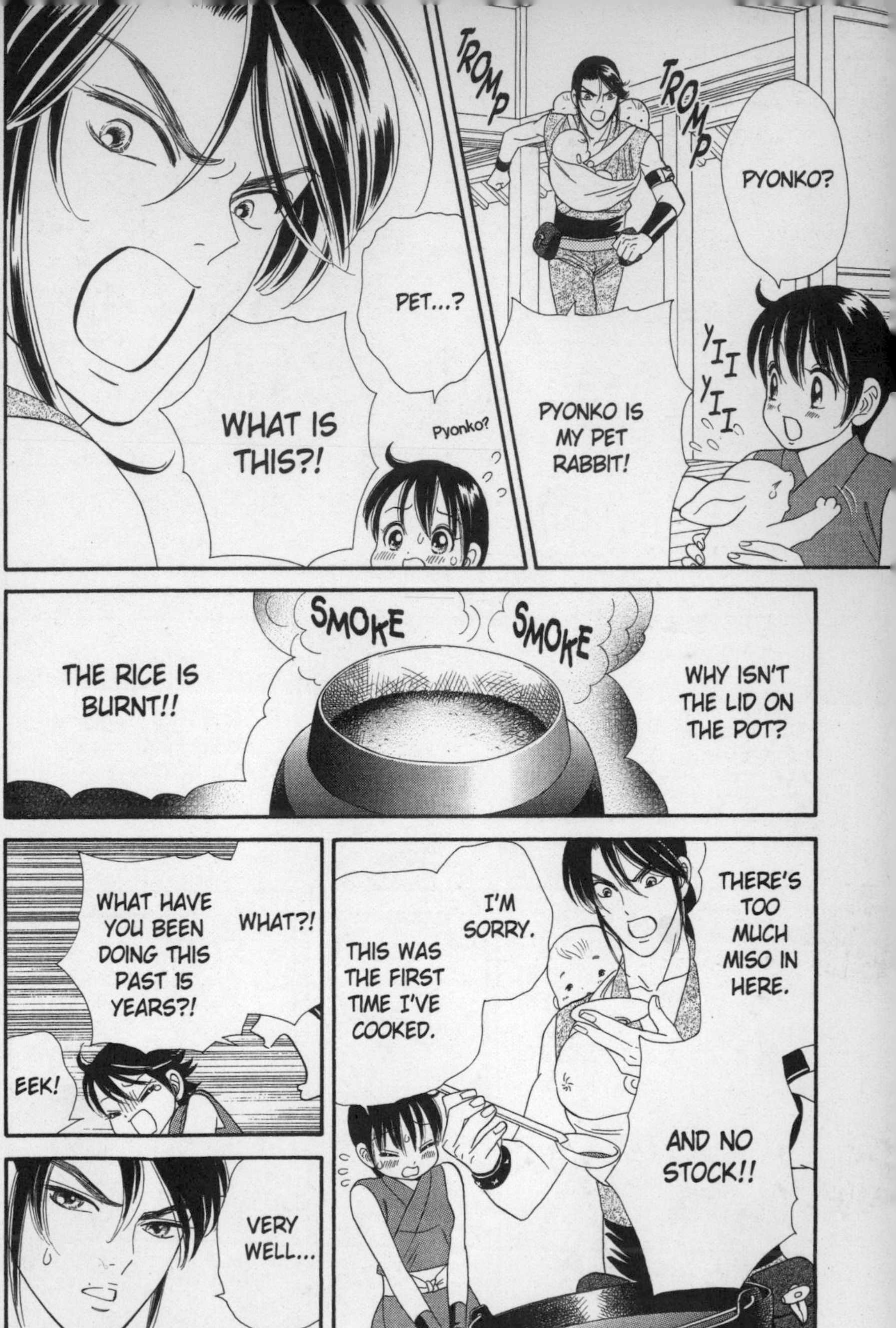
TROMP
TROMP
PYONKO?
YIII YIII
PYONKO IS MY PET RABBIT!
PET...?
Pyonko?
WHAT IS THIS?!
SMOKE
SMOKE
WHY ISN'T THE LID ON THE POT?
THE RICE IS BURNT!!
THERE'S TOO MUCH MISO IN HERE.
AND NO STOCK!!
I'M SORRY.
THIS WAS THE FIRST TIME I'VE COOKED.
WHAT?!
WHAT HAVE YOU BEEN DOING THIS PAST 15 YEARS?!
EEK!
VERY WELL...

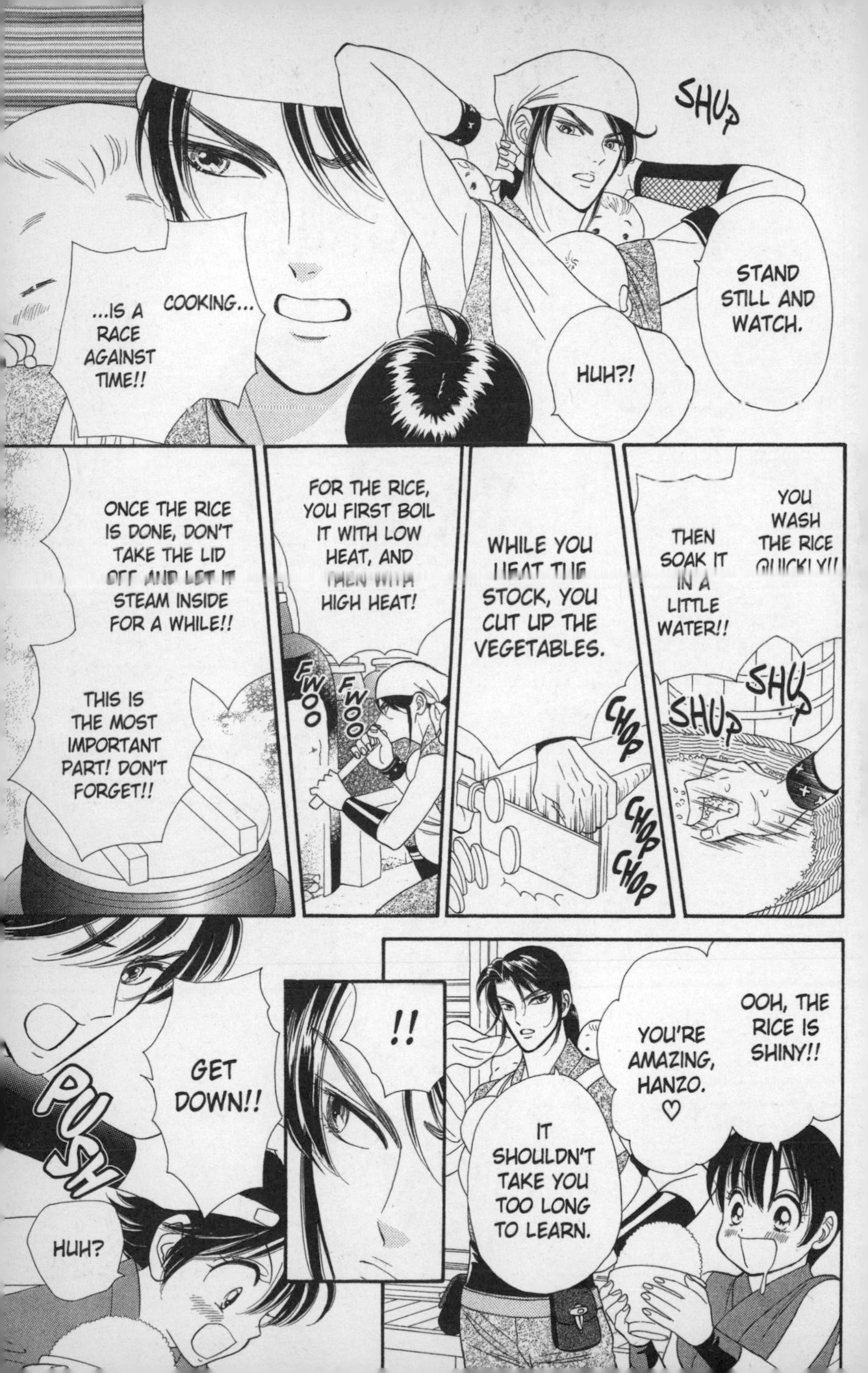
SHUP
STAND STILL AND WATCH.
HUH?!
COOKING...
...IS A RACE AGAINST TIME!!
YOU WASH THE RICE QUICKLY!!
THEN SOAK IT IN A LITTLE WATER!!
SHUP
SHUP
WHILE YOU HEAT THE STOCK, YOU CUT UP THE VEGETABLES.
CHOP
CHOP
CHOP
FOR THE RICE, YOU FIRST BOIL IT WITH LOW HEAT, AND THEN WITH HIGH HEAT!
FWOO
FWOO
ONCE THE RICE IS DONE, DON'T TAKE THE LID OFF AND LET IT STEAM INSIDE FOR A WHILE!!
THIS IS THE MOST IMPORTANT PART! DON'T FORGET!!
OOH, THE RICE IS SHINY!!
YOU'RE AMAZING, HANZO. ♡
IT SHOULDN'T TAKE YOU TOO LONG TO LEARN.
!!
GET DOWN!!
PUSH
HUH?

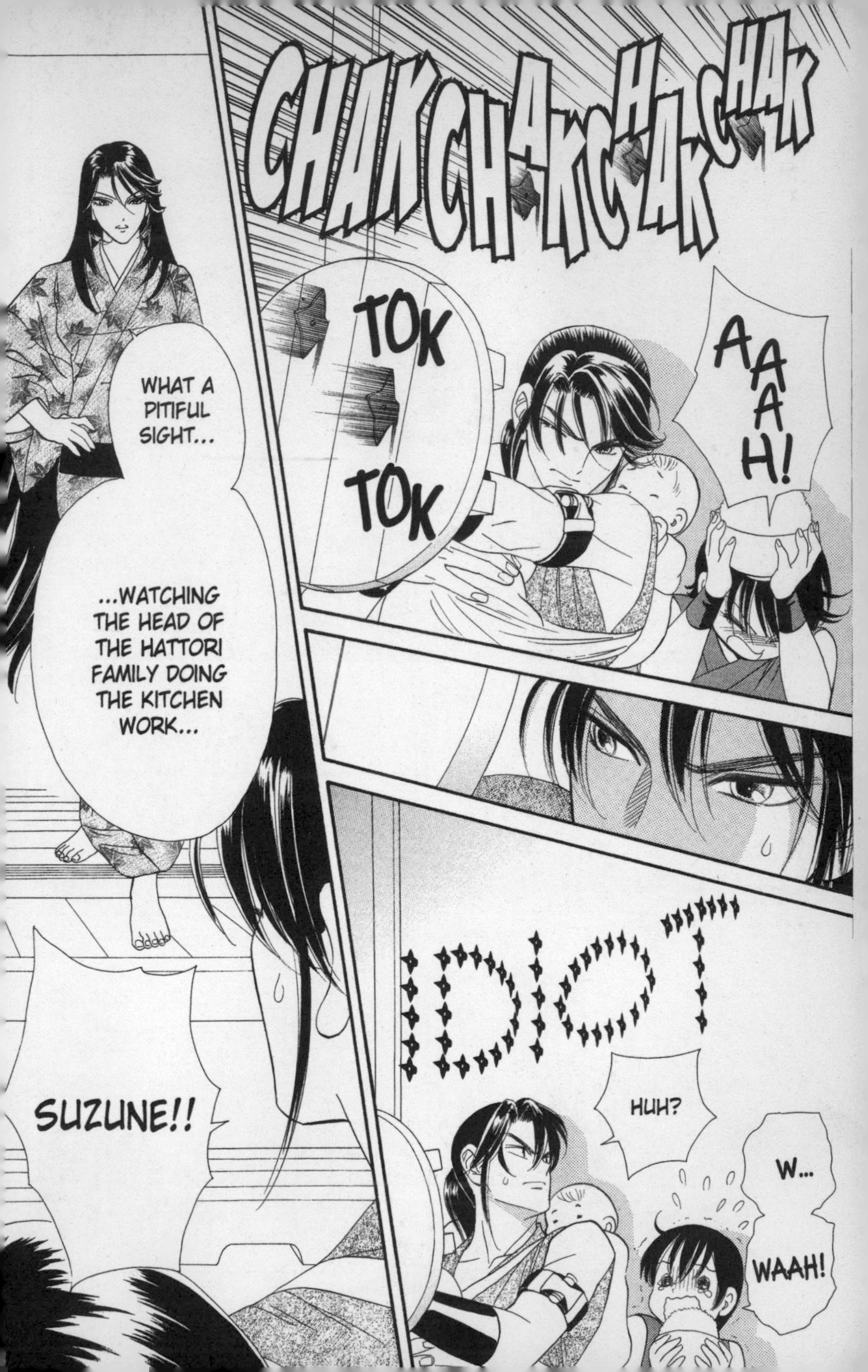
CHAKCHAKCHAKCHAK
TOK
TOK
AAAH!
WHAT A PITIFUL SIGHT...
...WATCHING THE HEAD OF THE HATTORI FAMILY DOING THE KITCHEN WORK...
SUZUNE!!
IDIOT
HUH?
W...
WAAH!

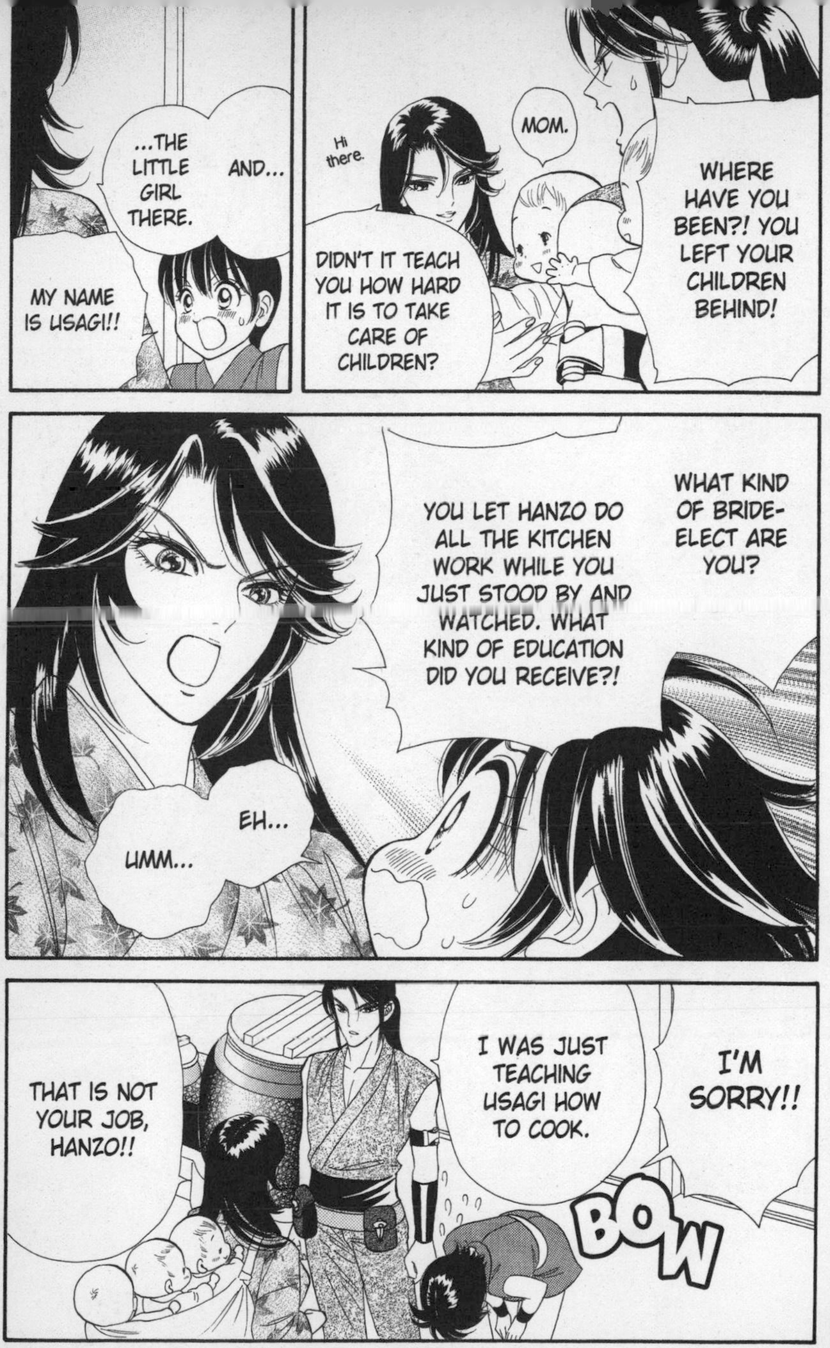
WHERE HAVE YOU BEEN?! YOU LEFT YOUR CHILDREN BEHIND!
MOM.
Hi there.
DIDN'T IT TEACH YOU HOW HARD IT IS TO TAKE CARE OF CHILDREN?
AND...
...THE LITTLE GIRL THERE.
MY NAME IS USAGI!!
WHAT KIND OF BRIDE-ELECT ARE YOU?
YOU LET HANZO DO ALL THE KITCHEN WORK WHILE YOU JUST STOOD BY AND WATCHED. WHAT KIND OF EDUCATION DID YOU RECEIVE?!
EH...
UMM...
I'M SORRY!!
BOW
I WAS JUST TEACHING USAGI HOW TO COOK.
THAT IS NOT YOUR JOB, HANZO!!

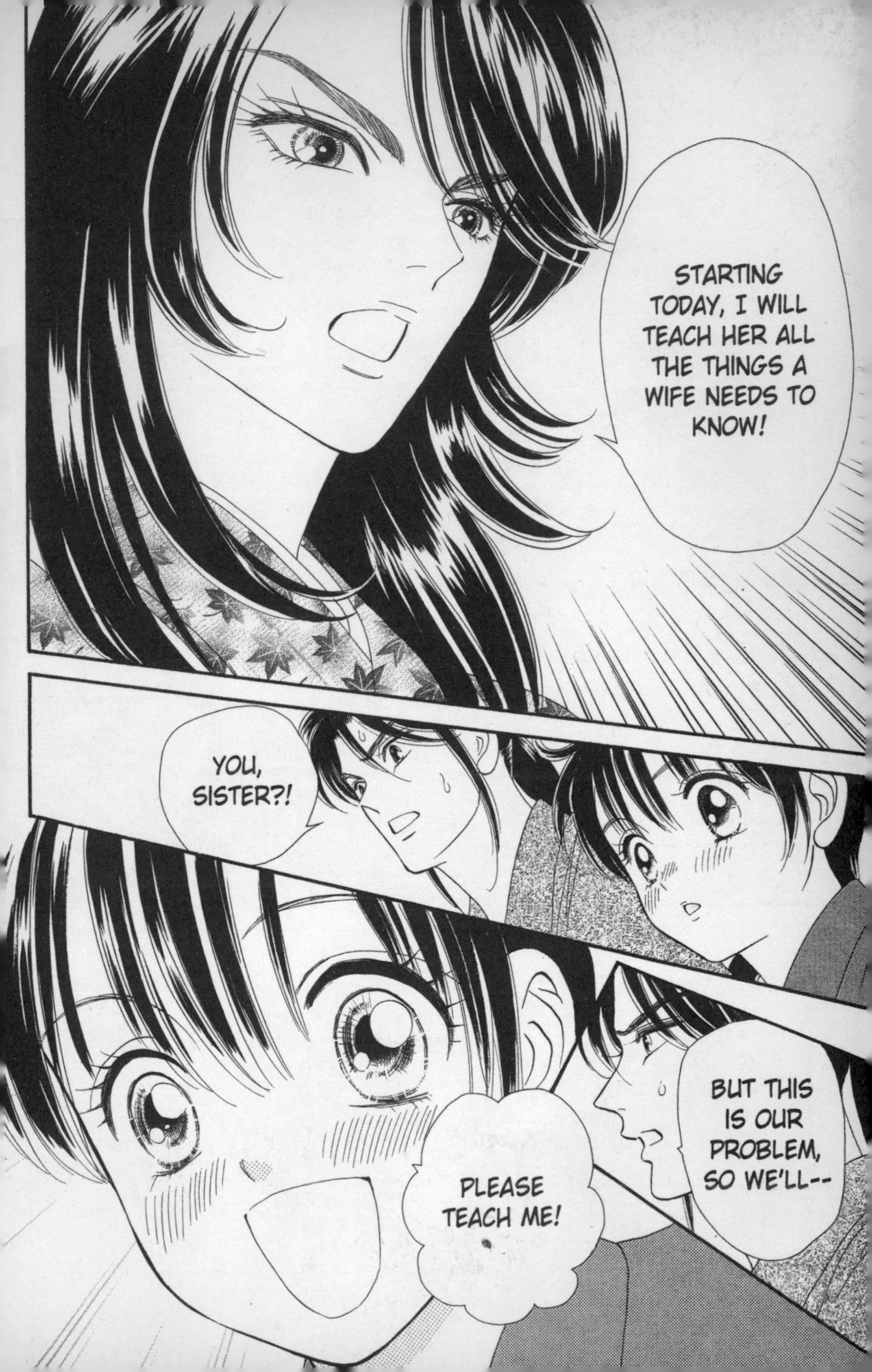
STARTING TODAY, I WILL TEACH HER ALL THE THINGS A WIFE NEEDS TO KNOW!
YOU, SISTER?!
BUT THIS IS OUR PROBLEM, SO WE'LL--
PLEASE TEACH ME!

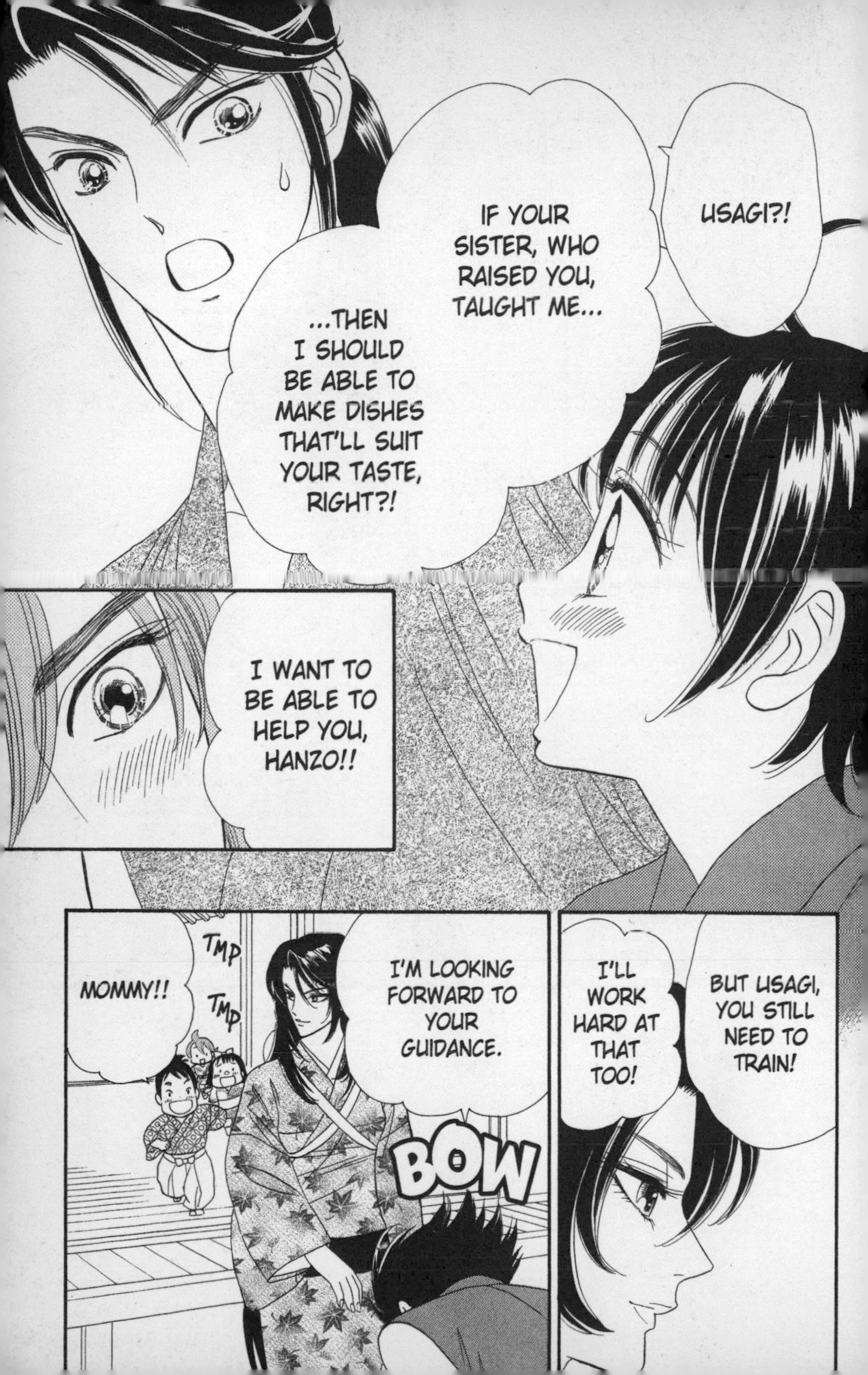
USAGI?!
IF YOUR SISTER, WHO RAISED YOU, TAUGHT ME...
...THEN I SHOULD BE ABLE TO MAKE DISHES THAT'LL SUIT YOUR TASTE, RIGHT?!
I WANT TO BE ABLE TO HELP YOU, HANZO!!
BUT USAGI, YOU STILL NEED TO TRAIN!
I'LL WORK HARD AT THAT TOO!
I'M LOOKING FORWARD TO YOUR GUIDANCE.
BOW
TMP
TMP
MOMMY!!

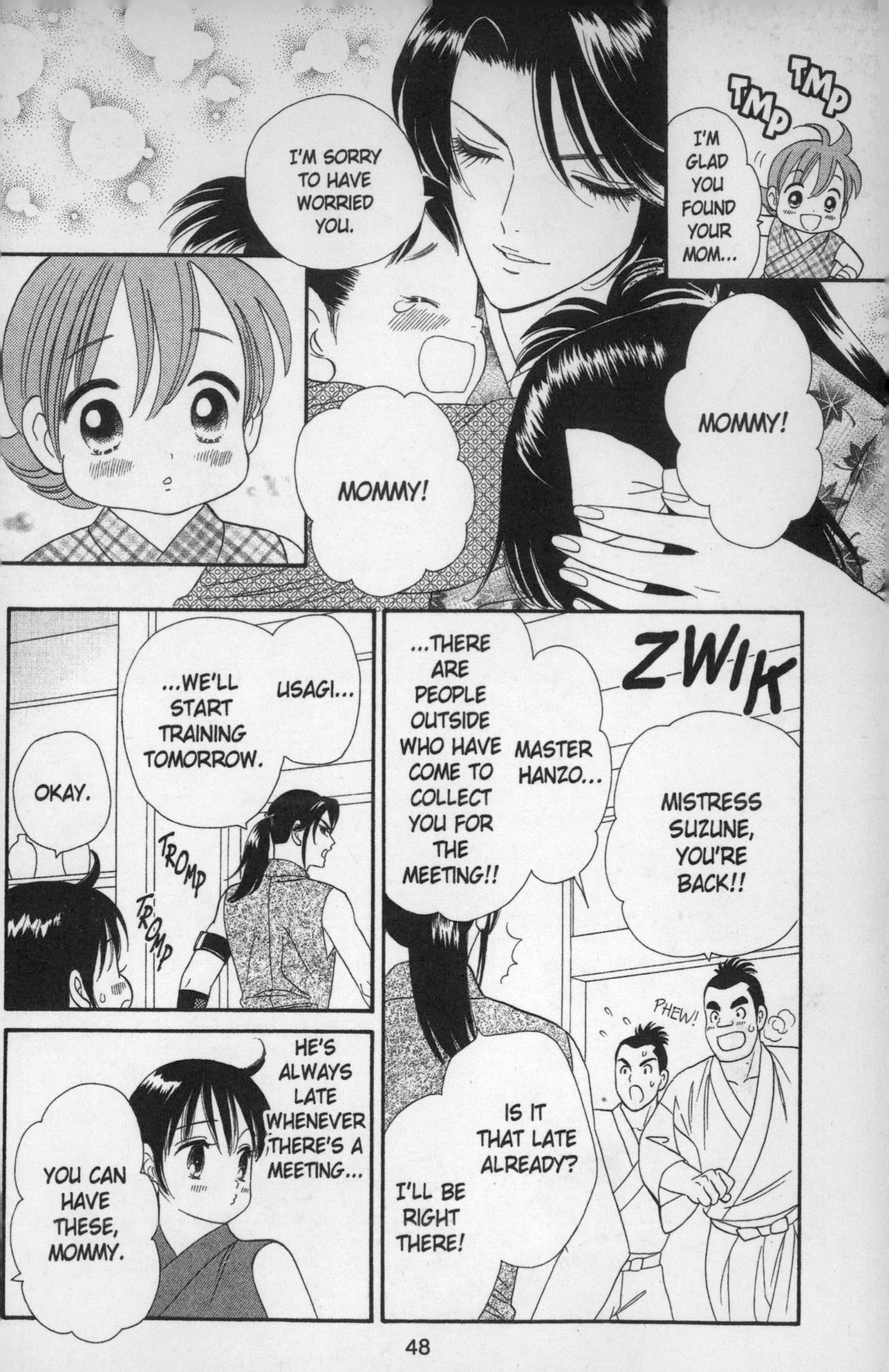
TMP TMP
I'M GLAD YOU FOUND YOUR MOM...
I'M SORRY TO HAVE WORRIED YOU.
MOMMY!
MOMMY!
ZWIK
MISTRESS SUZUNE, YOU'RE BACK!!
MASTER HANZO...
...THERE ARE PEOPLE OUTSIDE WHO HAVE COME TO COLLECT YOU FOR THE MEETING!!
PHEW!
IS IT THAT LATE ALREADY?
I'LL BE RIGHT THERE!
USAGI...
...WE'LL START TRAINING TOMORROW.
TROMP TROMP
OKAY.
HE'S ALWAYS LATE WHENEVER THERE'S A MEETING...
YOU CAN HAVE THESE, MOMMY.

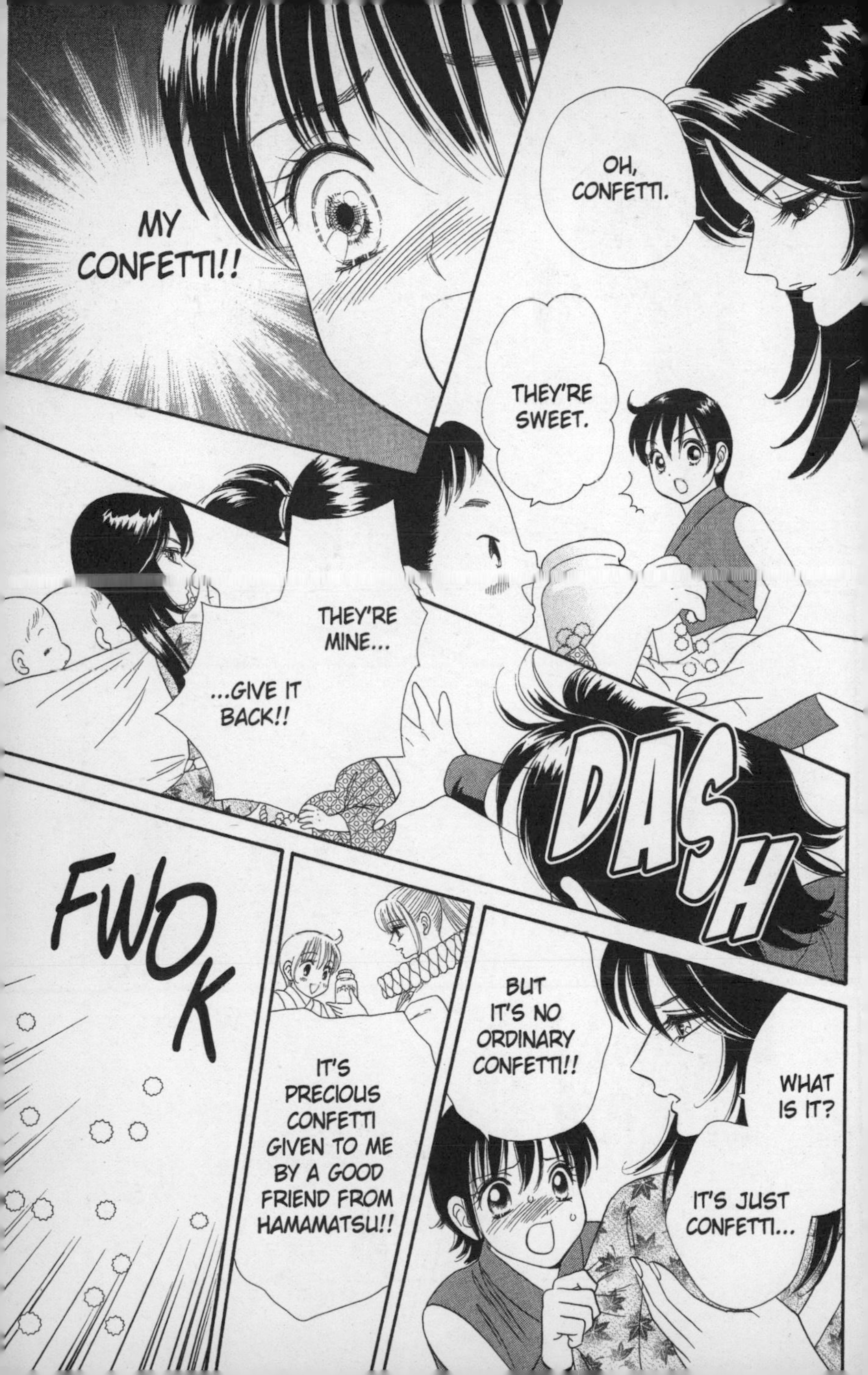
OH, CONFETTI.
THEY'RE SWEET.
MY CONFETTI!!
THEY'RE MINE...
...GIVE IT BACK!!
DASH
WHAT IS IT?
IT'S JUST CONFETTI...
BUT IT'S NO ORDINARY CONFETTI!!
IT'S PRECIOUS CONFETTI GIVEN TO ME BY A GOOD FRIEND FROM HAMAMATSU!!
FWOK

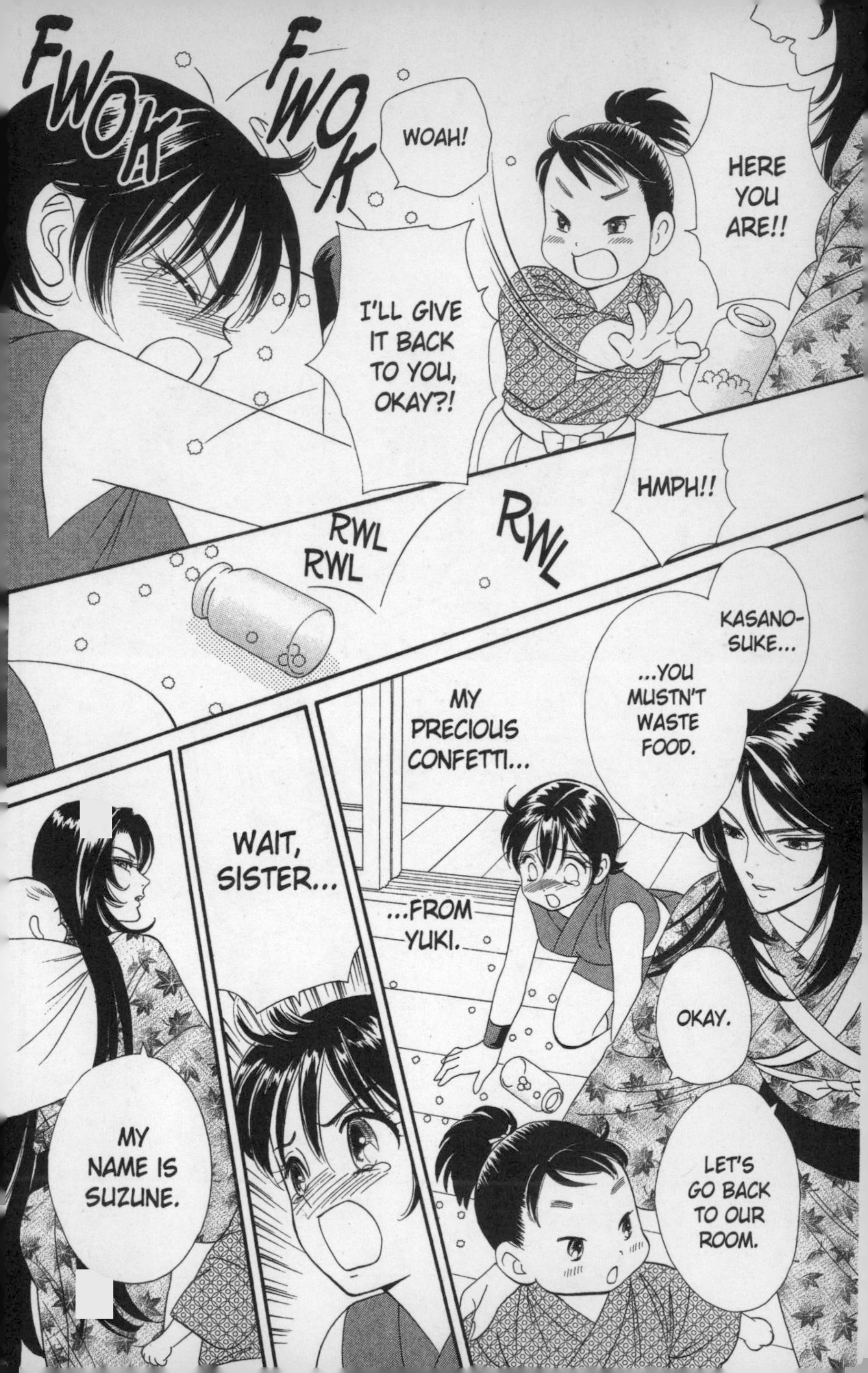
HERE YOU ARE!!
WOAH!
FWOK
FWOK
I'LL GIVE IT BACK TO YOU, OKAY?!
HMPH!!
RWL
RWL RWL
KASANO-SUKE...
...YOU MUSTN'T WASTE FOOD.
MY PRECIOUS CONFETTI...
...FROM YUKI.
OKAY.
LET'S GO BACK TO OUR ROOM.
WAIT, SISTER...
MY NAME IS SUZUNE.

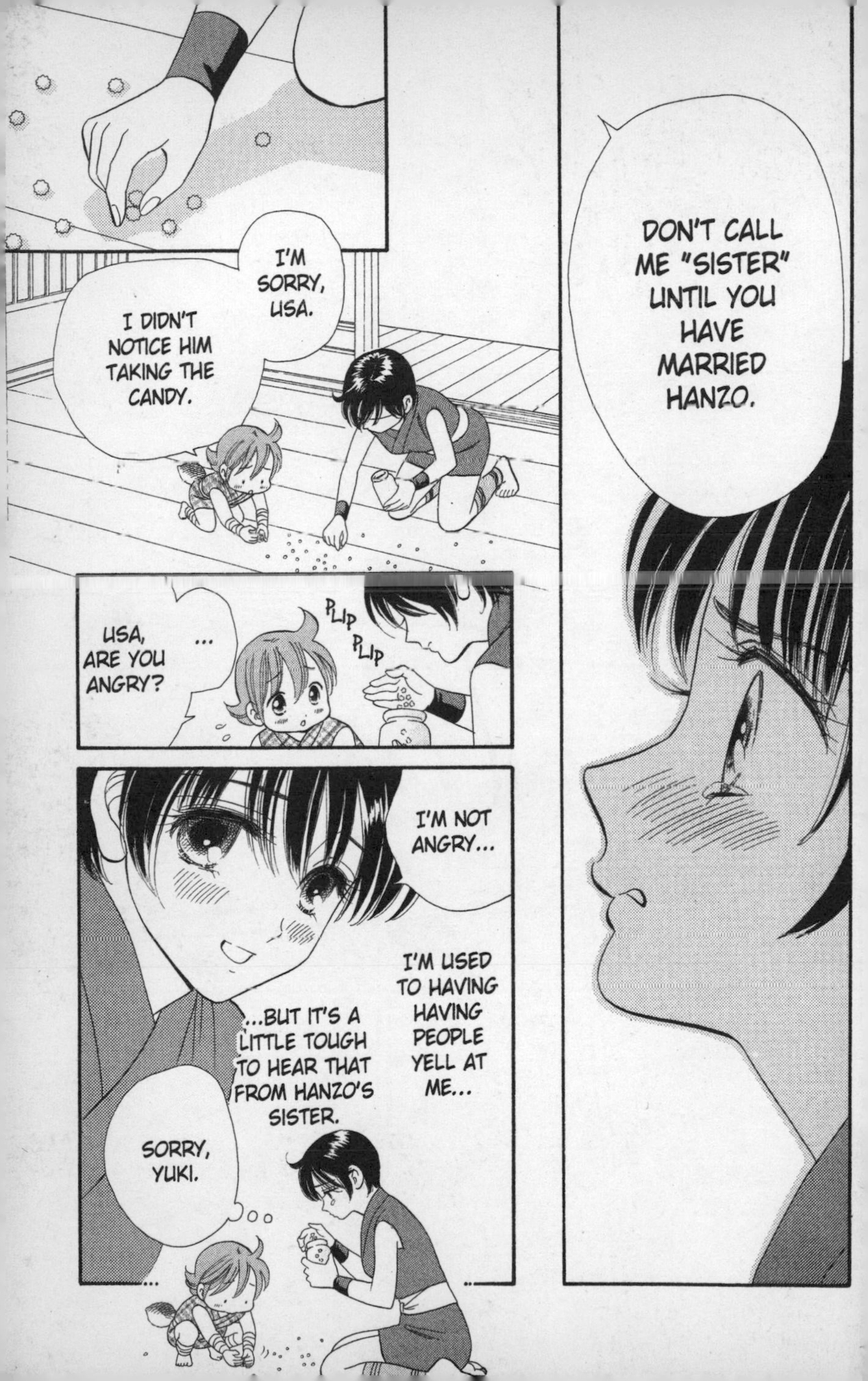
DON'T CALL ME "SISTER" UNTIL YOU HAVE MARRIED HANZO.
I'M SORRY, USA.
I DIDN'T NOTICE HIM TAKING THE CANDY.
...
USA, ARE YOU ANGRY?
PLIP PLIP
I'M NOT ANGRY...
I'M USED TO HAVING HAVING PEOPLE YELL AT ME...
...BUT IT'S A LITTLE TOUGH TO HEAR THAT FROM HANZO'S SISTER.
SORRY, YUKI.
...
...

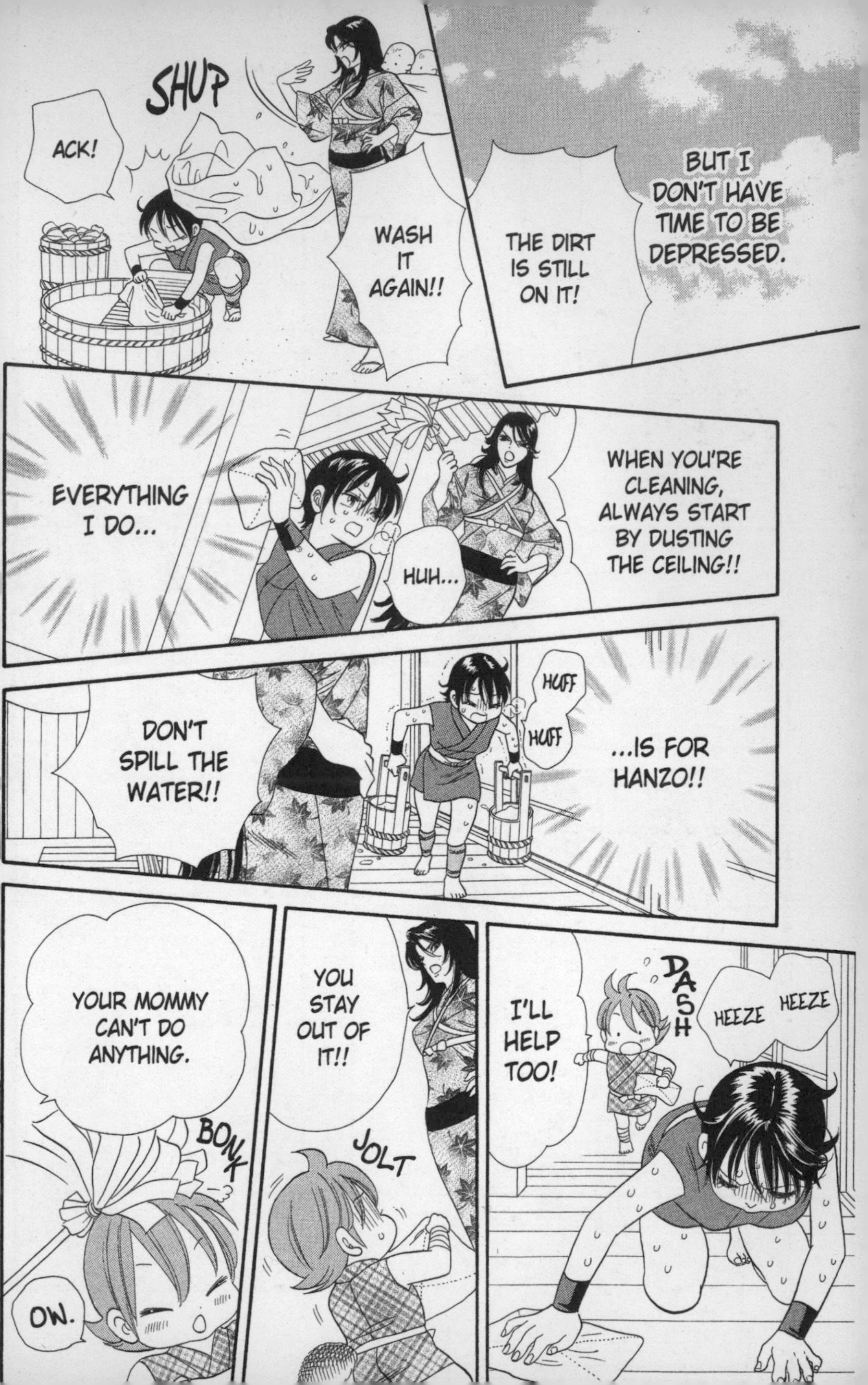
BUT I DON'T HAVE TIME TO BE DEPRESSED.
THE DIRT IS STILL ON IT!
WASH IT AGAIN!!
SHUP
ACK!
WHEN YOU'RE CLEANING, ALWAYS START BY DUSTING THE CEILING!!
HUH...
EVERYTHING I DO...
...IS FOR HANZO!!
HUFF
HUFF
DON'T SPILL THE WATER!!
HEEZE HEEZE
DASH
I'LL HELP TOO!
YOU STAY OUT OF IT!!
JOLT
YOUR MOMMY CAN'T DO ANYTHING.
BONK
OW.

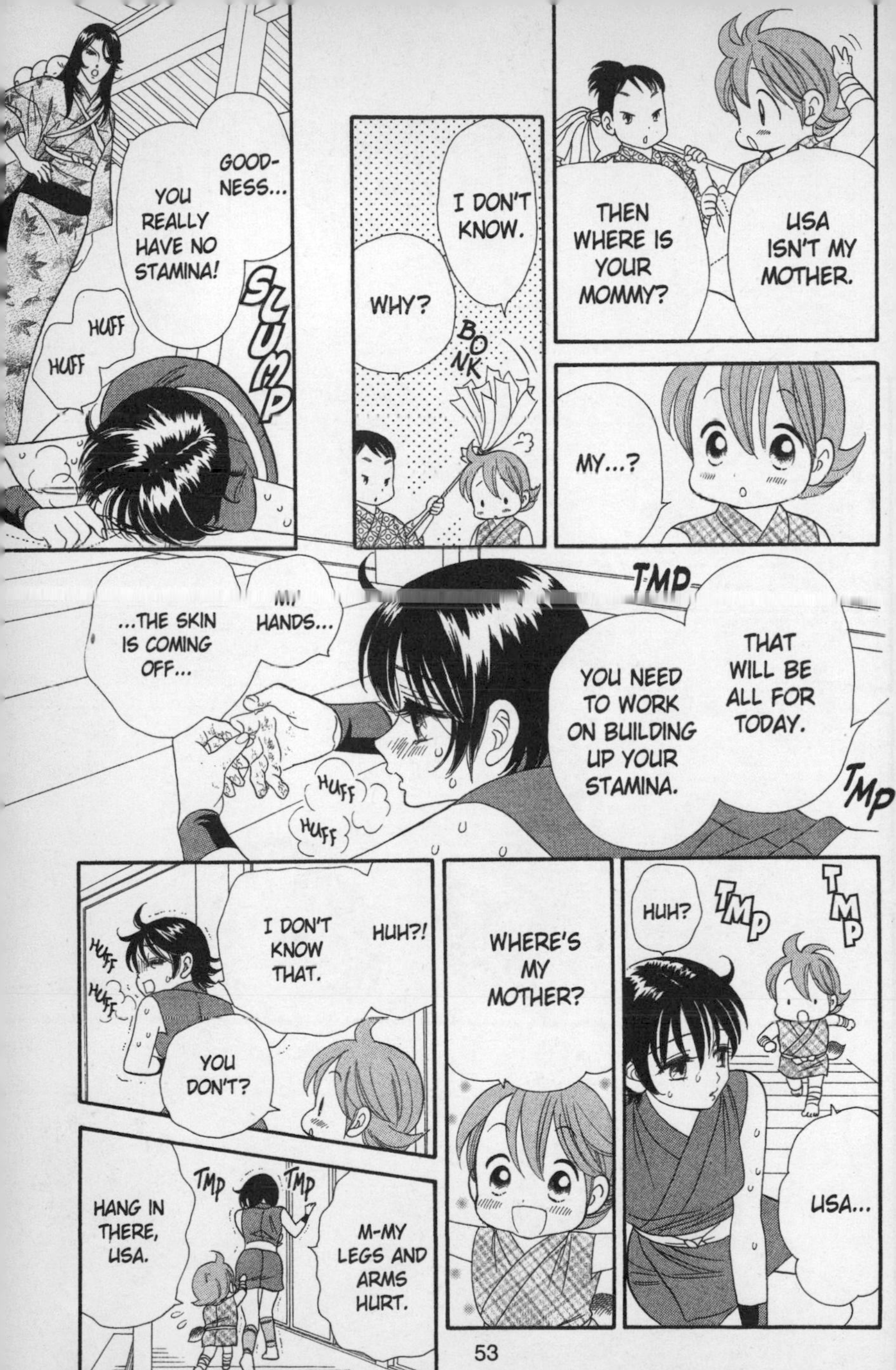
USA ISN'T MY MOTHER.
THEN WHERE IS YOUR MOMMY?
MY...?
I DON'T KNOW.
WHY?
BONK
GOOD-NESS...
YOU REALLY HAVE NO STAMINA!
SLUMP
HUFF
HUFF
TMP
THAT WILL BE ALL FOR TODAY.
YOU NEED TO WORK ON BUILDING UP YOUR STAMINA.
TMP
MY HANDS...
...THE SKIN IS COMING OFF...
HUFF
HUFF
HUH?
TMP
TMP
USA...
WHERE'S MY MOTHER?
HUH?!
I DON'T KNOW THAT.
YOU DON'T?
HUFF
HUFF
M-MY LEGS AND ARMS HURT.
TMP
TMP
HANG IN THERE, USA.

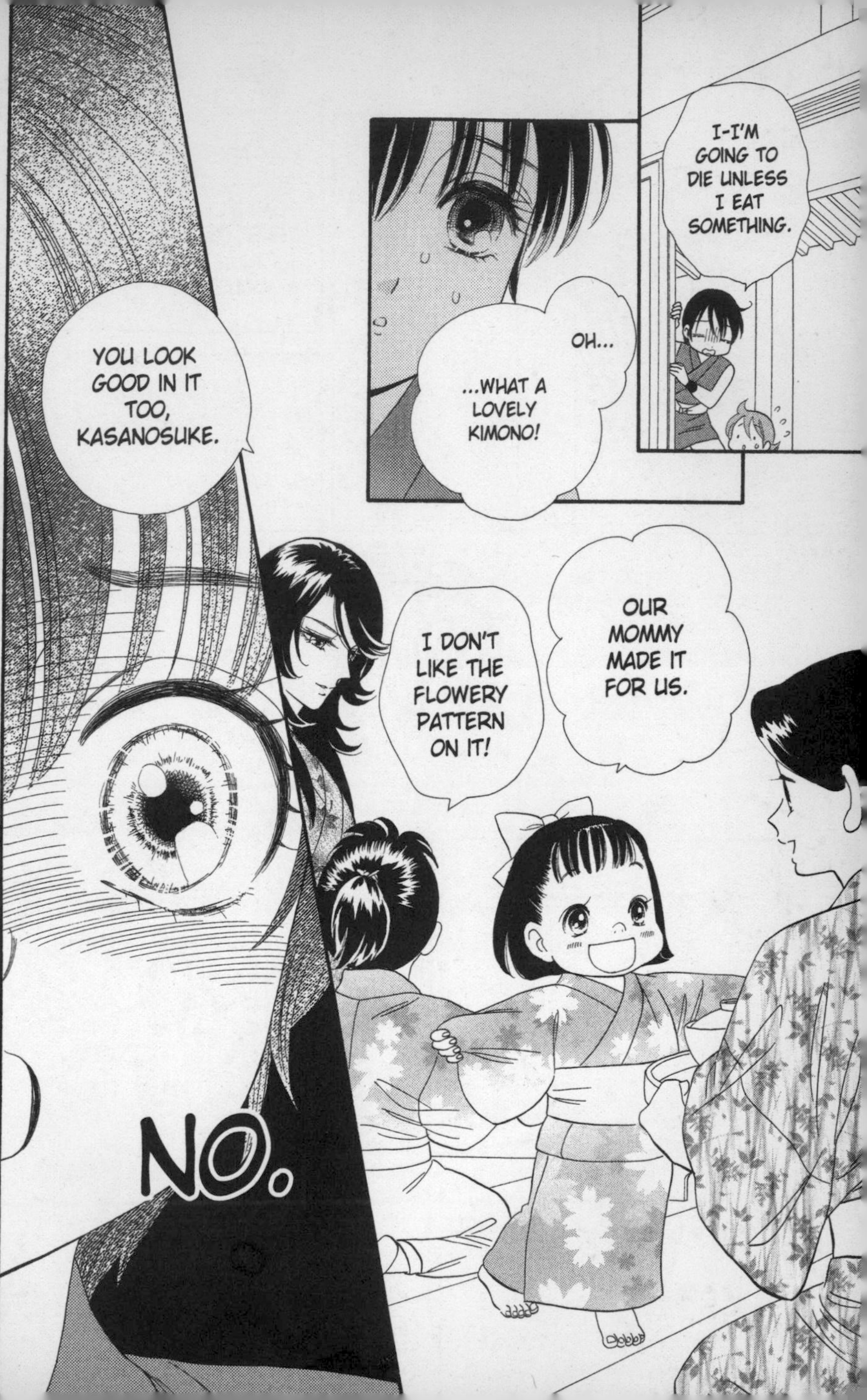
I-I'M GOING TO DIE UNLESS I EAT SOMETHING.
OH...
...WHAT A LOVELY KIMONO!
OUR MOMMY MADE IT FOR US.
I DON'T LIKE THE FLOWERY PATTERN ON IT!
YOU LOOK GOOD IN IT TOO, KASANOSUKE.
NO.

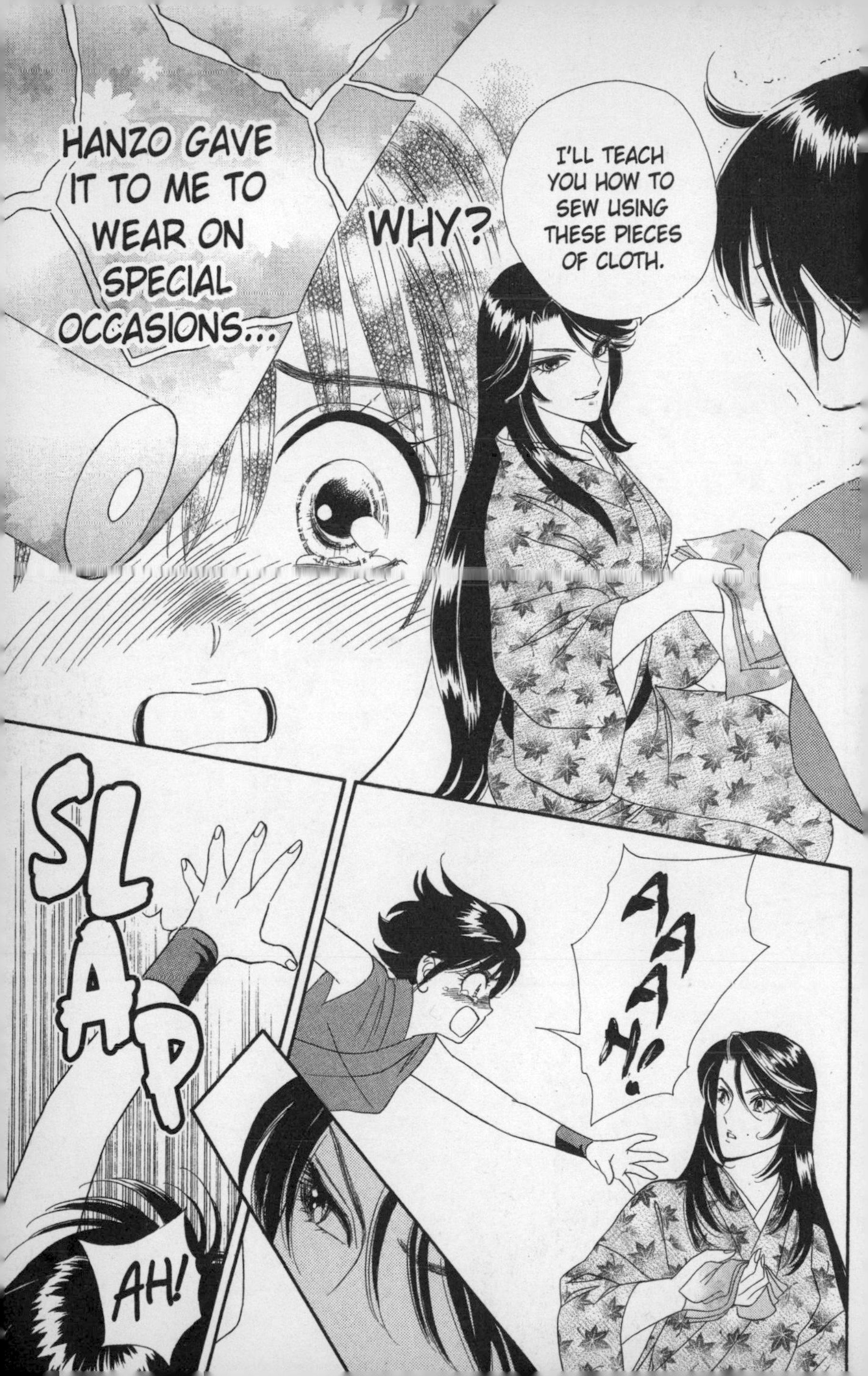
I'LL TEACH YOU HOW TO SEW USING THESE PIECES OF CLOTH.
WHY?
HANZO GAVE IT TO ME TO WEAR ON SPECIAL OCCASIONS...
AAAH!!
SLAP
AH!

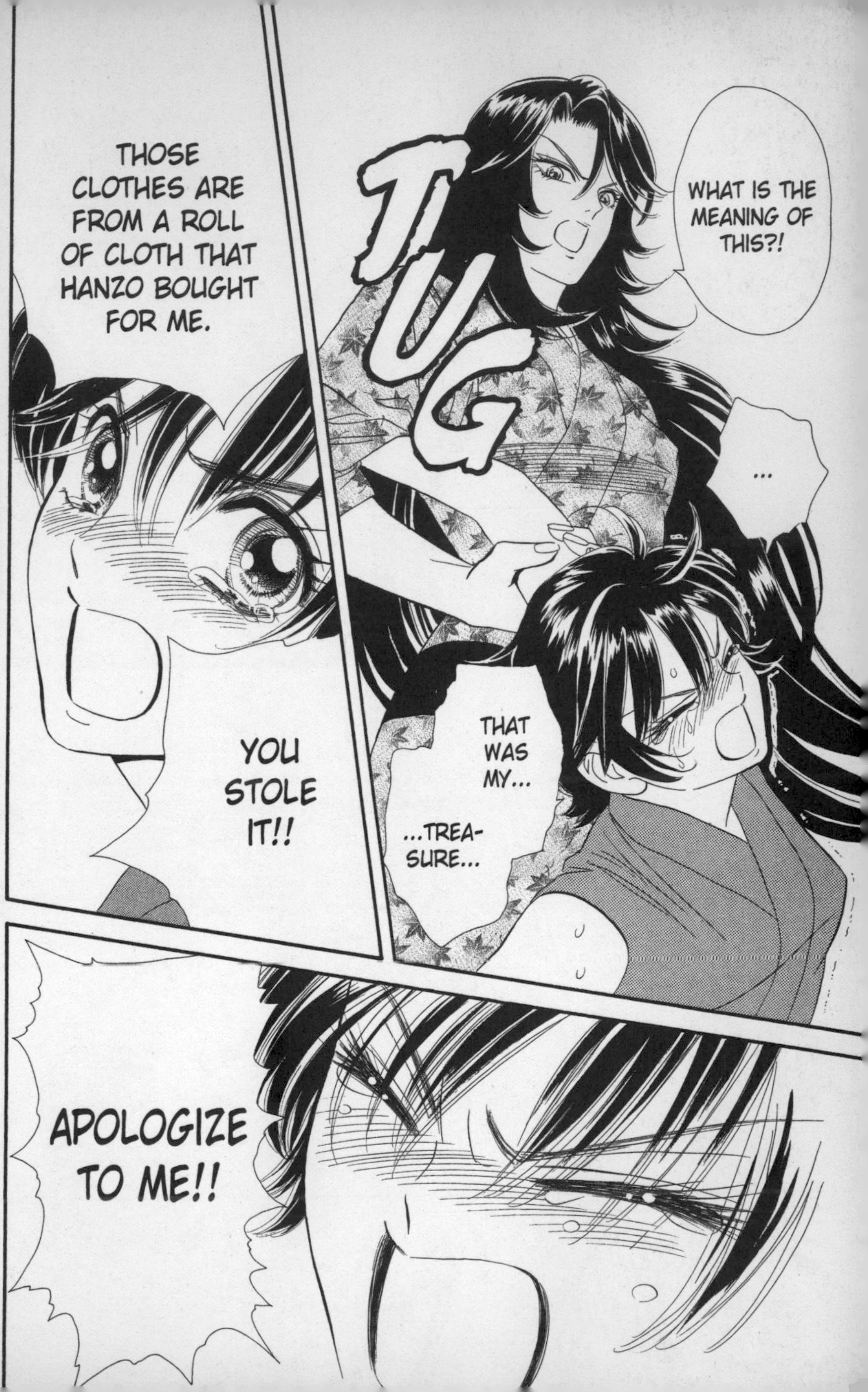
WHAT IS THE MEANING OF THIS?!
TUG
...
THAT WAS MY...
...TREA-SURE...
THOSE CLOTHES ARE FROM A ROLL OF CLOTH THAT HANZO BOUGHT FOR ME.
YOU STOLE IT!!
APOLOGIZE TO ME!!

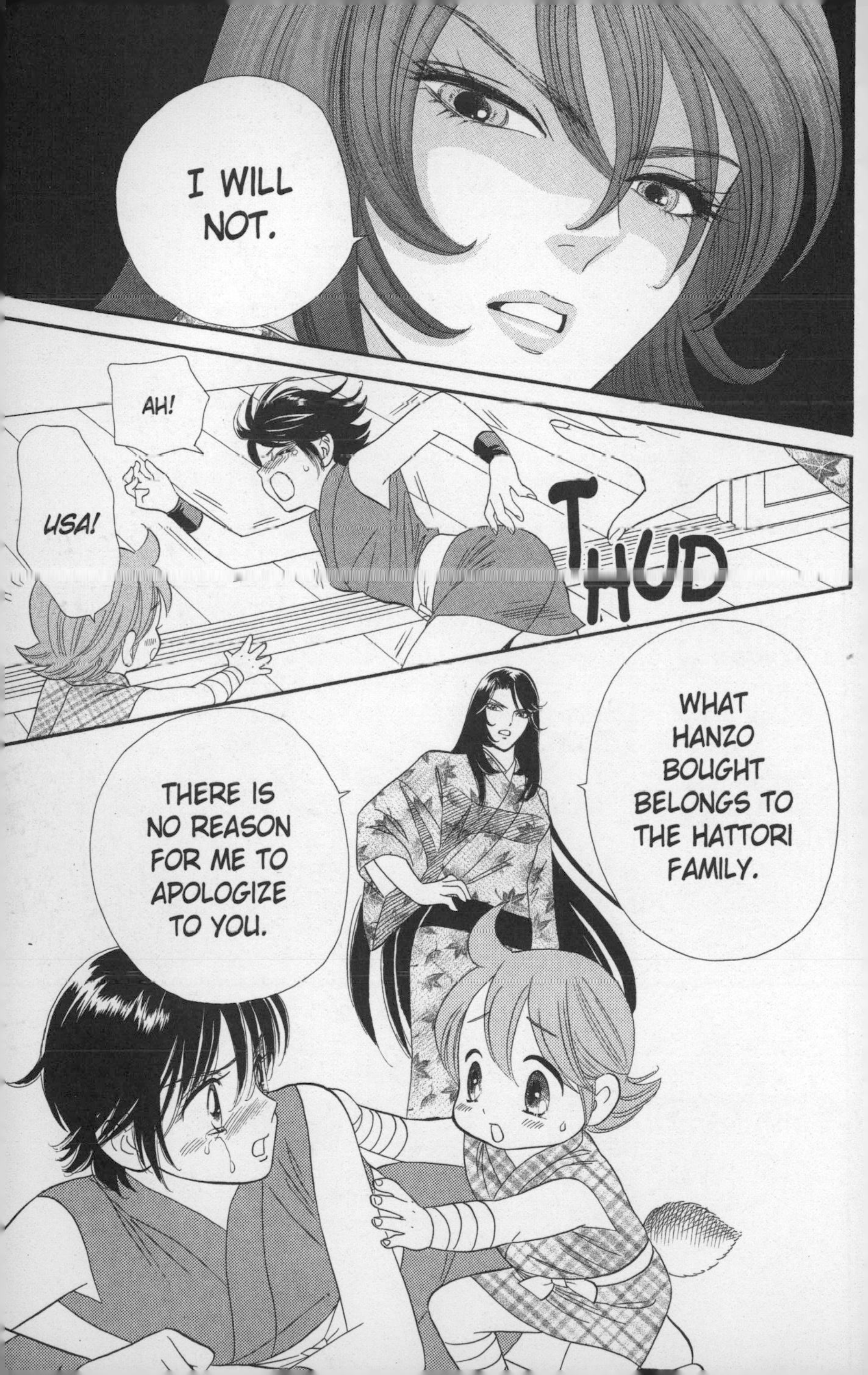
I WILL NOT.
THUD
AH!
USA!
WHAT HANZO BOUGHT BELONGS TO THE HATTORI FAMILY.
THERE IS NO REASON FOR ME TO APOLOGIZE TO YOU.

TAIL OF THE MOON EXTRA: TODAY'S MISSION

"I WANT HANZO IN A TUXEDO TO ESCORT ME!"

-TANAKA HINAKO, KANAGAWA PREFECTURE

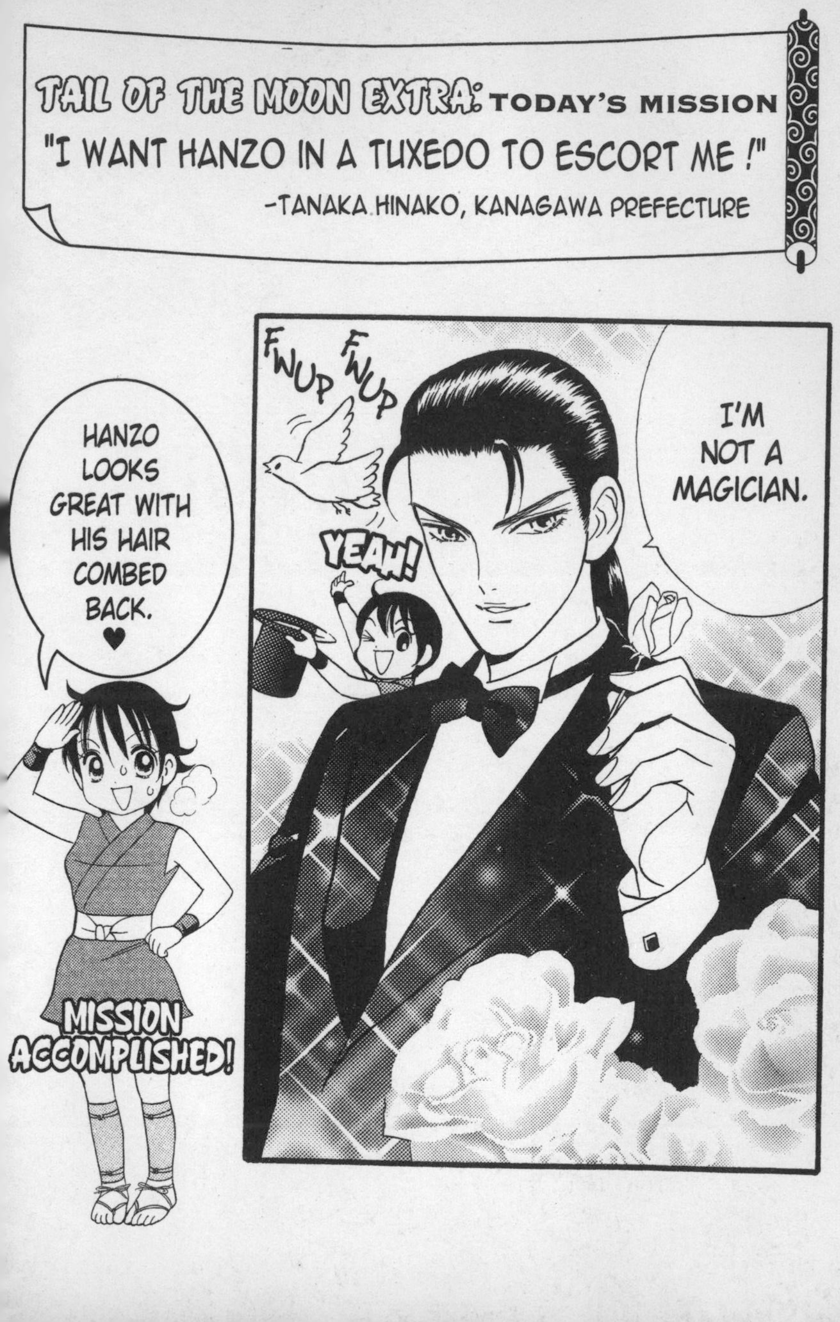
I'M NOT A MAGICIAN.
FWUP FWUP
YEAH!
HANZO LOOKS GREAT WITH HIS HAIR COMBED BACK. ♥
MISSION ACCOMPLISHED!

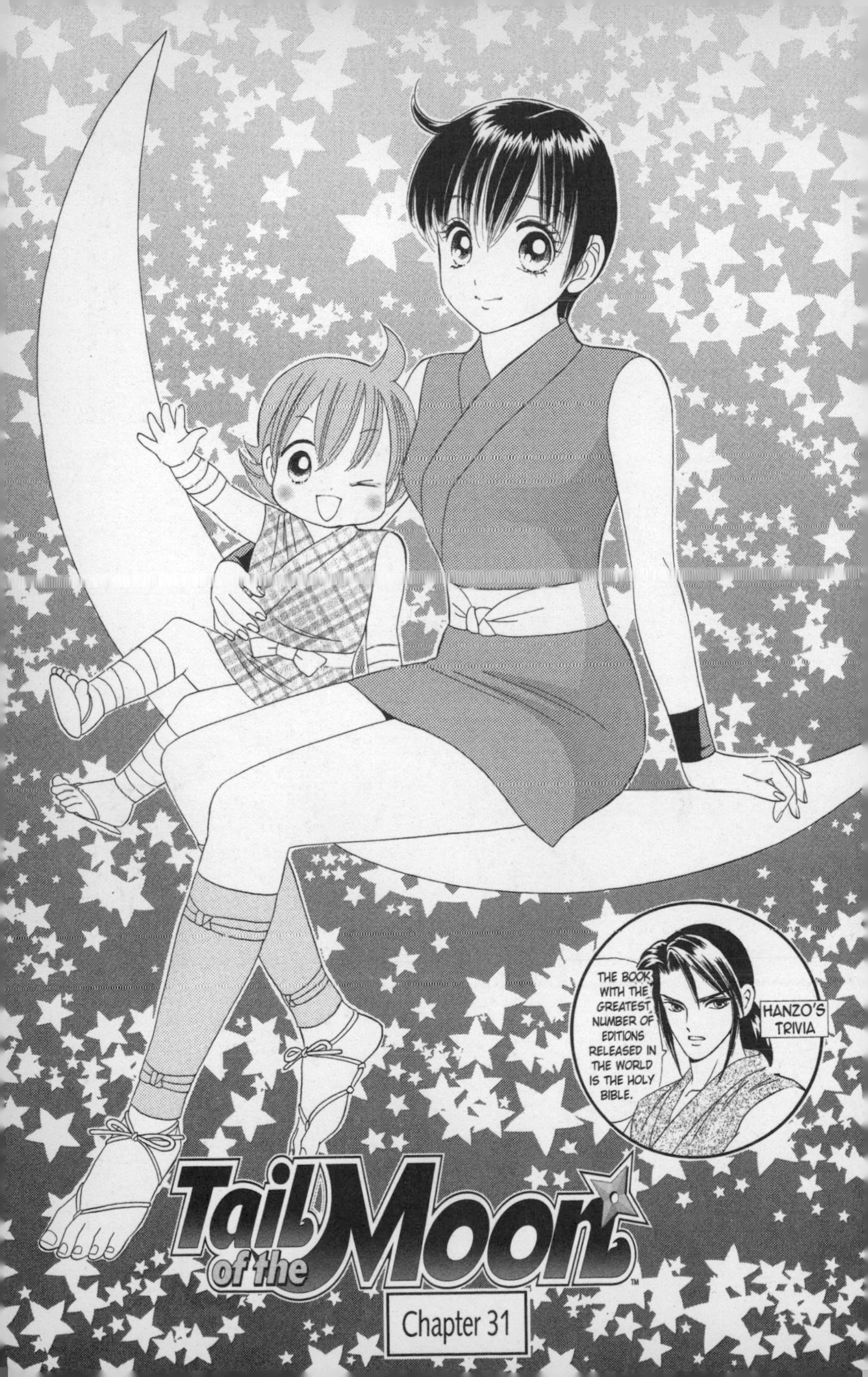
HANZO'S TRIVIA
THE BOOK WITH THE GREATEST NUMBER OF EDITIONS RELEASED IN THE WORLD IS THE HOLY BIBLE.
Tail of the Moon™
Chapter 31

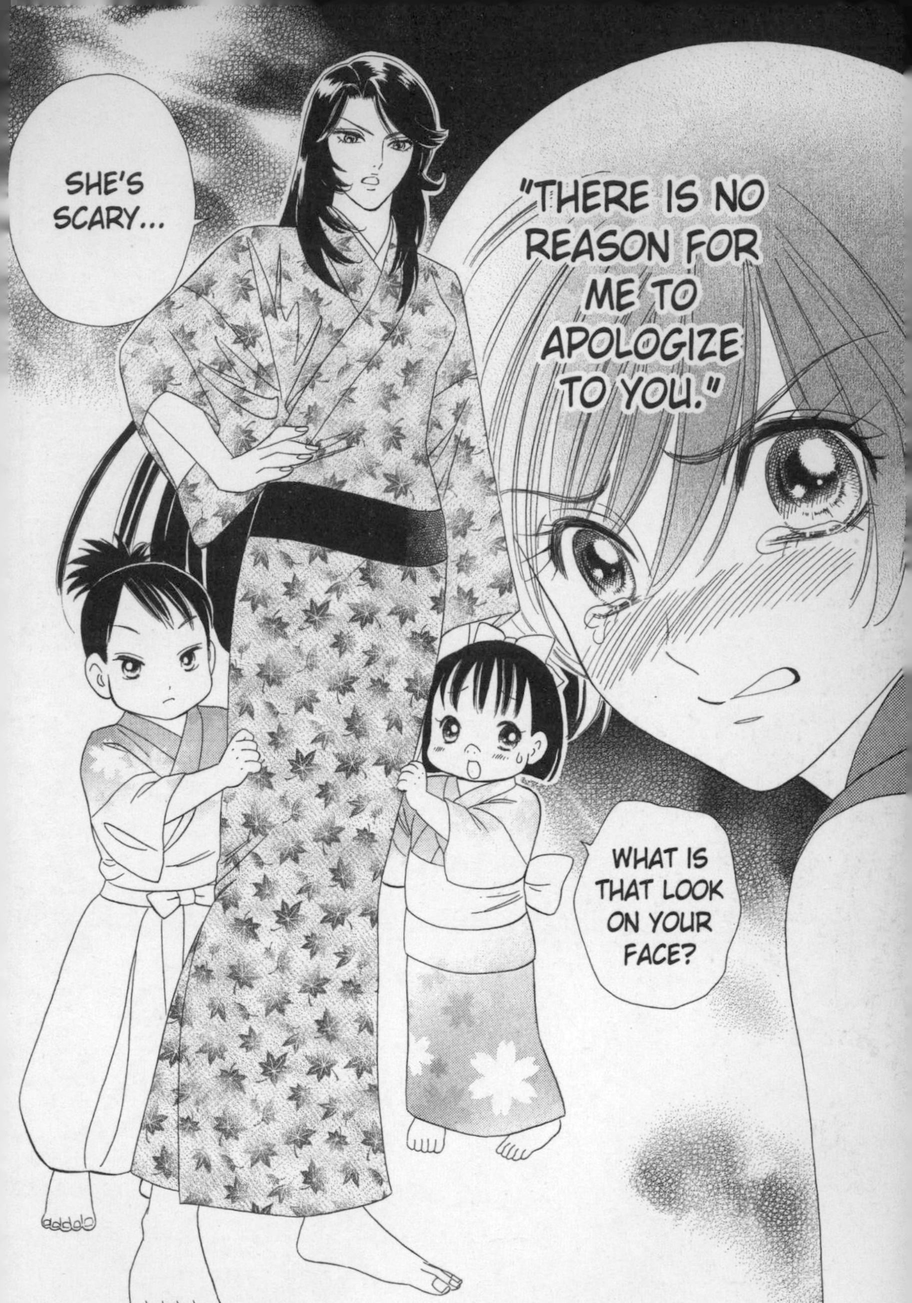
"THERE IS NO REASON FOR ME TO APOLOGIZE TO YOU."
SHE'S SCARY...
WHAT IS THAT LOOK ON YOUR FACE?

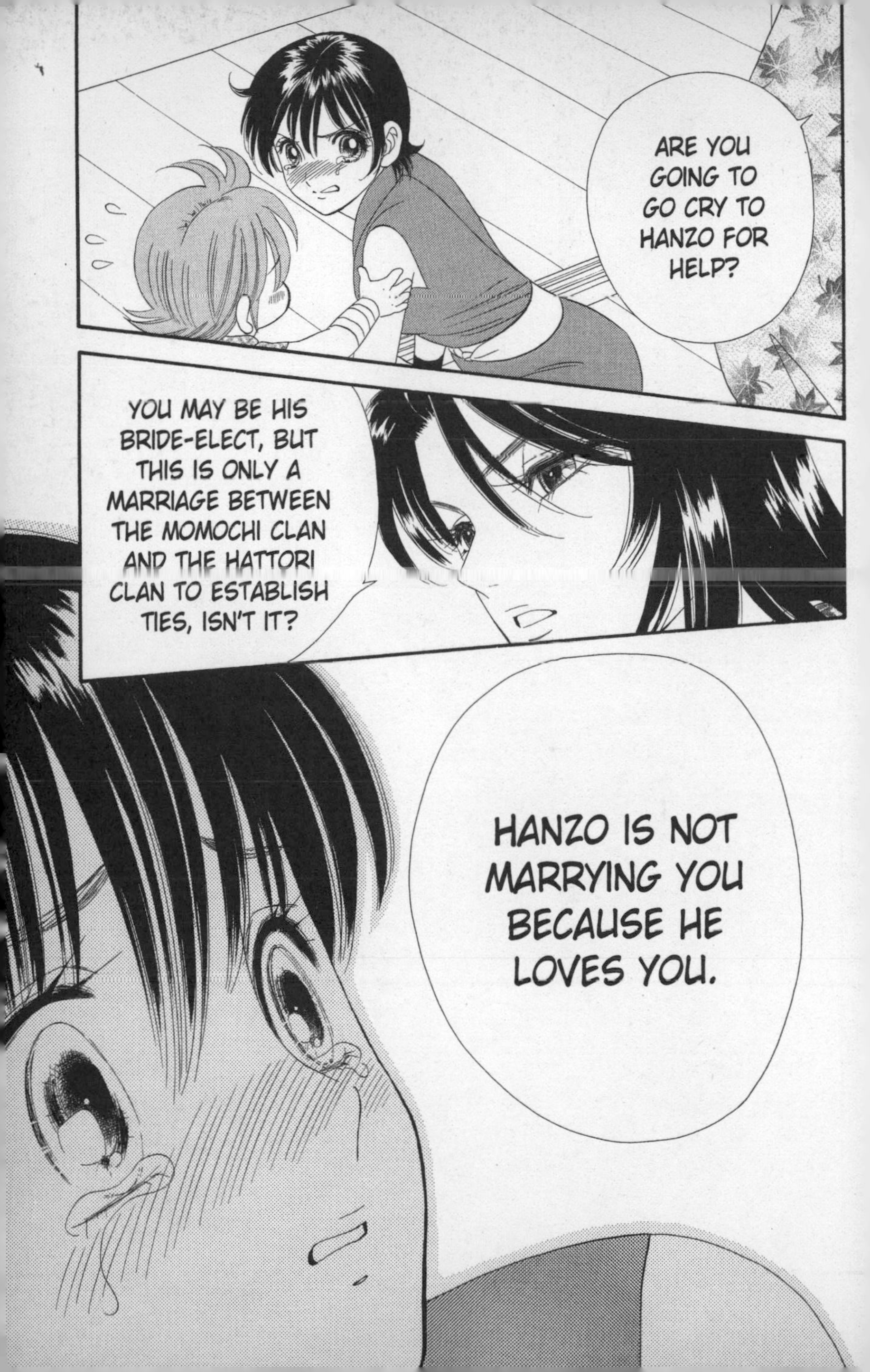
ARE YOU GOING TO GO CRY TO HANZO FOR HELP?
YOU MAY BE HIS BRIDE-ELECT, BUT THIS IS ONLY A MARRIAGE BETWEEN THE MOMOCHI CLAN AND THE HATTORI CLAN TO ESTABLISH TIES, ISN'T IT?
HANZO IS NOT MARRYING YOU BECAUSE HE LOVES YOU.

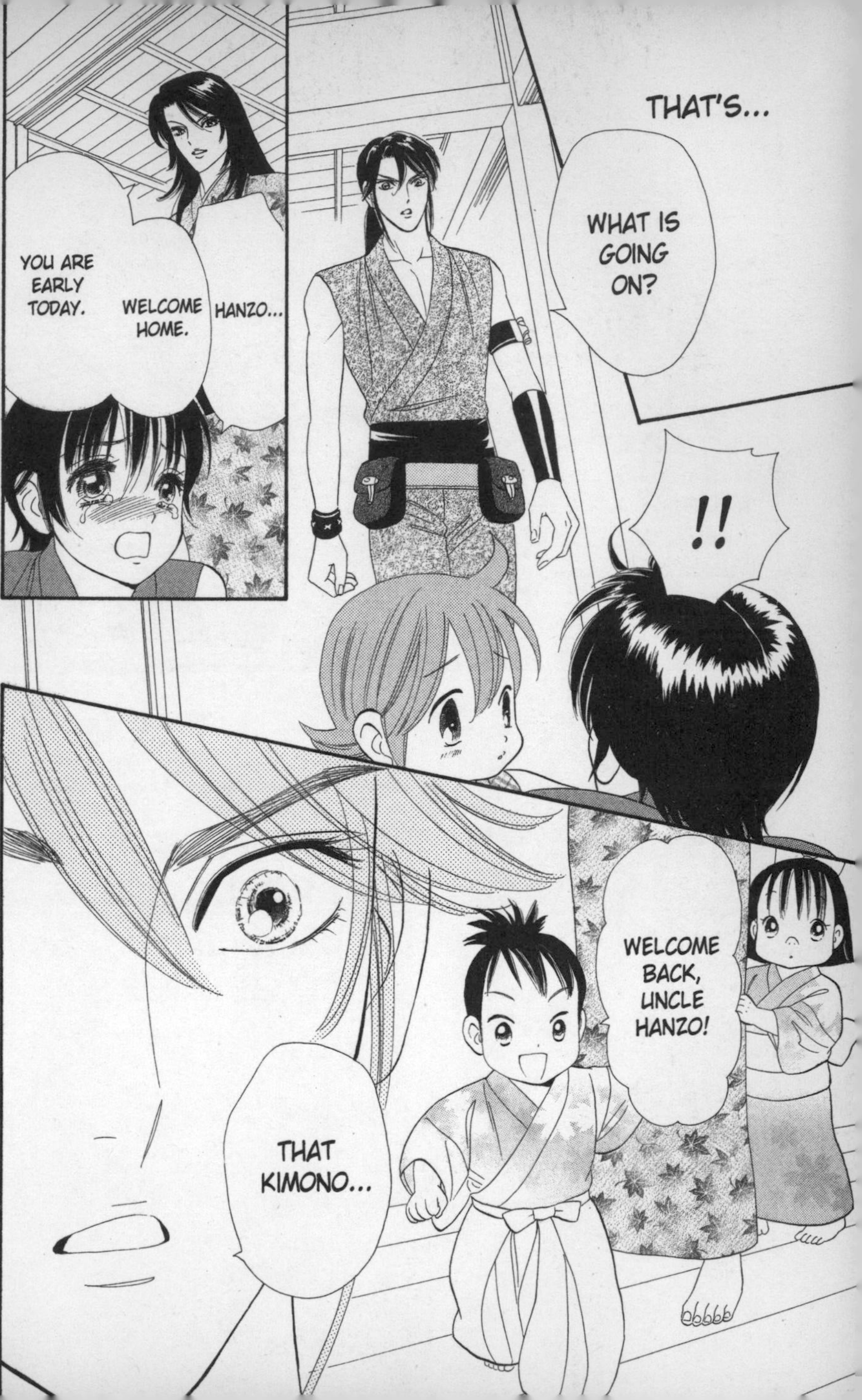
THAT'S...
WHAT IS GOING ON?
!!
HANZO...
WELCOME HOME.
YOU ARE EARLY TODAY.
WELCOME BACK, UNCLE HANZO!
THAT KIMONO...

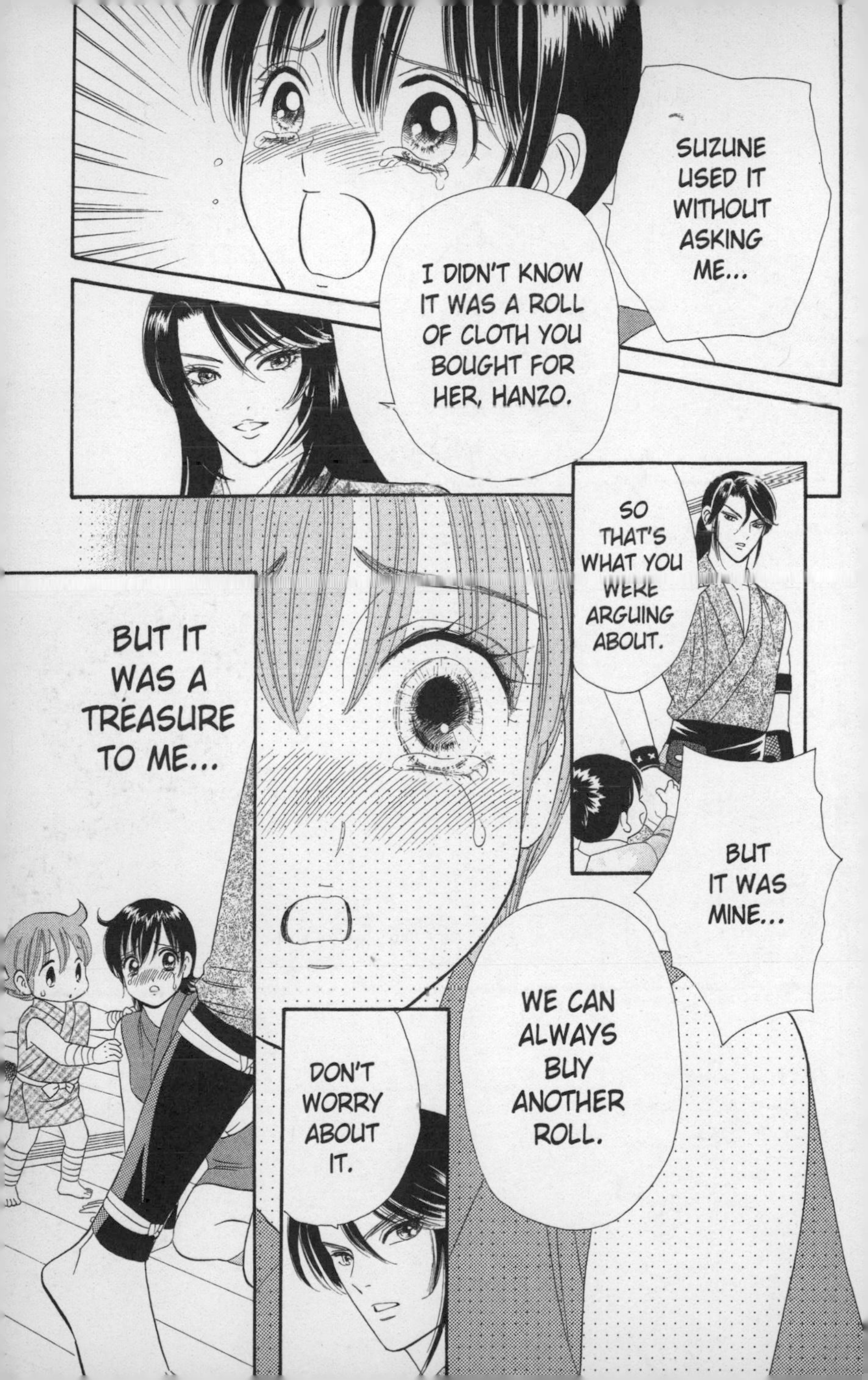
SUZUNE USED IT WITHOUT ASKING ME...
I DIDN'T KNOW IT WAS A ROLL OF CLOTH YOU BOUGHT FOR HER, HANZO.
SO THAT'S WHAT YOU WERE ARGUING ABOUT.
BUT IT WAS MINE...
WE CAN ALWAYS BUY ANOTHER ROLL.
DON'T WORRY ABOUT IT.
BUT IT WAS A TREASURE TO ME...

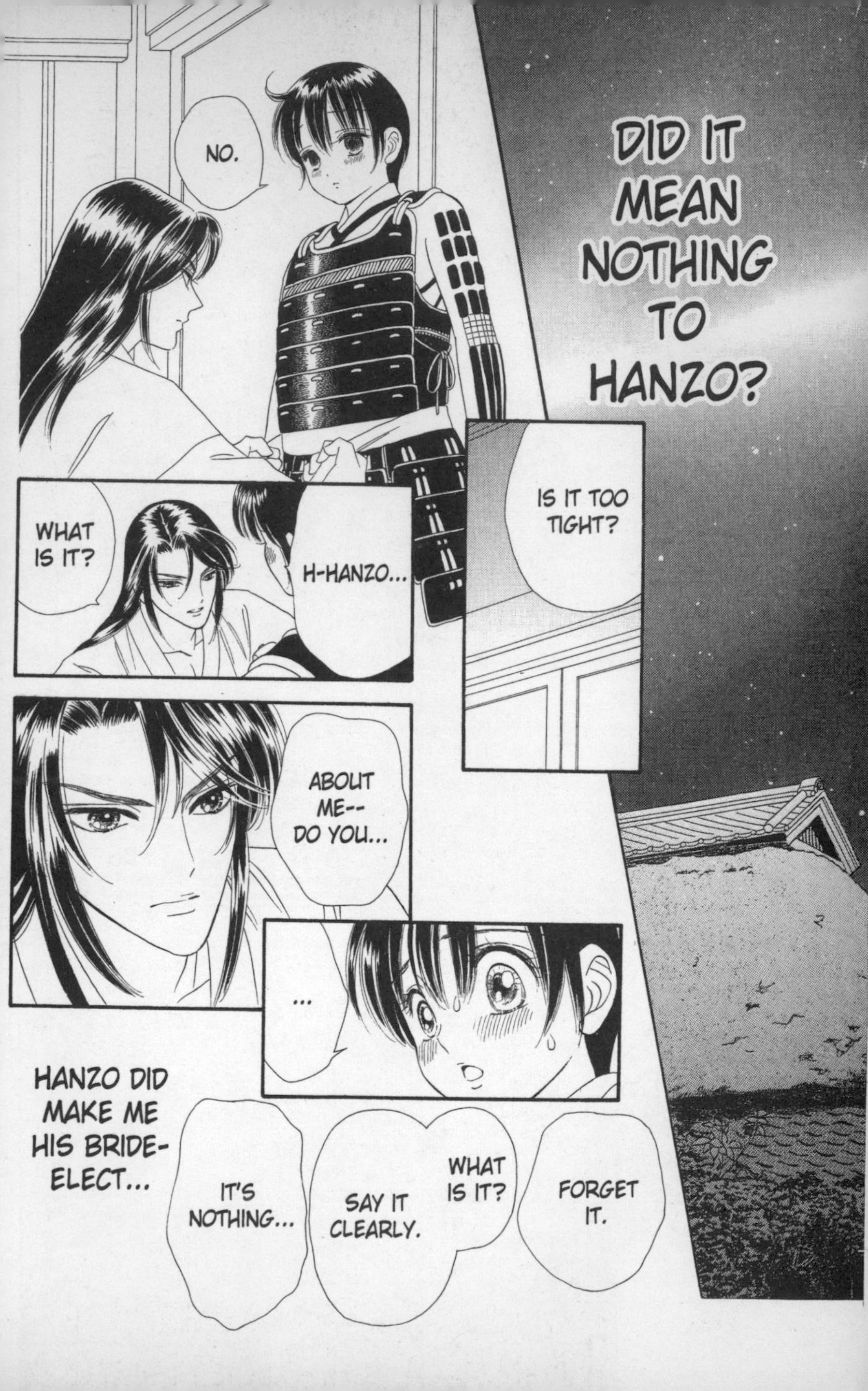
DID IT MEAN NOTHING TO HANZO?
IS IT TOO TIGHT?
NO.
H-HANZO...
WHAT IS IT?
ABOUT ME-- DO YOU...
...
FORGET IT.
WHAT IS IT?
SAY IT CLEARLY.
IT'S NOTHING...
HANZO DID MAKE ME HIS BRIDE-ELECT...

...BUT HE'S NEVER TOLD ME THAT HE LOVES ME.

I'M NOT SURE...

...HE'LL EVEN SAY THAT TO ME...

CAN'T YOU EVEN DO SUCH A SIMPLE TASK?!

YOU JUST NEED TO CONCENTRATE AND FOCUS ON GETTING THE THREAD THROUGH THE NEEDLE!

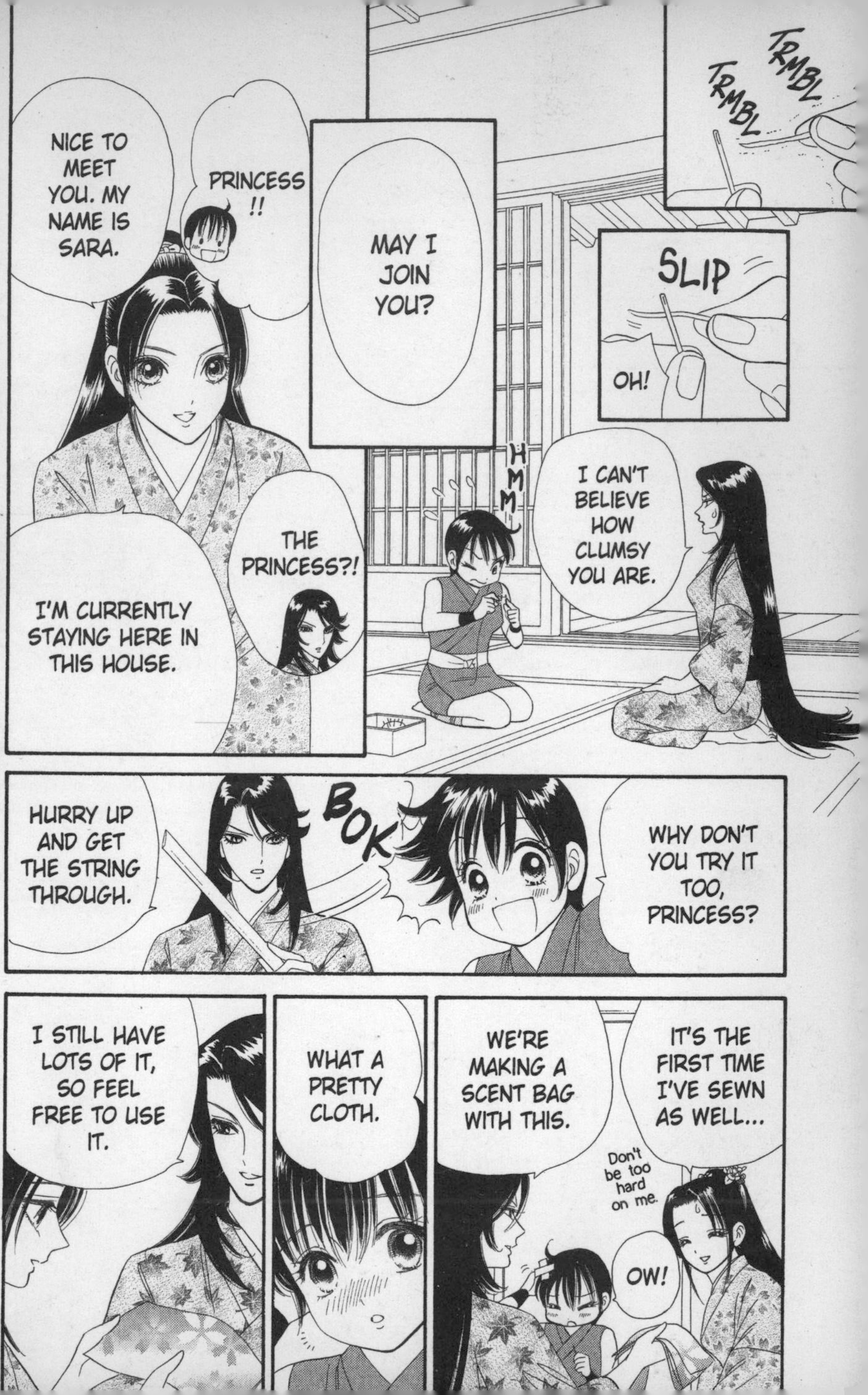
TRMBL
TRMBL
SLIP
OH!
I CAN'T BELIEVE HOW CLUMSY YOU ARE.
HMM
MAY I JOIN YOU?
PRINCESS !!
THE PRINCESS?!
NICE TO MEET YOU. MY NAME IS SARA.
I'M CURRENTLY STAYING HERE IN THIS HOUSE.
WHY DON'T YOU TRY IT TOO, PRINCESS?
BOK
HURRY UP AND GET THE STRING THROUGH.
IT'S THE FIRST TIME I'VE SEWN AS WELL...
Don't be too hard on me.
WE'RE MAKING A SCENT BAG WITH THIS.
OW!
WHAT A PRETTY CLOTH.
I STILL HAVE LOTS OF IT, SO FEEL FREE TO USE IT.

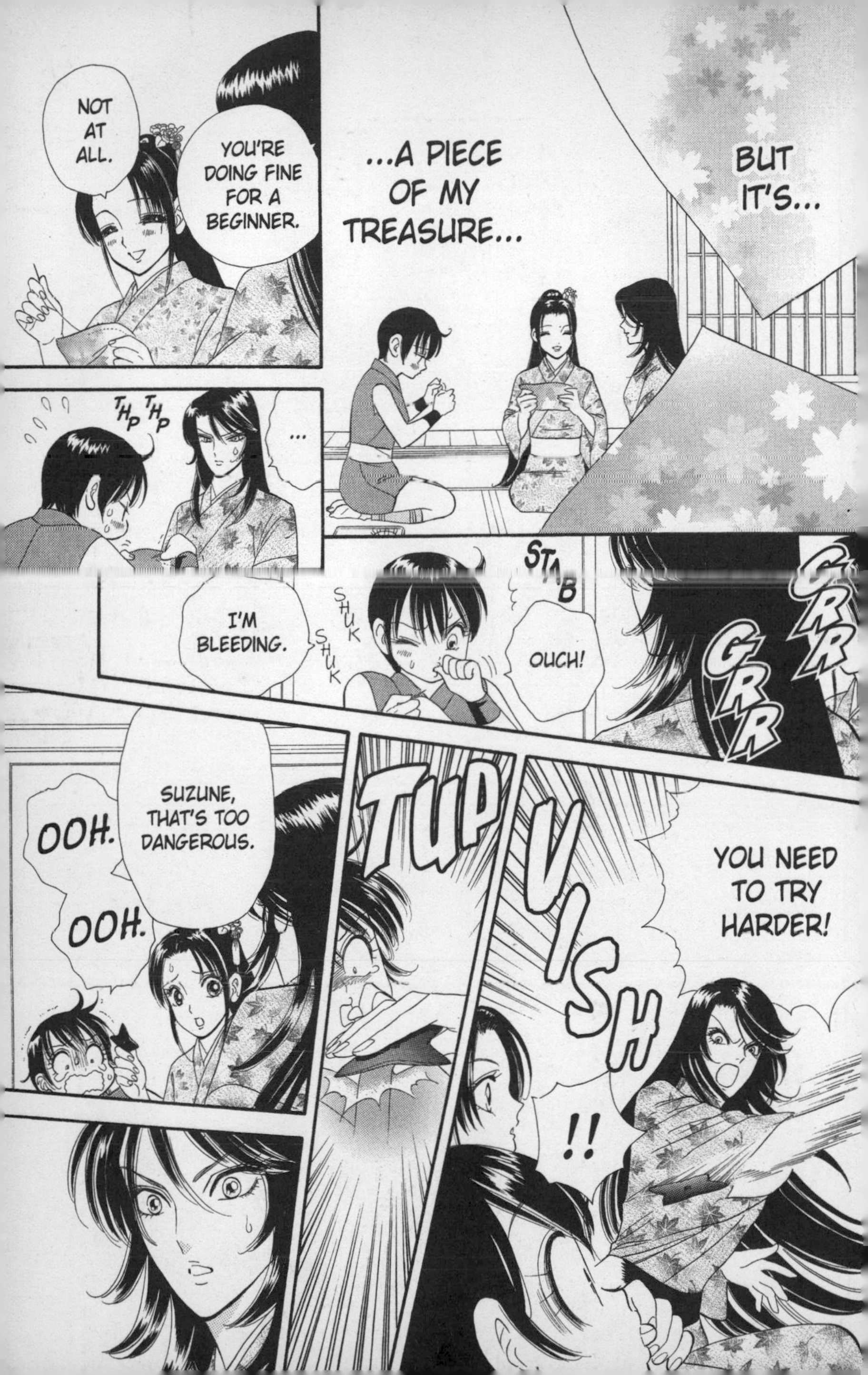
BUT IT'S...
...A PIECE OF MY TREASURE...
YOU'RE DOING FINE FOR A BEGINNER.
NOT AT ALL.
...
THP THP
GRR GRR
STAB
OUCH!
SHUK SHUK
I'M BLEEDING.
YOU NEED TO TRY HARDER!
VISH
!!
TUP
SUZUNE, THAT'S TOO DANGEROUS.
OOH.
OOH.

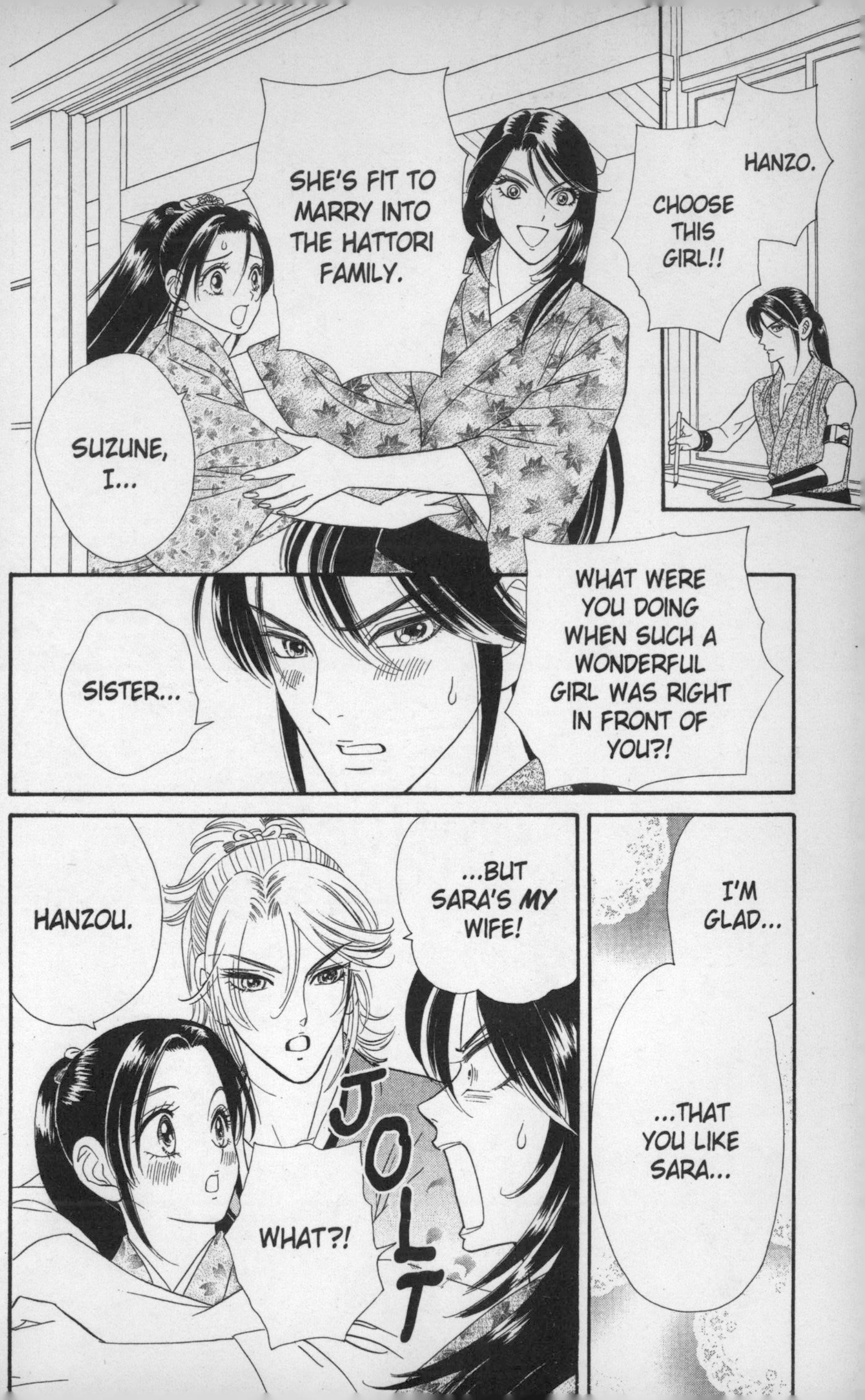
HANZO.
CHOOSE THIS GIRL!!
SHE'S FIT TO MARRY INTO THE HATTORI FAMILY.
SUZUNE, I...
WHAT WERE YOU DOING WHEN SUCH A WONDERFUL GIRL WAS RIGHT IN FRONT OF YOU?!
SISTER...
I'M GLAD...
...THAT YOU LIKE SARA...
...BUT SARA'S *MY* WIFE!
HANZOU.
JOLT
WHAT?!

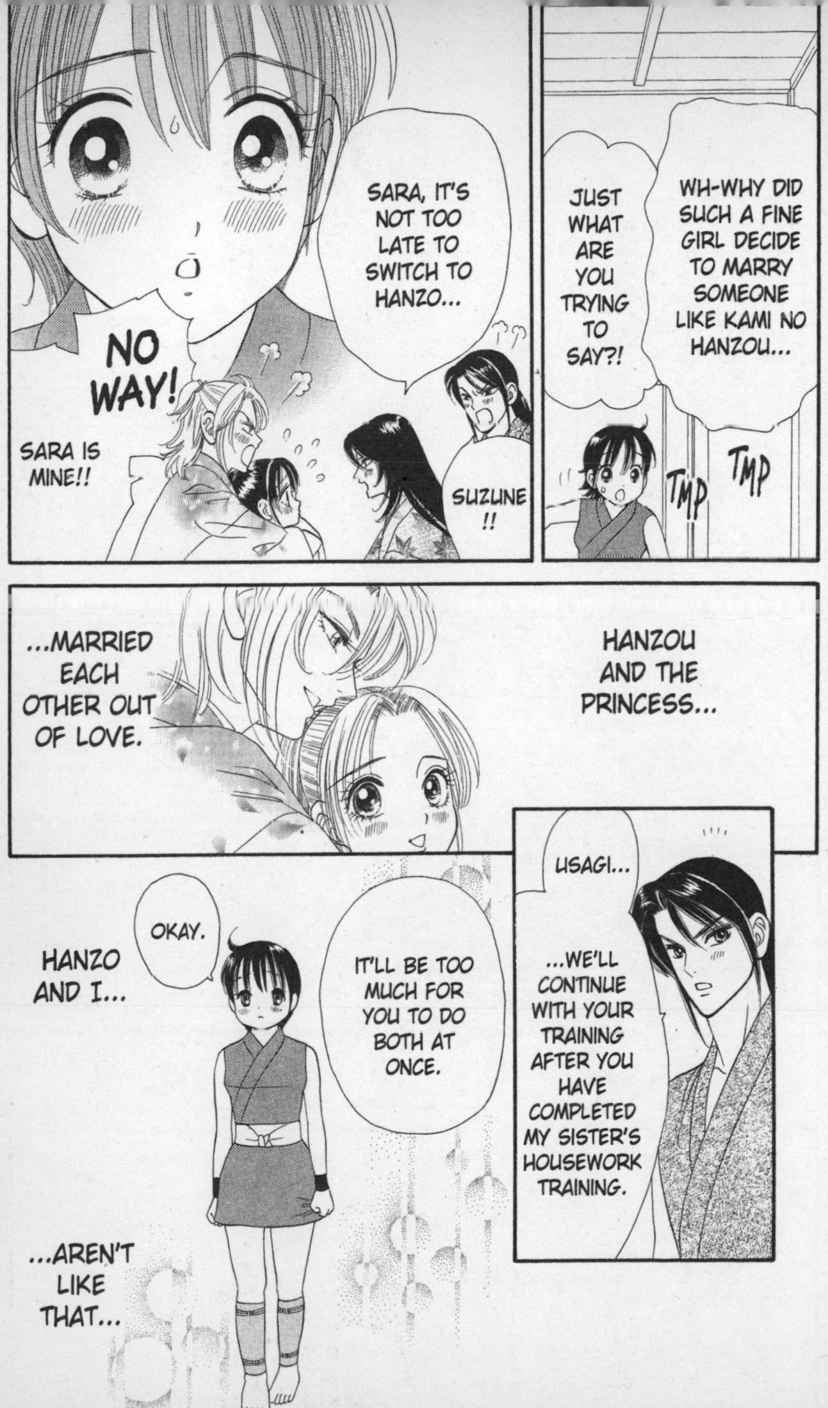
WH-WHY DID SUCH A FINE GIRL DECIDE TO MARRY SOMEONE LIKE KAMI NO HANZOU...
JUST WHAT ARE YOU TRYING TO SAY?!
TMP
TMP
SARA, IT'S NOT TOO LATE TO SWITCH TO HANZO...
SUZUNE !!
NO WAY!
SARA IS MINE!!
HANZOU AND THE PRINCESS...
...MARRIED EACH OTHER OUT OF LOVE.
USAGI...
...WE'LL CONTINUE WITH YOUR TRAINING AFTER YOU HAVE COMPLETED MY SISTER'S HOUSEWORK TRAINING.
IT'LL BE TOO MUCH FOR YOU TO DO BOTH AT ONCE.
OKAY.
HANZO AND I...
...AREN'T LIKE THAT...

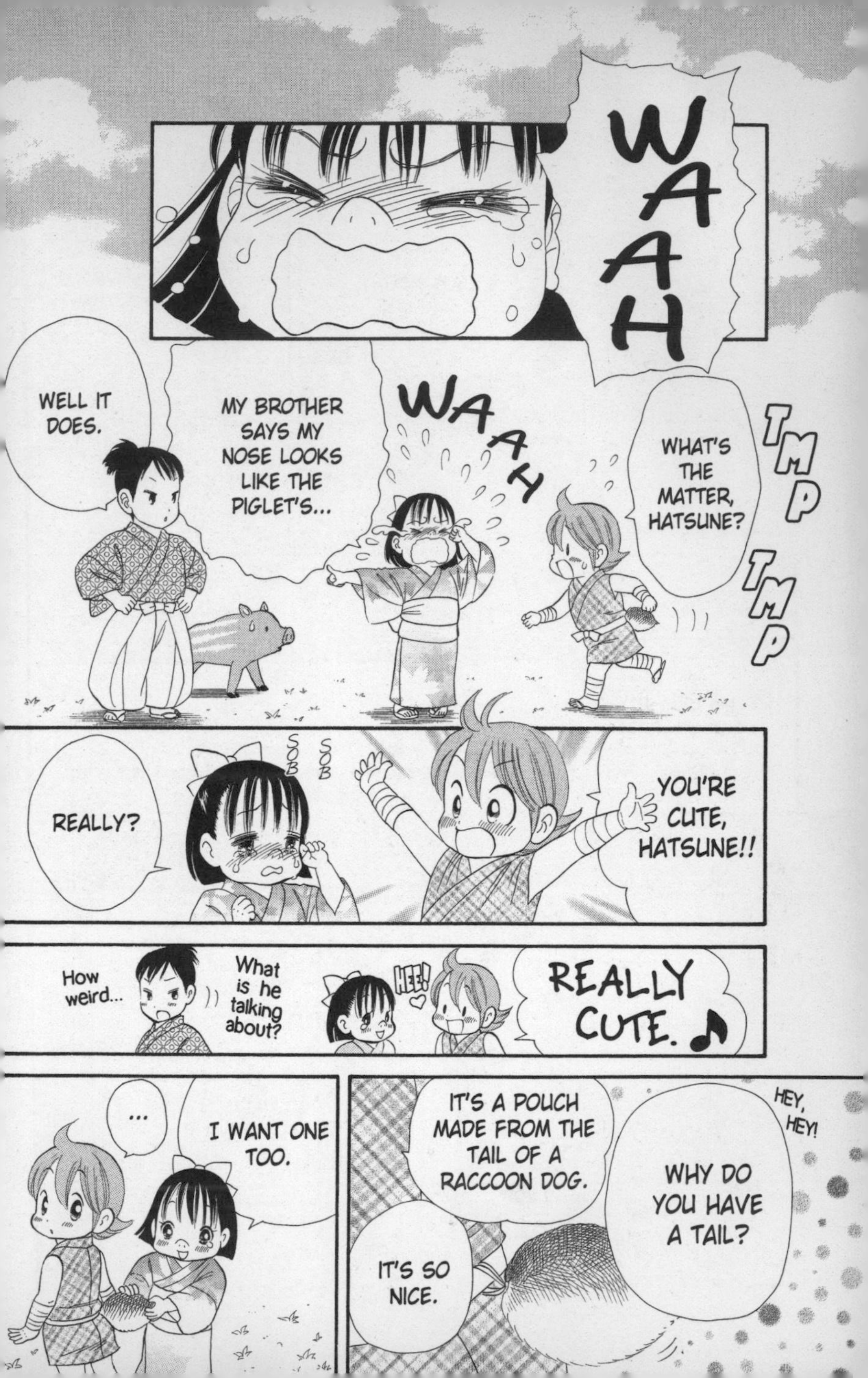
WAAH
TMP TMP
WHAT'S THE MATTER, HATSUNE?
WAAH
MY BROTHER SAYS MY NOSE LOOKS LIKE THE PIGLET'S...
WELL IT DOES.
YOU'RE CUTE, HATSUNE!!
SOB SOB
REALLY?
REALLY CUTE. ♪
HEE!
What is he talking about?
How weird...
HEY, HEY!
WHY DO YOU HAVE A TAIL?
IT'S A POUCH MADE FROM THE TAIL OF A RACCOON DOG.
IT'S SO NICE.
I WANT ONE TOO.
...

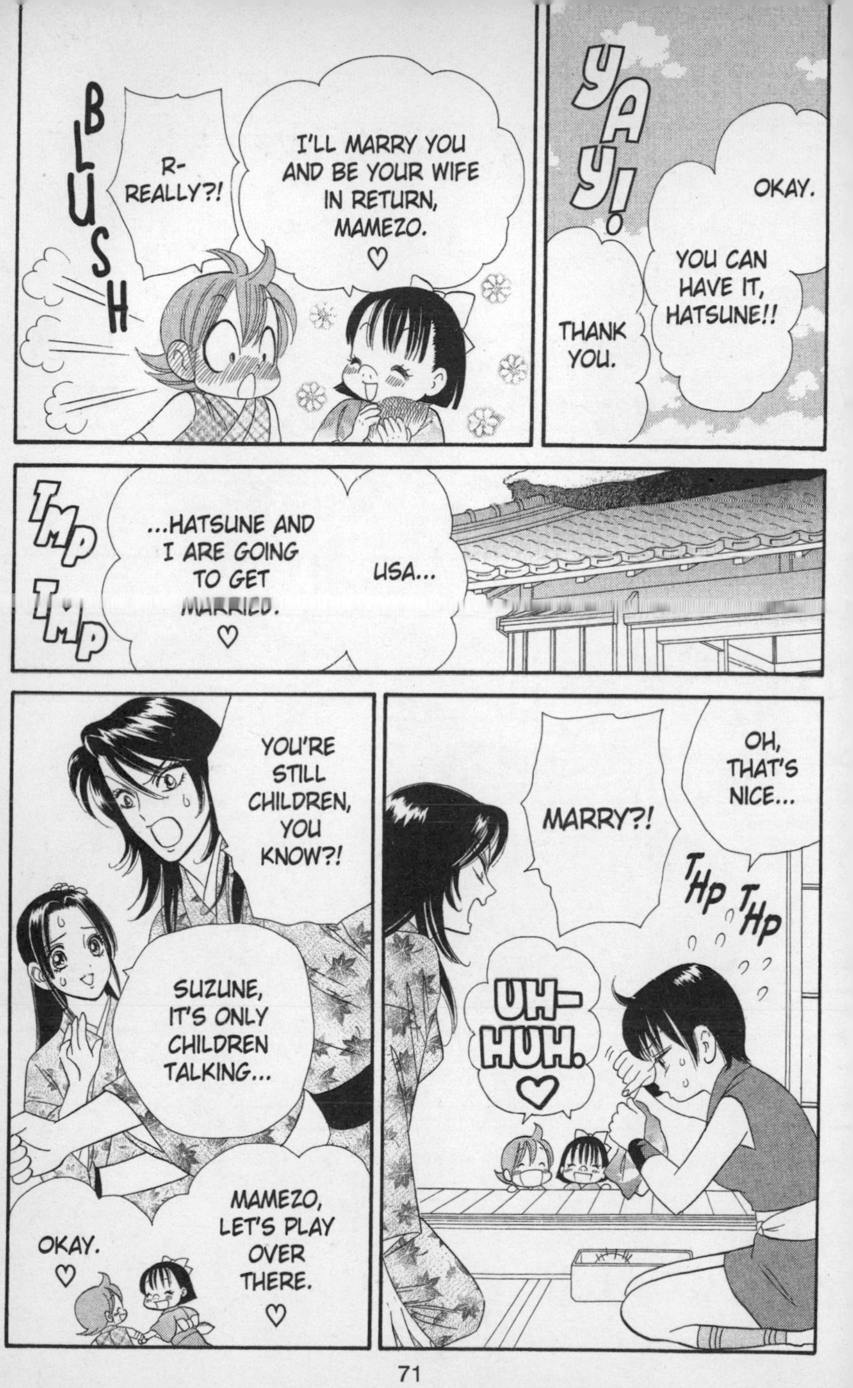
OKAY.
YOU CAN HAVE IT, HATSUNE!!
THANK YOU.
YAY!
I'LL MARRY YOU AND BE YOUR WIFE IN RETURN, MAMEZO. ♡
R-REALLY?!
BLUSH
USA...
...HATSUNE AND I ARE GOING TO GET MARRIED. ♡
TMP TMP
OH, THAT'S NICE...
MARRY?!
THP THP
UH-HUH. ♡
YOU'RE STILL CHILDREN, YOU KNOW?!
SUZUNE, IT'S ONLY CHILDREN TALKING...
MAMEZO, LET'S PLAY OVER THERE. ♡
OKAY. ♡

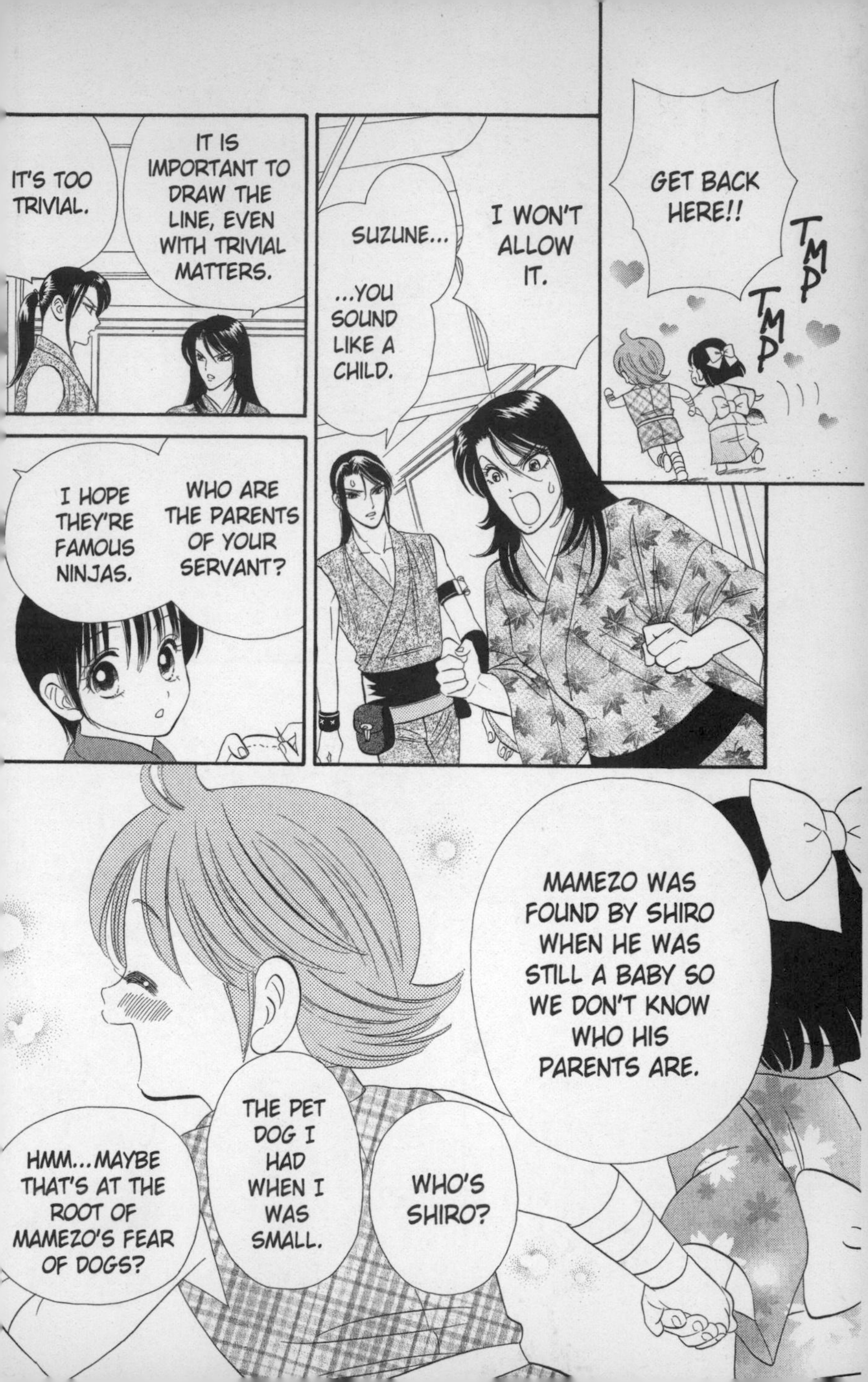
GET BACK HERE!!
TMP
TMP
I WON'T ALLOW IT.
SUZUNE...
...YOU SOUND LIKE A CHILD.
IT IS IMPORTANT TO DRAW THE LINE, EVEN WITH TRIVIAL MATTERS.
IT'S TOO TRIVIAL.
WHO ARE THE PARENTS OF YOUR SERVANT?
I HOPE THEY'RE FAMOUS NINJAS.
MAMEZO WAS FOUND BY SHIRO WHEN HE WAS STILL A BABY SO WE DON'T KNOW WHO HIS PARENTS ARE.
WHO'S SHIRO?
THE PET DOG I HAD WHEN I WAS SMALL.
HMM...MAYBE THAT'S AT THE ROOT OF MAMEZO'S FEAR OF DOGS?

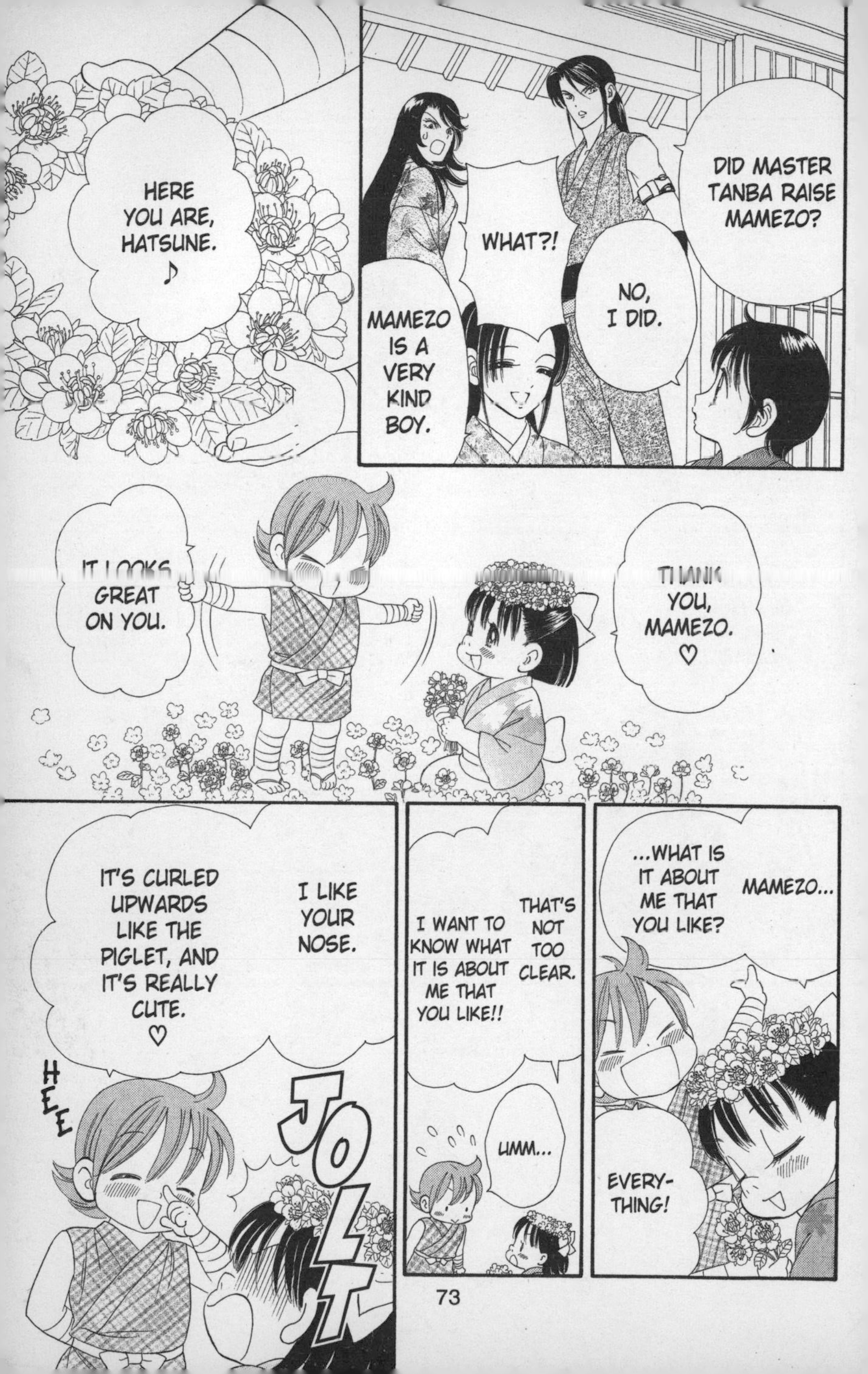
DID MASTER TANBA RAISE MAMEZO?
WHAT?!
NO, I DID.
MAMEZO IS A VERY KIND BOY.
HERE YOU ARE, HATSUNE. ♪
THANK YOU, MAMEZO. ♡
IT LOOKS GREAT ON YOU.
MAMEZO...
...WHAT IS IT ABOUT ME THAT YOU LIKE?
EVERY-THING!
THAT'S NOT TOO CLEAR.
I WANT TO KNOW WHAT IT IS ABOUT ME THAT YOU LIKE!!
UMM...
I LIKE YOUR NOSE.
IT'S CURLED UPWARDS LIKE THE PIGLET, AND IT'S REALLY CUTE. ♡
HEE
JOLT

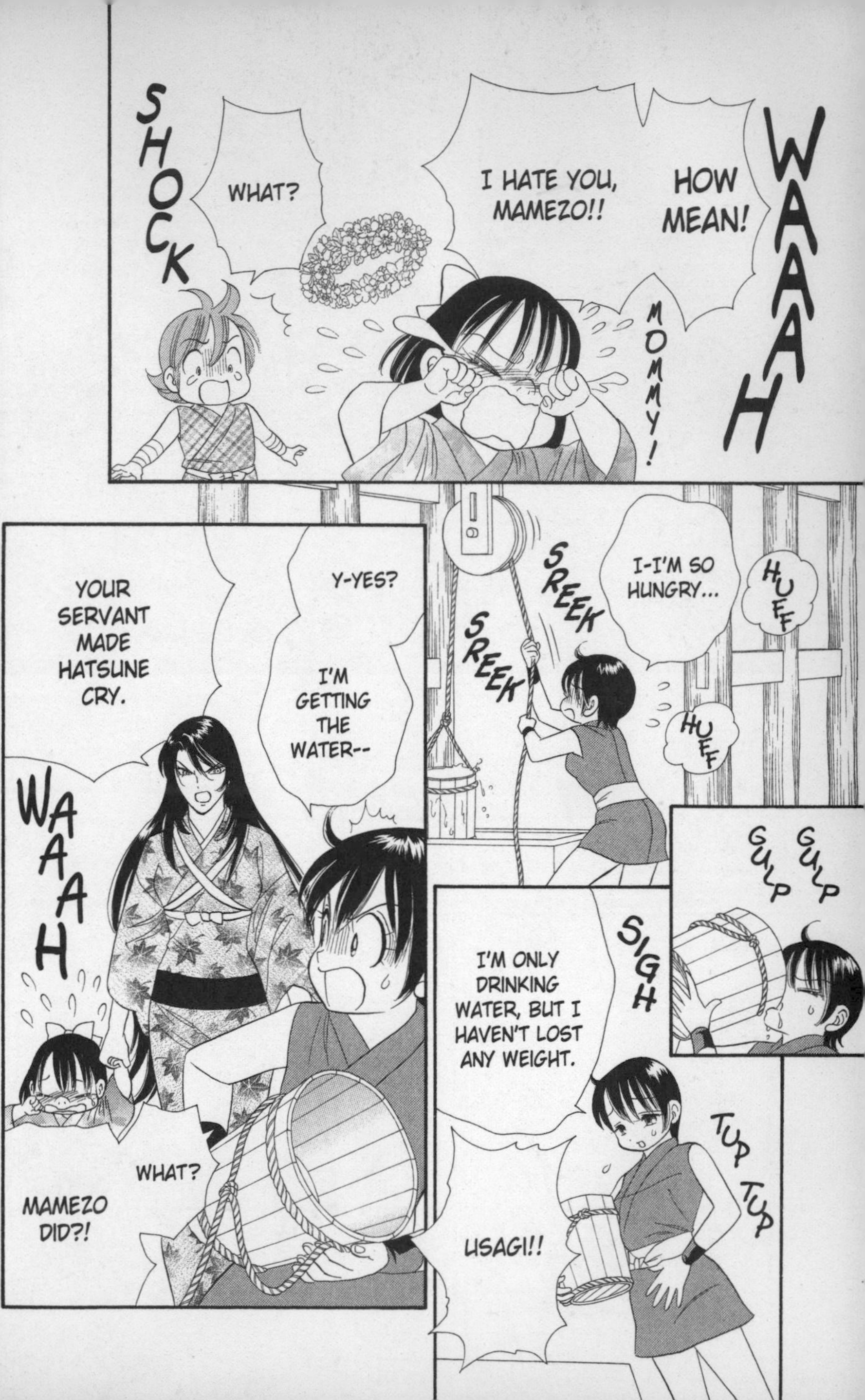
WAAAH
HOW MEAN!
MOMMY!
I HATE YOU, MAMEZO!!
WHAT?
SHOCK
I-I'M SO HUNGRY...
HUFF HUFF
SREEK SREEK
GULP GULP
SIGH
I'M ONLY DRINKING WATER, BUT I HAVEN'T LOST ANY WEIGHT.
TUP TUP
USAGI!!
Y-YES?
I'M GETTING THE WATER--
YOUR SERVANT MADE HATSUNE CRY.
WAAAH
WHAT?
MAMEZO DID?!

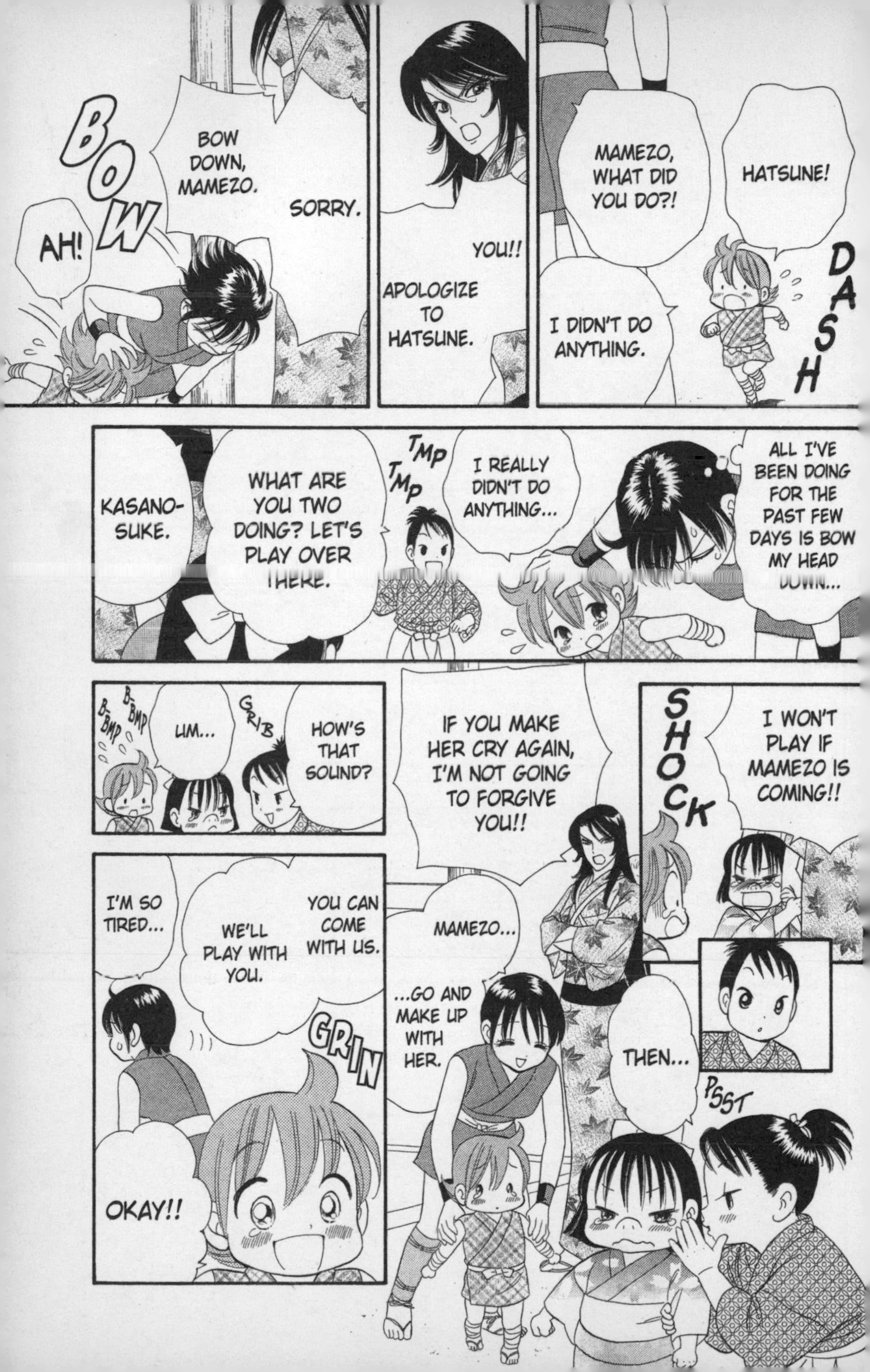
HATSUNE!
DASH
MAMEZO, WHAT DID YOU DO?!
I DIDN'T DO ANYTHING.
YOU!!
APOLOGIZE TO HATSUNE.
SORRY.
BOW DOWN, MAMEZO.
BOW
AH!
ALL I'VE BEEN DOING FOR THE PAST FEW DAYS IS BOW MY HEAD DOWN...
I REALLY DIDN'T DO ANYTHING...
TMP TMP
WHAT ARE YOU TWO DOING? LET'S PLAY OVER THERE.
KASANO-SUKE.
I WON'T PLAY IF MAMEZO IS COMING!!
SHOCK
IF YOU MAKE HER CRY AGAIN, I'M NOT GOING TO FORGIVE YOU!!
HOW'S THAT SOUND?
GRIB
UM...
B-BMP B-BMP
PSST
THEN...
MAMEZO...
...GO AND MAKE UP WITH HER.
YOU CAN COME WITH US.
WE'LL PLAY WITH YOU.
I'M SO TIRED...
GRIN
OKAY!!

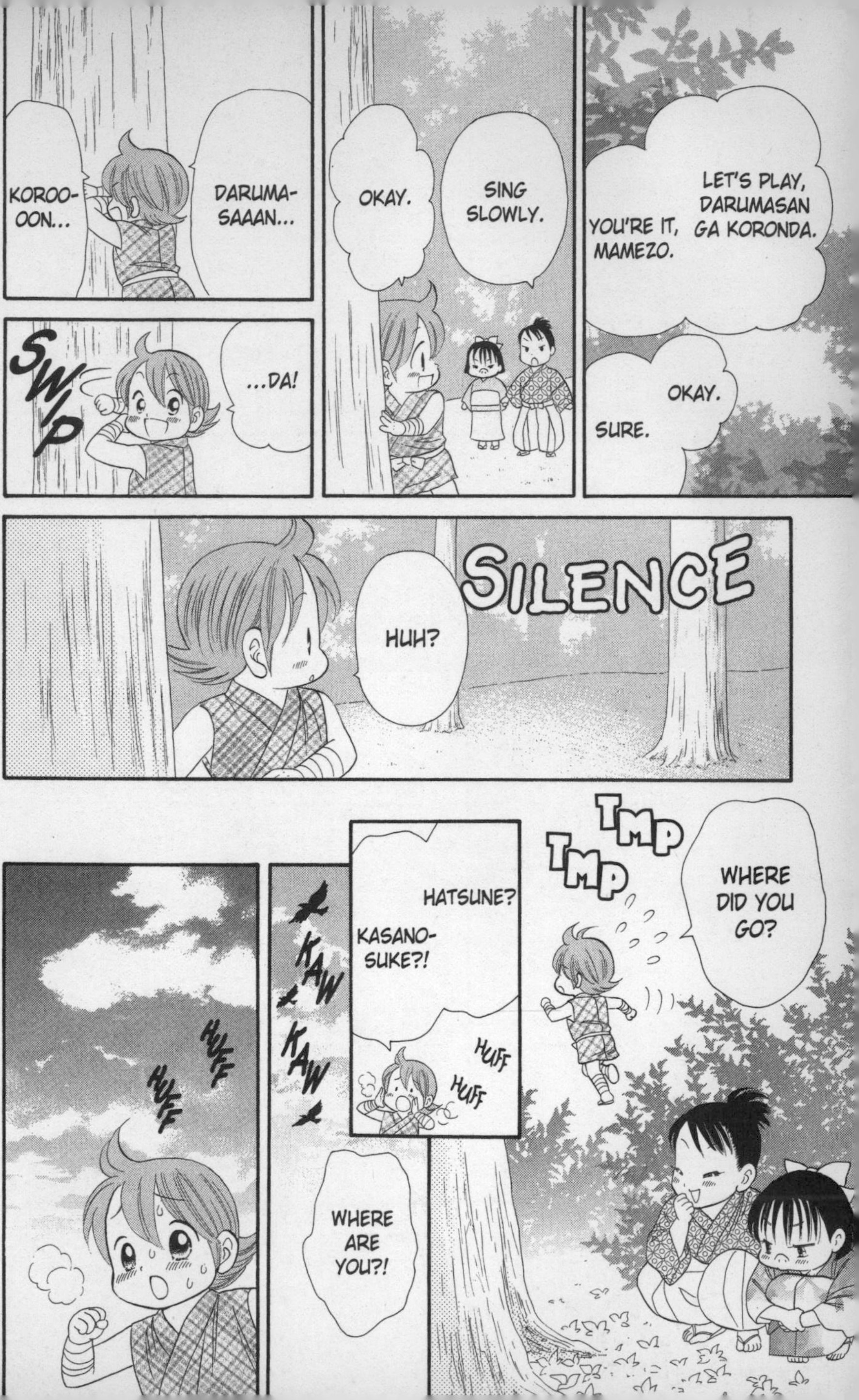
LET'S PLAY, DARUMASAN GA KORONDA.
YOU'RE IT, MAMEZO.
OKAY.
SURE.
SING SLOWLY.
OKAY.
DARUMA-SAAAN...
KOROOO-OON...
SWIP
...DA!
SILENCE
HUH?
TMP TMP
WHERE DID YOU GO?
HATSUNE?
KASANO-SUKE?!
HUFF HUFF
KAW KAW
HUFF HUFF
WHERE ARE YOU?!

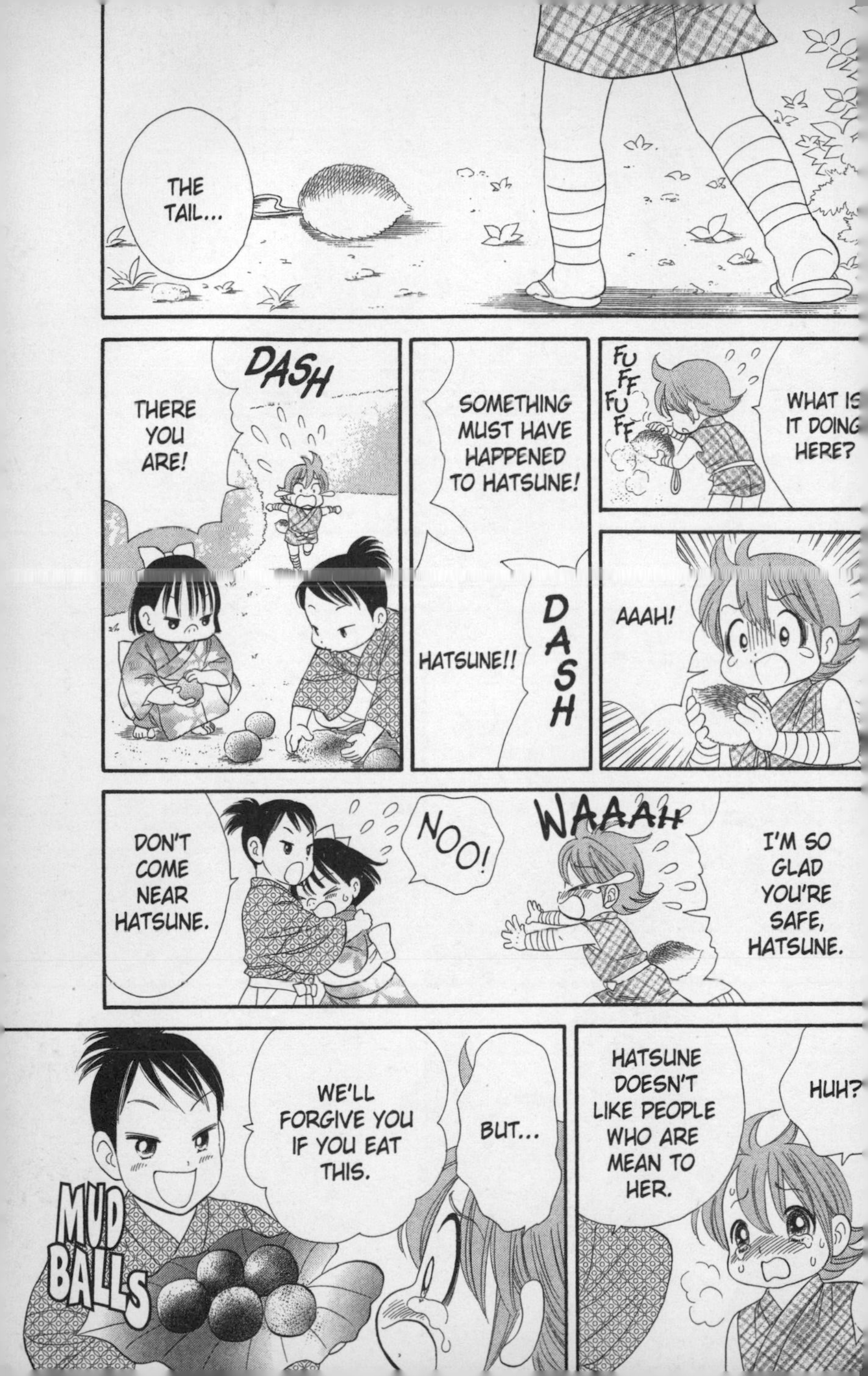
THE TAIL...
WHAT IS IT DOING HERE?
FUFF FUFF
AAAH!
SOMETHING MUST HAVE HAPPENED TO HATSUNE!
DASH
HATSUNE!!
DASH
THERE YOU ARE!
I'M SO GLAD YOU'RE SAFE, HATSUNE.
WAAAH
NOO!
DON'T COME NEAR HATSUNE.
HUH?
HATSUNE DOESN'T LIKE PEOPLE WHO ARE MEAN TO HER.
BUT...
WE'LL FORGIVE YOU IF YOU EAT THIS.
MUD BALLS

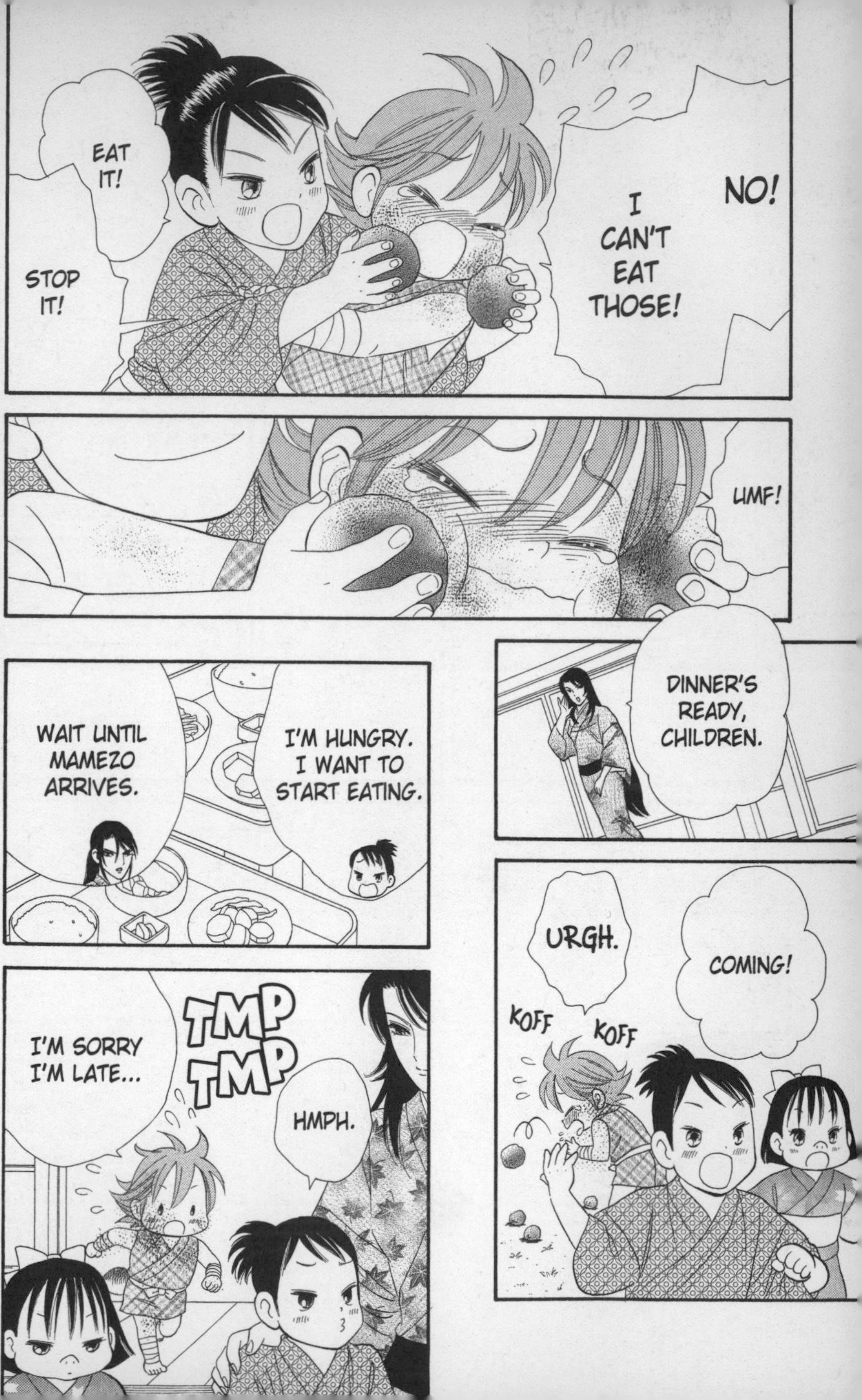
NO!
I CAN'T EAT THOSE!
EAT IT!
STOP IT!
UMF!
DINNER'S READY, CHILDREN.
COMING!
URGH.
KOFF
KOFF
I'M HUNGRY. I WANT TO START EATING.
WAIT UNTIL MAMEZO ARRIVES.
TMP TMP
HMPH.
I'M SORRY I'M LATE...

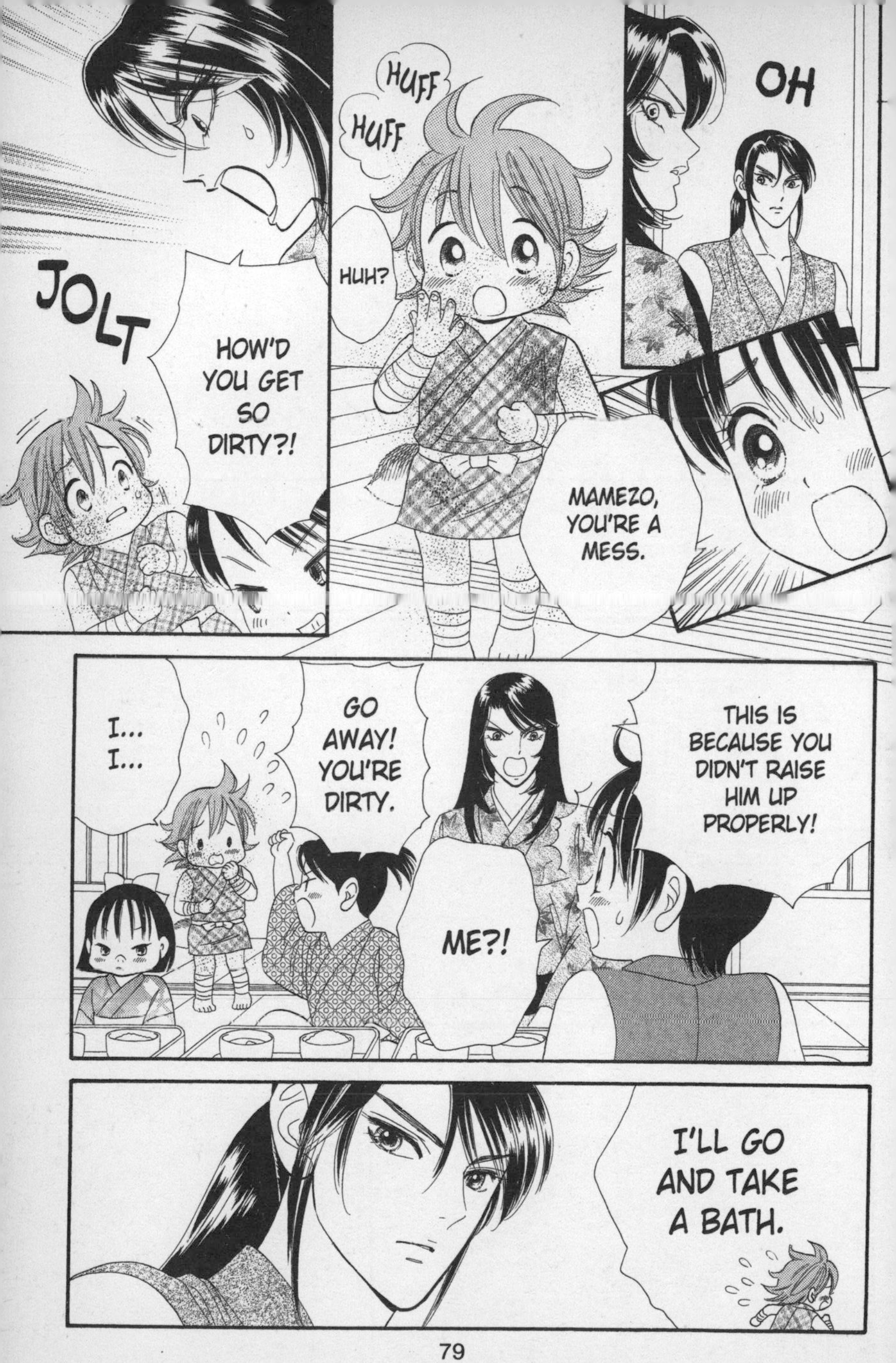
OH
MAMEZO, YOU'RE A MESS.
HUFF
HUFF
HUH?
JOLT
HOW'D YOU GET SO DIRTY?!
THIS IS BECAUSE YOU DIDN'T RAISE HIM UP PROPERLY!
ME?!
GO AWAY! YOU'RE DIRTY.
I... I...
I'LL GO AND TAKE A BATH.

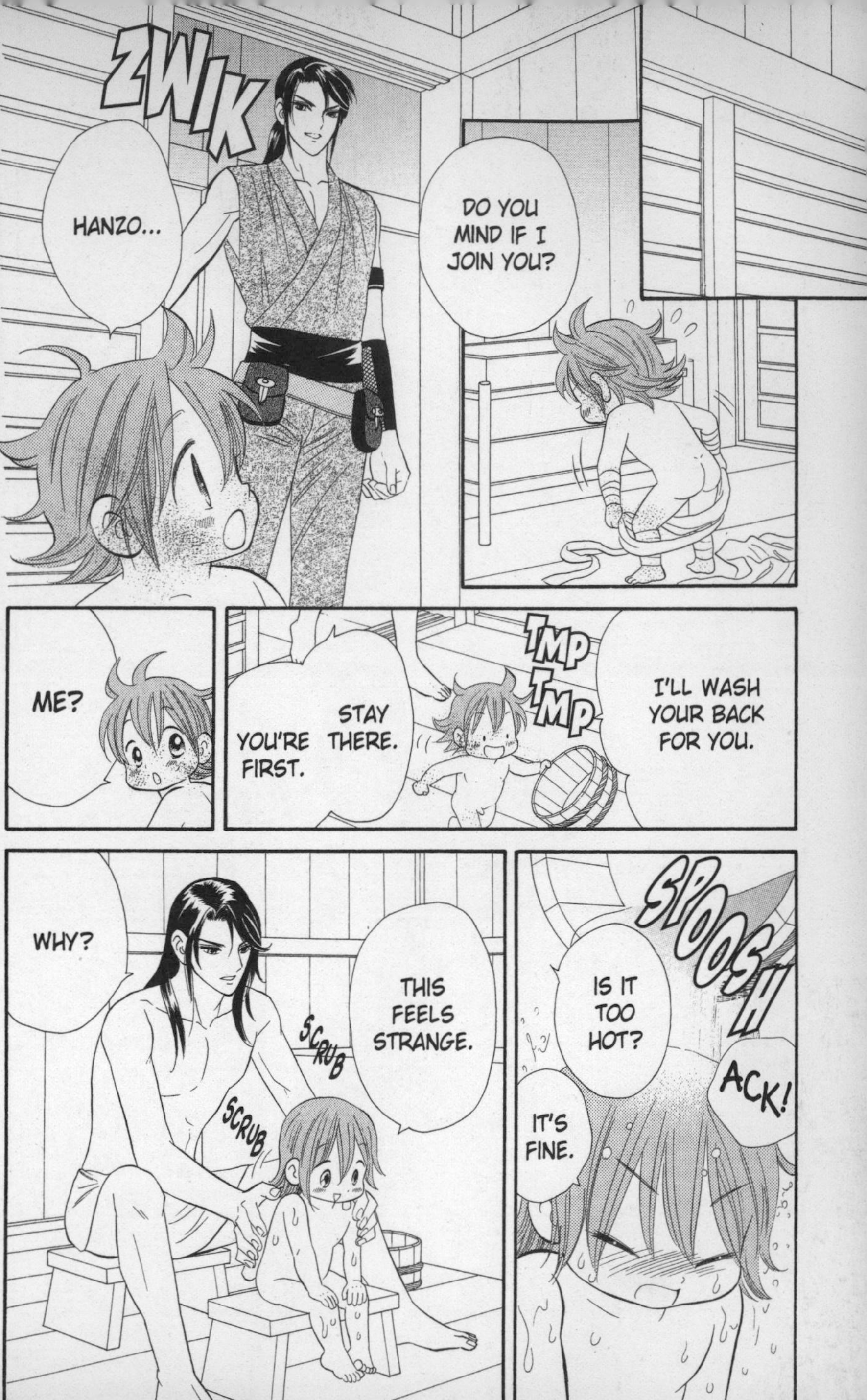
ZWIK
DO YOU MIND IF I JOIN YOU?
HANZO...
TMP TMP
I'LL WASH YOUR BACK FOR YOU.
STAY THERE. YOU'RE FIRST.
ME?
SPOOSH
ACK!
IS IT TOO HOT?
IT'S FINE.
THIS FEELS STRANGE.
SCRUB
SCRUB
WHY?

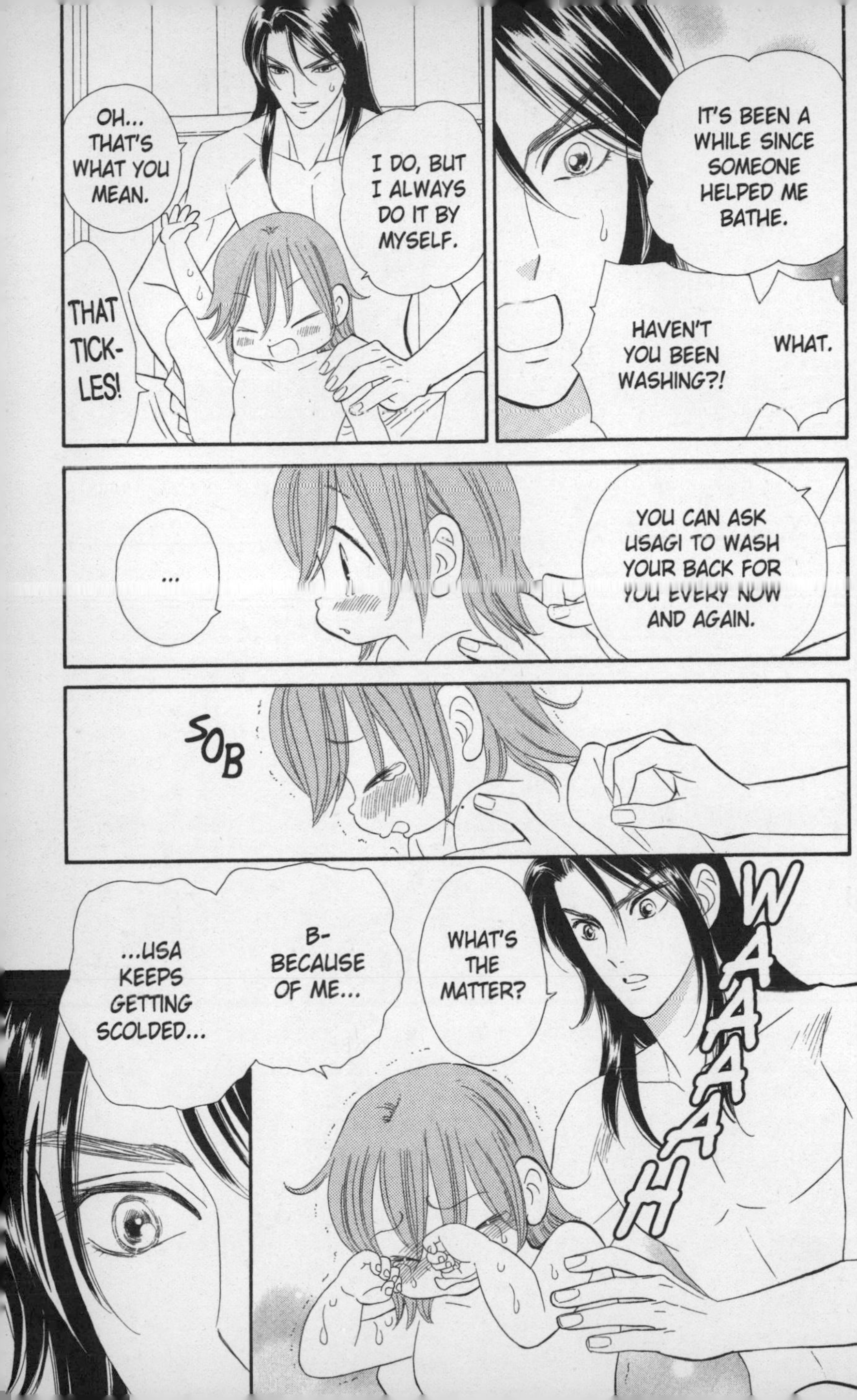
IT'S BEEN A WHILE SINCE SOMEONE HELPED ME BATHE.
WHAT.
HAVEN'T YOU BEEN WASHING?!
I DO, BUT I ALWAYS DO IT BY MYSELF.
OH... THAT'S WHAT YOU MEAN.
THAT TICK-LES!
YOU CAN ASK USAGI TO WASH YOUR BACK FOR YOU EVERY NOW AND AGAIN.
...
SOB
WAAAAH
WHAT'S THE MATTER?
B-BECAUSE OF ME...
...USA KEEPS GETTING SCOLDED...

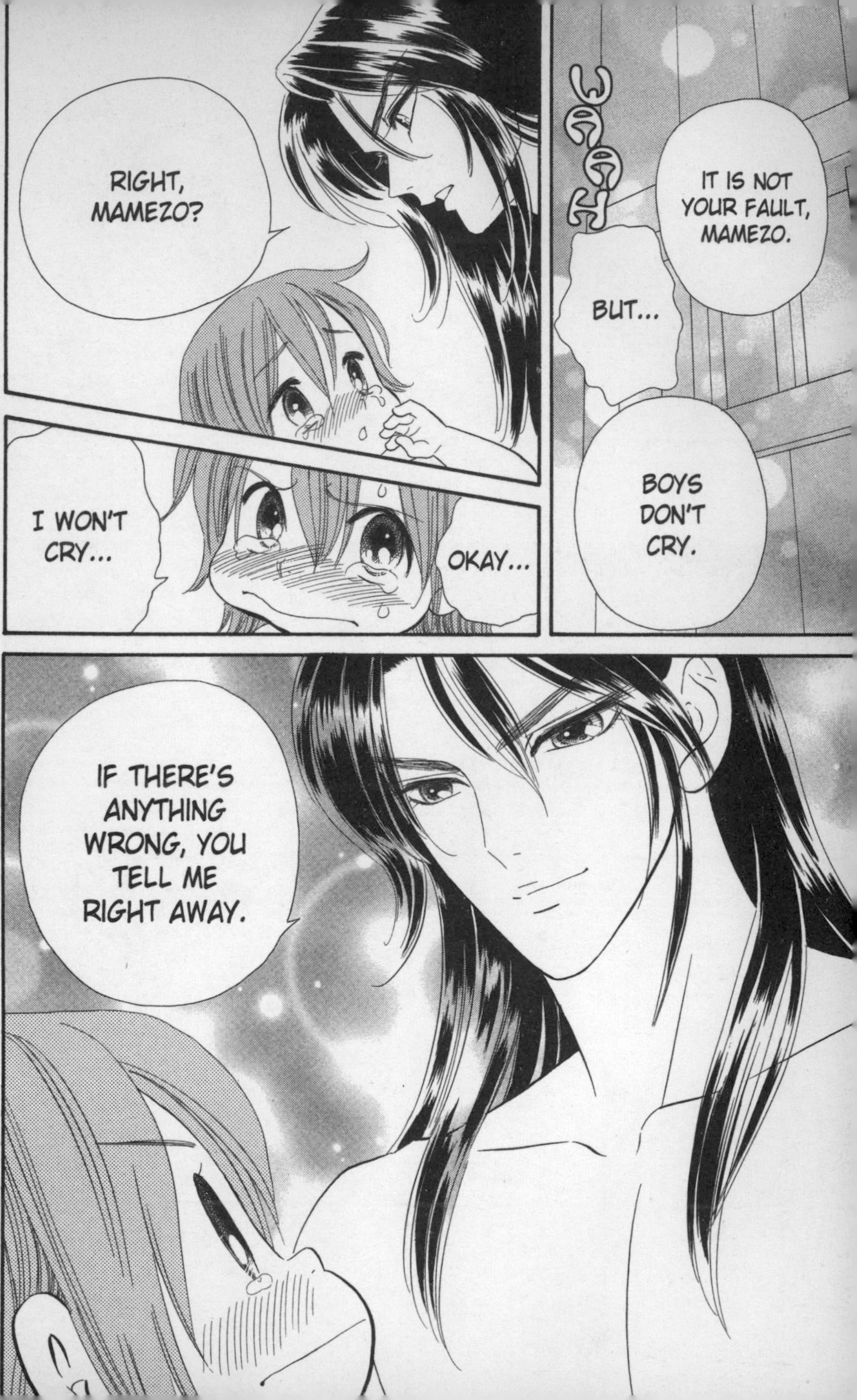
IT IS NOT YOUR FAULT, MAMEZO.
WAAH
BUT...
BOYS DON'T CRY.
RIGHT, MAMEZO?
OKAY...
I WON'T CRY...
IF THERE'S ANYTHING WRONG, YOU TELL ME RIGHT AWAY.

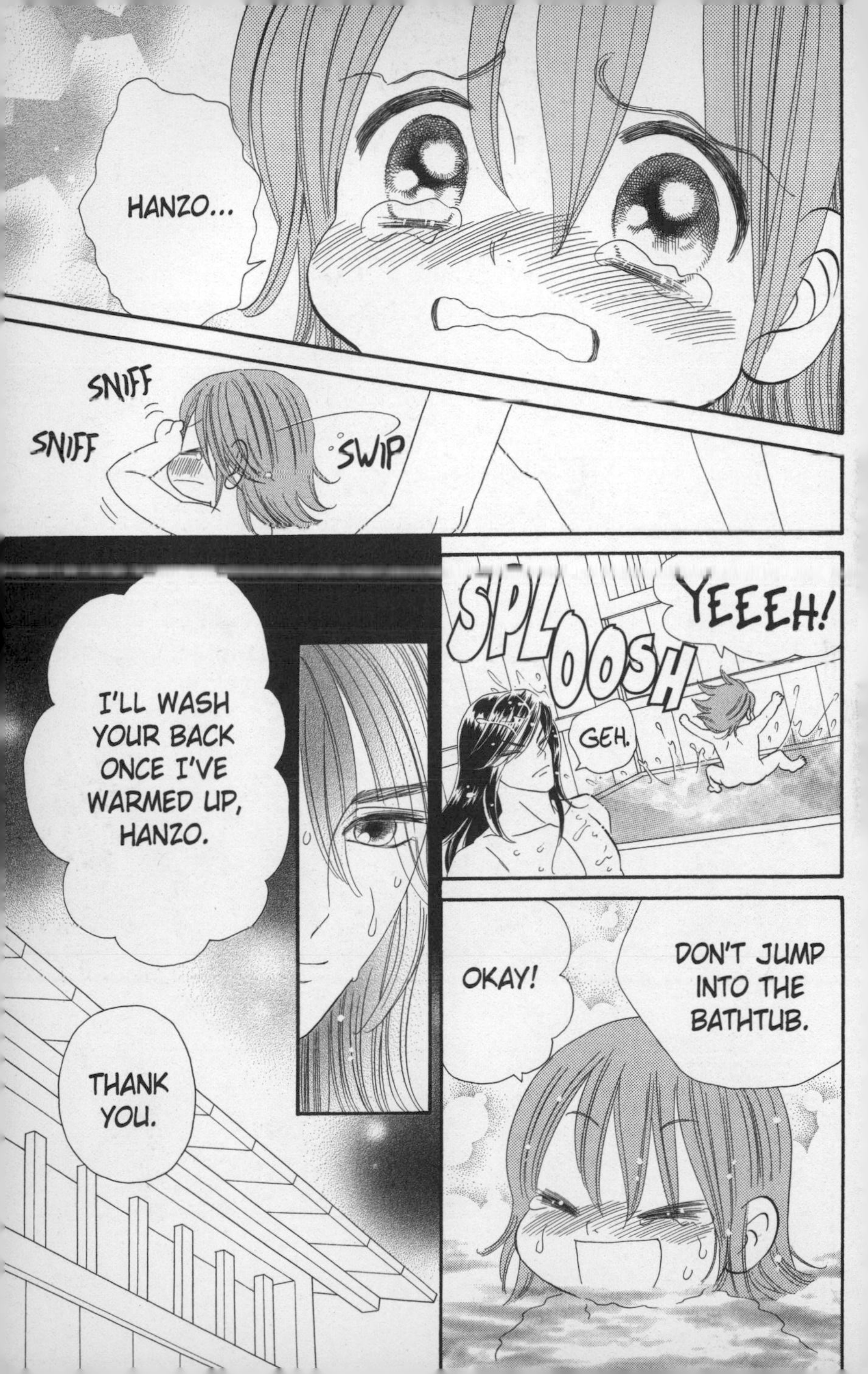
HANZO...
SWIP
SNIFF
SNIFF
YEEEH!
SPLOOSH
GEH.
DON'T JUMP INTO THE BATHTUB.
OKAY!
I'LL WASH YOUR BACK ONCE I'VE WARMED UP, HANZO.
THANK YOU.

TAIL OF THE MOON EXTRA: TODAY'S MISSION

"I WANT TO SEE HANZO IN A VAMPIRE OUTFIT!"

-GRIFFITH, WAKAYAMA PREFECTURE & DOTE MASAKO, KOUCHI PREFECTURE

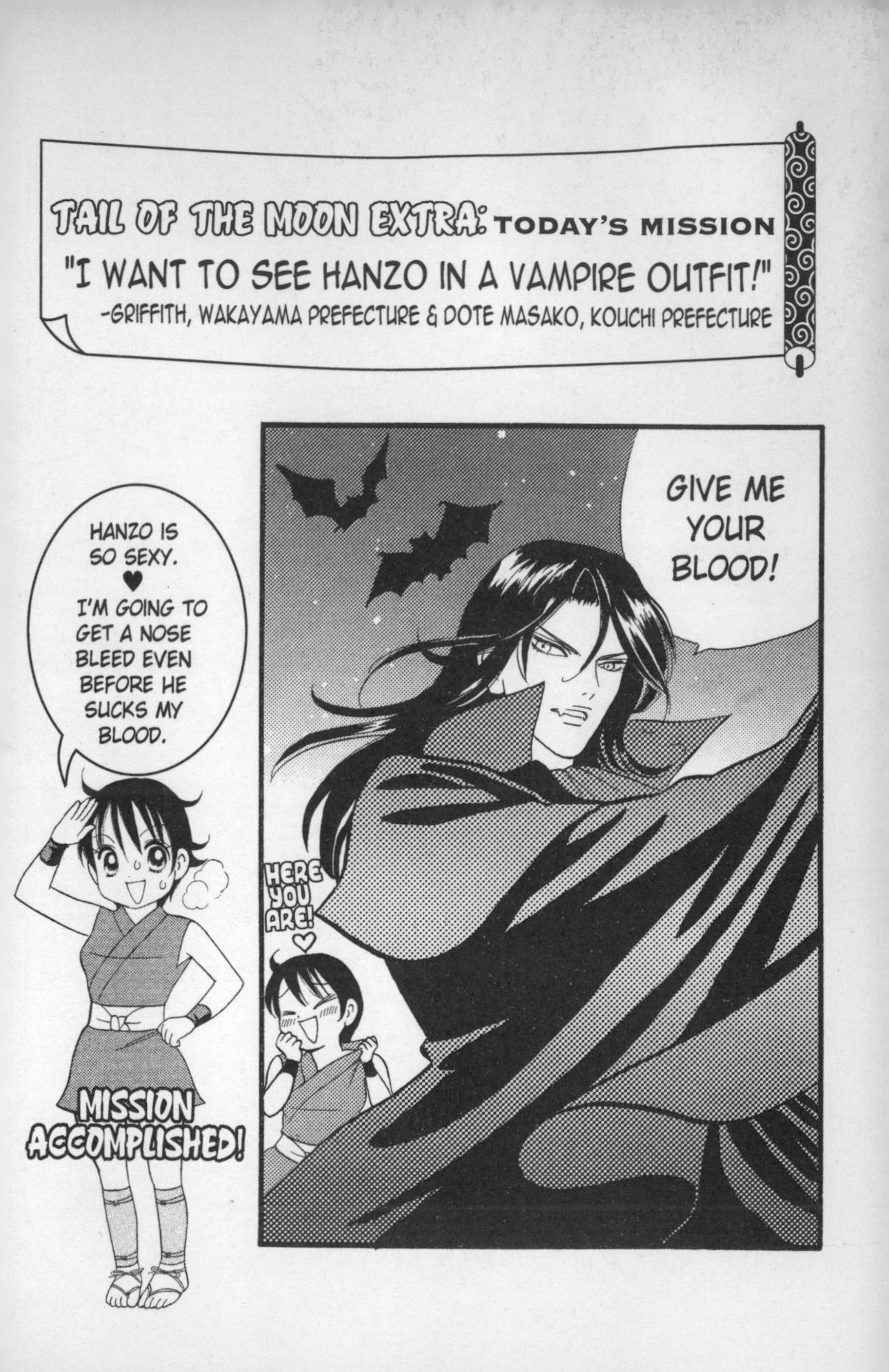
GIVE ME YOUR BLOOD!
HERE YOU ARE! ♥
HANZO IS SO SEXY. ♥ I'M GOING TO GET A NOSE BLEED EVEN BEFORE HE SUCKS MY BLOOD.
MISSION ACCOMPLISHED!

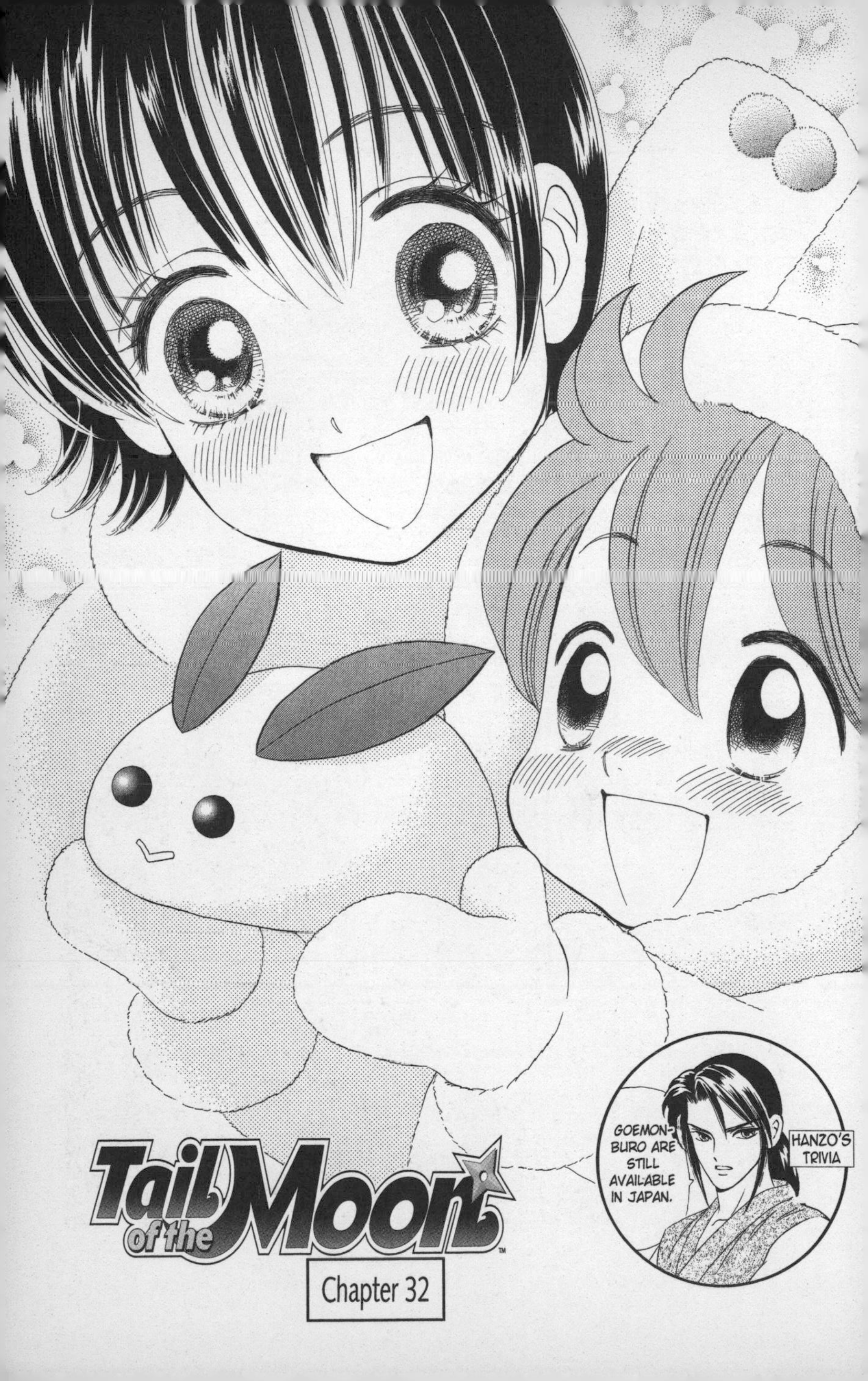
Tail of the Moon
Chapter 32
HANZO'S TRIVIA
GOEMON-BURO ARE STILL AVAILABLE IN JAPAN.

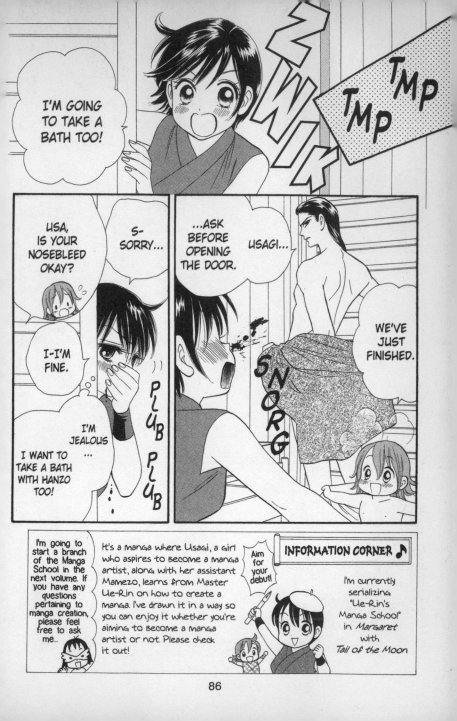

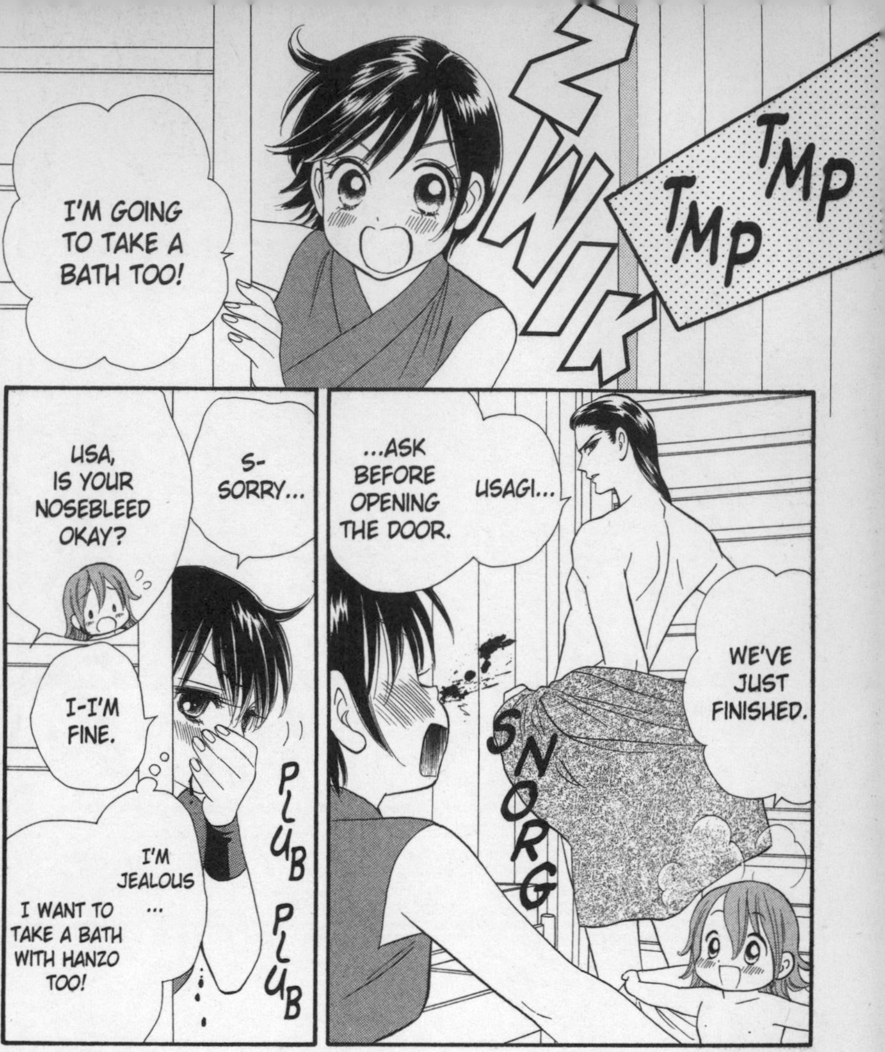
TMP TMP TMP
ZWIK
I'M GOING TO TAKE A BATH TOO!
WE'VE JUST FINISHED.
USAGI...
...ASK BEFORE OPENING THE DOOR.
SNORG
S-SORRY...
USA, IS YOUR NOSEBLEED OKAY?
I-I'M FINE.
PLUB PLUB
I'M JEALOUS...
I WANT TO TAKE A BATH WITH HANZO TOO!

INFORMATION CORNER ♪

I'm currently serializing "Ue-Rin's Manga School" in *Margaret* with *Tail of the Moon*

Aim for your debut!

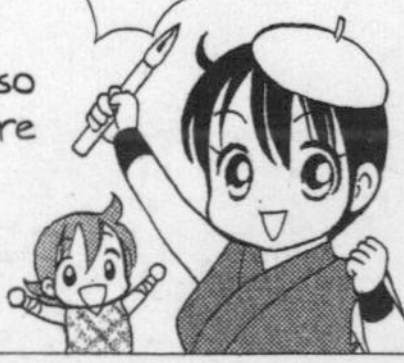

It's a manga where Usagi, a girl who aspires to become a manga artist, along with her assistant Mamezo, learns from Master Ue-Rin on how to create a manga. I've drawn it in a way so you can enjoy it whether you're aiming to become a manga artist or not. Please check it out!

I'm going to start a branch of the Manga School in the next volume. If you have any questions pertaining to manga creation, please feel free to ask me..

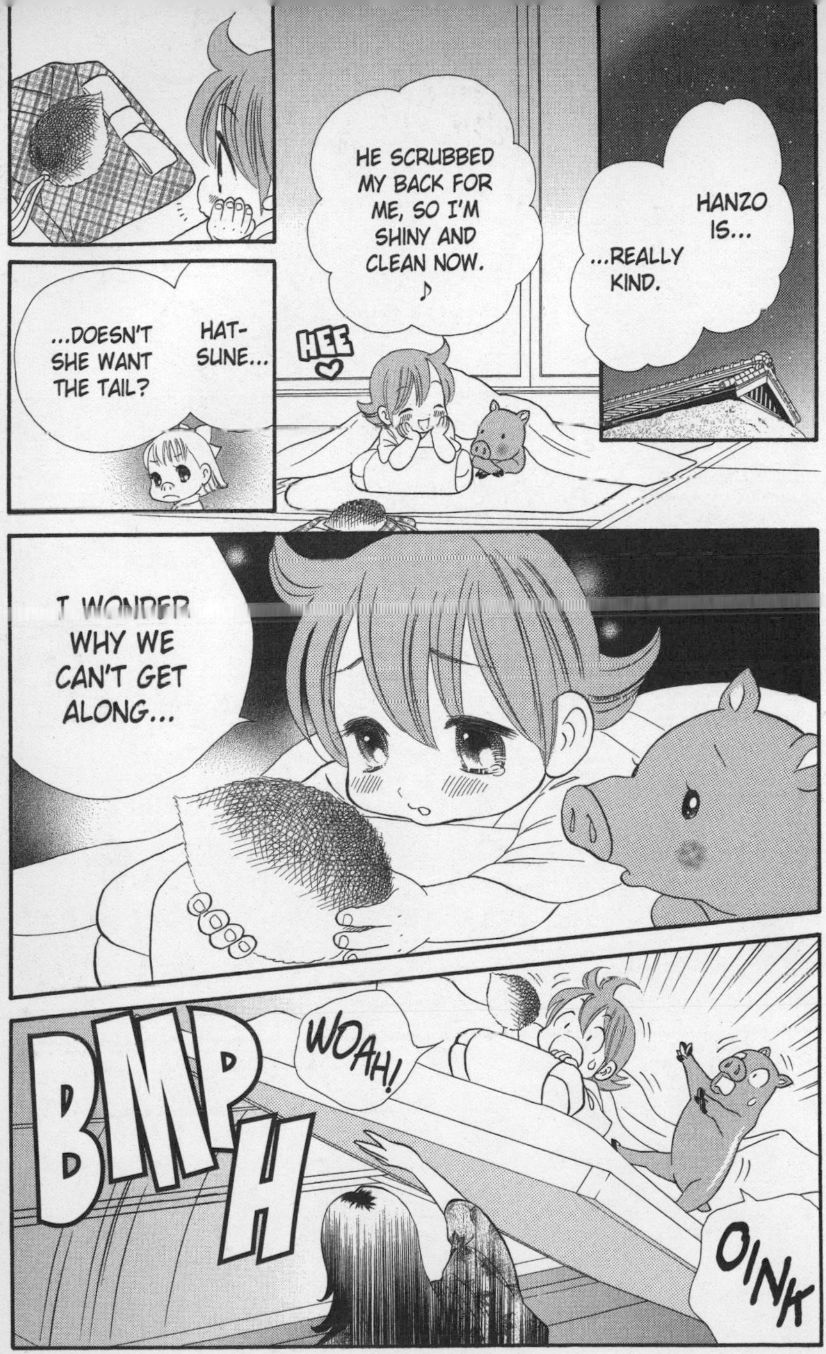
HANZO IS...
...REALLY KIND.
HE SCRUBBED MY BACK FOR ME, SO I'M SHINY AND CLEAN NOW. ♪
HEE ♡
HAT-SUNE...
...DOESN'T SHE WANT THE TAIL?
I WONDER WHY WE CAN'T GET ALONG...
WOAH!
BMPH
OINK

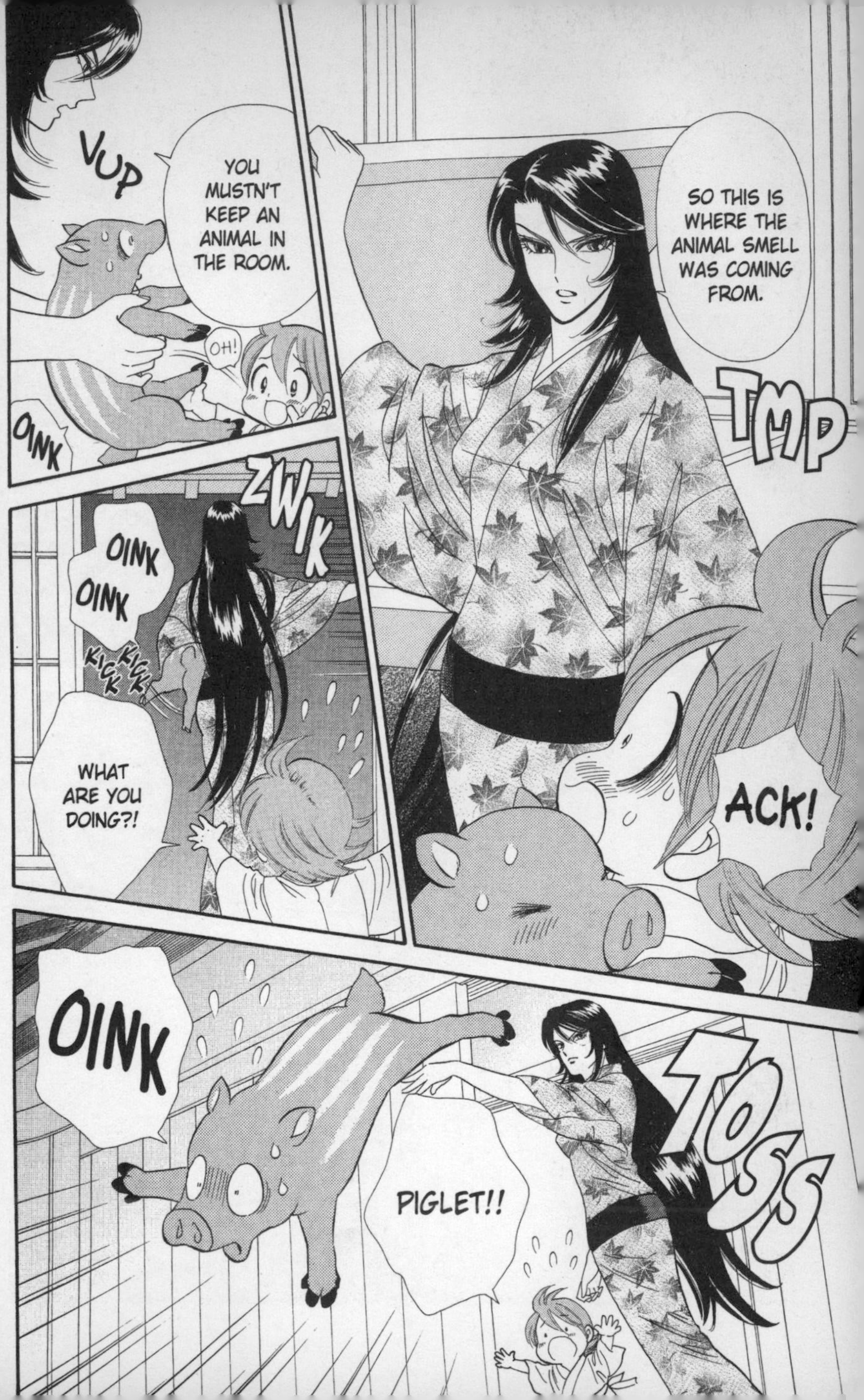
SO THIS IS WHERE THE ANIMAL SMELL WAS COMING FROM.
TMP
ACK!
VUP
YOU MUSTN'T KEEP AN ANIMAL IN THE ROOM.
OH!
OINK
ZWIK
OINK OINK
KICK KICK
WHAT ARE YOU DOING?!
TOSS
PIGLET!!
OINK

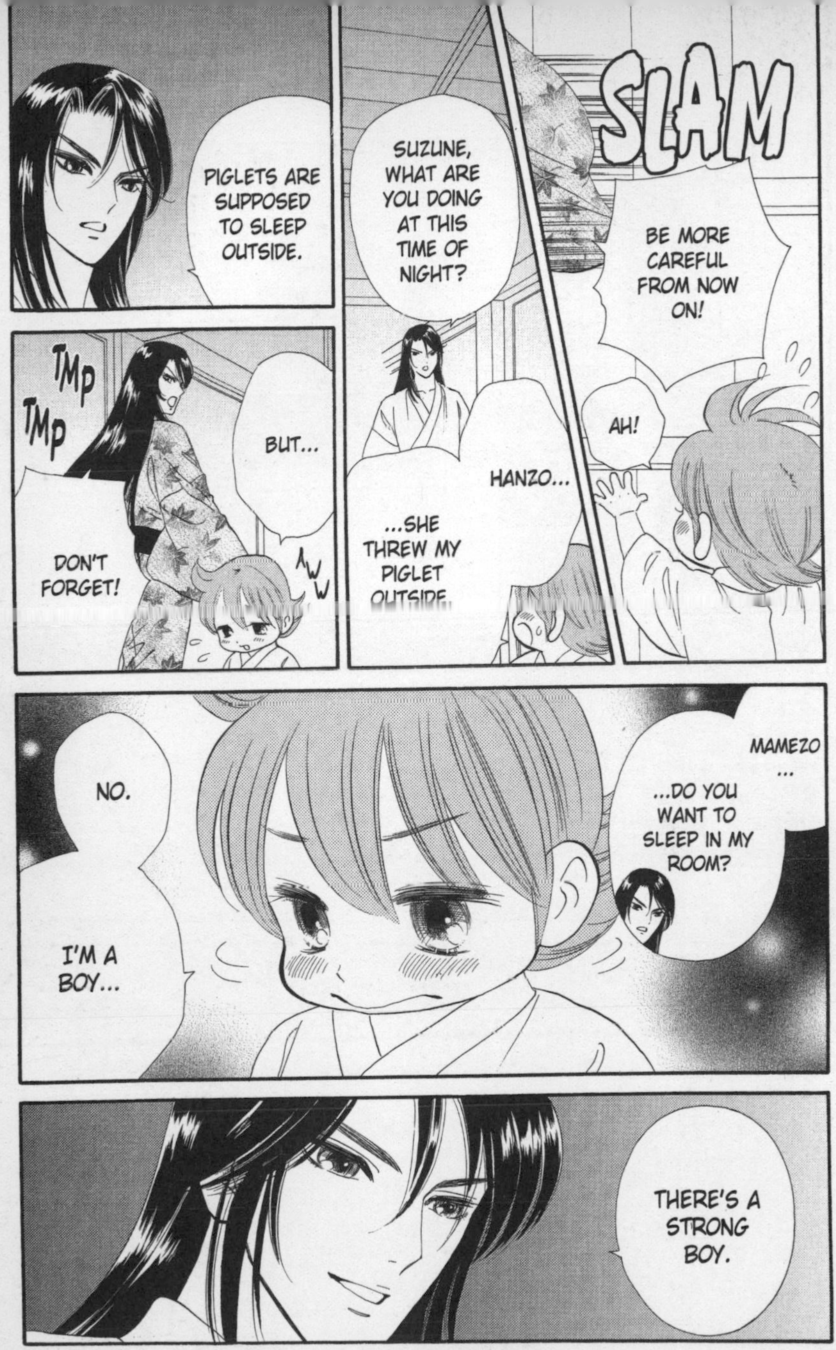

SLAM
BE MORE CAREFUL FROM NOW ON!
AH!
SUZUNE, WHAT ARE YOU DOING AT THIS TIME OF NIGHT?
HANZO...
...SHE THREW MY PIGLET OUTSIDE.
PIGLETS ARE SUPPOSED TO SLEEP OUTSIDE.
BUT...
TMP TMP
DON'T FORGET!
AWW
MAMEZO...
...DO YOU WANT TO SLEEP IN MY ROOM?
NO.
I'M A BOY...
THERE'S A STRONG BOY.

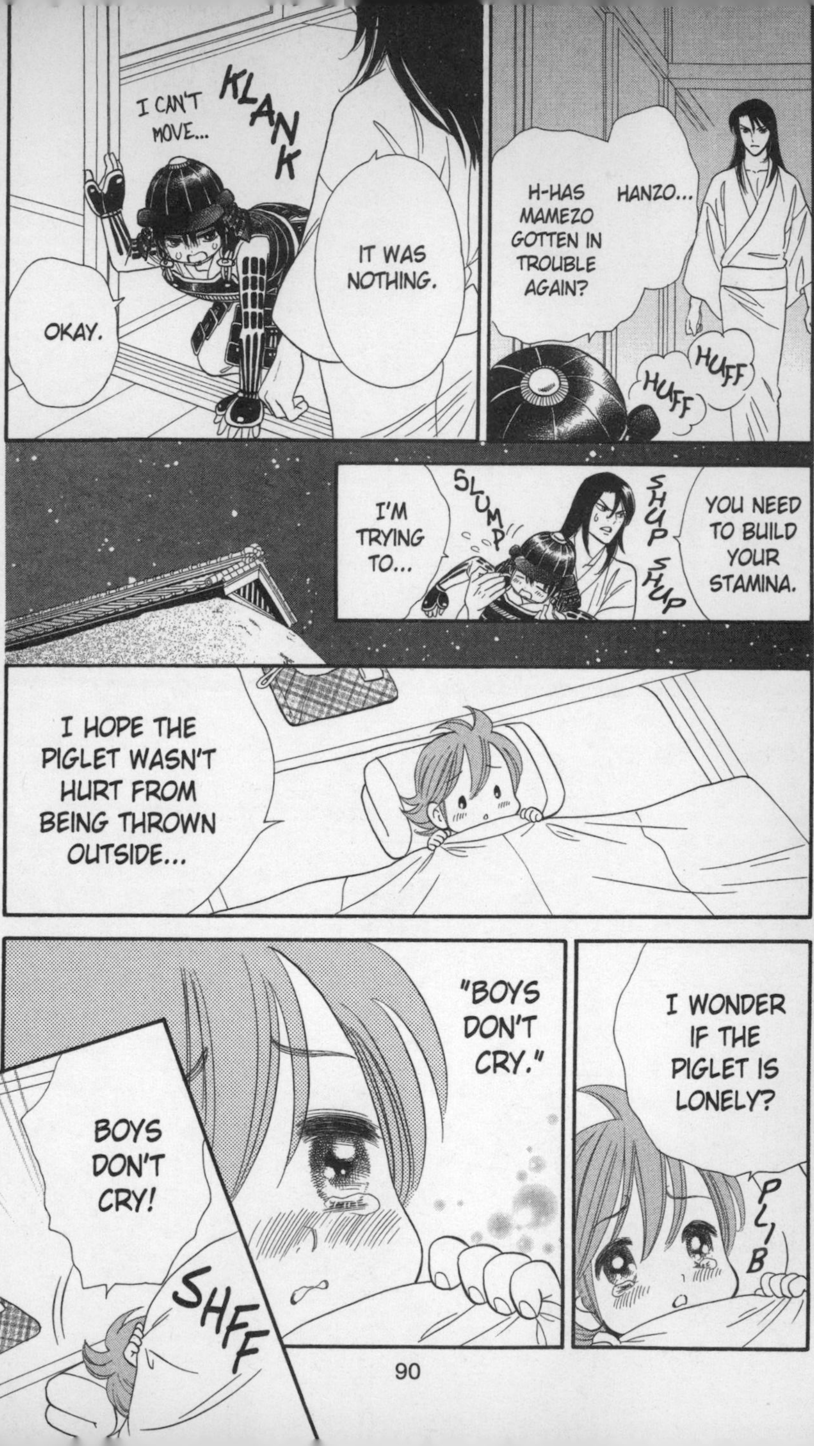
HANZO...
H-HAS MAMEZO GOTTEN IN TROUBLE AGAIN?
HUFF HUFF
IT WAS NOTHING.
OKAY.
I CAN'T MOVE...
KLANK
YOU NEED TO BUILD YOUR STAMINA.
SHUP SHUP
SLUMP
I'M TRYING TO...
I HOPE THE PIGLET WASN'T HURT FROM BEING THROWN OUTSIDE...
I WONDER IF THE PIGLET IS LONELY?
PLIB
"BOYS DON'T CRY."
BOYS DON'T CRY!
SHFF

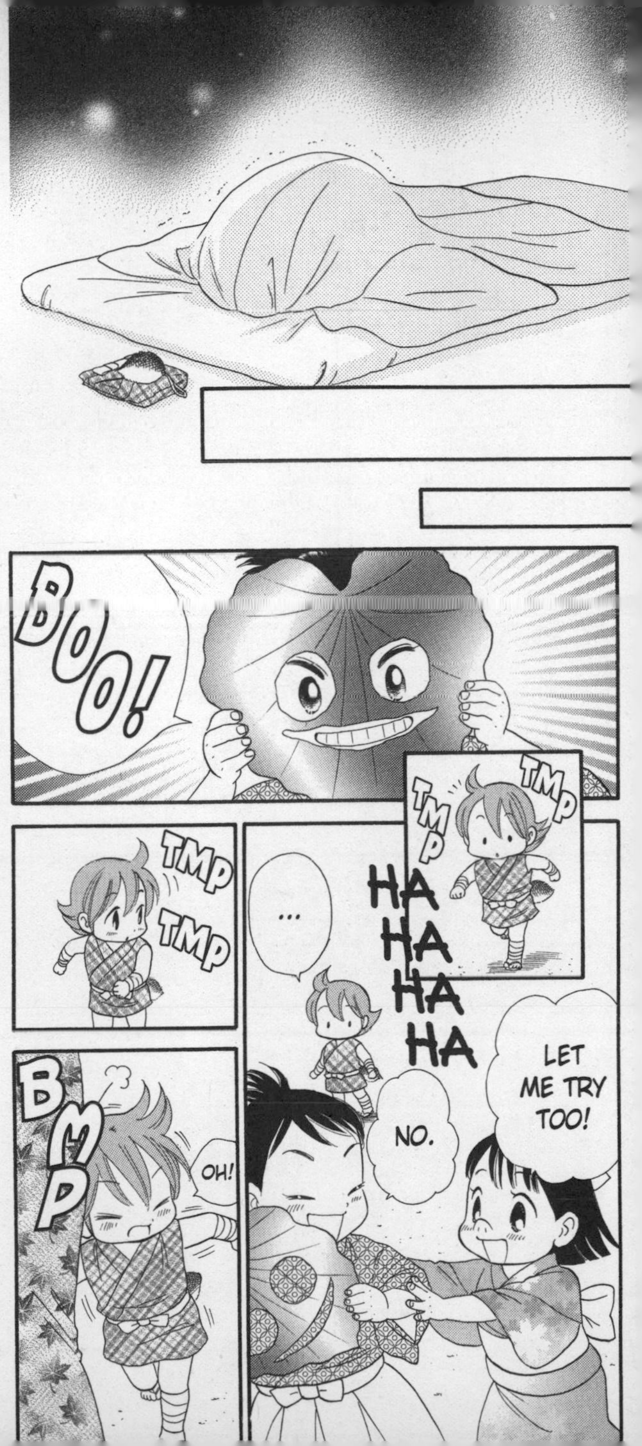
BOO!
TMP TMP
HA HA HA HA HA
...
LET ME TRY TOO!
NO.
TMP TMP
BMP
OH!

Stories About My Research Trip #3

When I was choosing what ninja souvenirs to buy, the lady suggested that I get the Hatomugi tea!! As I stood there with a ? mark over my head...

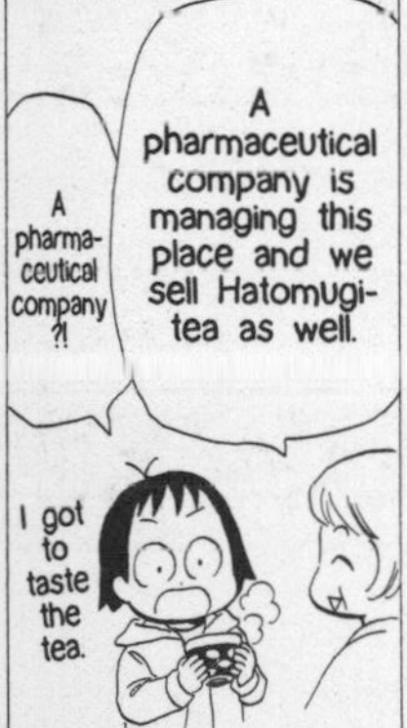
A pharmaceutical company is managing this place and we sell Hatomugi-tea as well.
A pharma-ceutical company?!
I got to taste the tea.

I wrote about this in volume 2 before, but after Japan became peaceful, many ninjas were out of jobs. They decided to use their knowledge of herbs and medicine to create what has become present-day pharmaceutical companies.

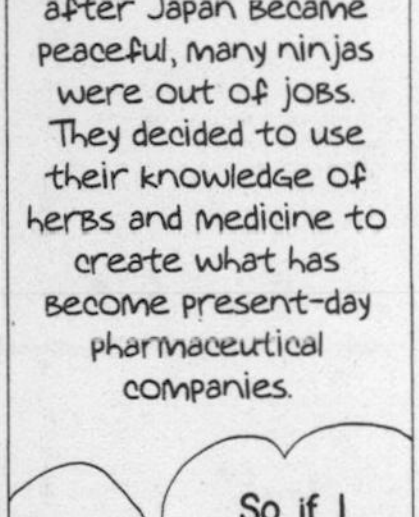
So if I lived in the modern world, I would be a pharmacist or a doctor?!
That's if you pass the national exam...
HEE!

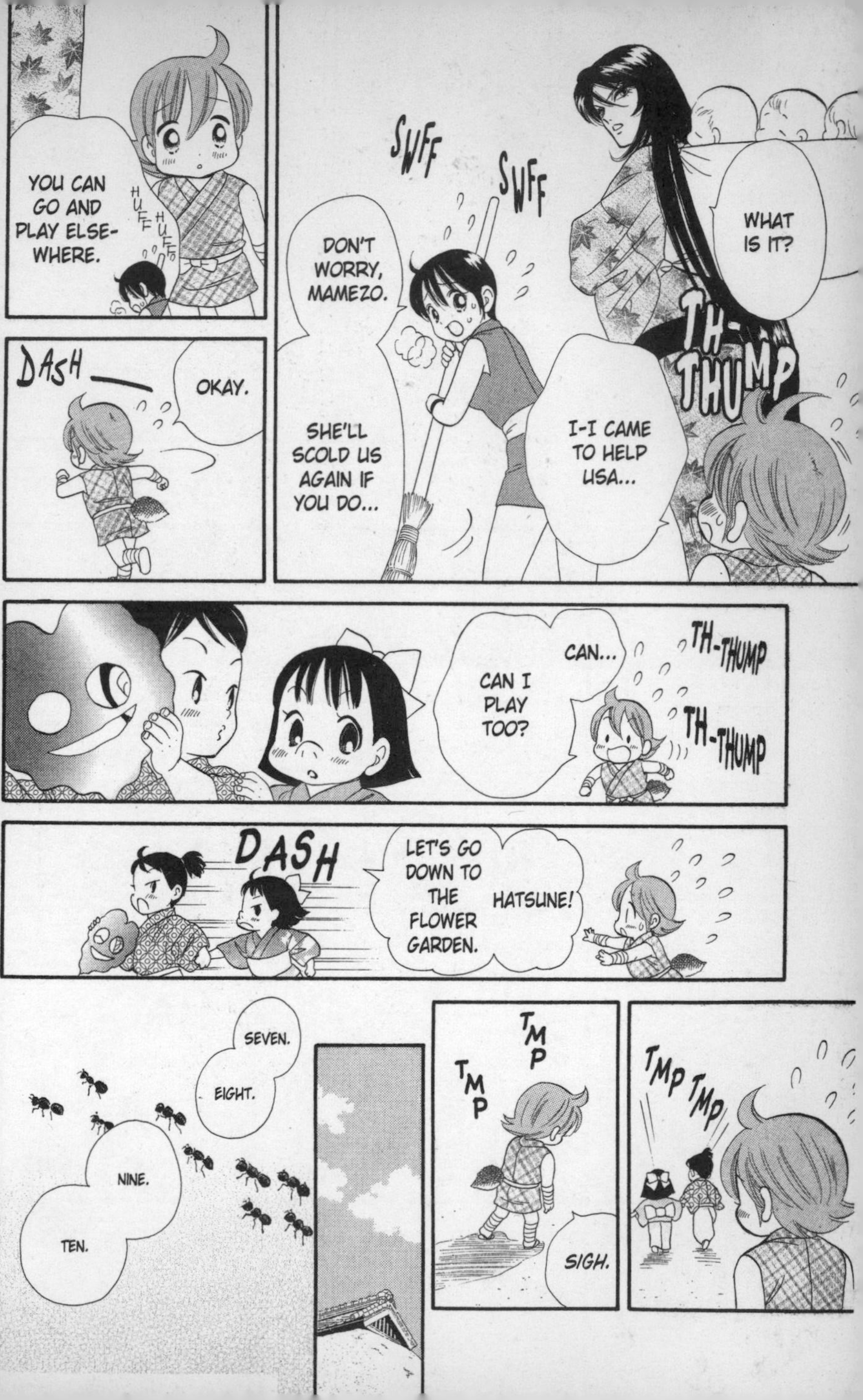
WHAT IS IT?
TH-THUMP
I-I CAME TO HELP USA...
SWFF
SWFF
DON'T WORRY, MAMEZO.
SHE'LL SCOLD US AGAIN IF YOU DO...
YOU CAN GO AND PLAY ELSE-WHERE.
HUFF HUFF
OKAY.
DASH
TH-THUMP
TH-THUMP
CAN...
CAN I PLAY TOO?
HATSUNE!
LET'S GO DOWN TO THE FLOWER GARDEN.
DASH
TMP TMP
TMP
TMP
SIGH.
SEVEN.
EIGHT.
NINE.
TEN.

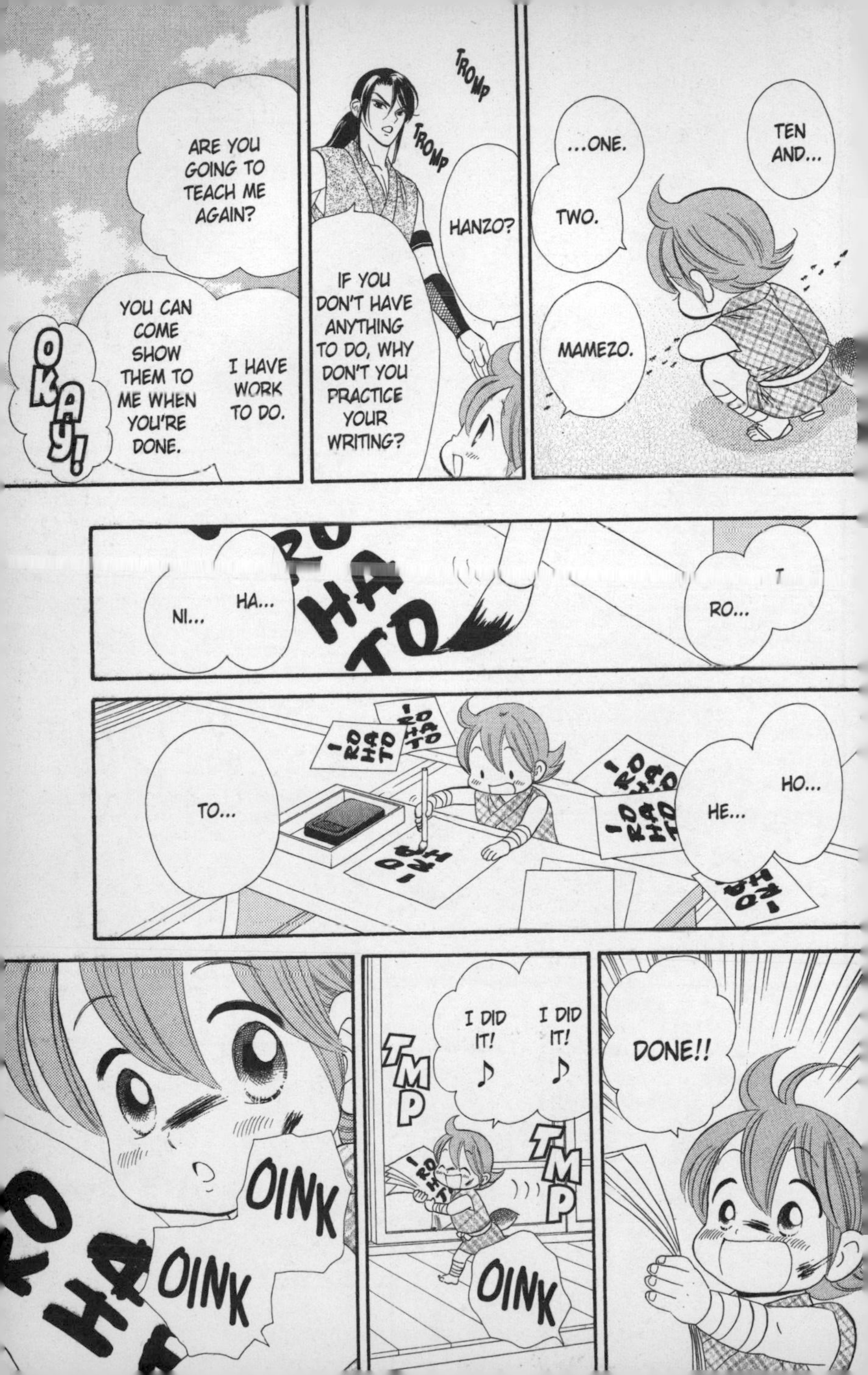
TEN AND...
...ONE.
TWO.
MAMEZO.
TROMP
TROMP
HANZO?
IF YOU DON'T HAVE ANYTHING TO DO, WHY DON'T YOU PRACTICE YOUR WRITING?
ARE YOU GOING TO TEACH ME AGAIN?
I HAVE WORK TO DO.
YOU CAN COME SHOW THEM TO ME WHEN YOU'RE DONE.
OKAY!
RO...
HA...
NI...
HO...
HE...
TO...
DONE!!
I DID IT! ♪
I DID IT! ♪
TMP
TMP
OINK
OINK
OINK

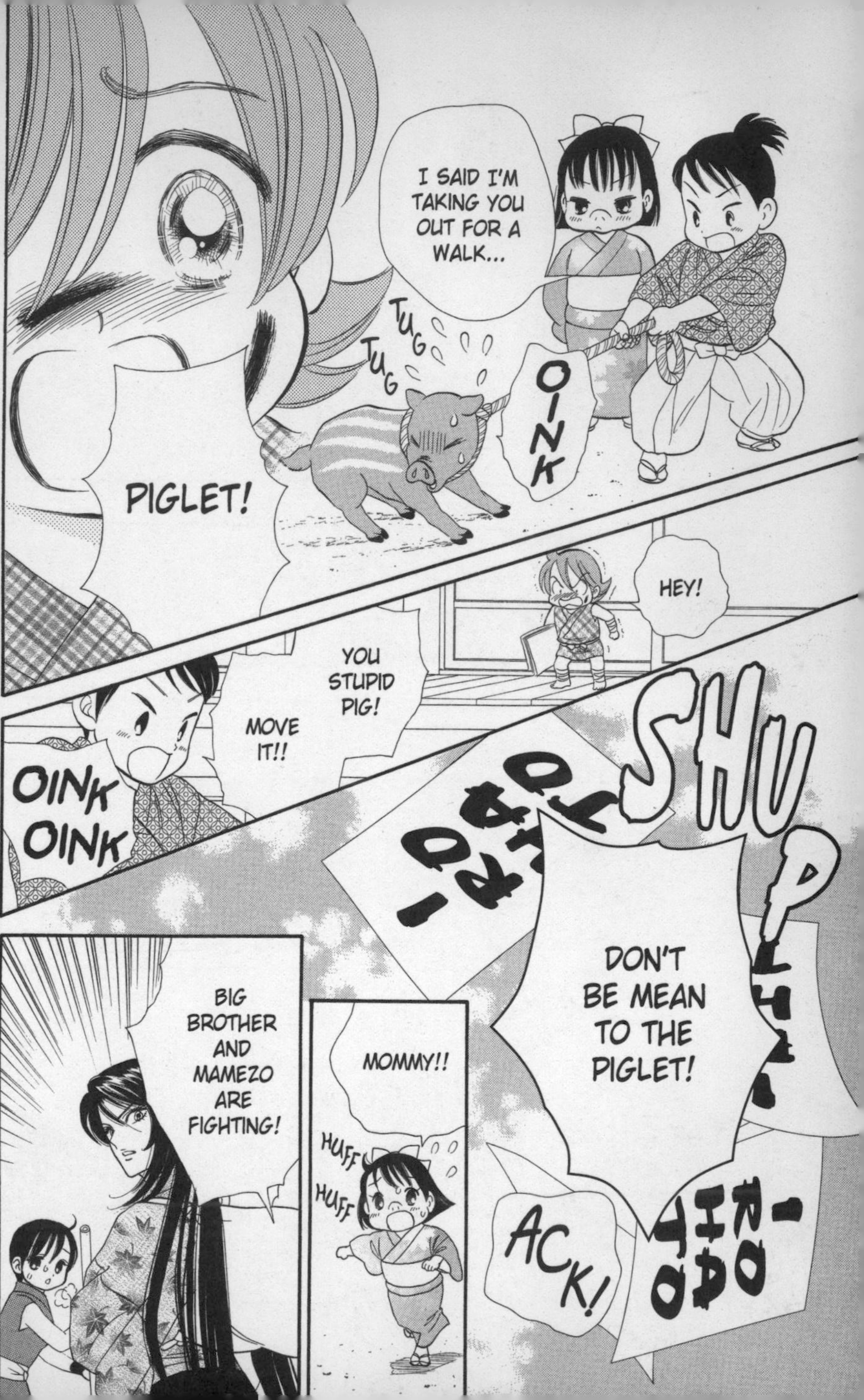
I SAID I'M TAKING YOU OUT FOR A WALK...
OINK
TUG TUG
PIGLET!
HEY!
YOU STUPID PIG!
MOVE IT!!
OINK OINK
SHUP
DON'T BE MEAN TO THE PIGLET!
ACK!
MOMMY!!
HUFF HUFF
BIG BROTHER AND MAMEZO ARE FIGHTING!

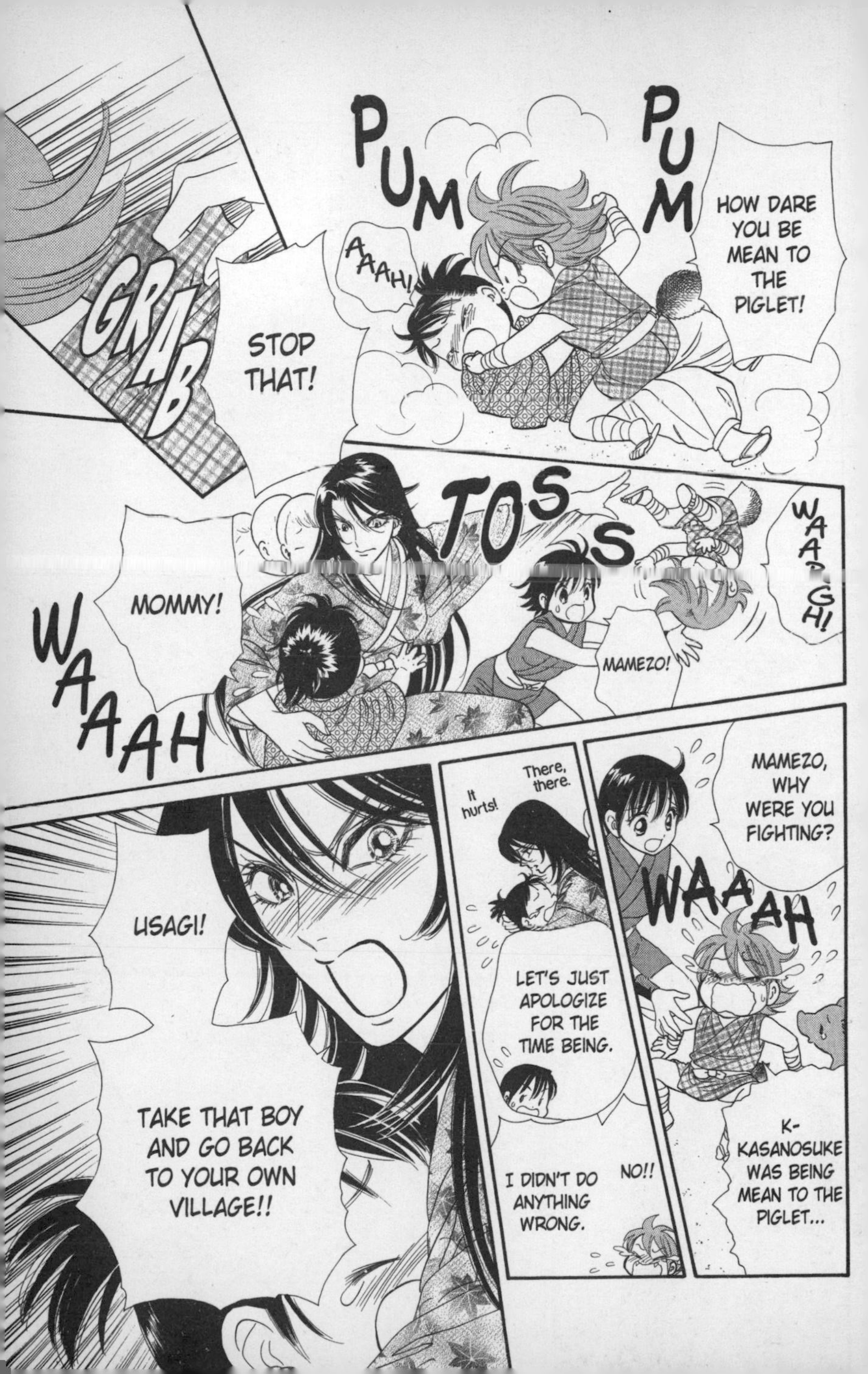
PUM PUM
HOW DARE YOU BE MEAN TO THE PIGLET!
AAAAH!
STOP THAT!
GRAB
TOSS
WAARGH!
MAMEZO!
MOMMY!
WAAAH
MAMEZO, WHY WERE YOU FIGHTING?
WAAAH
K-KASANOSUKE WAS BEING MEAN TO THE PIGLET...
There, there.
It hurts!
LET'S JUST APOLOGIZE FOR THE TIME BEING.
NO!!
I DIDN'T DO ANYTHING WRONG.
USAGI!
TAKE THAT BOY AND GO BACK TO YOUR OWN VILLAGE!!

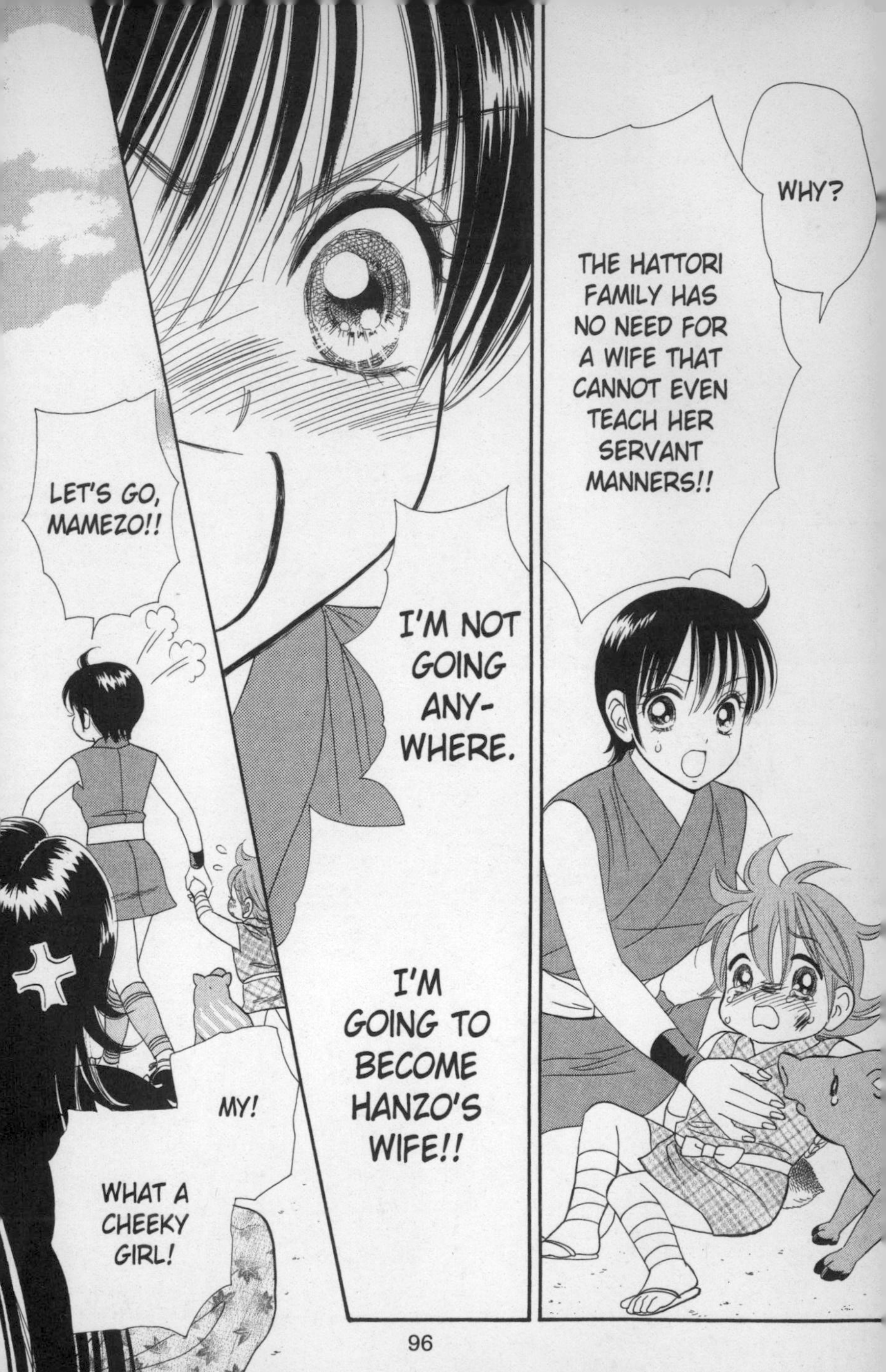
WHY?
THE HATTORI FAMILY HAS NO NEED FOR A WIFE THAT CANNOT EVEN TEACH HER SERVANT MANNERS!!
I'M NOT GOING ANY-WHERE.
I'M GOING TO BECOME HANZO'S WIFE!!
LET'S GO, MAMEZO!!
MY!
WHAT A CHEEKY GIRL!

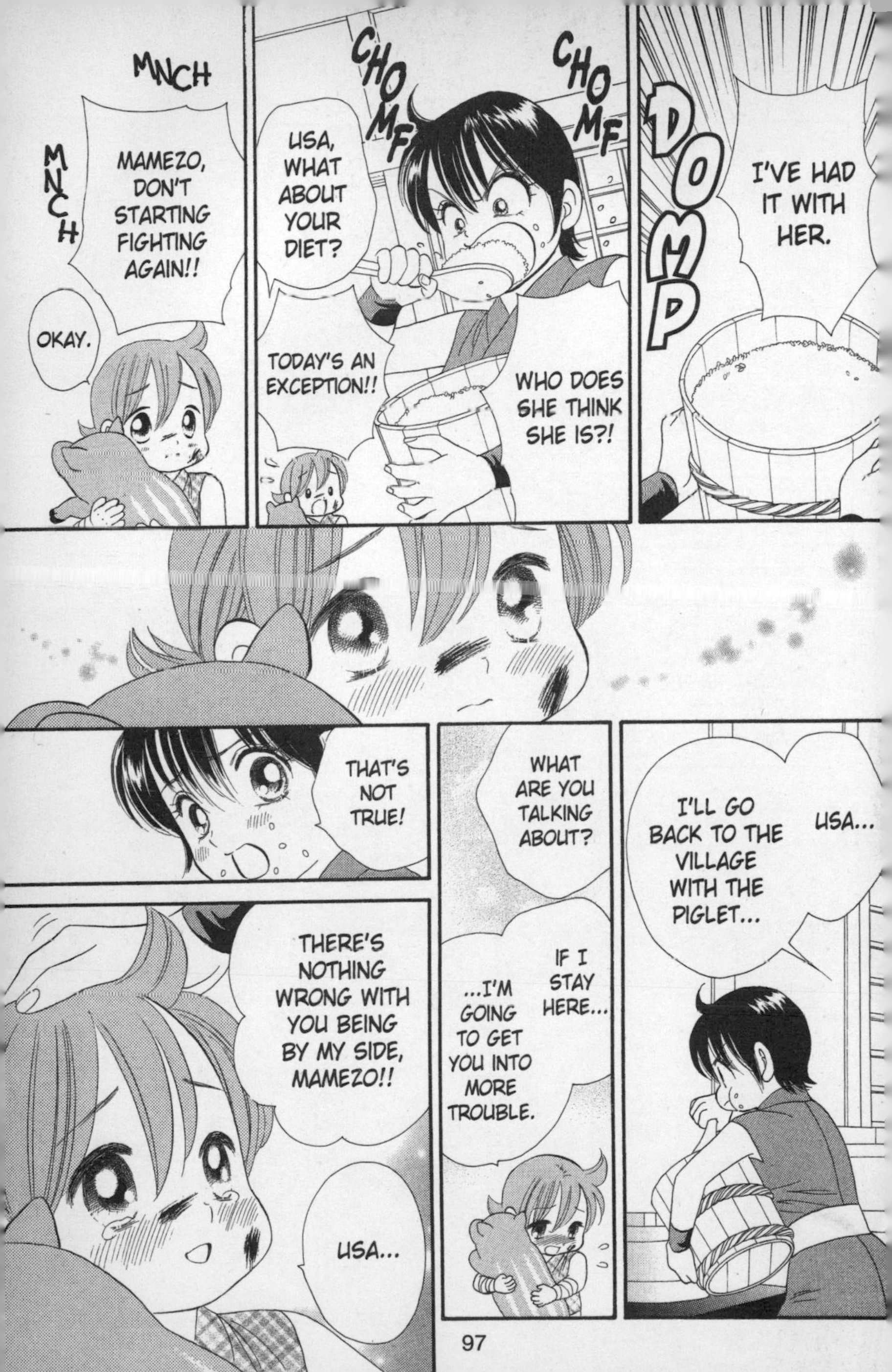
DOMP
I'VE HAD IT WITH HER.
CHOMF
CHOMF
USA, WHAT ABOUT YOUR DIET?
TODAY'S AN EXCEPTION!!
WHO DOES SHE THINK SHE IS?!
MNCH
MNCH
MAMEZO, DON'T STARTING FIGHTING AGAIN!!
OKAY.
USA...
I'LL GO BACK TO THE VILLAGE WITH THE PIGLET...
WHAT ARE YOU TALKING ABOUT?
IF I STAY HERE...
...I'M GOING TO GET YOU INTO MORE TROUBLE.
THAT'S NOT TRUE!
THERE'S NOTHING WRONG WITH YOU BEING BY MY SIDE, MAMEZO!!
USA...

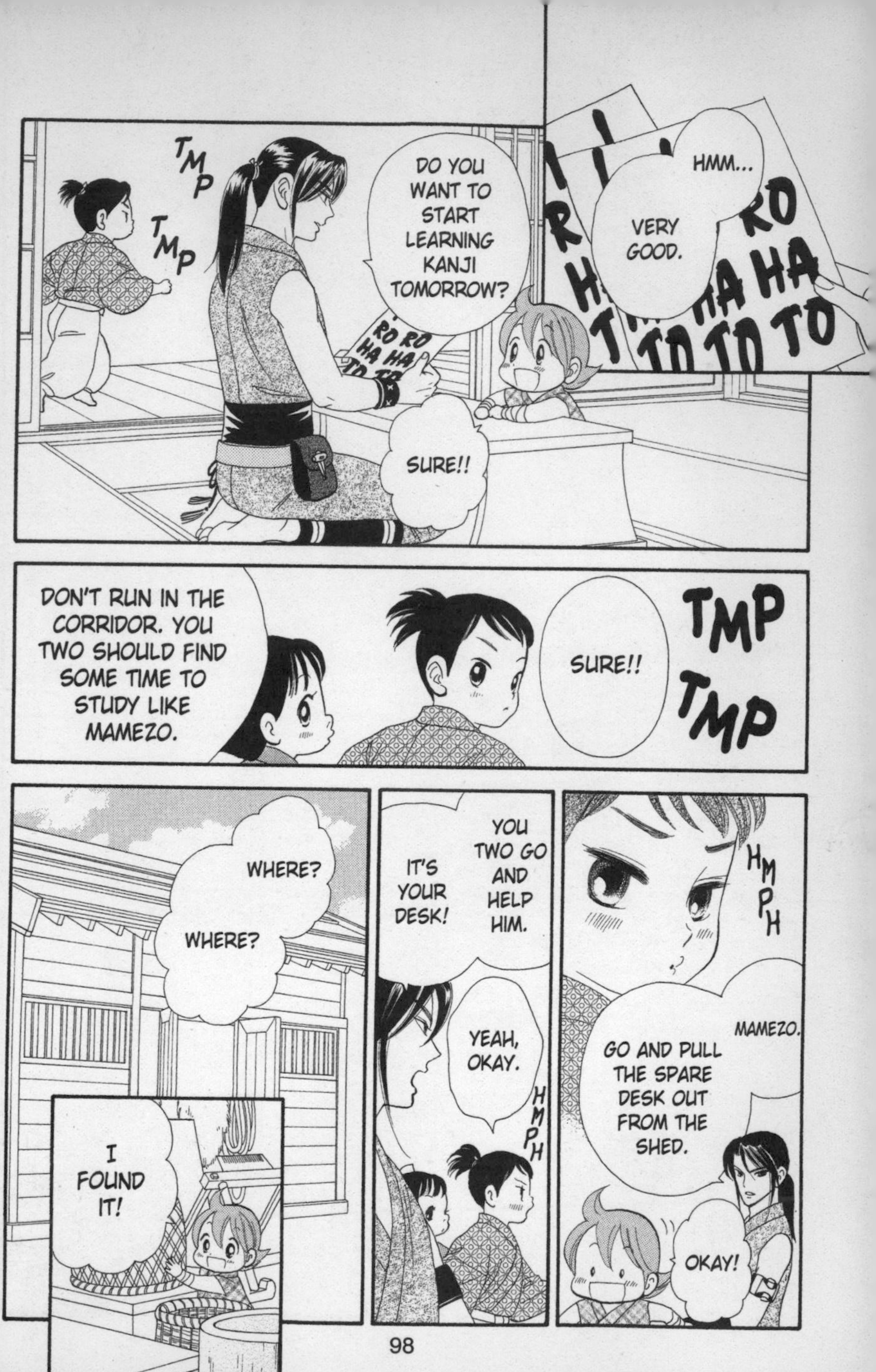
HMM...
VERY GOOD.
RO
HA HA
TO TO TO
DO YOU WANT TO START LEARNING KANJI TOMORROW?
TMP TMP
SURE!!
TMP TMP
SURE!!
DON'T RUN IN THE CORRIDOR. YOU TWO SHOULD FIND SOME TIME TO STUDY LIKE MAMEZO.
HMPH
MAMEZO.
GO AND PULL THE SPARE DESK OUT FROM THE SHED.
OKAY!
YOU TWO GO AND HELP HIM.
IT'S YOUR DESK!
YEAH, OKAY.
HMPH
WHERE?
WHERE?
I FOUND IT!

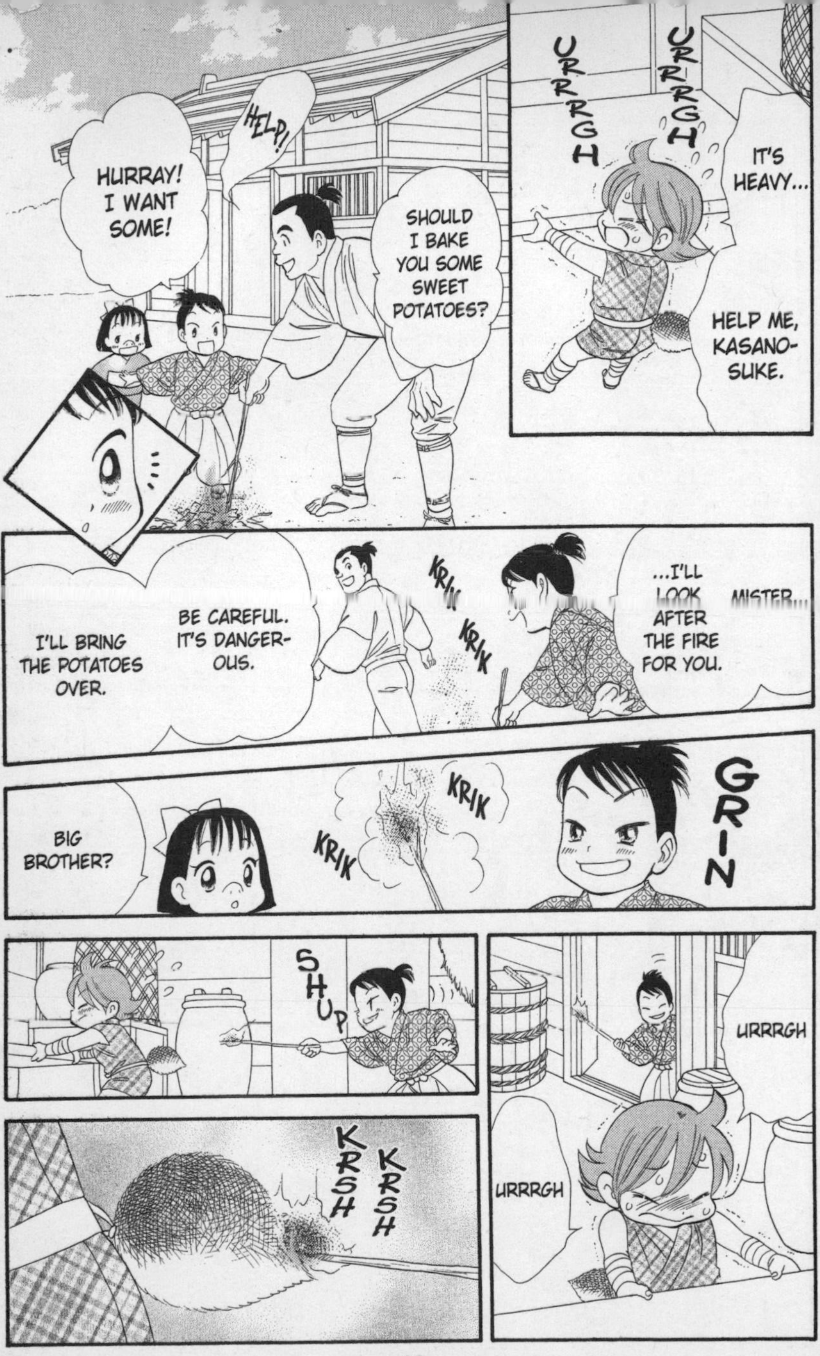
URRRGH
URRRGH
IT'S HEAVY...
HELP ME, KASANO-SUKE.
SHOULD I BAKE YOU SOME SWEET POTATOES?
HELP!
HURRAY! I WANT SOME!
MISTER...
...I'LL LOOK AFTER THE FIRE FOR YOU.
KRIK
KRIK
BE CAREFUL. IT'S DANGER-OUS.
I'LL BRING THE POTATOES OVER.
GRIN
KRIK
KRIK
BIG BROTHER?
URRRGH
URRRGH
SHUP
KRSH
KRSH

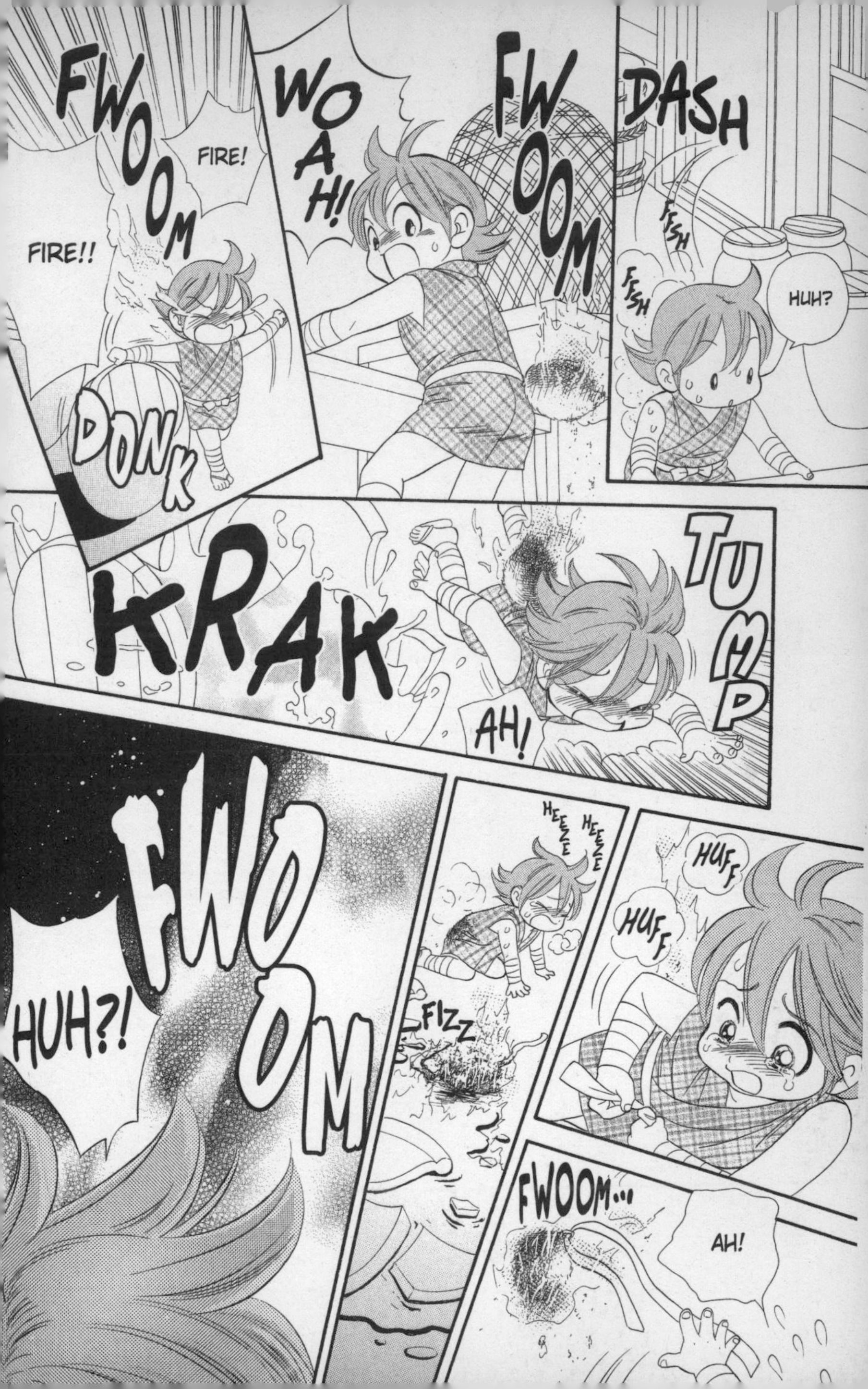
DASH
FFSH
FFSH
HUH?
FWOOOM
WOAH!
FWOOM
FIRE!
FIRE!!
DONK
TUMP
AH!
KRAK
HUFF
HUFF
FWOOM...
AH!
HEEZE
HEEZE
FIZZ
FWOOOM
HUH?!

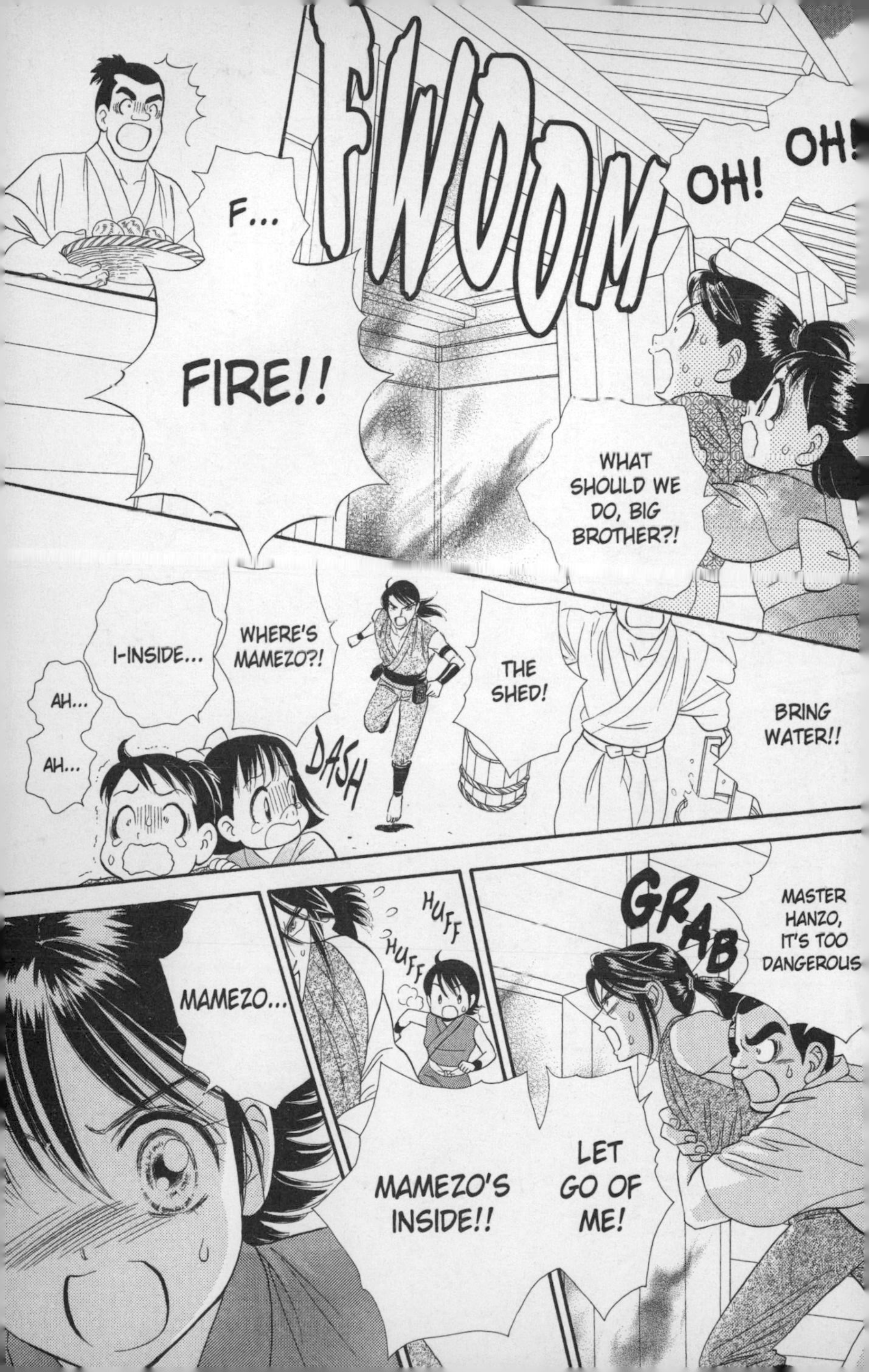
OH! OH!
FWOOM
F...
FIRE!!
WHAT SHOULD WE DO, BIG BROTHER?!
BRING WATER!!
THE SHED!
WHERE'S MAMEZO?!
DASH
I-INSIDE...
AH...
AH...
MASTER HANZO, IT'S TOO DANGEROUS
GRAB
LET GO OF ME!
MAMEZO'S INSIDE!!
HUFF
HUFF
MAMEZO...

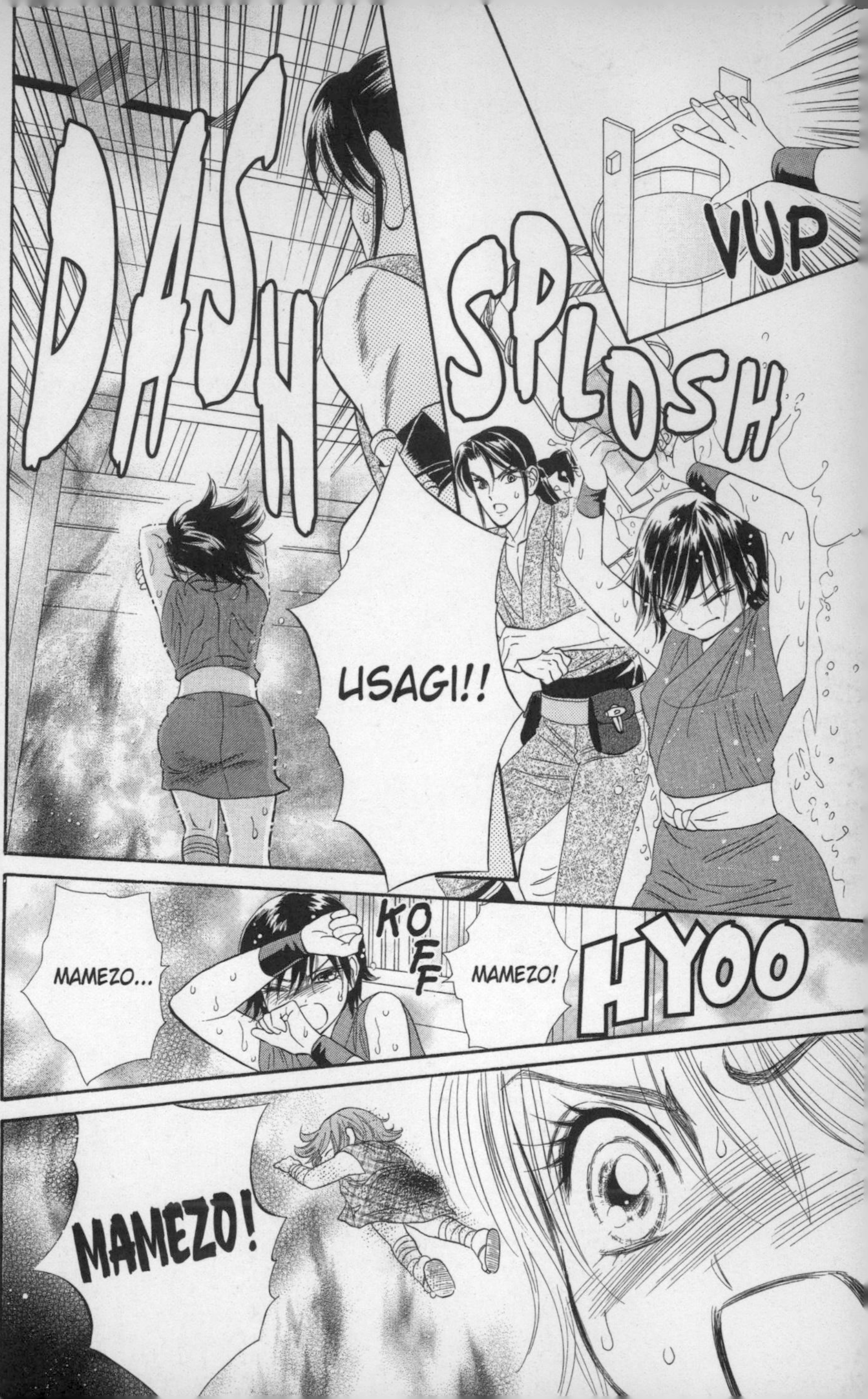
VUP
SPLOSH
USAGI!!
DASH
HYOO
MAMEZO!
KOFF
MAMEZO...
MAMEZO!

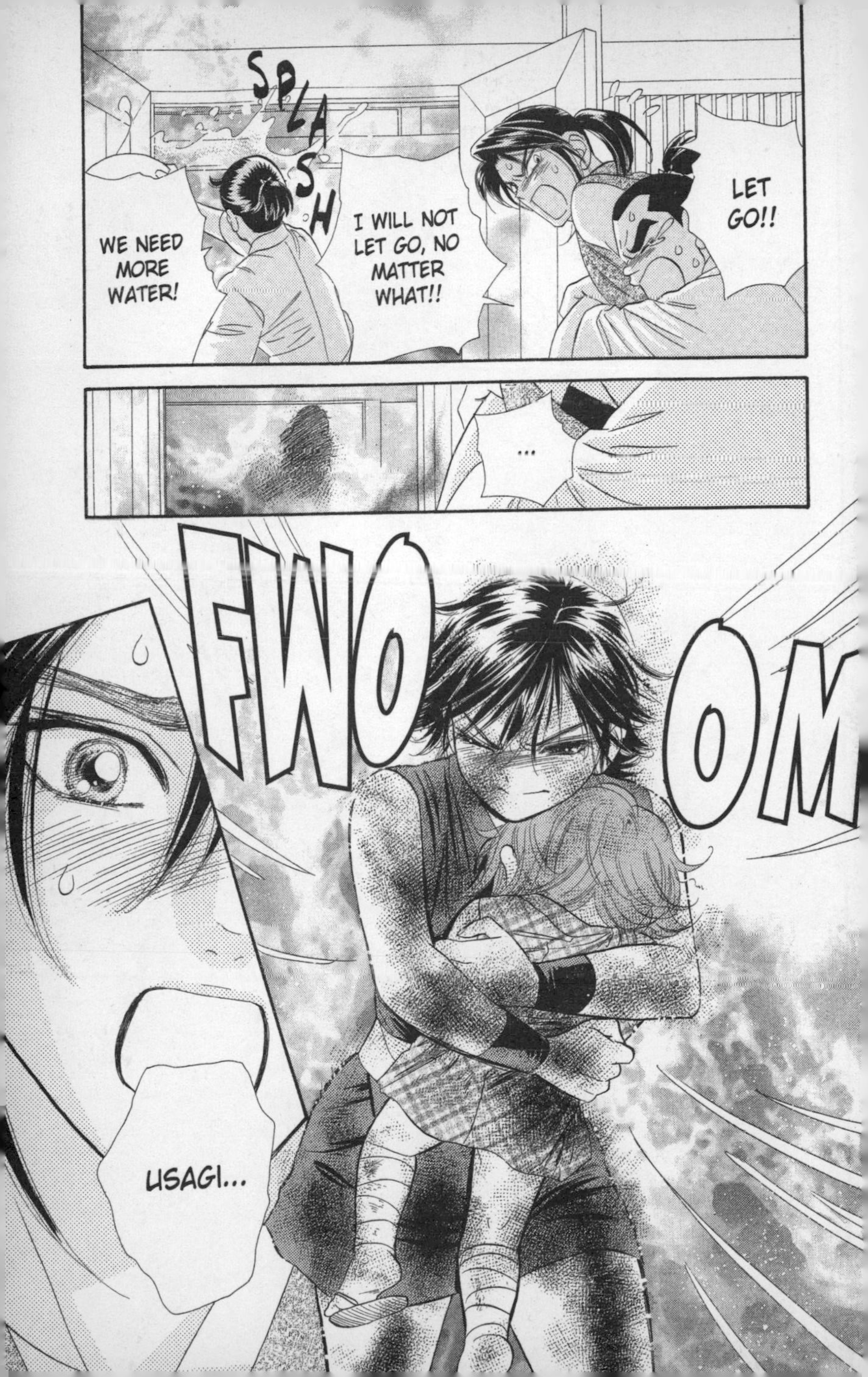
LET GO!!
I WILL NOT LET GO, NO MATTER WHAT!!
SPLASH
WE NEED MORE WATER!
...
FWOOM
USAGI...

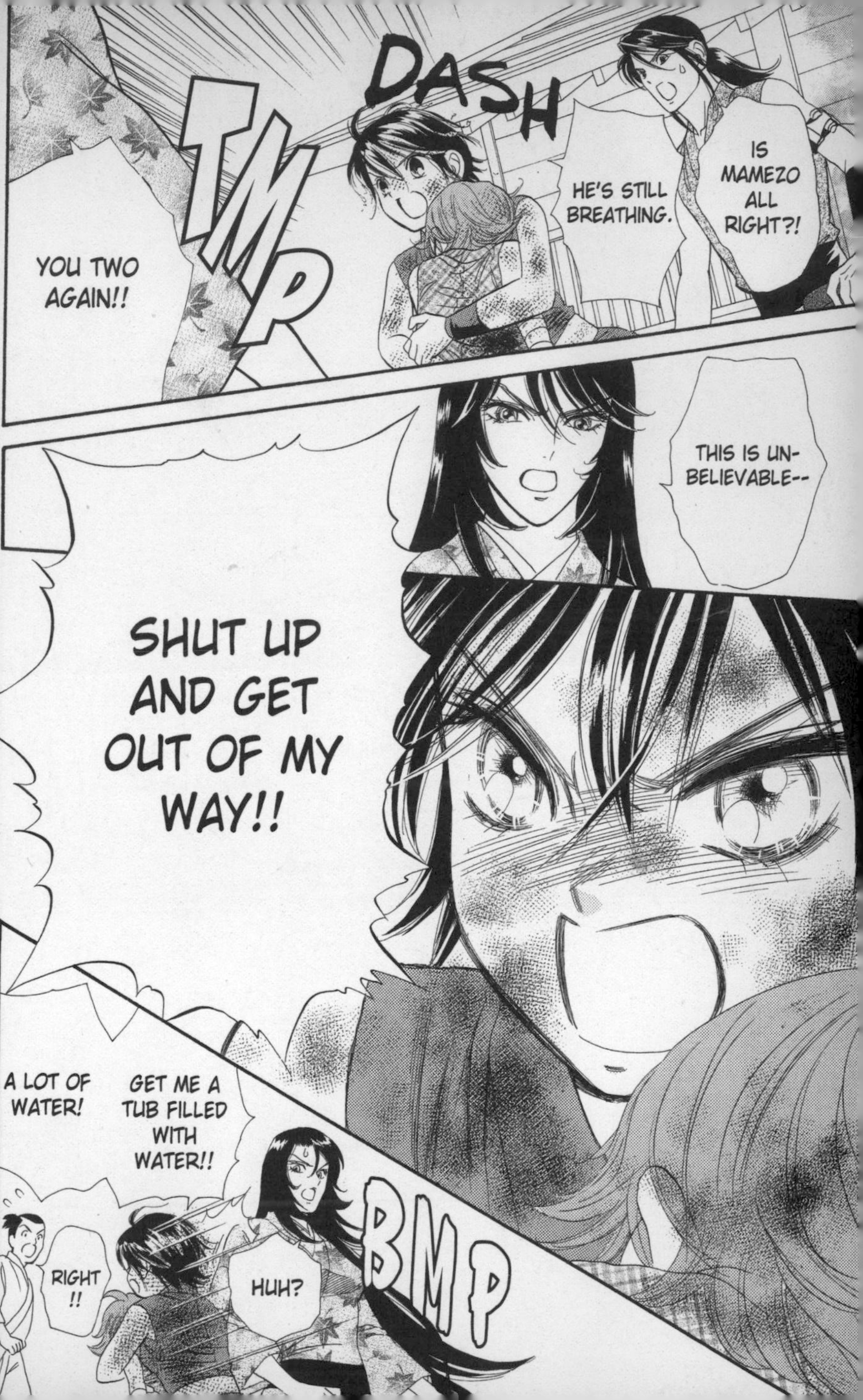
IS MAMEZO ALL RIGHT?!
HE'S STILL BREATHING.
DASH
TMP
YOU TWO AGAIN!!
THIS IS UN-BELIEVABLE--
SHUT UP AND GET OUT OF MY WAY!!
GET ME A TUB FILLED WITH WATER!!
A LOT OF WATER!
BMP
HUH?
RIGHT!!

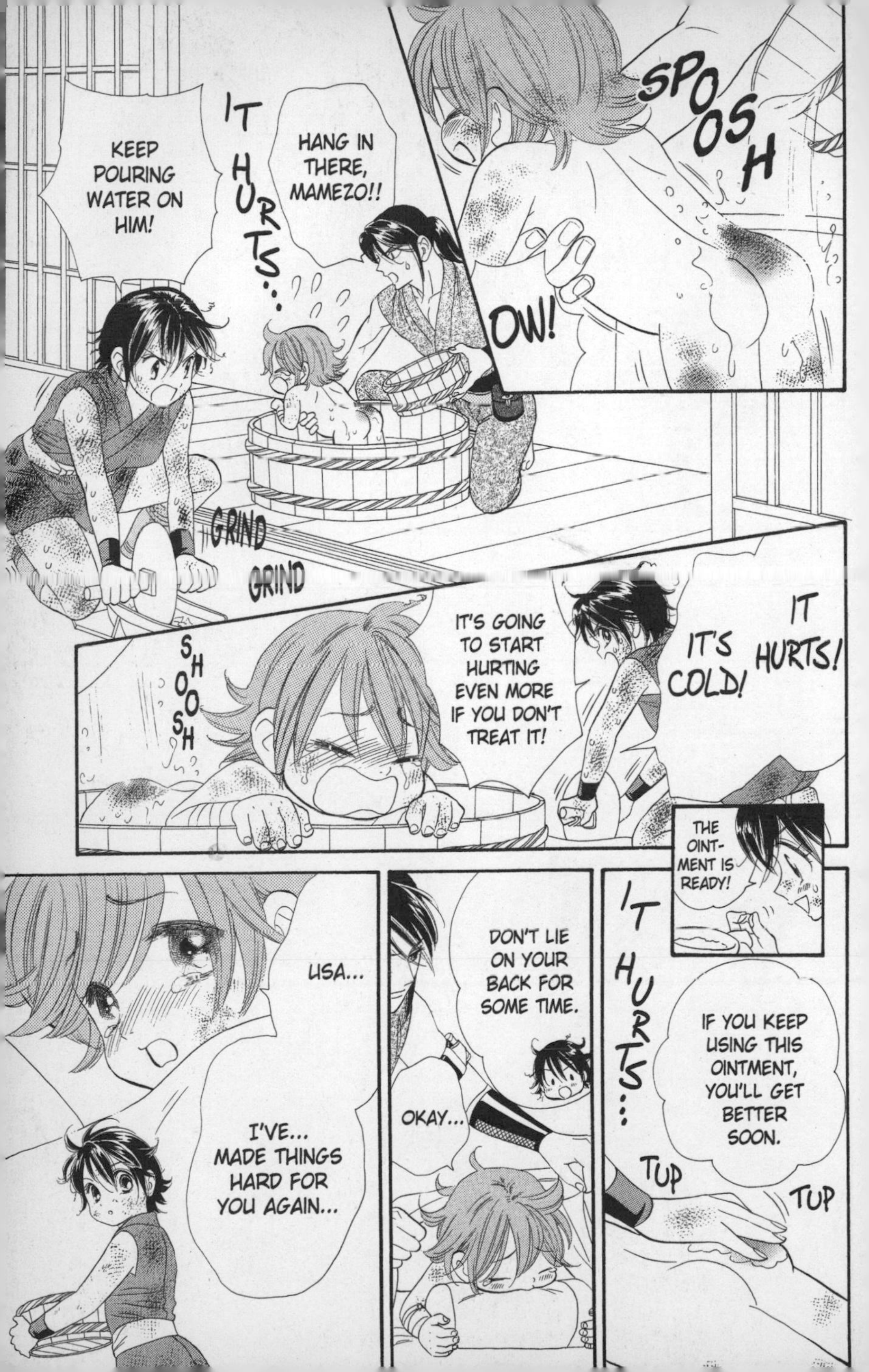
SPOOSH
OW!
IT HURTS...
HANG IN THERE, MAMEZO!!
KEEP POURING WATER ON HIM!
GRIND
GRIND
IT HURTS!
IT'S COLD!
IT'S GOING TO START HURTING EVEN MORE IF YOU DON'T TREAT IT!
SHOOSH
THE OINT-MENT IS READY!
IT HURTS...
IF YOU KEEP USING THIS OINTMENT, YOU'LL GET BETTER SOON.
TUP
TUP
DON'T LIE ON YOUR BACK FOR SOME TIME.
OKAY...
USA...
I'VE... MADE THINGS HARD FOR YOU AGAIN...

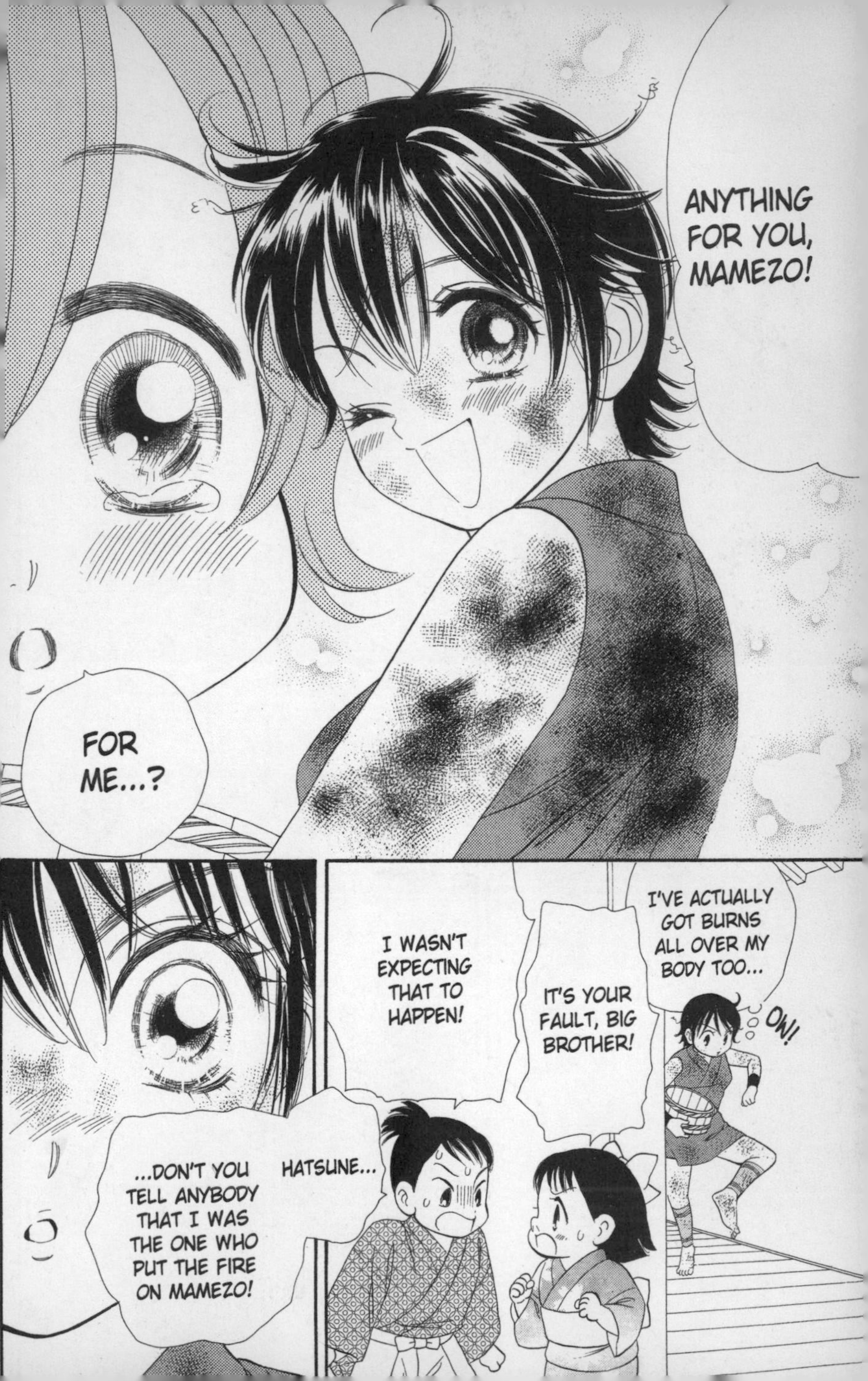
ANYTHING FOR YOU, MAMEZO!
FOR ME...?
I'VE ACTUALLY GOT BURNS ALL OVER MY BODY TOO...
ON!
IT'S YOUR FAULT, BIG BROTHER!
I WASN'T EXPECTING THAT TO HAPPEN!
HATSUNE...
...DON'T YOU TELL ANYBODY THAT I WAS THE ONE WHO PUT THE FIRE ON MAMEZO!

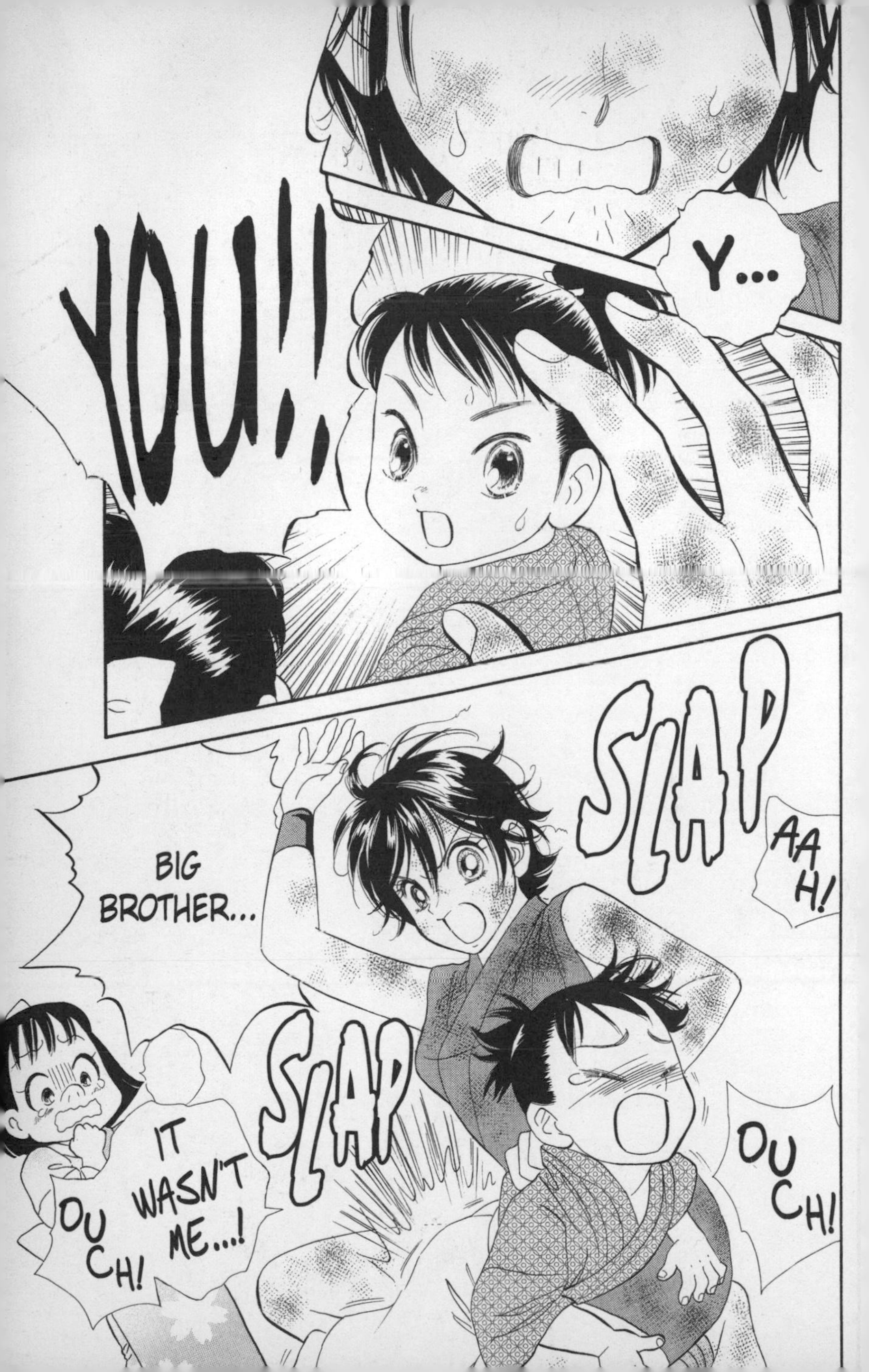
Y...
YOU!!
SLAP
AAH!
BIG BROTHER...
SLAP
OUCH!
IT WASN'T ME...!
OUCH!

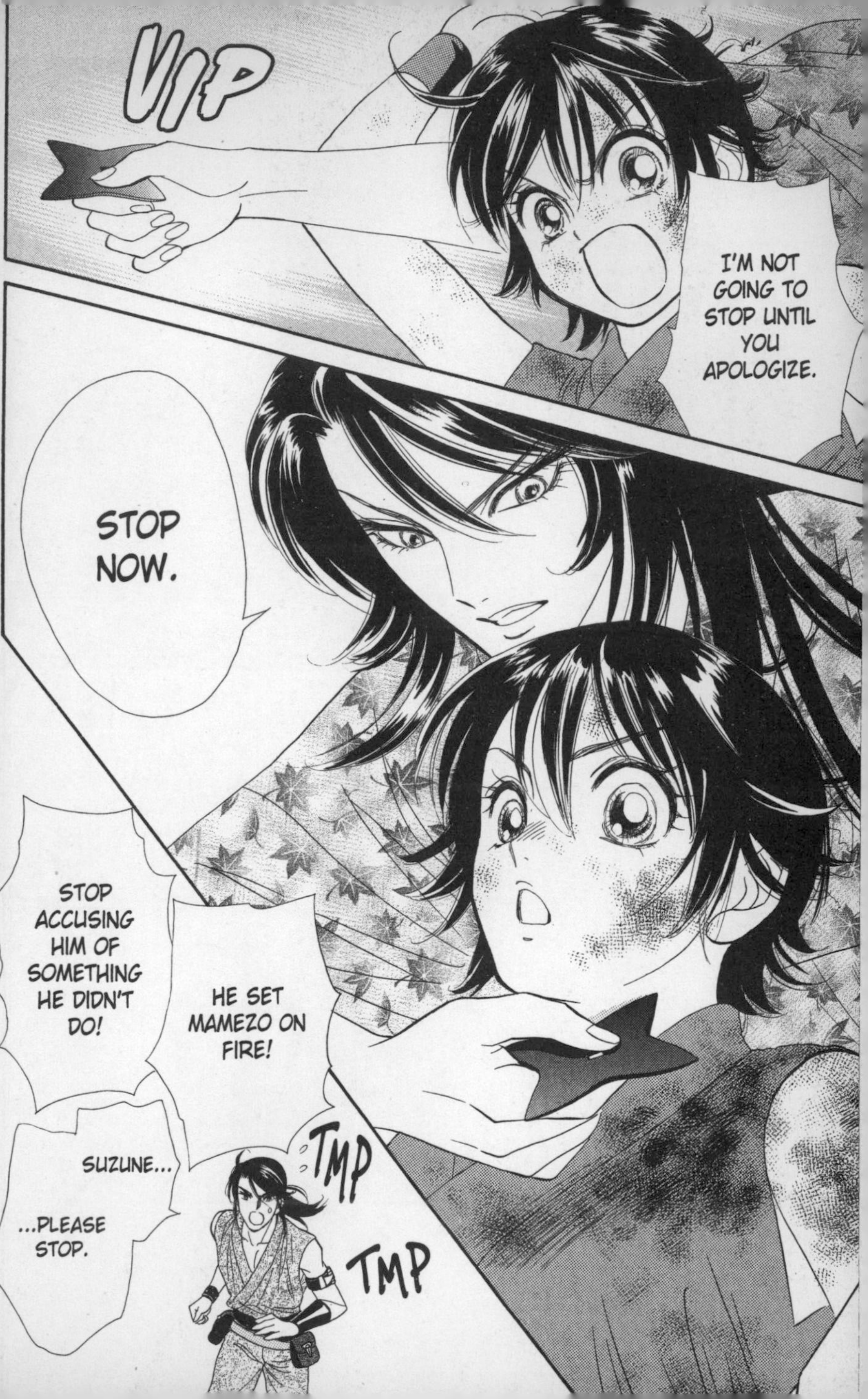
VIP
I'M NOT GOING TO STOP UNTIL YOU APOLOGIZE.
STOP NOW.
HE SET MAMEZO ON FIRE!
STOP ACCUSING HIM OF SOMETHING HE DIDN'T DO!
TMP
TMP
SUZUNE...
...PLEASE STOP.

TAIL OF THE MOON EXTRA: TODAY'S MISSION

"I WANT HANZO TO BE A TOUGH COACH." ♡

-AYA UENO, KANAGAWA PREFECTURE

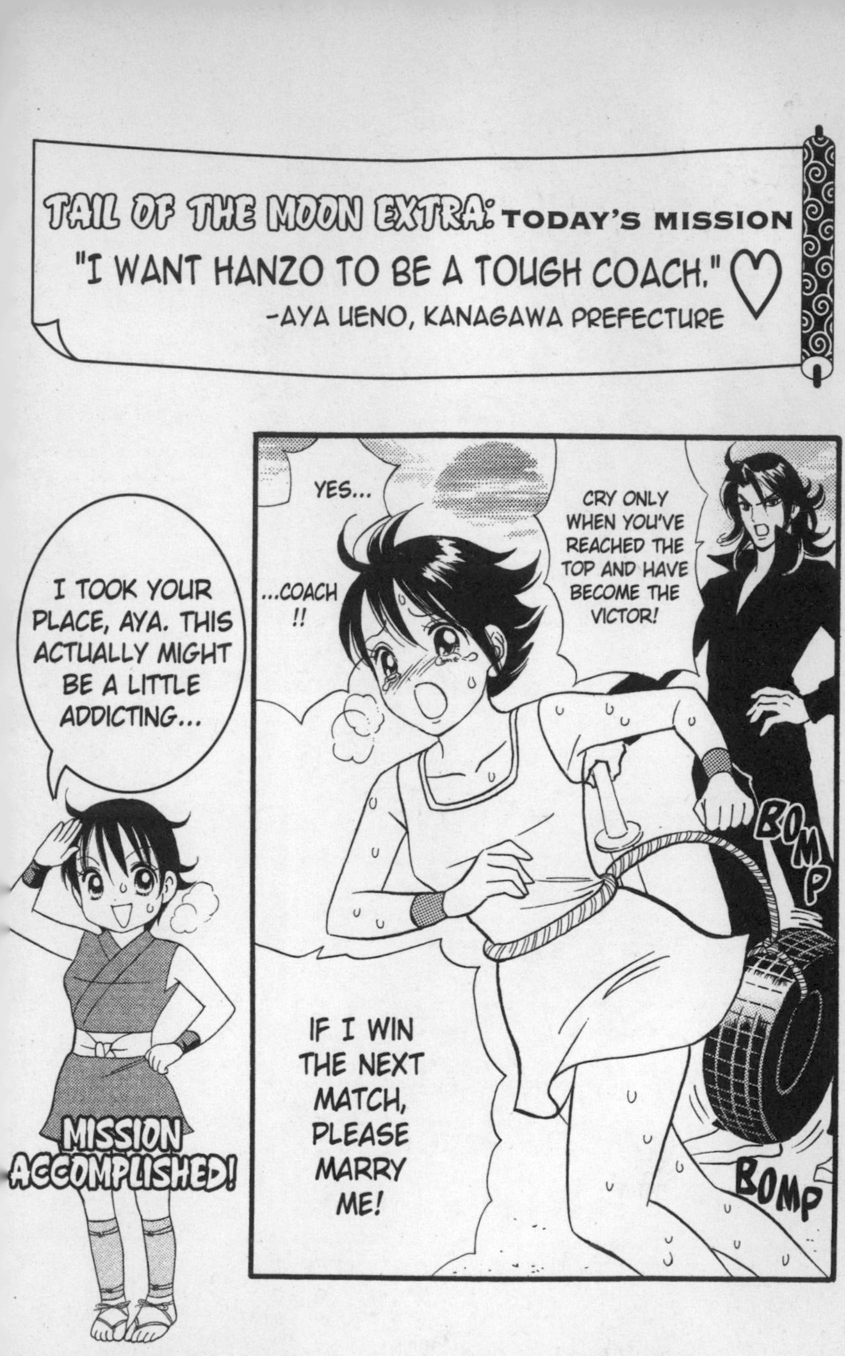
CRY ONLY WHEN YOU'VE REACHED THE TOP AND HAVE BECOME THE VICTOR!
YES...
...COACH !!
BOMP
BOMP
IF I WIN THE NEXT MATCH, PLEASE MARRY ME!
I TOOK YOUR PLACE, AYA. THIS ACTUALLY MIGHT BE A LITTLE ADDICTING...
MISSION ACCOMPLISHED!

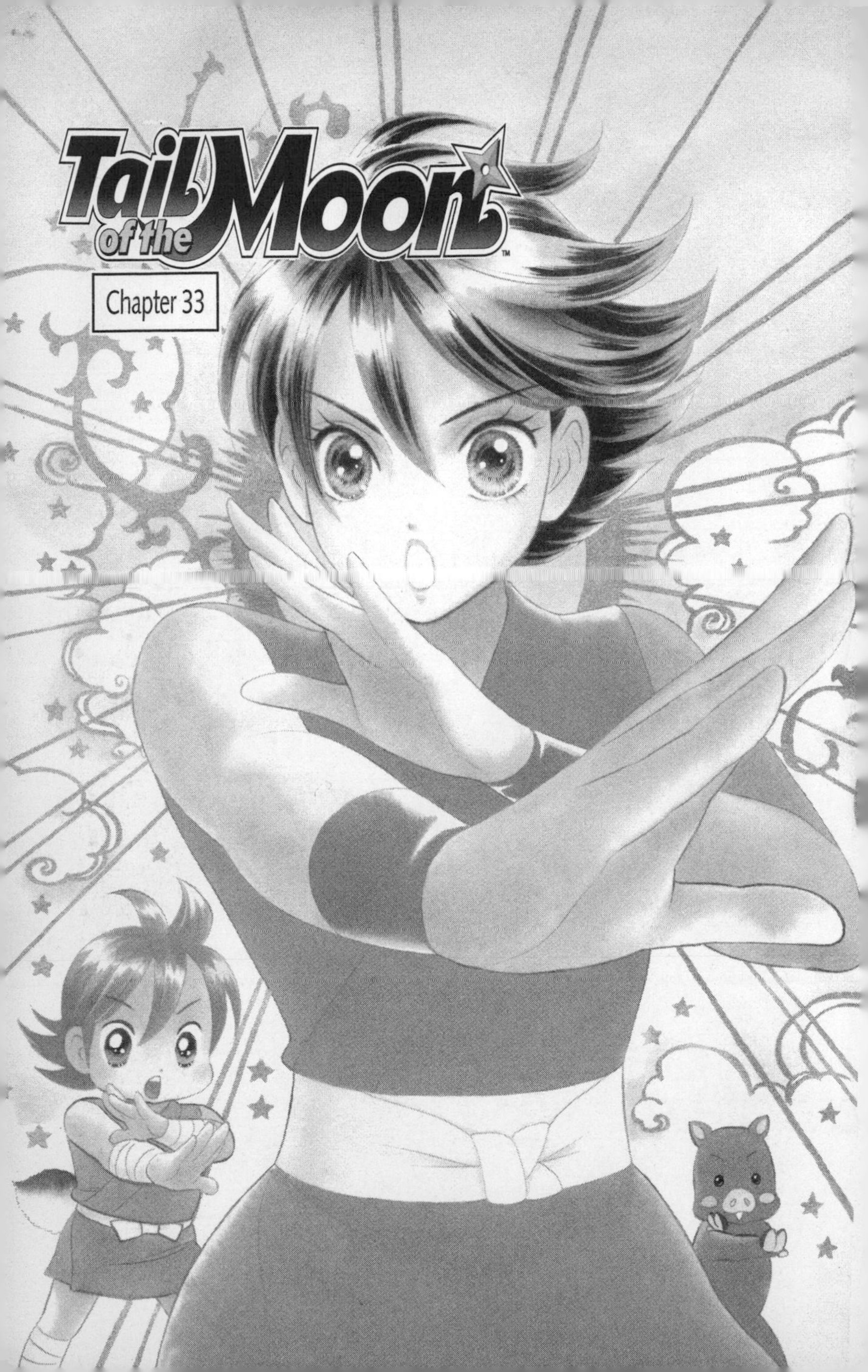
Tail of the Moon™
Chapter 33

TAIL OF THE MOON EXTRA: TODAY'S MISSION

"I WANT TO HAVE TEA AT A CAFÉ WITH GOOD-LOOKING MEN!"

-KE-CHAN-SAN, IWATE PREFECTURE

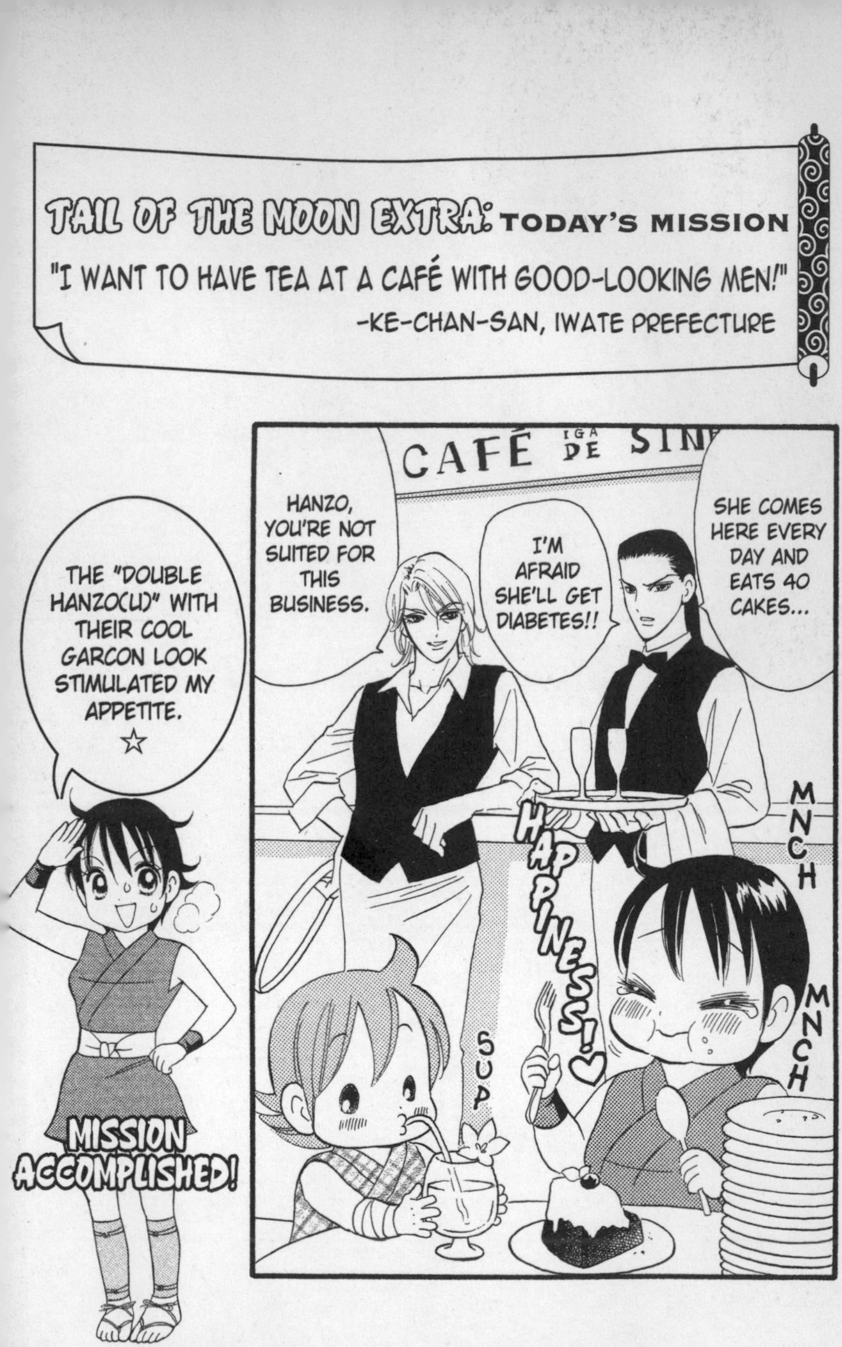
CAFÉ IGA DE SIN
SHE COMES HERE EVERY DAY AND EATS 40 CAKES...
I'M AFRAID SHE'LL GET DIABETES!!
HANZO, YOU'RE NOT SUITED FOR THIS BUSINESS.
MNCH
HAPPINESS!♥
MNCH
SUP
THE "DOUBLE HANZO(U)" WITH THEIR COOL GARCON LOOK STIMULATED MY APPETITE. ☆
MISSION ACCOMPLISHED!

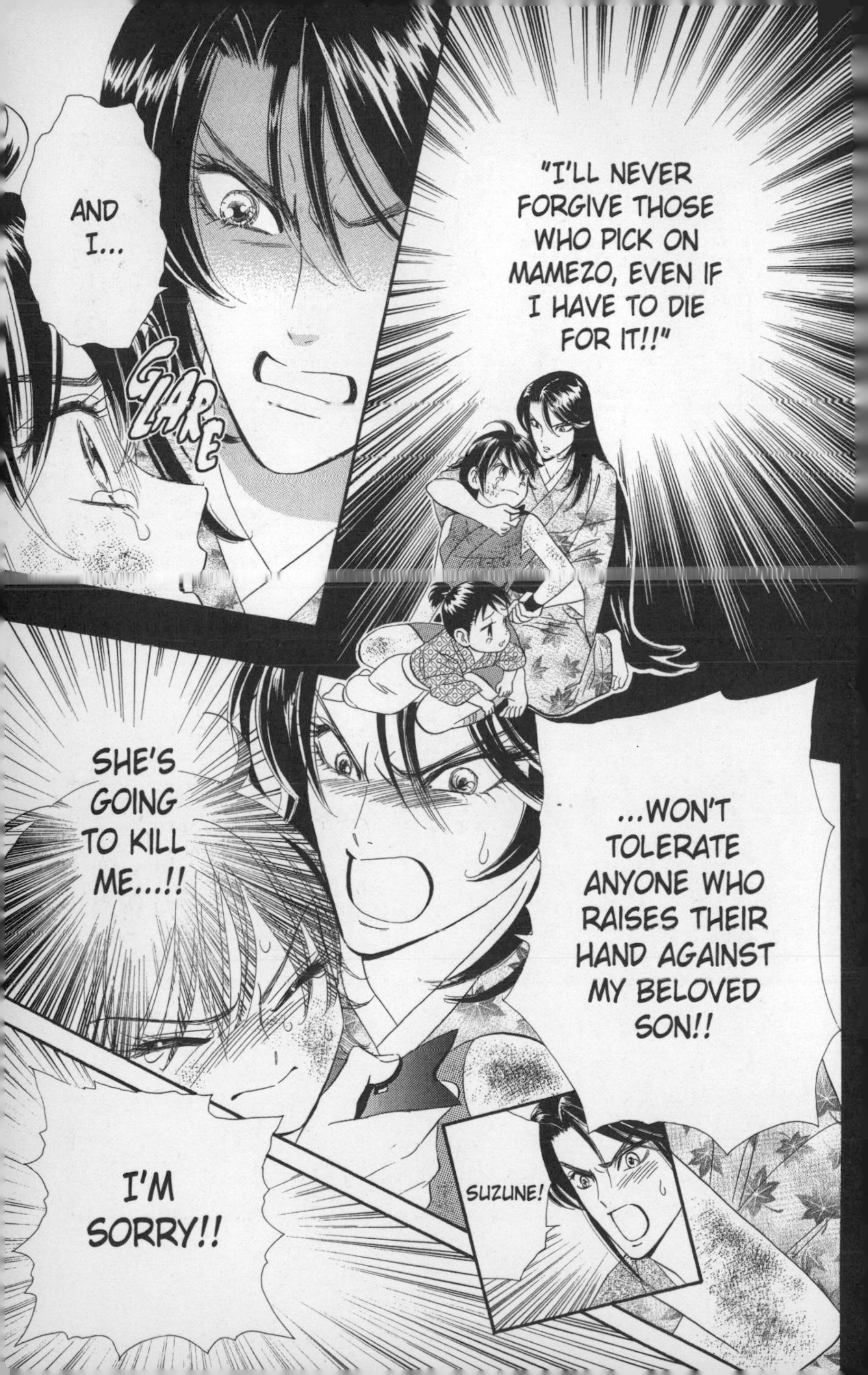
"I'LL NEVER FORGIVE THOSE WHO PICK ON MAMEZO, EVEN IF I HAVE TO DIE FOR IT!!"
AND I...
GLARE
...WON'T TOLERATE ANYONE WHO RAISES THEIR HAND AGAINST MY BELOVED SON!!
SHE'S GOING TO KILL ME...!!
SUZUNE!
I'M SORRY!!

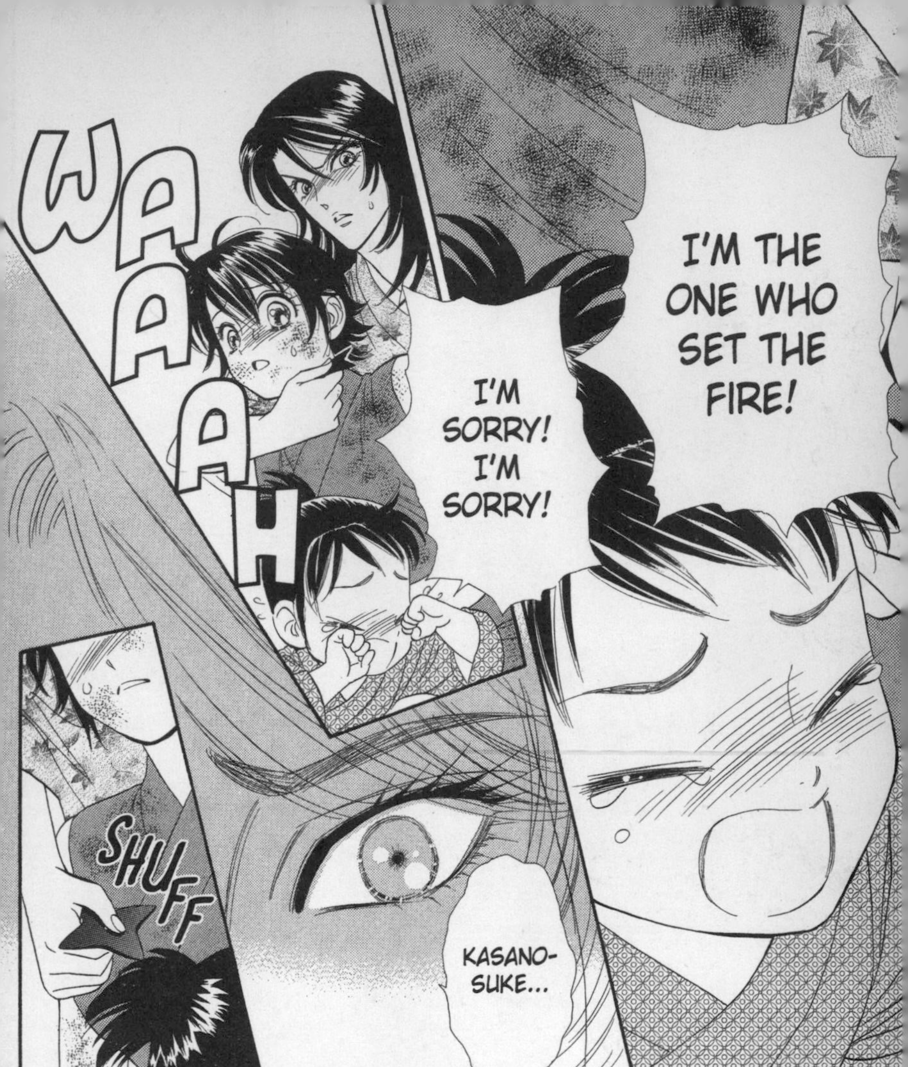
I'M THE ONE WHO SET THE FIRE!
I'M SORRY! I'M SORRY!
WAAAH
KASANO-SUKE...
SHUFF

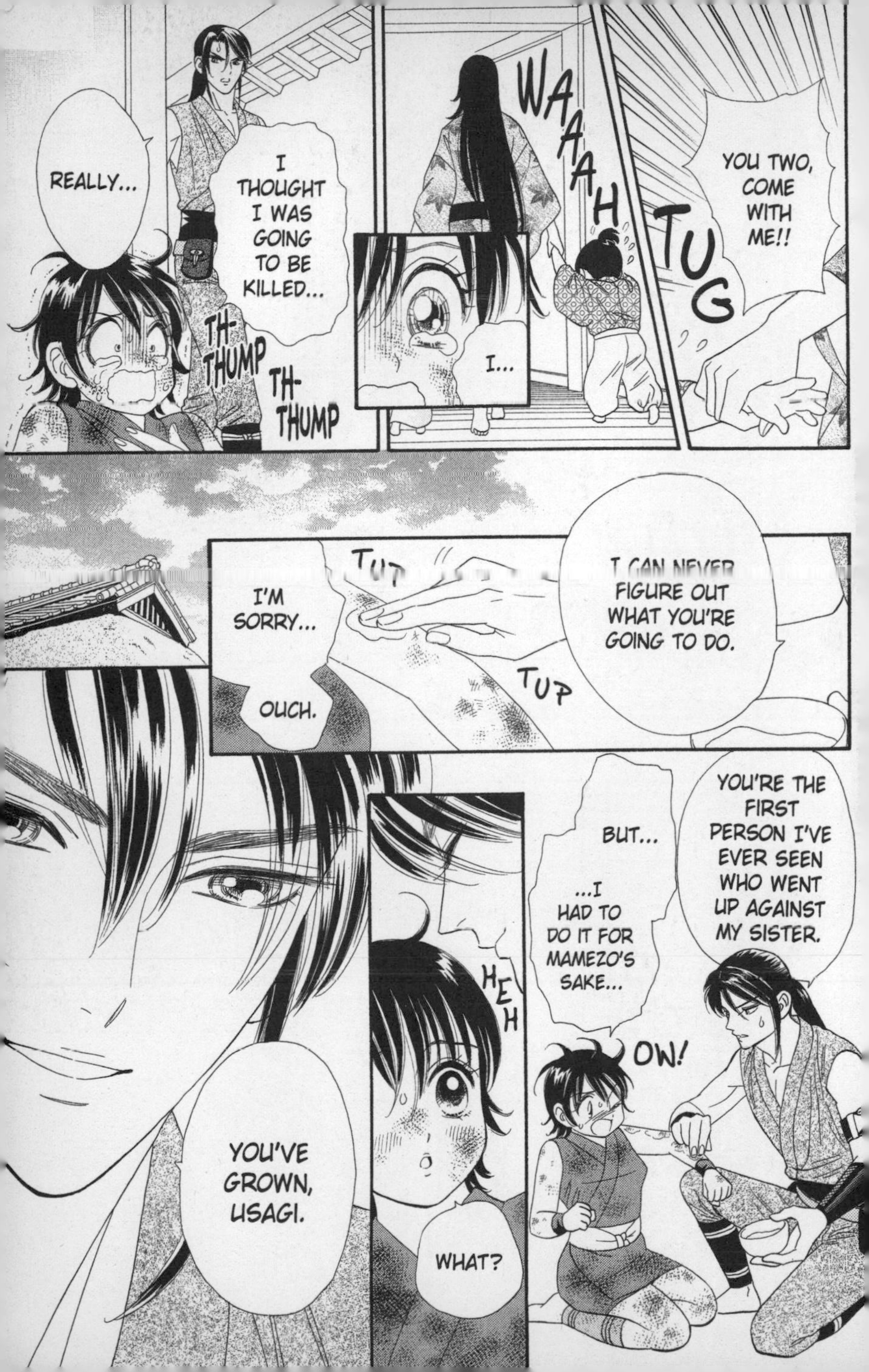
YOU TWO, COME WITH ME!!
TUG
WAAAAH
I...
I THOUGHT I WAS GOING TO BE KILLED...
REALLY...
TH-THUMP
TH-THUMP
I CAN NEVER FIGURE OUT WHAT YOU'RE GOING TO DO.
TUP
TUP
I'M SORRY...
OUCH.
YOU'RE THE FIRST PERSON I'VE EVER SEEN WHO WENT UP AGAINST MY SISTER.
BUT...
...I HAD TO DO IT FOR MAMEZO'S SAKE...
OW!
HEH
YOU'VE GROWN, USAGI.
WHAT?

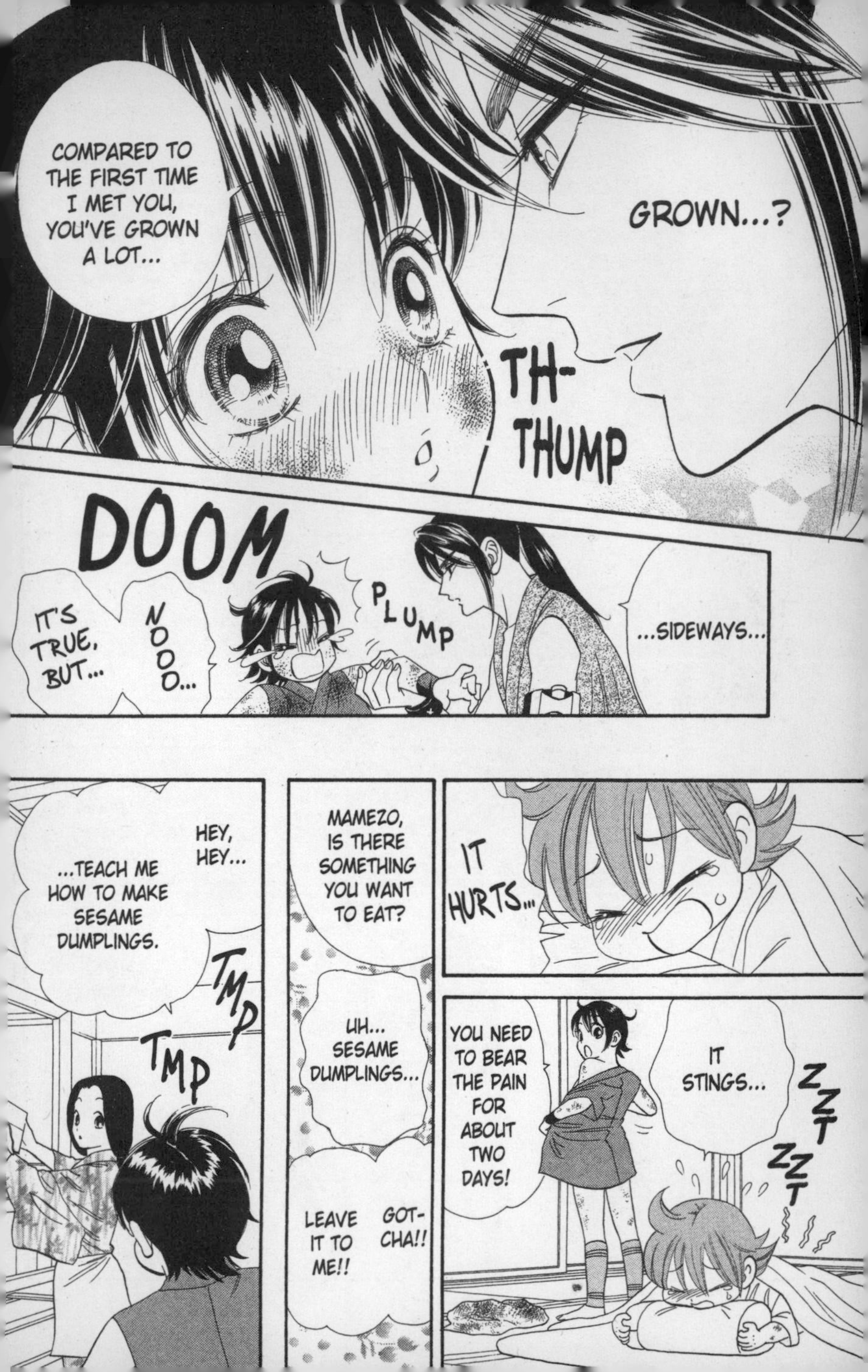
COMPARED TO THE FIRST TIME I MET YOU, YOU'VE GROWN A LOT...
GROWN...?
TH-THUMP
...SIDEWAYS...
PLUMP
DOOM
NOOOO...
IT'S TRUE, BUT...
IT HURTS...
IT STINGS...
ZZT ZZT
YOU NEED TO BEAR THE PAIN FOR ABOUT TWO DAYS!
MAMEZO, IS THERE SOMETHING YOU WANT TO EAT?
UH... SESAME DUMPLINGS...
GOT-CHA!!
LEAVE IT TO ME!!
HEY, HEY...
...TEACH ME HOW TO MAKE SESAME DUMPLINGS.
TMP TMP

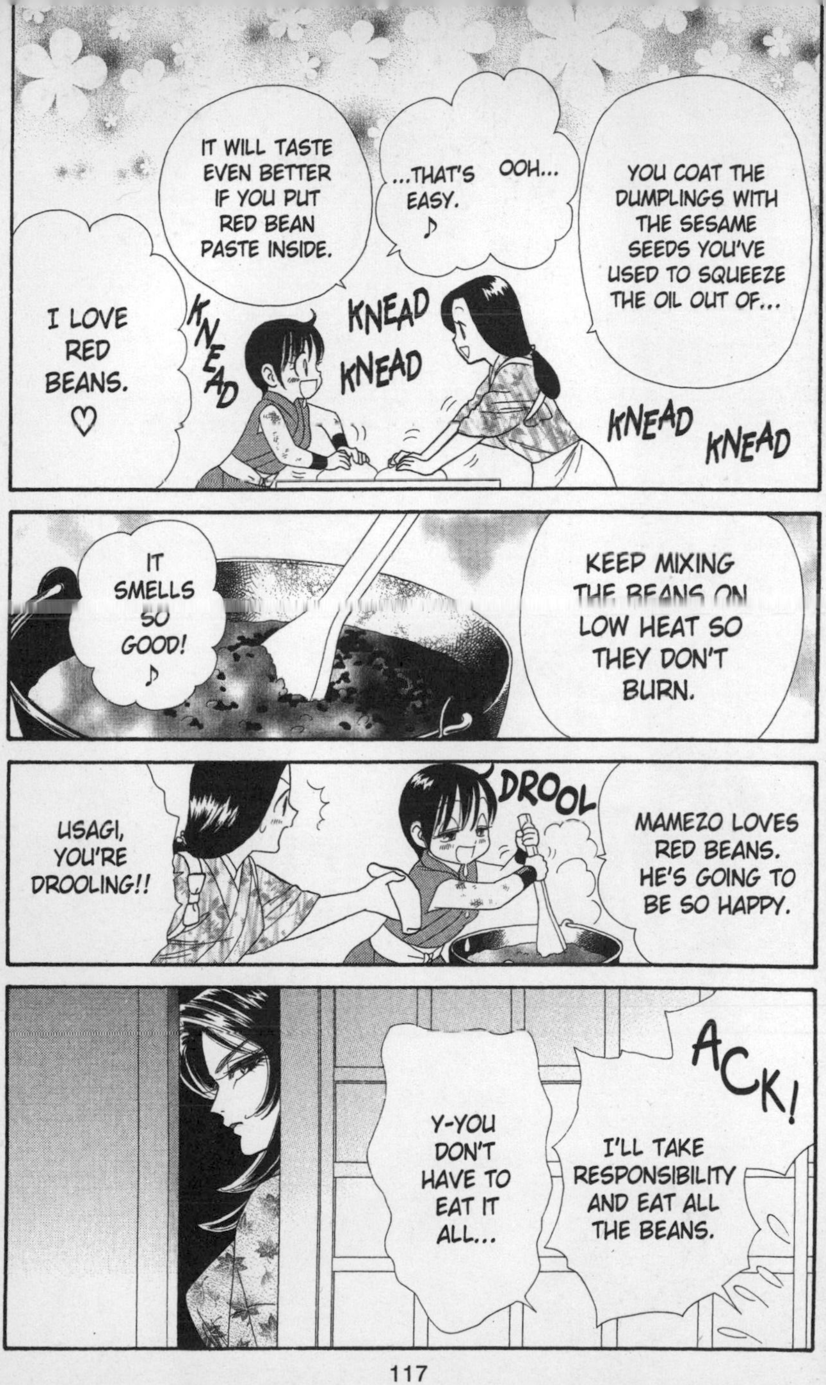

YOU COAT THE DUMPLINGS WITH THE SESAME SEEDS YOU'VE USED TO SQUEEZE THE OIL OUT OF...
OOH...
...THAT'S EASY. ♪
IT WILL TASTE EVEN BETTER IF YOU PUT RED BEAN PASTE INSIDE.
KNEAD KNEAD
KNEAD KNEAD
KNEAD
I LOVE RED BEANS. ♡
KEEP MIXING THE BEANS ON LOW HEAT SO THEY DON'T BURN.
IT SMELLS SO GOOD! ♪
MAMEZO LOVES RED BEANS. HE'S GOING TO BE SO HAPPY.
DROOL
USAGI, YOU'RE DROOLING!!
ACK!
I'LL TAKE RESPONSIBILITY AND EAT ALL THE BEANS.
Y-YOU DON'T HAVE TO EAT IT ALL...

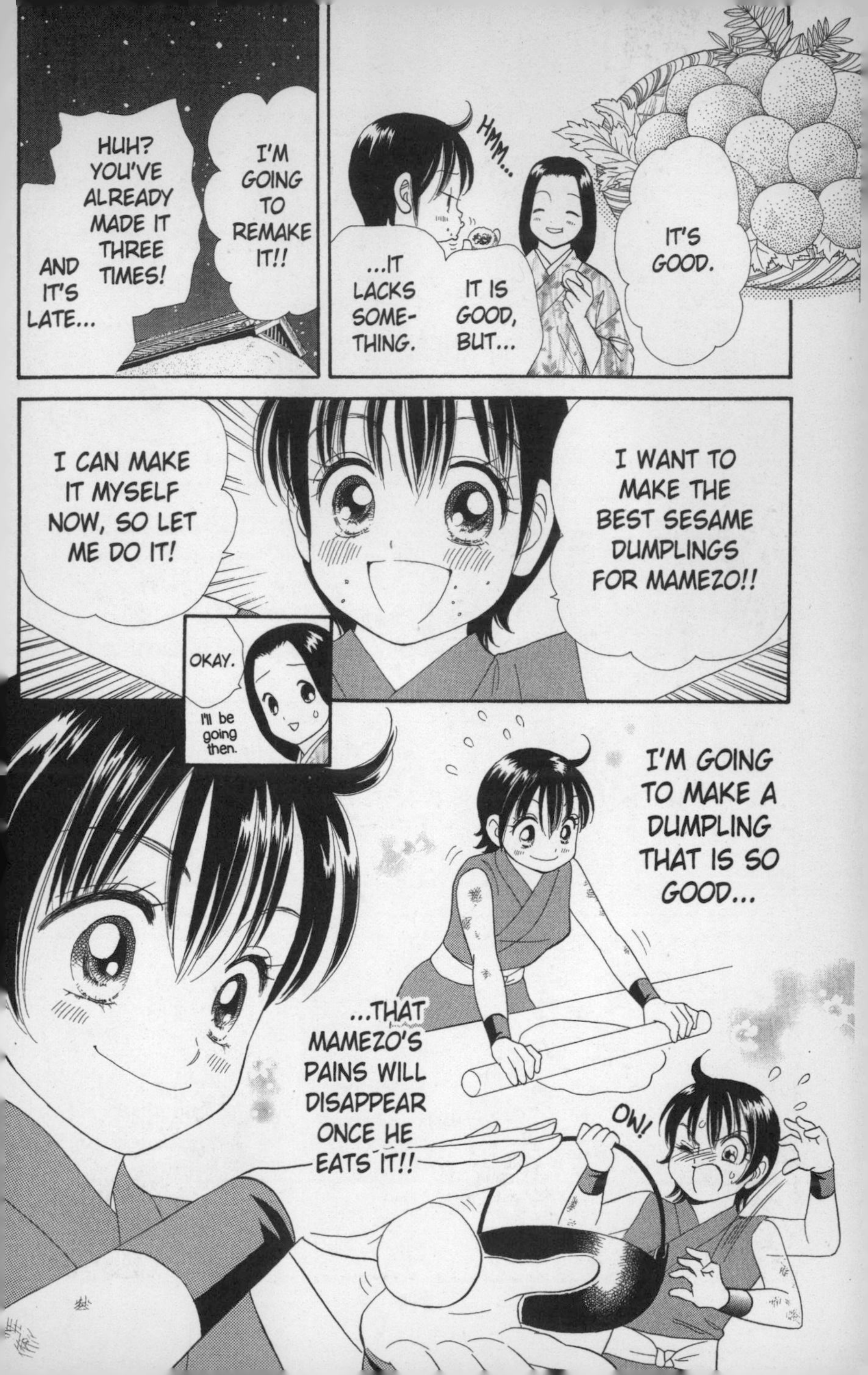
HMM...
IT'S GOOD.
IT IS GOOD, BUT...
...IT LACKS SOMETHING.
I'M GOING TO REMAKE IT!!
HUH? YOU'VE ALREADY MADE IT THREE TIMES!
AND IT'S LATE...
I WANT TO MAKE THE BEST SESAME DUMPLINGS FOR MAMEZO!!
I CAN MAKE IT MYSELF NOW, SO LET ME DO IT!
OKAY.
I'll be going then.
I'M GOING TO MAKE A DUMPLING THAT IS SO GOOD...
OW!
...THAT MAMEZO'S PAINS WILL DISAPPEAR ONCE HE EATS IT!!

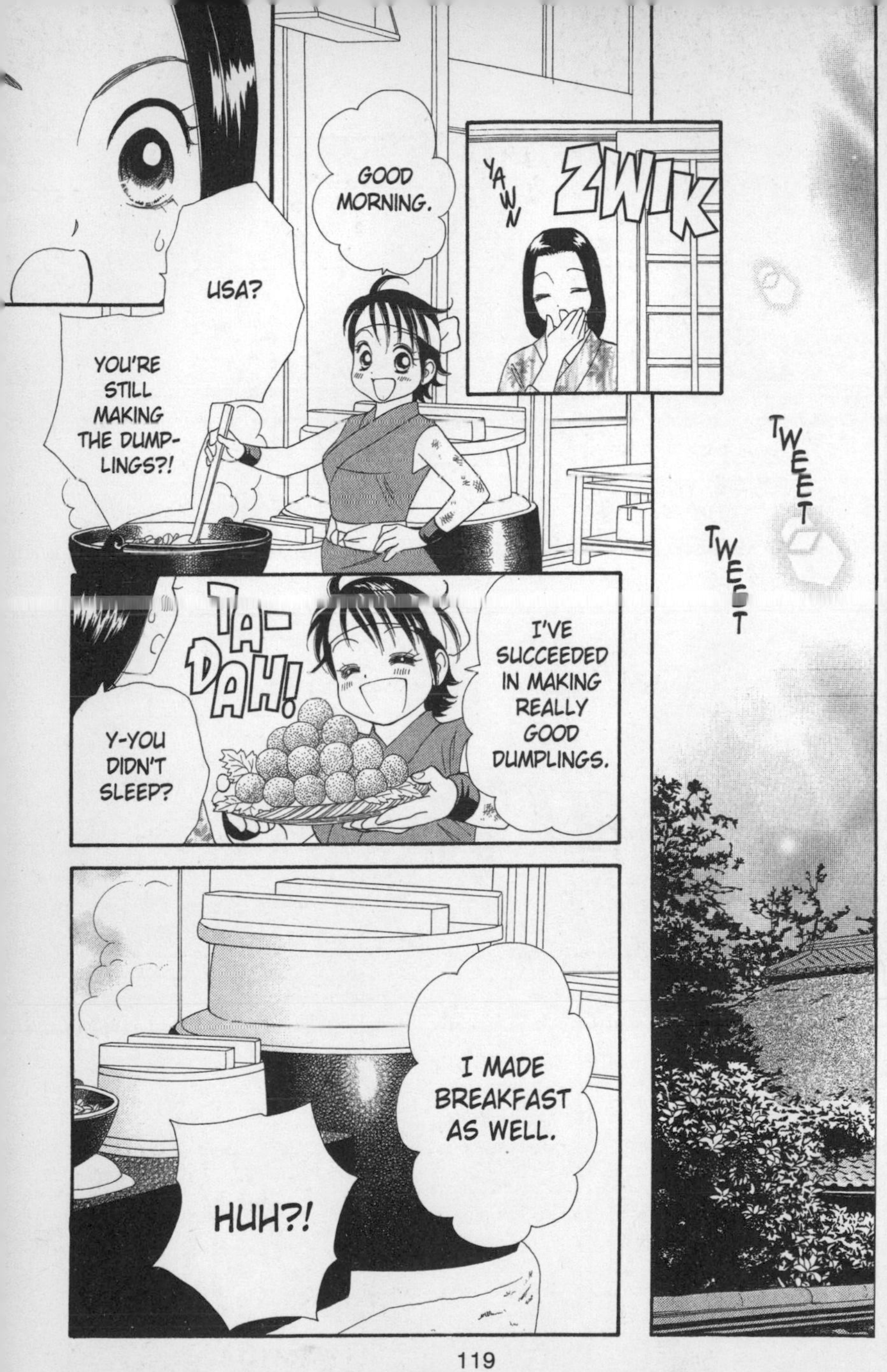
TWEET
TWEET
YAWN
ZWIK
GOOD MORNING.
USA?
YOU'RE STILL MAKING THE DUMP-LINGS?!
I'VE SUCCEEDED IN MAKING REALLY GOOD DUMPLINGS.
TA-DAH!
Y-YOU DIDN'T SLEEP?
I MADE BREAKFAST AS WELL.
HUH?!

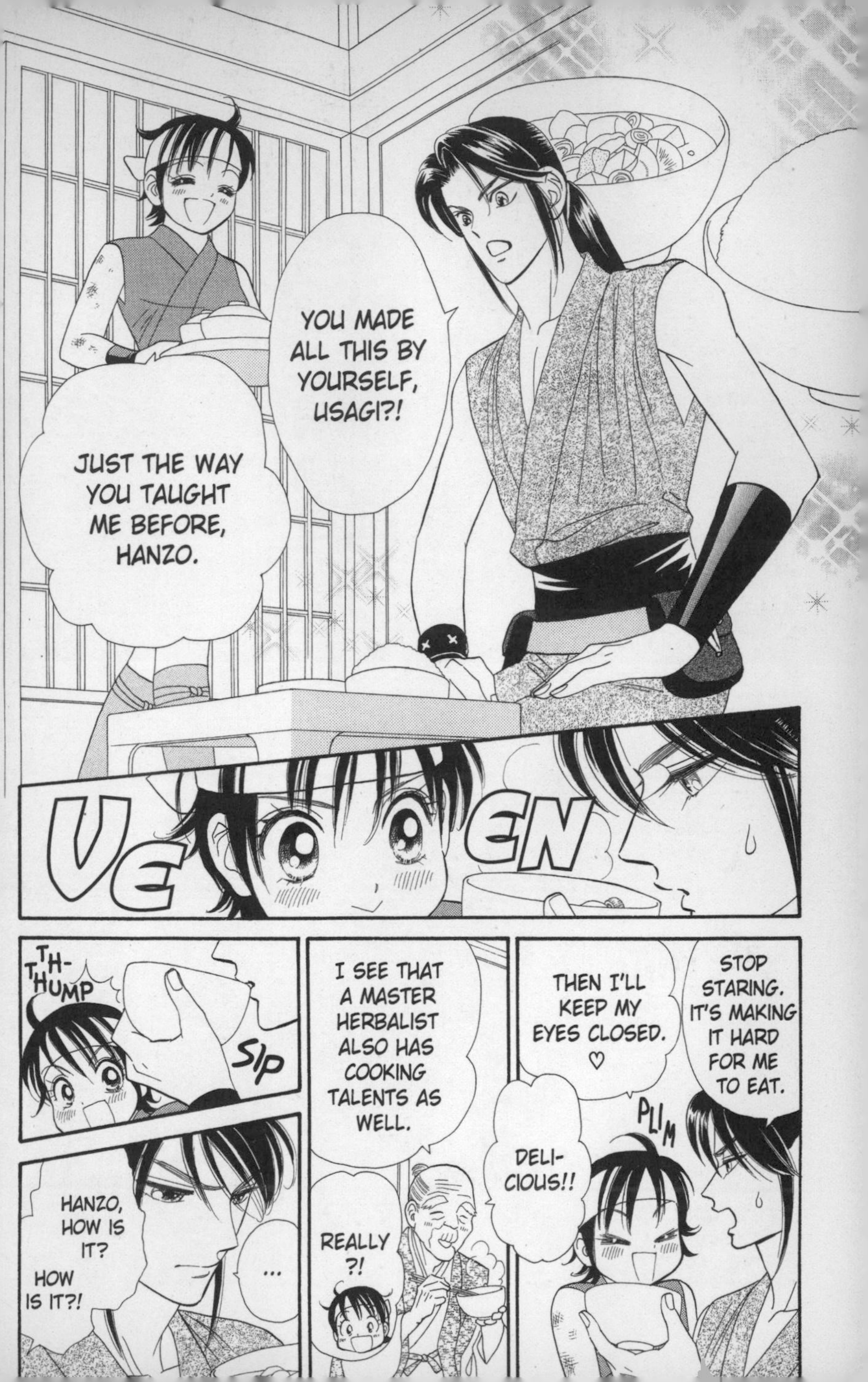
YOU MADE ALL THIS BY YOURSELF, USAGI?!
JUST THE WAY YOU TAUGHT ME BEFORE, HANZO.
VE EN
STOP STARING. IT'S MAKING IT HARD FOR ME TO EAT.
THEN I'LL KEEP MY EYES CLOSED. ♡
PLIM
DELICIOUS!!
I SEE THAT A MASTER HERBALIST ALSO HAS COOKING TALENTS AS WELL.
REALLY?!
TH-THUMP
SIP
...
HANZO, HOW IS IT?
HOW IS IT?!

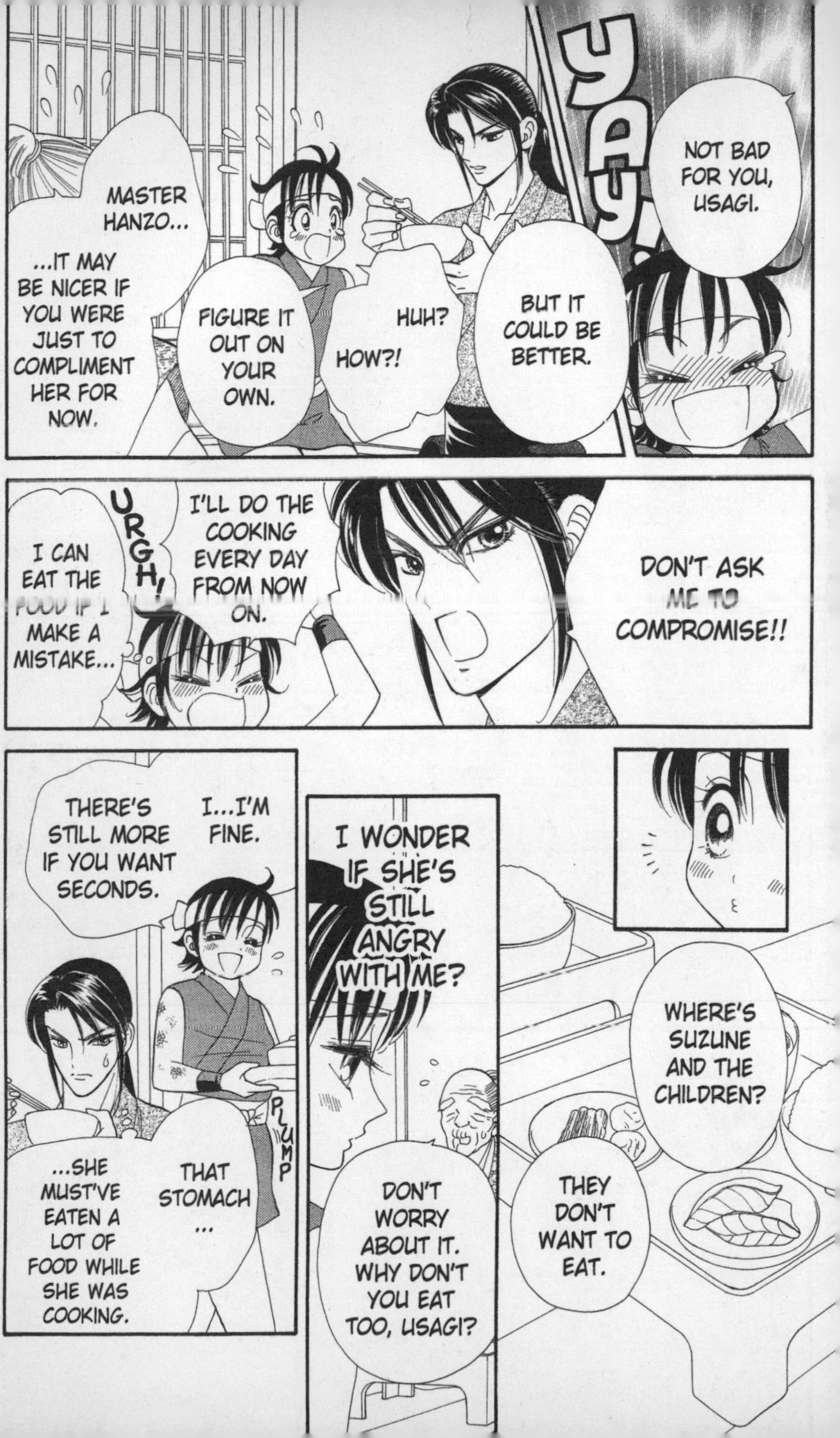
YAY!
NOT BAD FOR YOU, USAGI.
BUT IT COULD BE BETTER.
HUH?
HOW?!
FIGURE IT OUT ON YOUR OWN.
MASTER HANZO...
...IT MAY BE NICER IF YOU WERE JUST TO COMPLIMENT HER FOR NOW.
DON'T ASK ME TO COMPROMISE!!
I'LL DO THE COOKING EVERY DAY FROM NOW ON.
URGH!
I CAN EAT THE FOOD IF I MAKE A MISTAKE...
WHERE'S SUZUNE AND THE CHILDREN?
THEY DON'T WANT TO EAT.
DON'T WORRY ABOUT IT. WHY DON'T YOU EAT TOO, USAGI?
I WONDER IF SHE'S STILL ANGRY WITH ME?
I...I'M FINE.
THERE'S STILL MORE IF YOU WANT SECONDS.
PLUMP
THAT STOMACH...
...SHE MUST'VE EATEN A LOT OF FOOD WHILE SHE WAS COOKING.

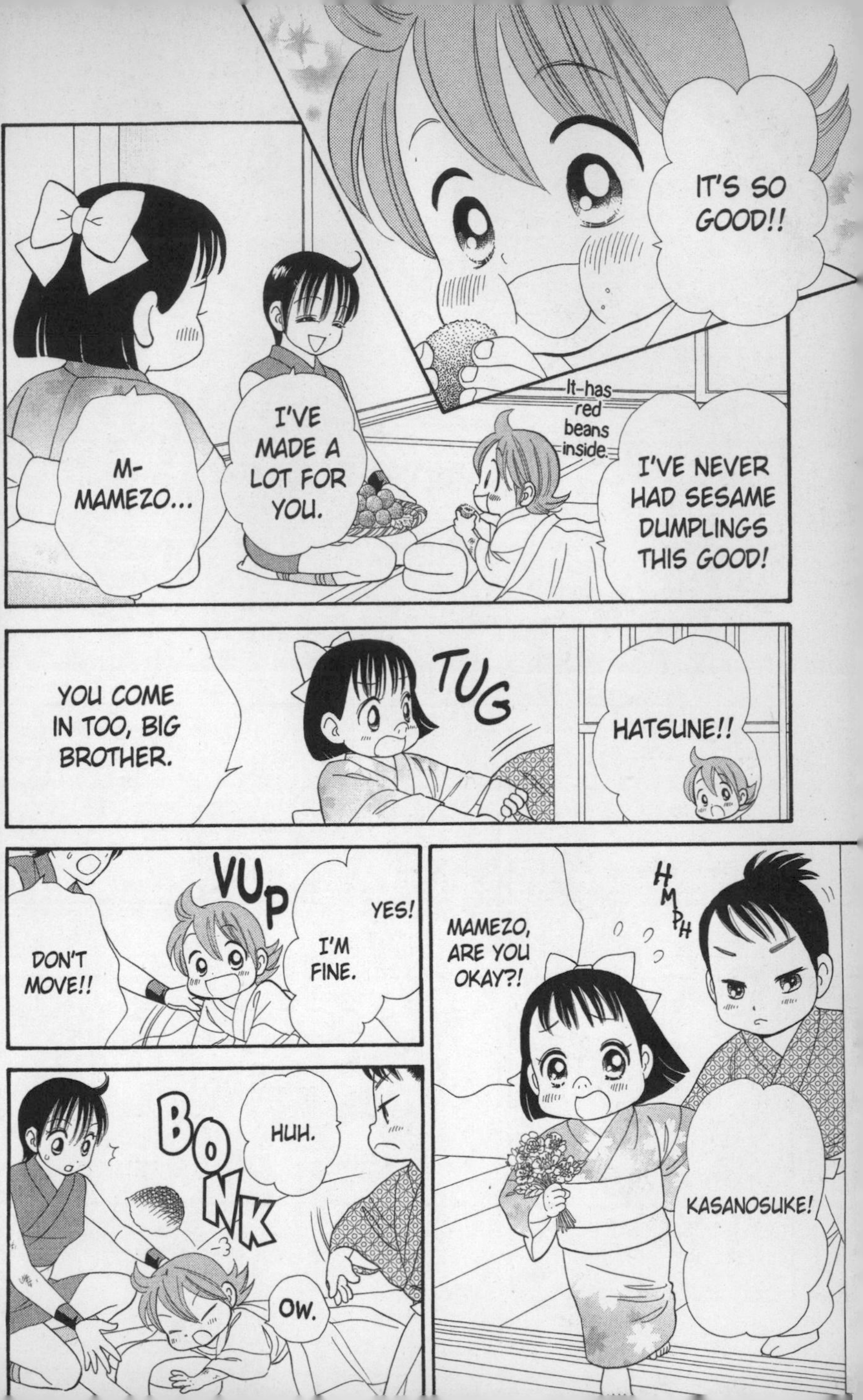
IT'S SO GOOD!!
I'VE NEVER HAD SESAME DUMPLINGS THIS GOOD!
It has red beans inside.
I'VE MADE A LOT FOR YOU.
M-MAMEZO...
HATSUNE!!
TUG
YOU COME IN TOO, BIG BROTHER.
HMPH
MAMEZO, ARE YOU OKAY?!
KASANOSUKE!
VUP
YES!
I'M FINE.
DON'T MOVE!!
BONK
HUH.
OW.

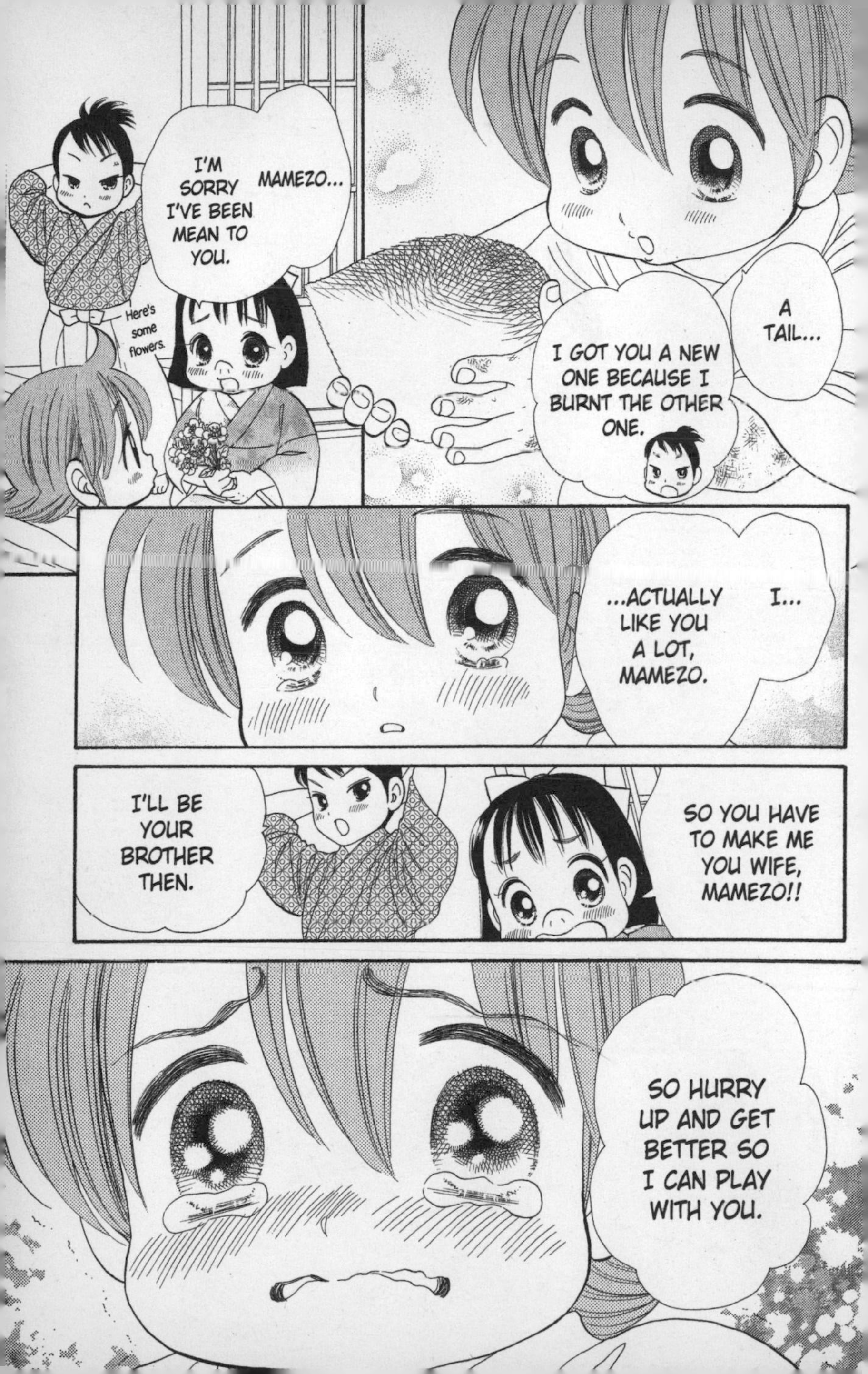
A TAIL...
I GOT YOU A NEW ONE BECAUSE I BURNT THE OTHER ONE.
MAMEZO...
I'M SORRY I'VE BEEN MEAN TO YOU.
Here's some flowers.
I...
...ACTUALLY LIKE YOU A LOT, MAMEZO.
SO YOU HAVE TO MAKE ME YOU WIFE, MAMEZO!!
I'LL BE YOUR BROTHER THEN.
SO HURRY UP AND GET BETTER SO I CAN PLAY WITH YOU.

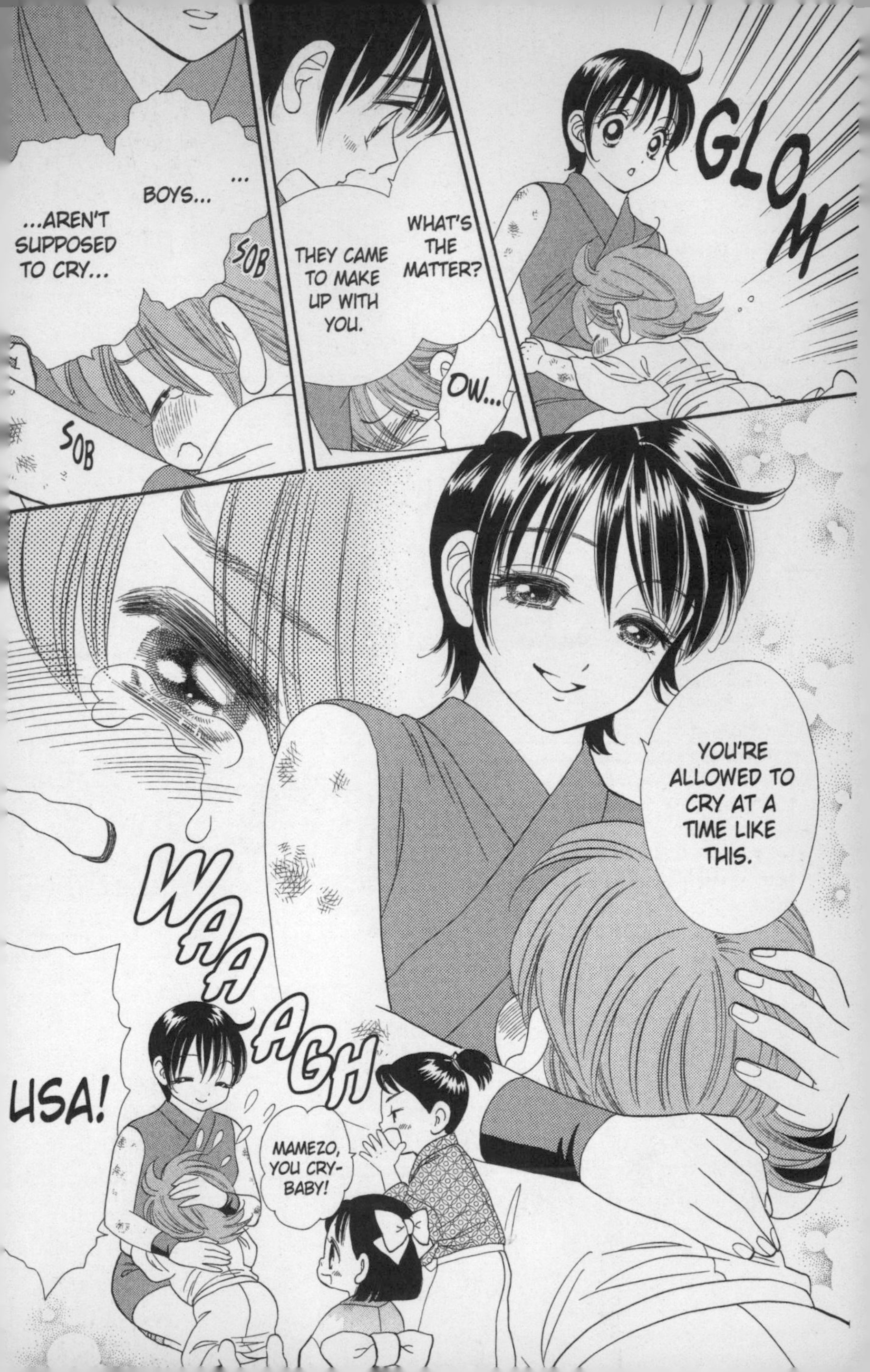
GLOM
WHAT'S THE MATTER?
THEY CAME TO MAKE UP WITH YOU.
OW...
SOB
...
BOYS...
...AREN'T SUPPOSED TO CRY...
SOB
YOU'RE ALLOWED TO CRY AT A TIME LIKE THIS.
WAAAGH
MAMEZO, YOU CRY-BABY!
USA!

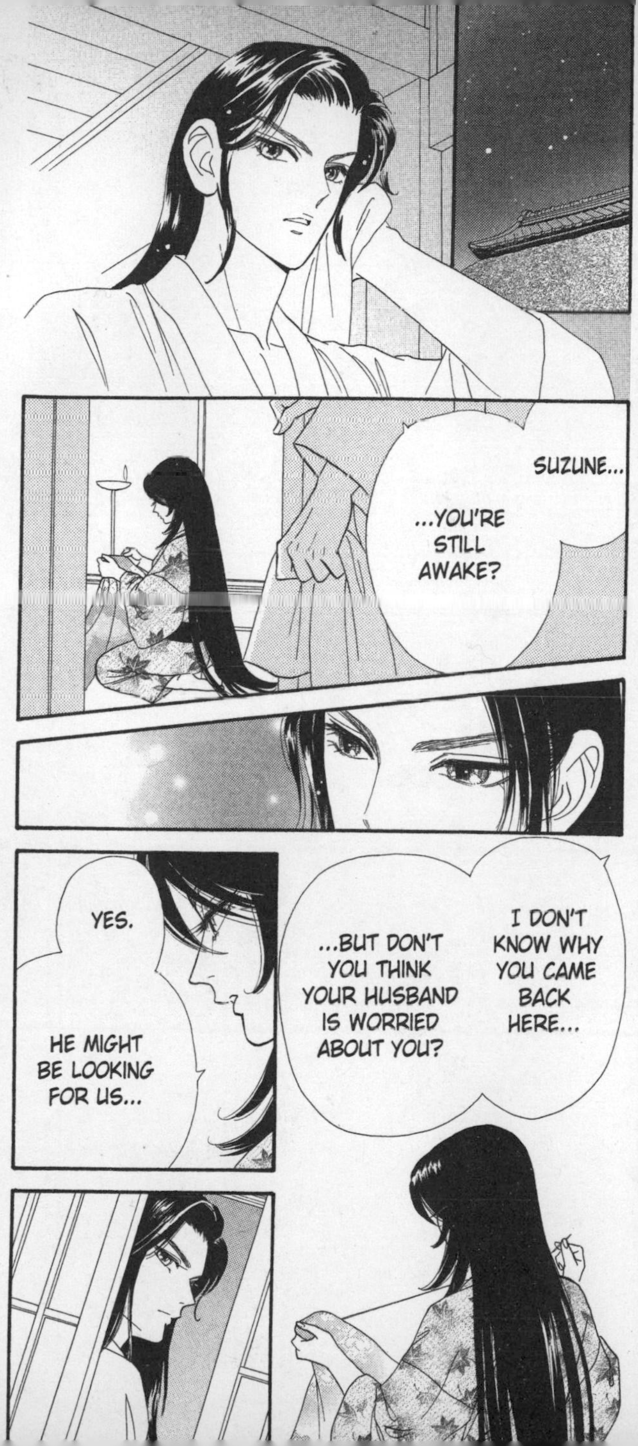
SUZUNE...
...YOU'RE STILL AWAKE?
I DON'T KNOW WHY YOU CAME BACK HERE...
...BUT DON'T YOU THINK YOUR HUSBAND IS WORRIED ABOUT YOU?
YES.
HE MIGHT BE LOOKING FOR US...

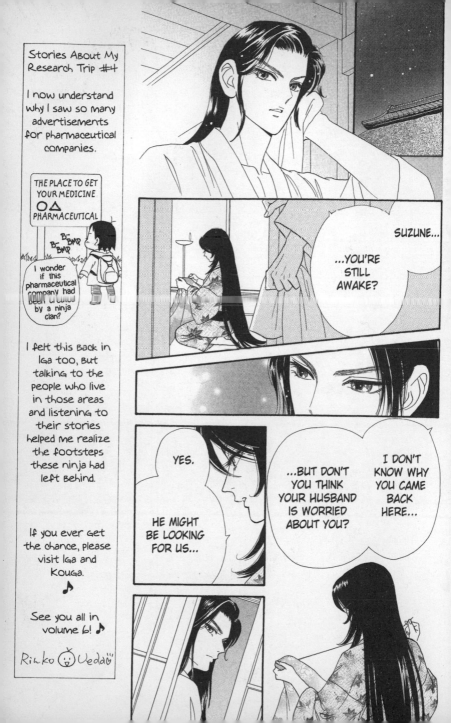

Stories About My Research Trip #4

I now understand why I saw so many advertisements for pharmaceutical companies.

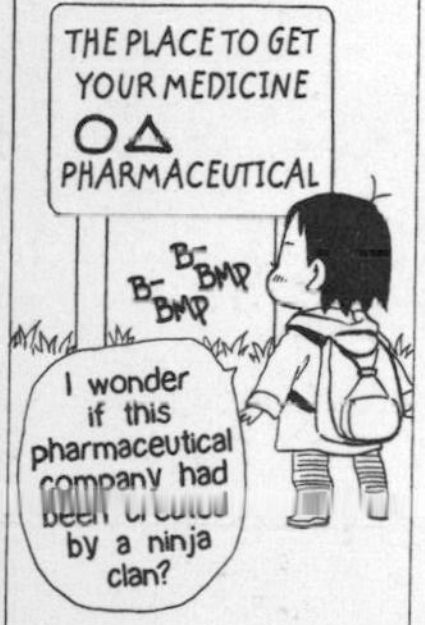
THE PLACE TO GET YOUR MEDICINE
○△ PHARMACEUTICAL
B-BMP B-BMP
I wonder if this pharmaceutical company had
by a ninja clan?

I felt this back in Iga too, but talking to the people who live in those areas and listening to their stories helped me realize the footsteps these ninja had left behind.

If you ever get the chance, please visit Iga and Kouga. ♪

See you all in volume 6! ♪

Rinko Ueda

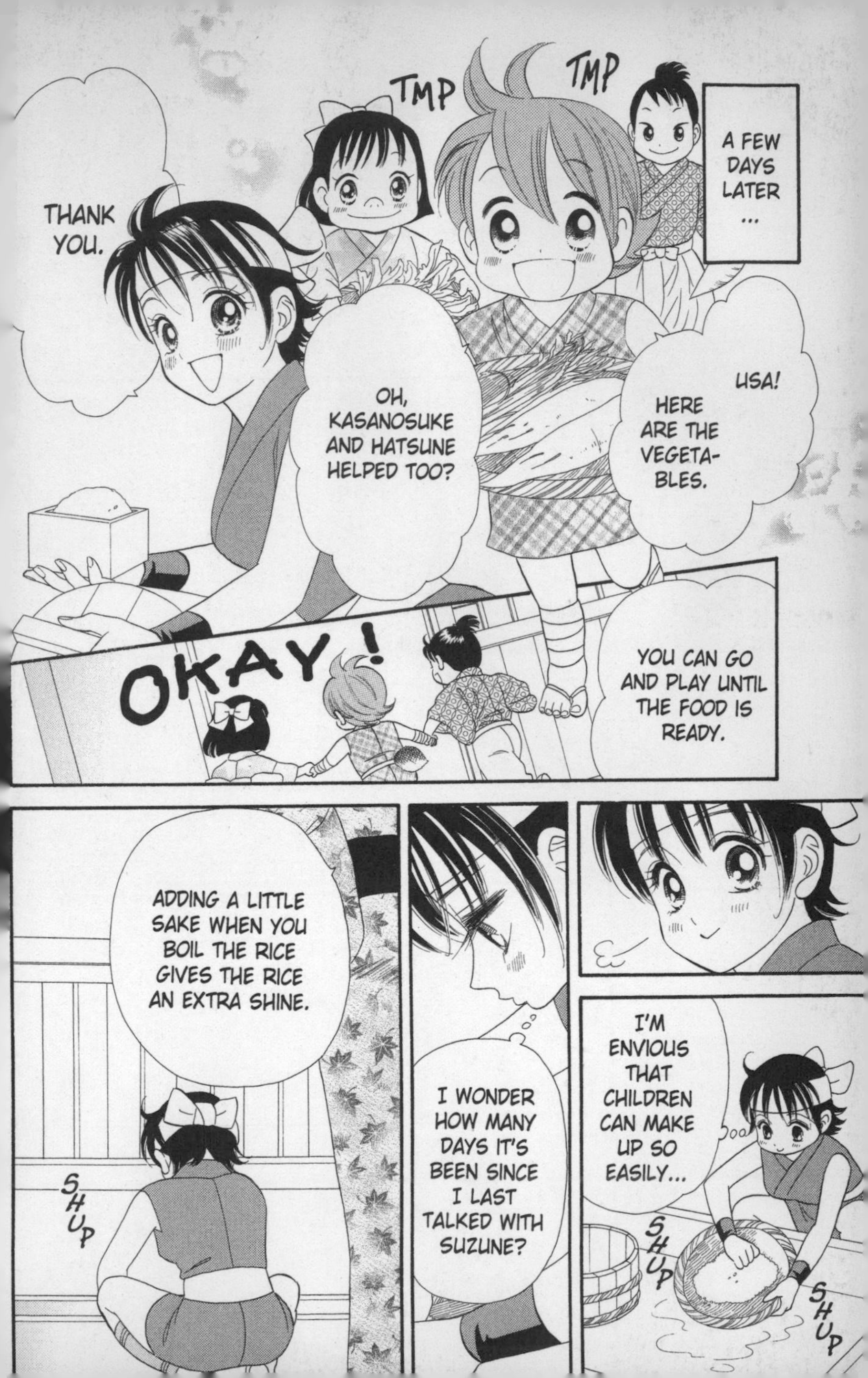
A FEW DAYS LATER ...
TMP
TMP
USA! HERE ARE THE VEGETA-BLES.
OH, KASANOSUKE AND HATSUNE HELPED TOO?
THANK YOU.
YOU CAN GO AND PLAY UNTIL THE FOOD IS READY.
OKAY!
I'M ENVIOUS THAT CHILDREN CAN MAKE UP SO EASILY...
SHUP
SHUP
I WONDER HOW MANY DAYS IT'S BEEN SINCE I LAST TALKED WITH SUZUNE?
ADDING A LITTLE SAKE WHEN YOU BOIL THE RICE GIVES THE RICE AN EXTRA SHINE.
SHUP

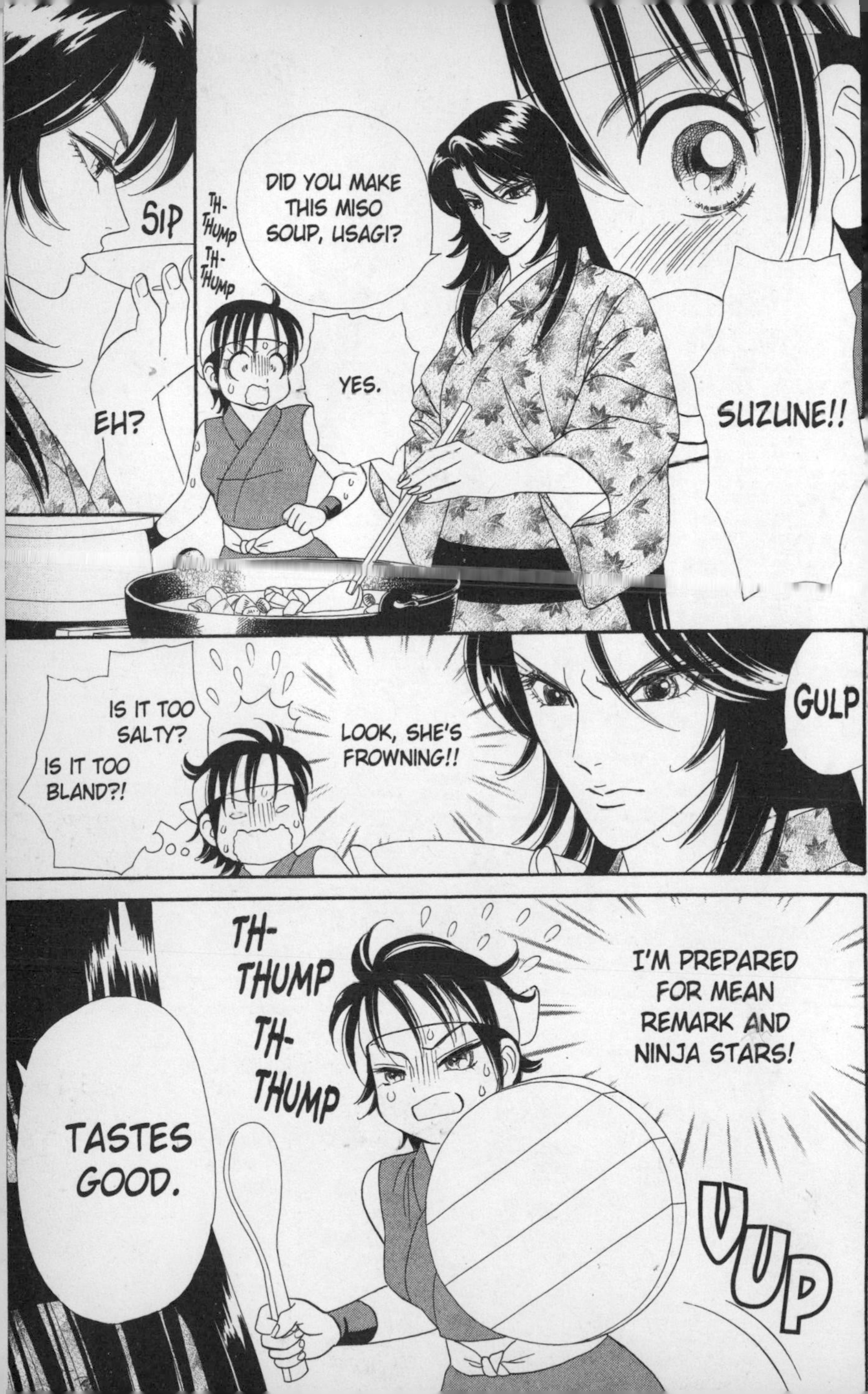
SUZUNE!!
DID YOU MAKE THIS MISO SOUP, USAGI?
YES.
SIP
TH-THUMP TH-THUMP
EH?
GULP
LOOK, SHE'S FROWNING!!
IS IT TOO SALTY?
IS IT TOO BLAND?!
I'M PREPARED FOR MEAN REMARK AND NINJA STARS!
VUUP
TH-THUMP TH-THUMP
TASTES GOOD.

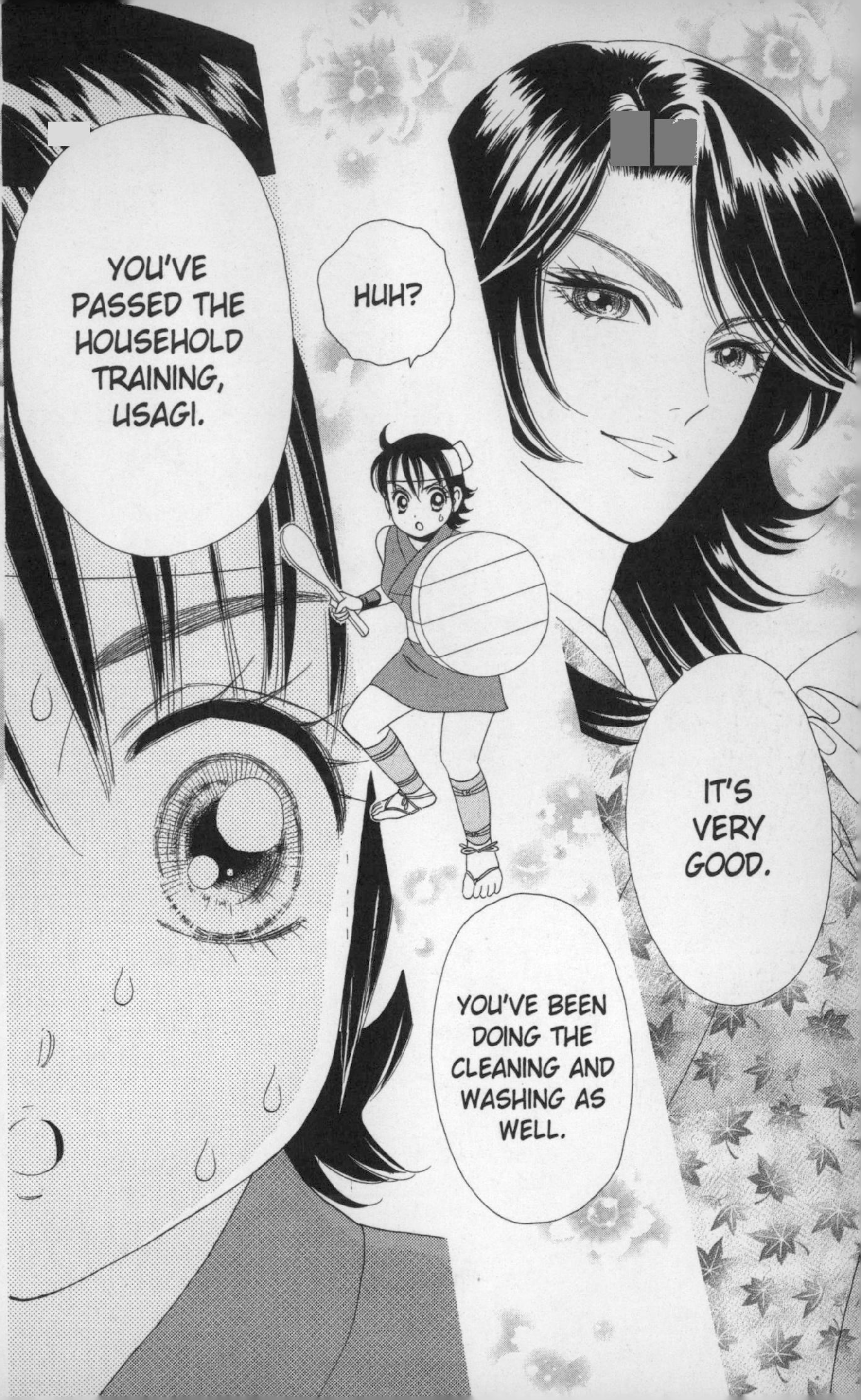
YOU'VE PASSED THE HOUSEHOLD TRAINING, USAGI.
HUH?
IT'S VERY GOOD.
YOU'VE BEEN DOING THE CLEANING AND WASHING AS WELL.

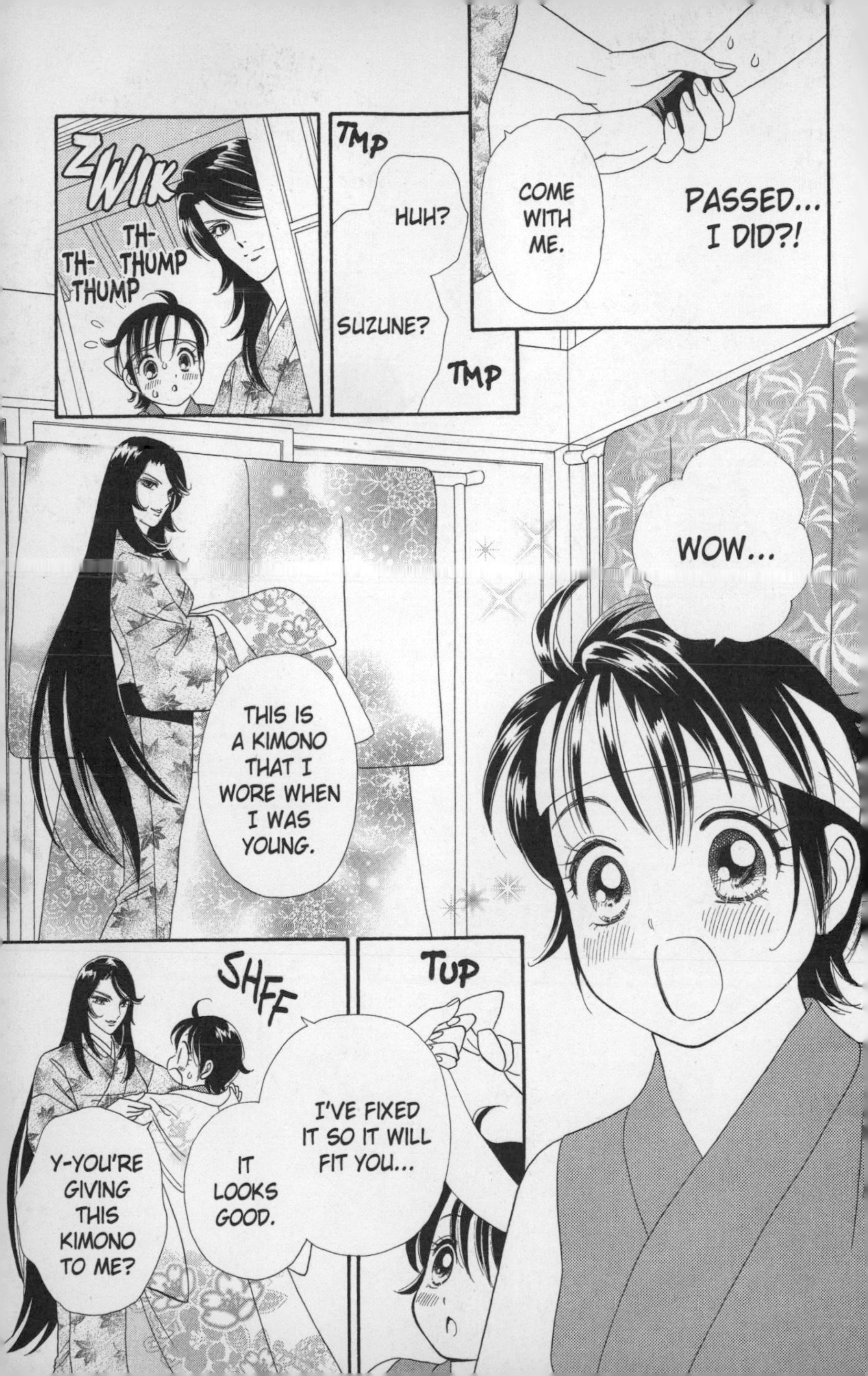
PASSED... I DID?!
COME WITH ME.
TMP
HUH?
SUZUNE?
TMP
ZWIK
TH-THUMP
TH-THUMP
WOW...
THIS IS A KIMONO THAT I WORE WHEN I WAS YOUNG.
TUP
I'VE FIXED IT SO IT WILL FIT YOU...
SHFF
IT LOOKS GOOD.
Y-YOU'RE GIVING THIS KIMONO TO ME?

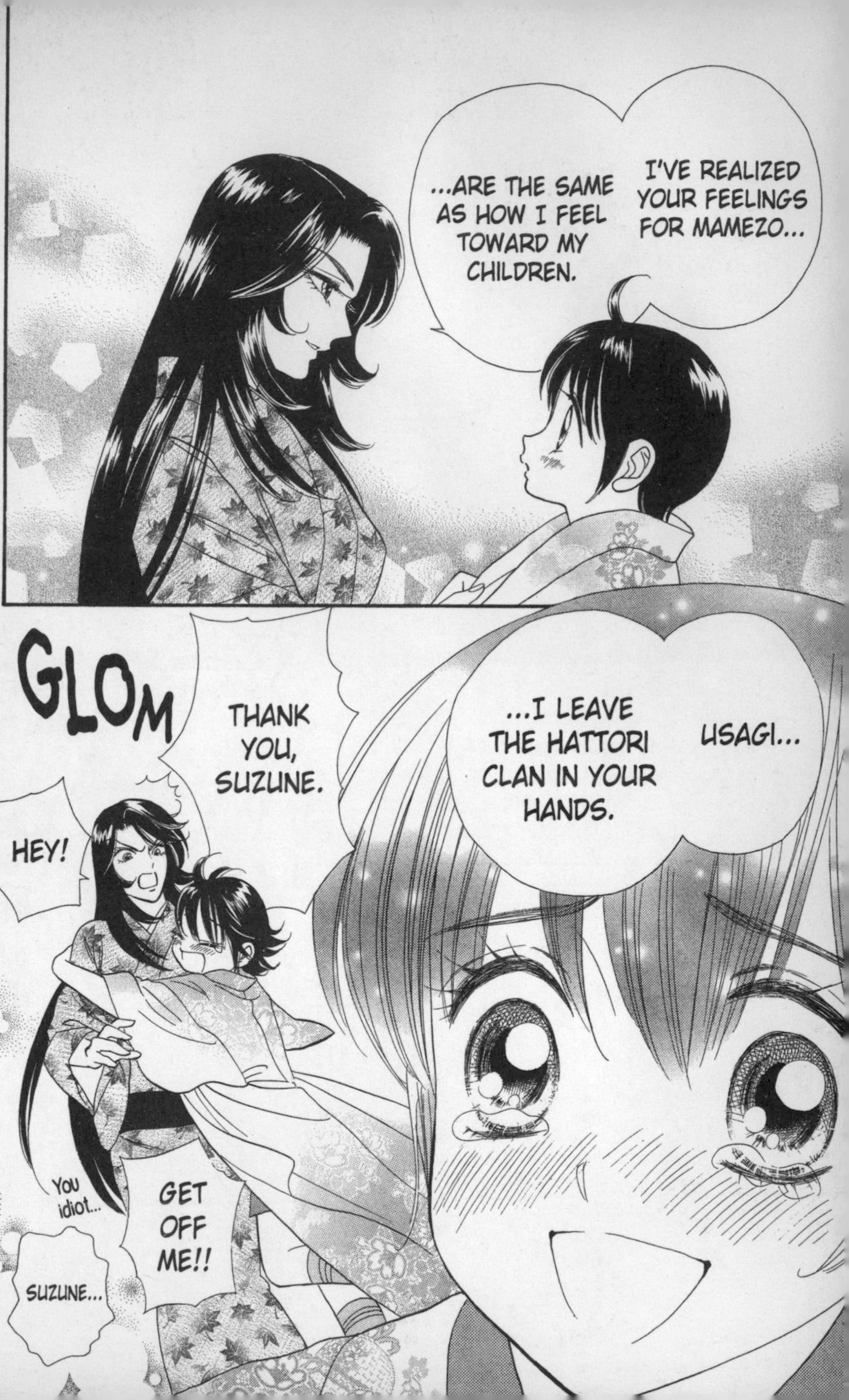
I'VE REALIZED YOUR FEELINGS FOR MAMEZO...
...ARE THE SAME AS HOW I FEEL TOWARD MY CHILDREN.
USAGI...
...I LEAVE THE HATTORI CLAN IN YOUR HANDS.
THANK YOU, SUZUNE.
GLOM
HEY!
GET OFF ME!!
You idiot...
SUZUNE...

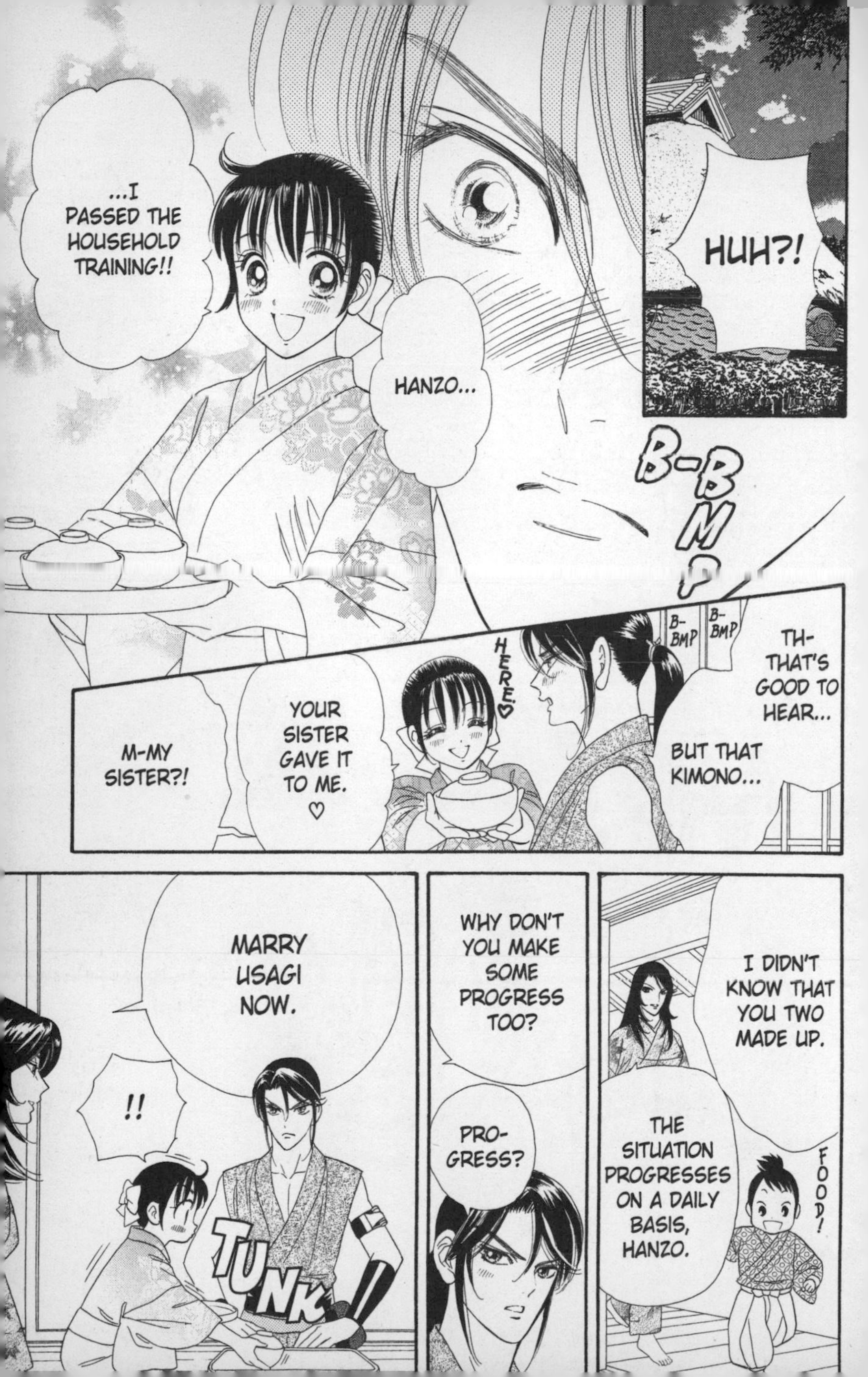
HUH?!
HANZO...
...I PASSED THE HOUSEHOLD TRAINING!!
B-BMP
B-BMP
B-BMP
TH-THAT'S GOOD TO HEAR...
BUT THAT KIMONO...
HERE.♡
YOUR SISTER GAVE IT TO ME. ♡
M-MY SISTER?!
I DIDN'T KNOW THAT YOU TWO MADE UP.
FOOD!
THE SITUATION PROGRESSES ON A DAILY BASIS, HANZO.
WHY DON'T YOU MAKE SOME PROGRESS TOO?
PRO-GRESS?
MARRY USAGI NOW.
!!
TUNK!

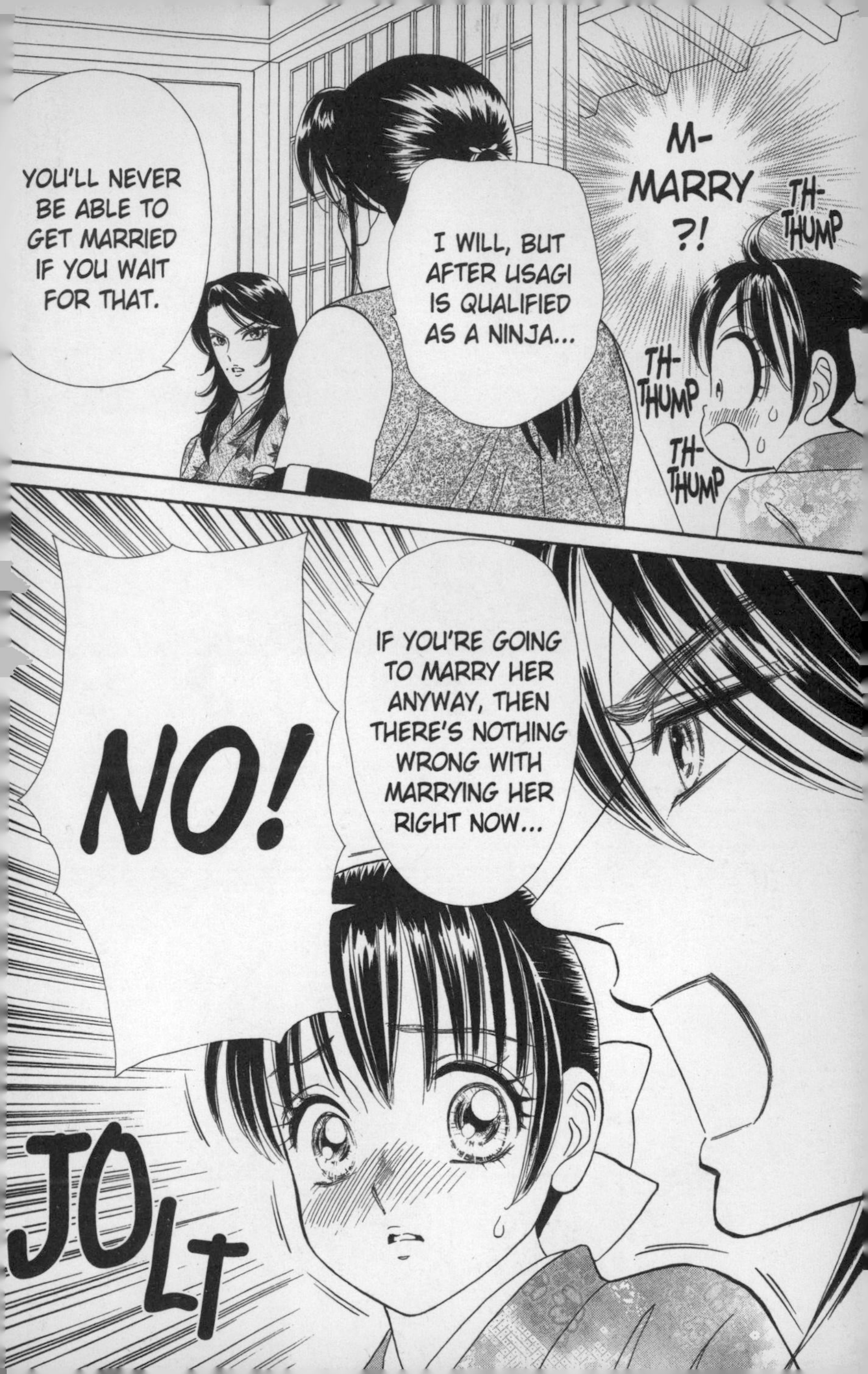
M- MARRY ?!
TH-THUMP
TH-THUMP
TH-THUMP
I WILL, BUT AFTER USAGI IS QUALIFIED AS A NINJA...
YOU'LL NEVER BE ABLE TO GET MARRIED IF YOU WAIT FOR THAT.
IF YOU'RE GOING TO MARRY HER ANYWAY, THEN THERE'S NOTHING WRONG WITH MARRYING HER RIGHT NOW...
NO!
JOLT

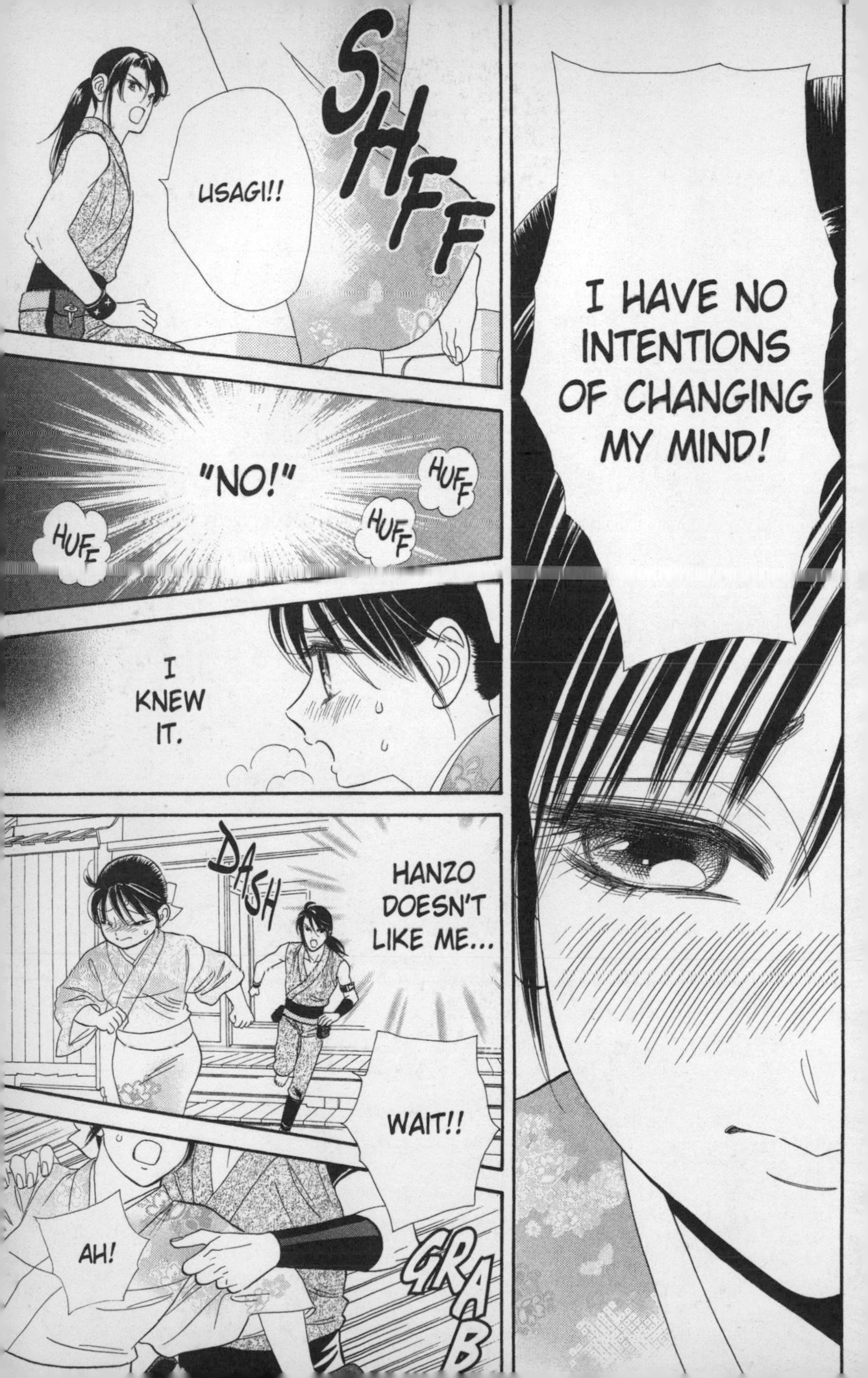
I HAVE NO INTENTIONS OF CHANGING MY MIND!
SHFF
USAGI!!
HUFF
HUFF
"NO!"
HUFF
I KNEW IT.
HANZO DOESN'T LIKE ME...
DASH
WAIT!!
GRAB
AH!

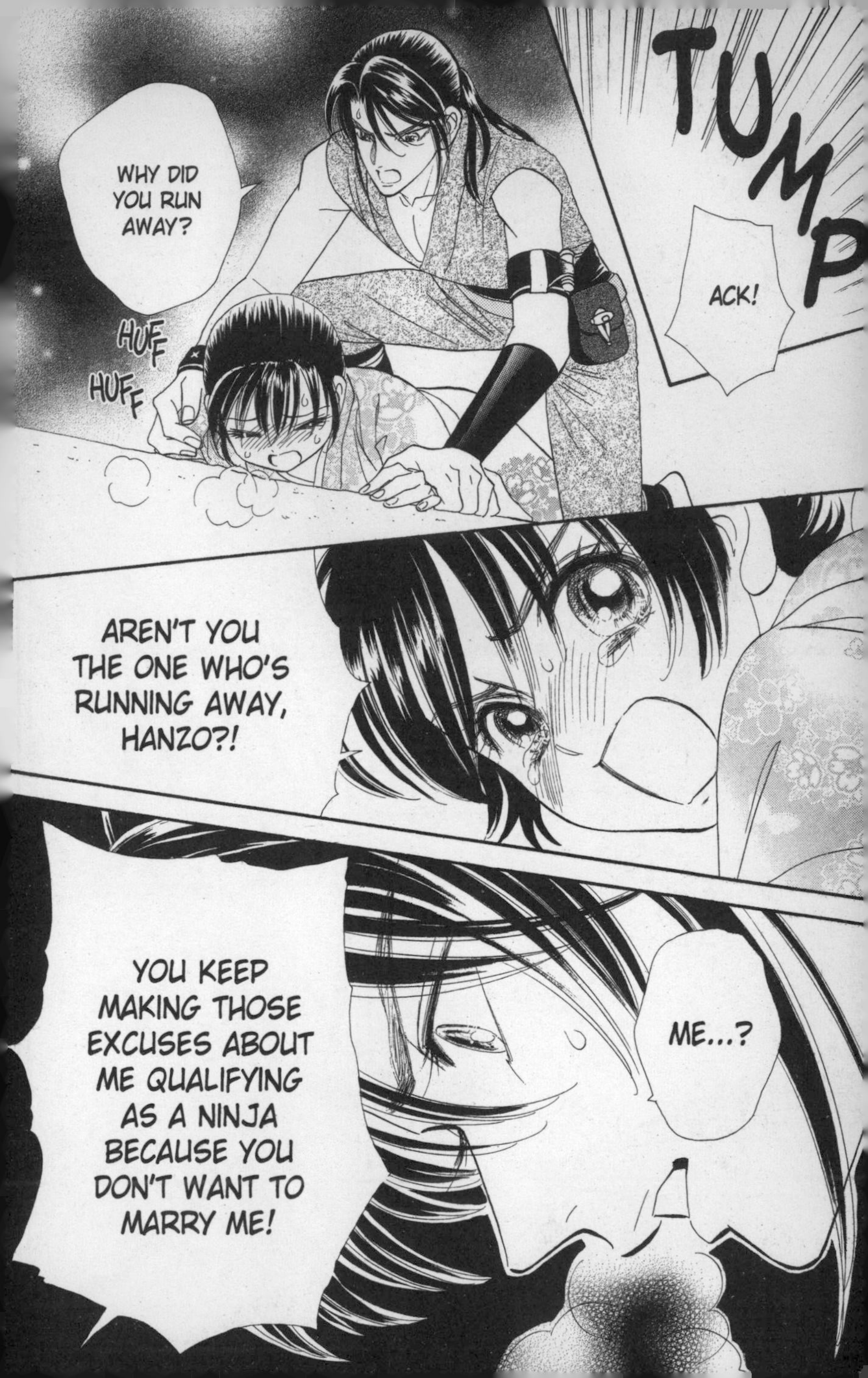
TUMP
ACK!
WHY DID YOU RUN AWAY?
HUFF HUFF
AREN'T YOU THE ONE WHO'S RUNNING AWAY, HANZO?!
ME...?
YOU KEEP MAKING THOSE EXCUSES ABOUT ME QUALIFYING AS A NINJA BECAUSE YOU DON'T WANT TO MARRY ME!

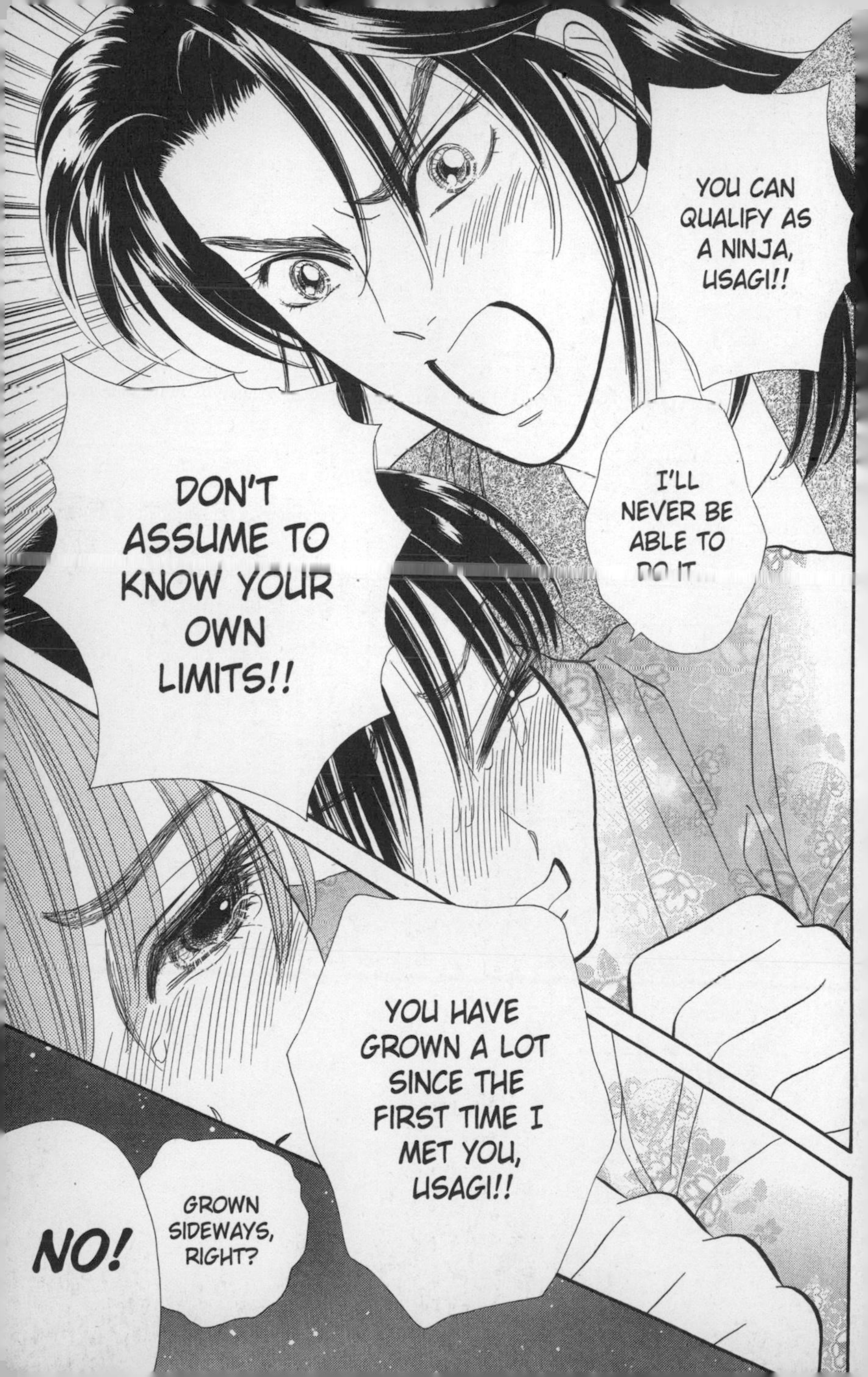
YOU CAN QUALIFY AS A NINJA, USAGI!!
I'LL NEVER BE ABLE TO DO IT...
DON'T ASSUME TO KNOW YOUR OWN LIMITS!!
YOU HAVE GROWN A LOT SINCE THE FIRST TIME I MET YOU, USAGI!!
GROWN SIDEWAYS, RIGHT?
NO!

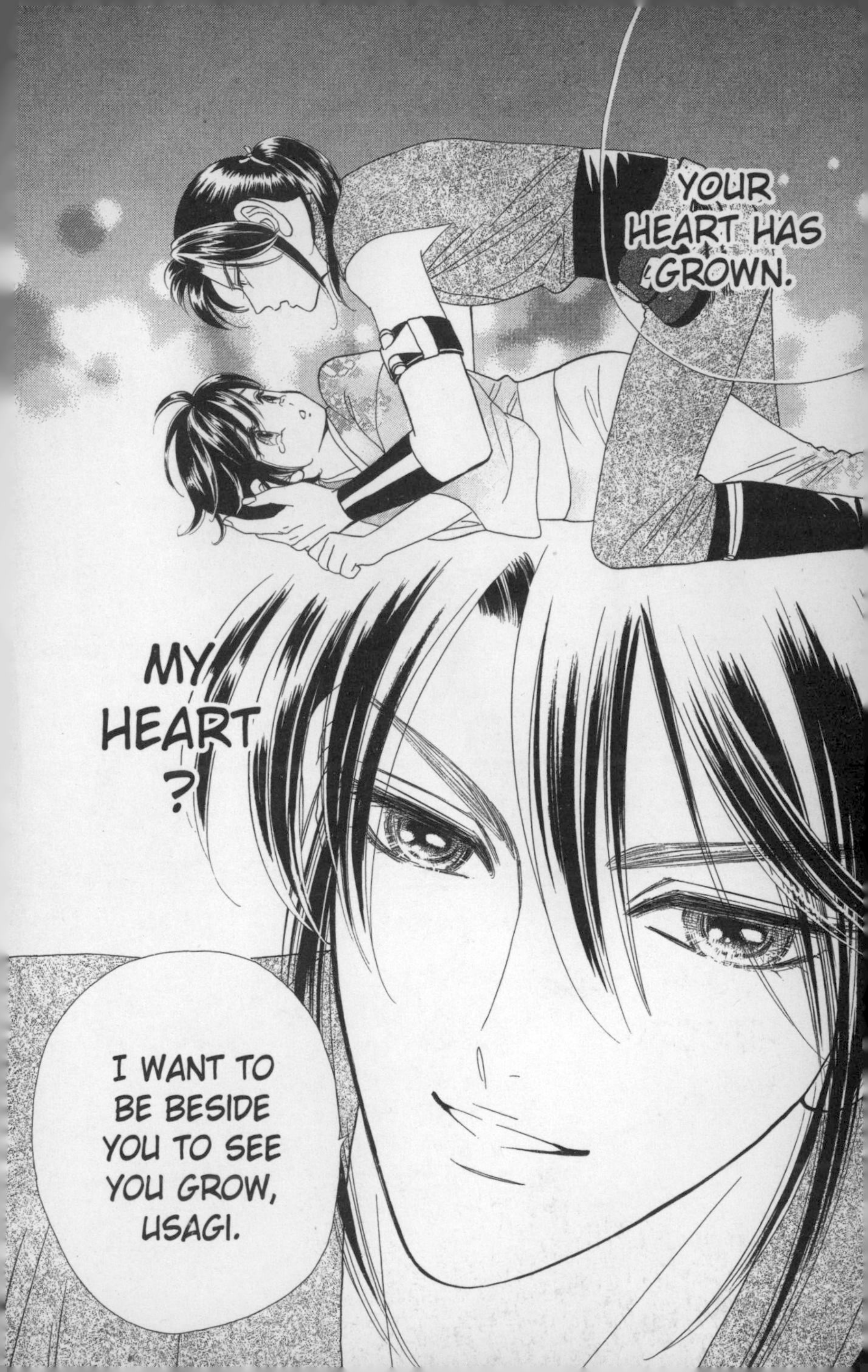
YOUR HEART HAS GROWN.
MY HEART?
I WANT TO BE BESIDE YOU TO SEE YOU GROW, USAGI.

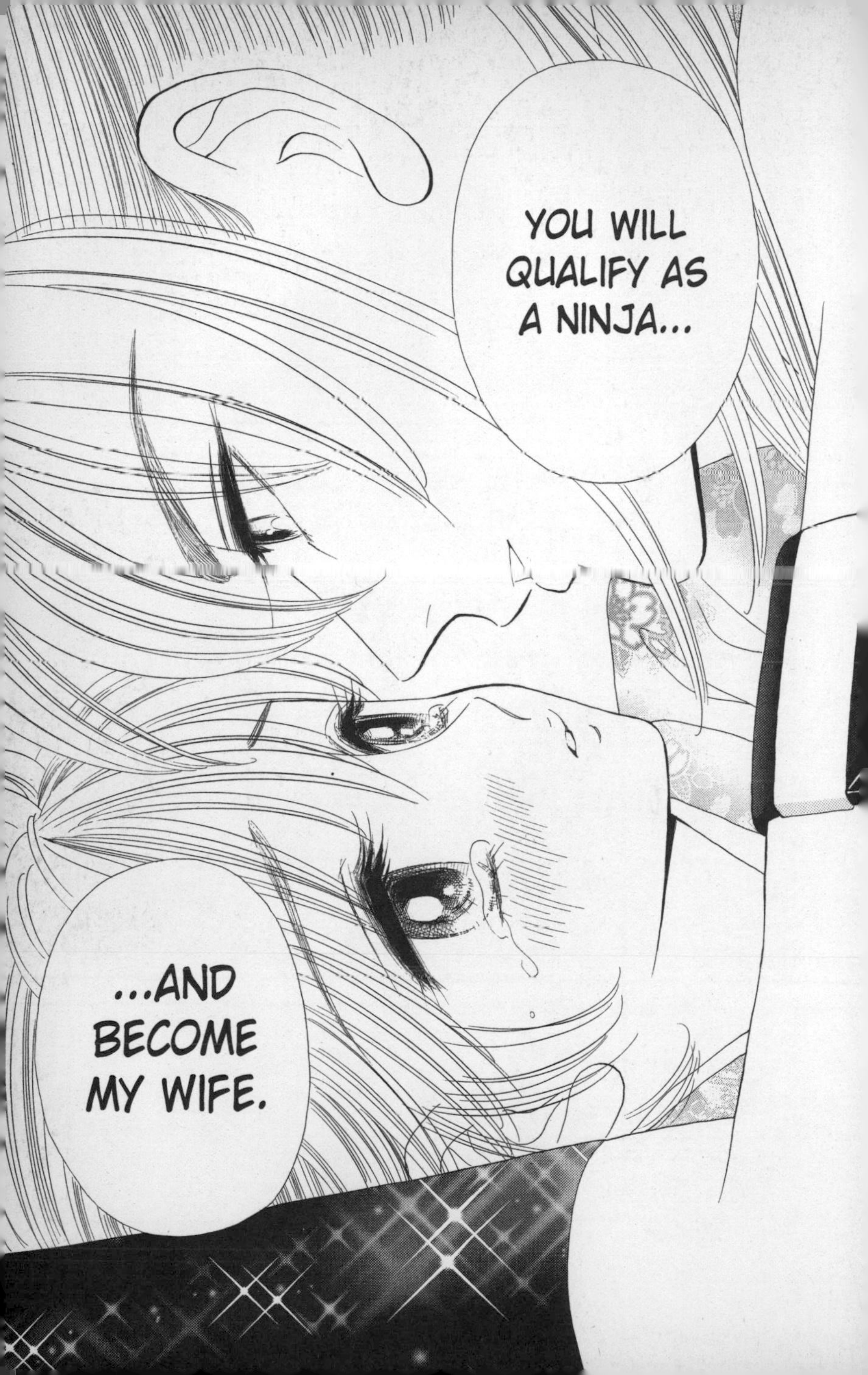
YOU WILL QUALIFY AS A NINJA...
...AND BECOME MY WIFE.

TAIL OF THE MOON EXTRA: TODAY'S MISSION

"I WANT TO SEE HANZO WORKING AT A PRESCHOOL."

-MACHAKO-SAN, FUKUSHIMA PREFECTURE

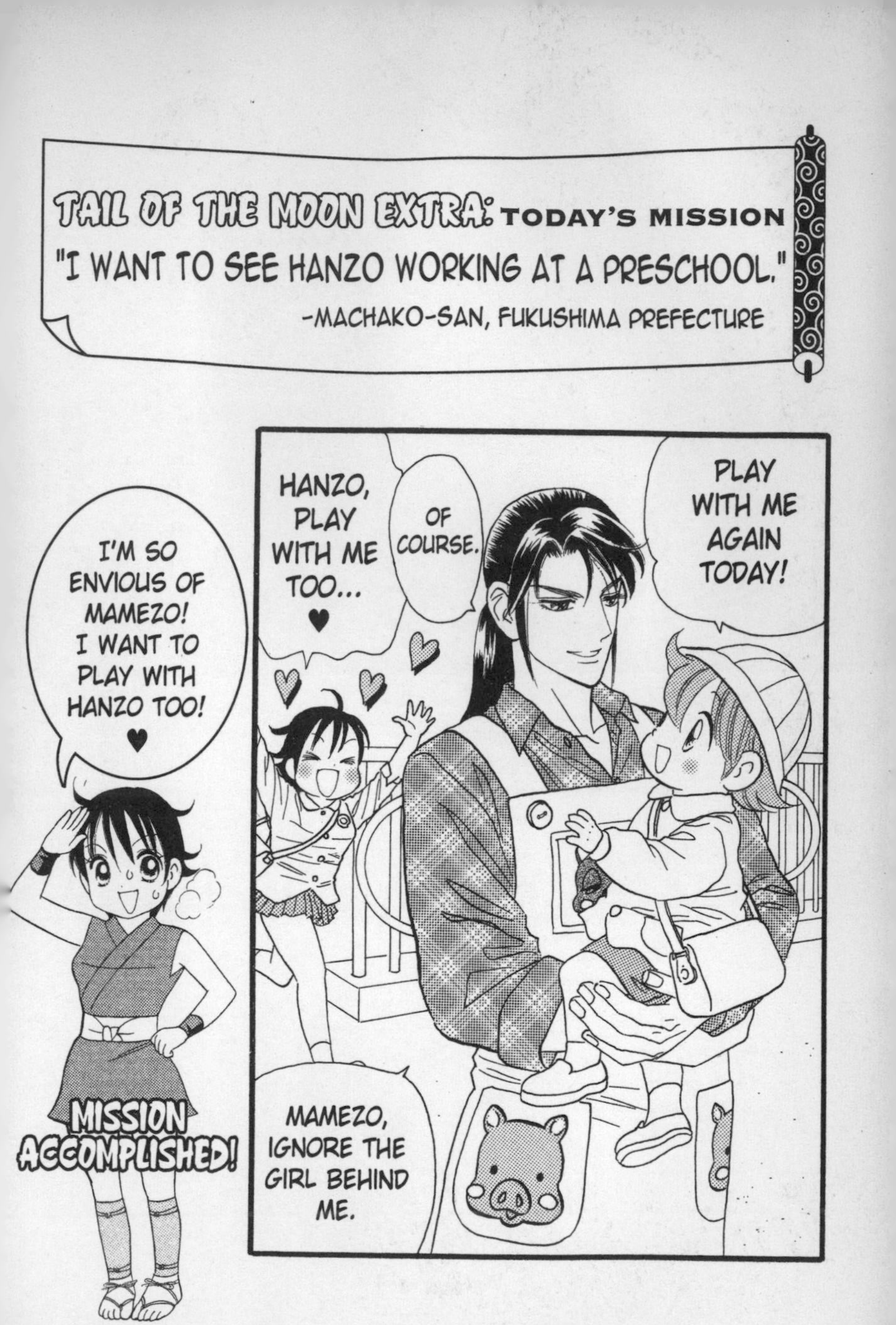
PLAY WITH ME AGAIN TODAY!
OF COURSE.
HANZO, PLAY WITH ME TOO... ♥
MAMEZO, IGNORE THE GIRL BEHIND ME.
I'M SO ENVIOUS OF MAMEZO! I WANT TO PLAY WITH HANZO TOO! ♥
MISSION ACCOMPLISHED!

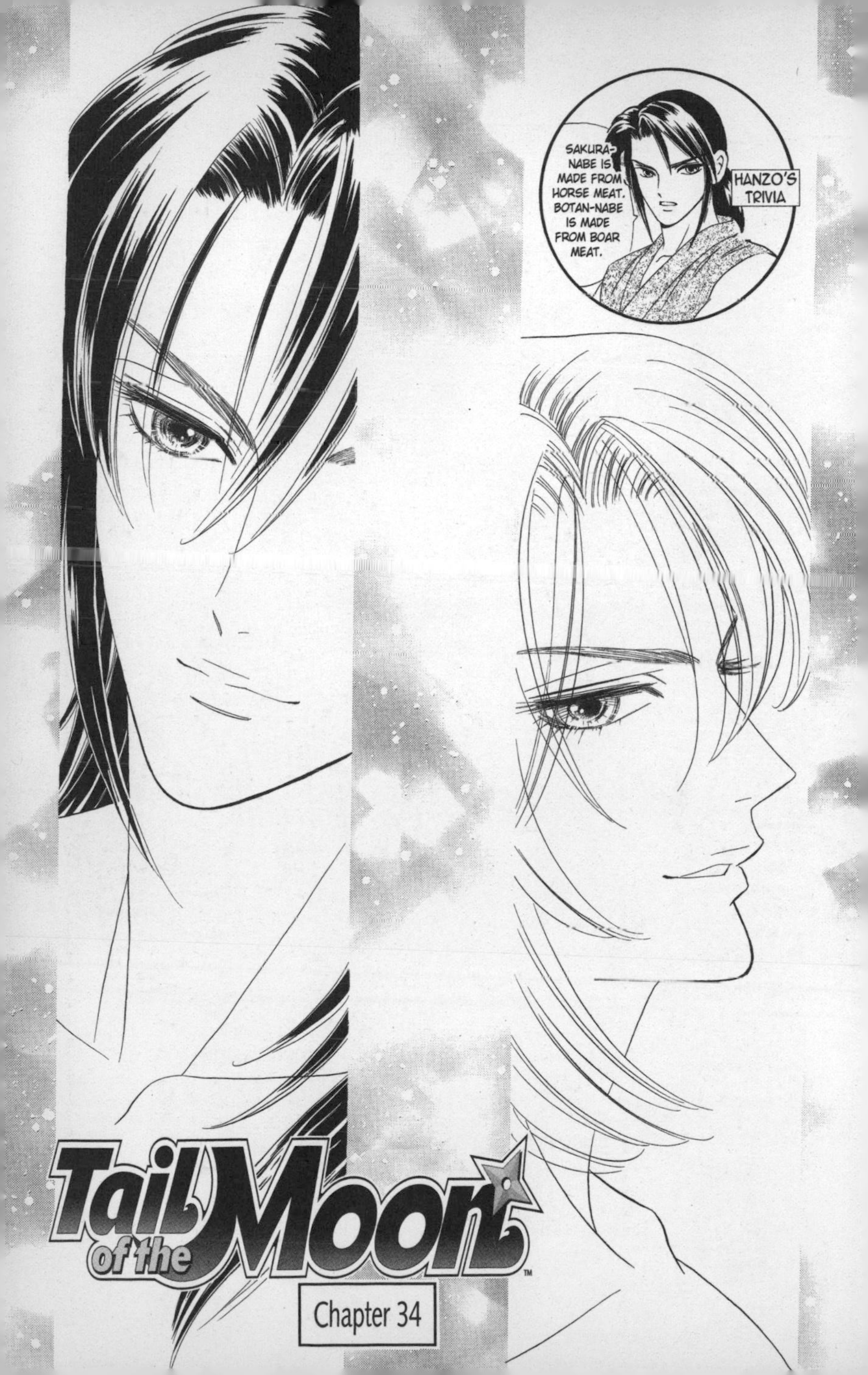
HANZO'S TRIVIA
SAKURA-NABE IS MADE FROM HORSE MEAT. BOTAN-NABE IS MADE FROM BOAR MEAT.
Tail of the Moon™
Chapter 34

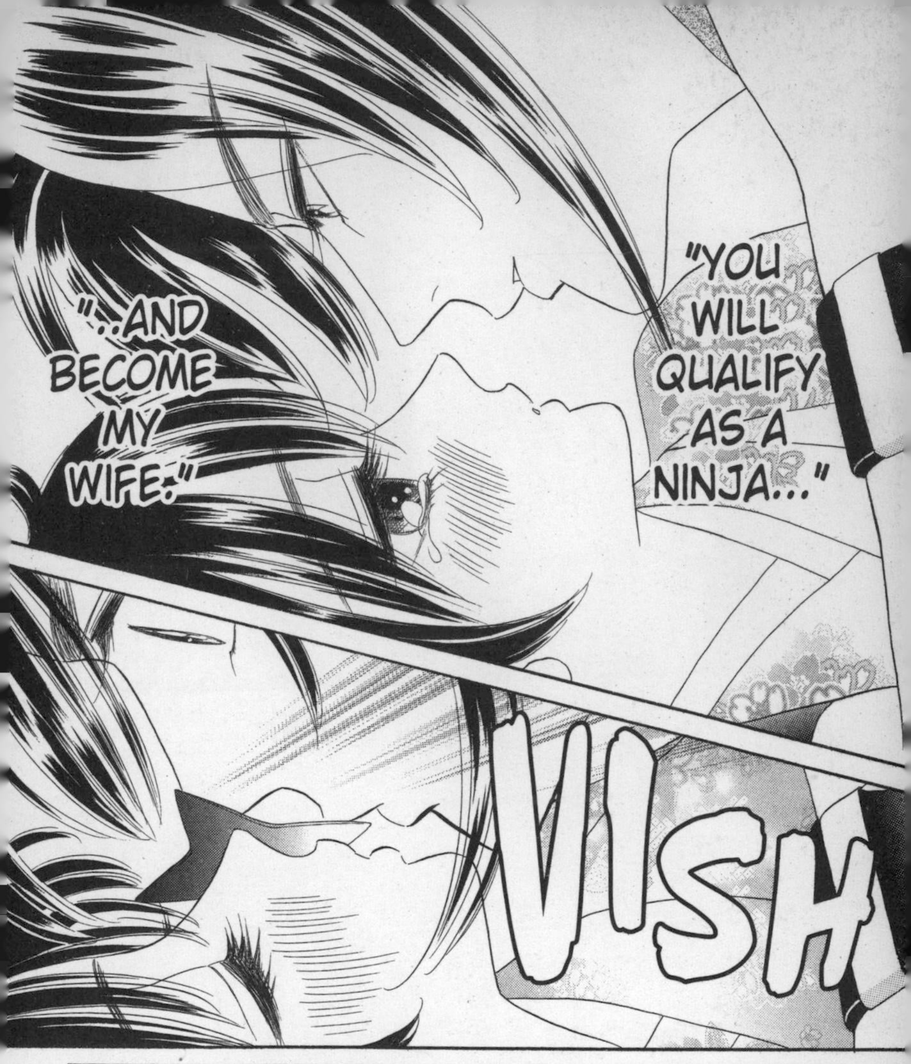
"YOU WILL QUALIFY AS A NINJA..."
"...AND BECOME MY WIFE."
VISH

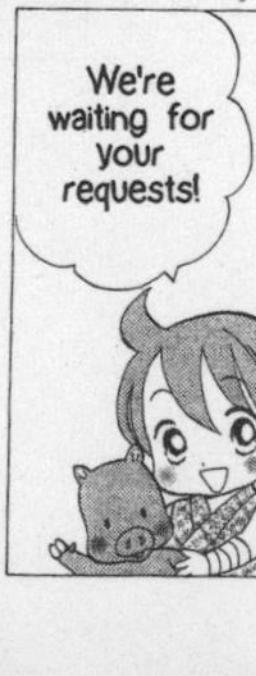
We're waiting for your requests!

INFORMATION CORNER ♪

The "Tail of the Moon Extra" that started appearing in this volume is a hands-on project for the *Tail of the Moon* fans who read *Margaret* magazine. This corner is always open to your wishes of "I want to see a scene like this with these characters," and "I want to see these characters say these lines!" It is a versatile project that will answer any request by the readers. In addition there's "Hattori Hanzo's Counseling Room," "Tips on a Better Romance by Three Handsome Men," "Mamezo's Trivia," and much, much more, so please feel free to make requests!!

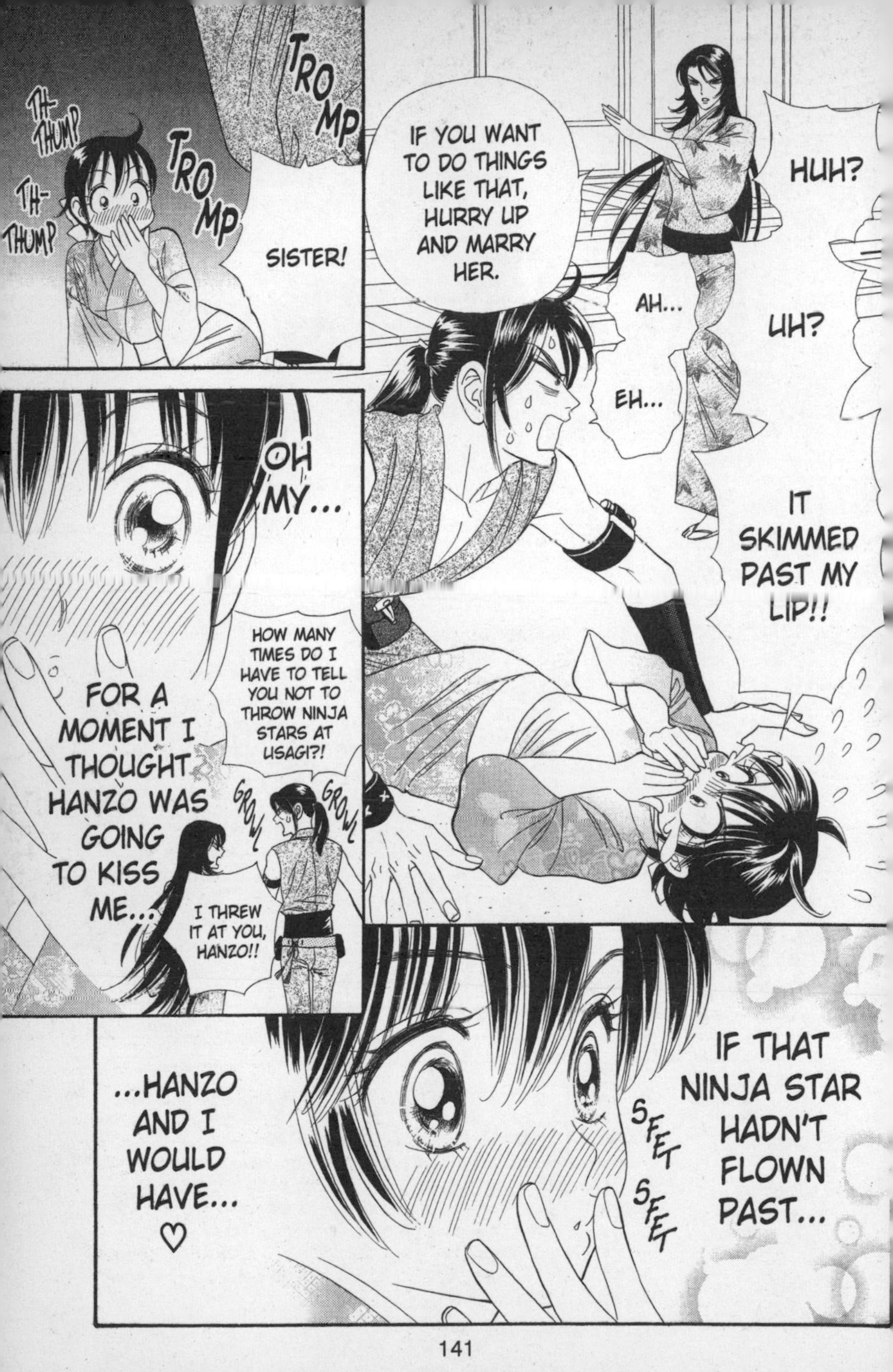
TROMP
TROMP
SISTER!
TH-THUMP
TH-THUMP
IF YOU WANT TO DO THINGS LIKE THAT, HURRY UP AND MARRY HER.
HUH?
AH...
UH?
EH...
IT SKIMMED PAST MY LIP!!
OH MY...
HOW MANY TIMES DO I HAVE TO TELL YOU NOT TO THROW NINJA STARS AT USAGI?!
GROWL
GROWL
I THREW IT AT YOU, HANZO!!
FOR A MOMENT I THOUGHT HANZO WAS GOING TO KISS ME...
IF THAT NINJA STAR HADN'T FLOWN PAST...
SFET
SFET
...HANZO AND I WOULD HAVE... ♡

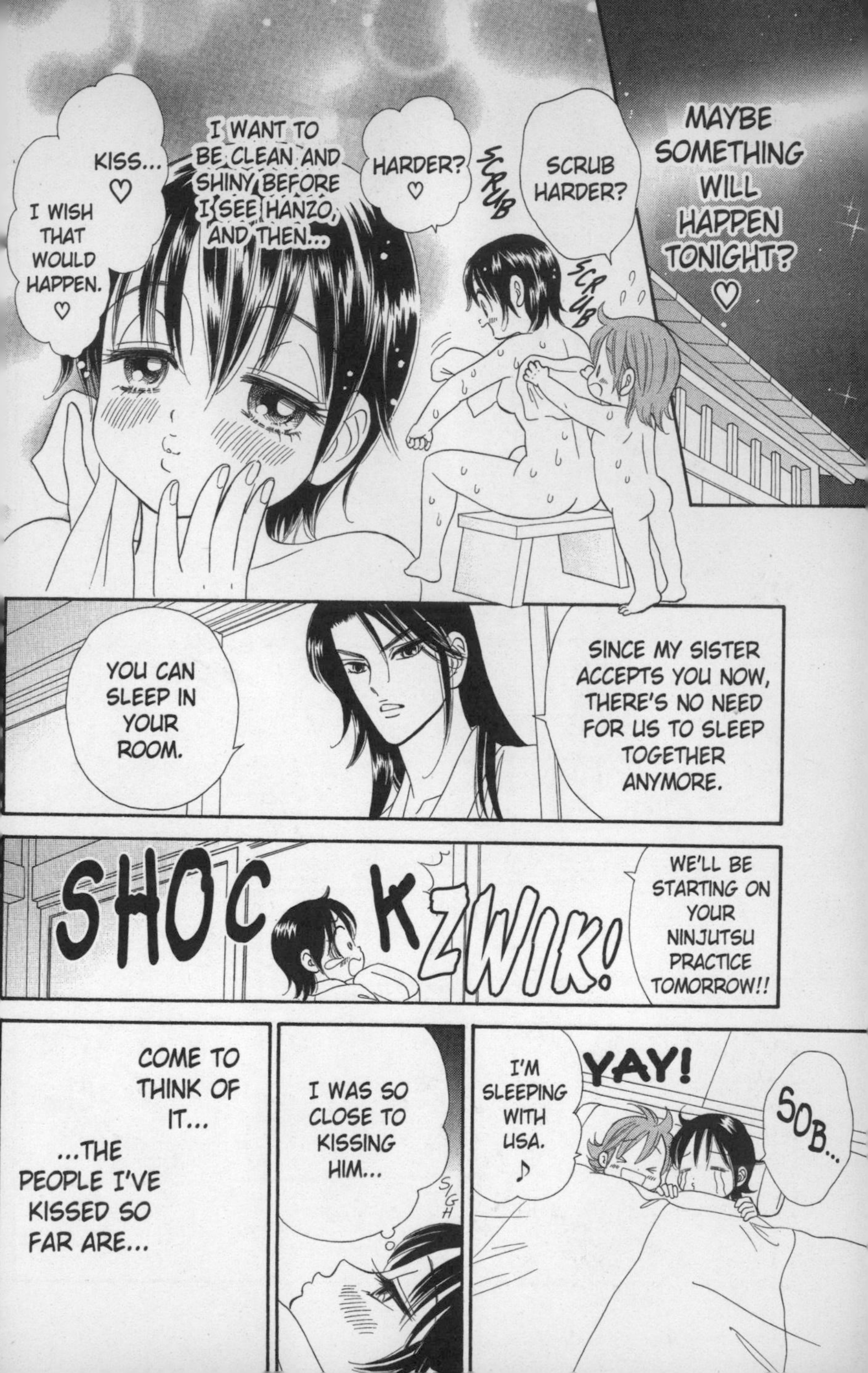
MAYBE SOMETHING WILL HAPPEN TONIGHT? ♡
SCRUB HARDER?
SCRUB
SCRUB
HARDER? ♡
I WANT TO BE CLEAN AND SHINY BEFORE I SEE HANZO, AND THEN...
KISS... ♡
I WISH THAT WOULD HAPPEN. ♡
SINCE MY SISTER ACCEPTS YOU NOW, THERE'S NO NEED FOR US TO SLEEP TOGETHER ANYMORE.
YOU CAN SLEEP IN YOUR ROOM.
WE'LL BE STARTING ON YOUR NINJUTSU PRACTICE TOMORROW!!
ZWIK!
SHOCK
SOB...
YAY!
I'M SLEEPING WITH USA. ♪
I WAS SO CLOSE TO KISSING HIM...
SIGH
COME TO THINK OF IT...
...THE PEOPLE I'VE KISSED SO FAR ARE...

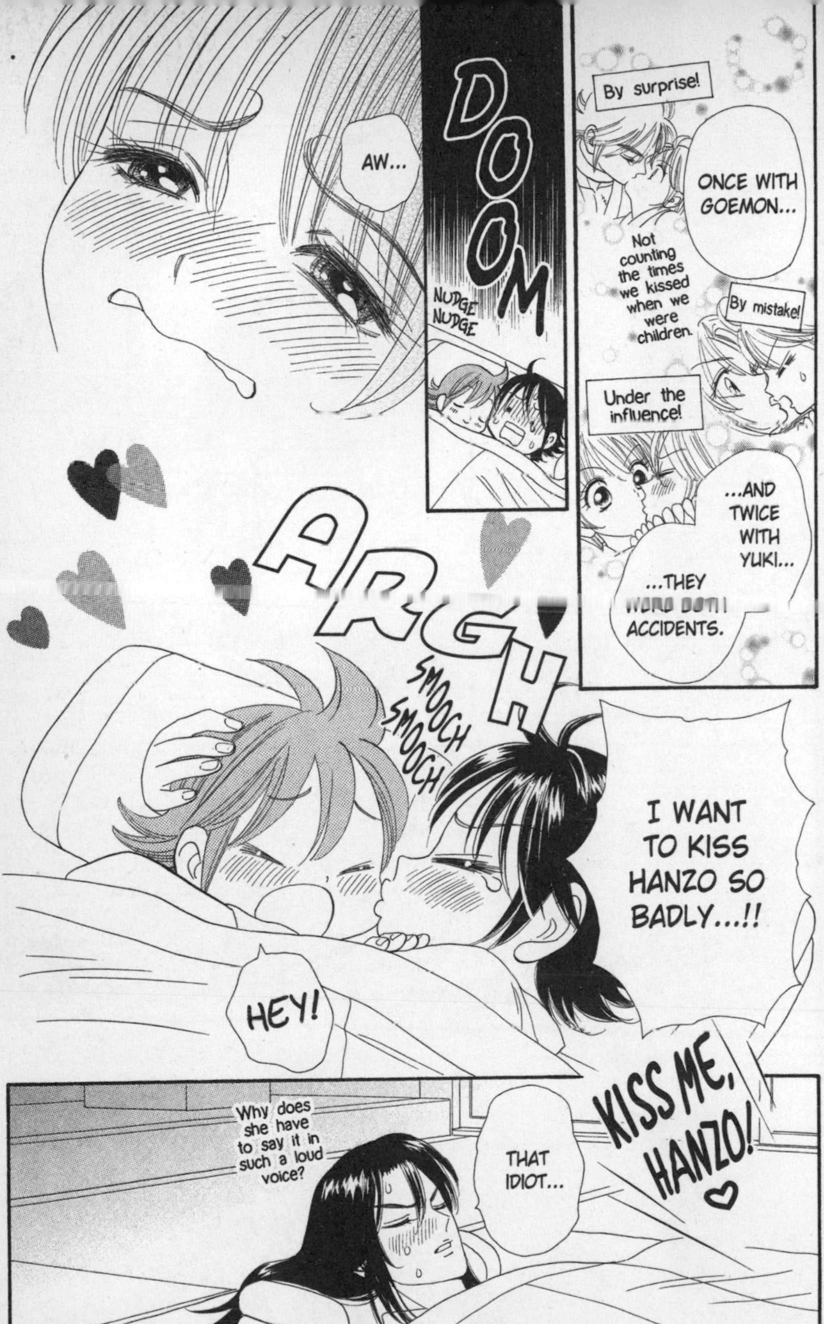
By surprise!
ONCE WITH GOEMON...
Not counting the times we kissed when we were children.
By mistake!
Under the influence!
...AND TWICE WITH YUKI...
...THEY WERE BOTH ACCIDENTS.
DOOM
NUDGE NUDGE
AW...
ARGH
SMOOCH SMOOCH
I WANT TO KISS HANZO SO BADLY...!!
HEY!
KISS ME, HANZO!
THAT IDIOT...
Why does she have to say it in such a loud voice?

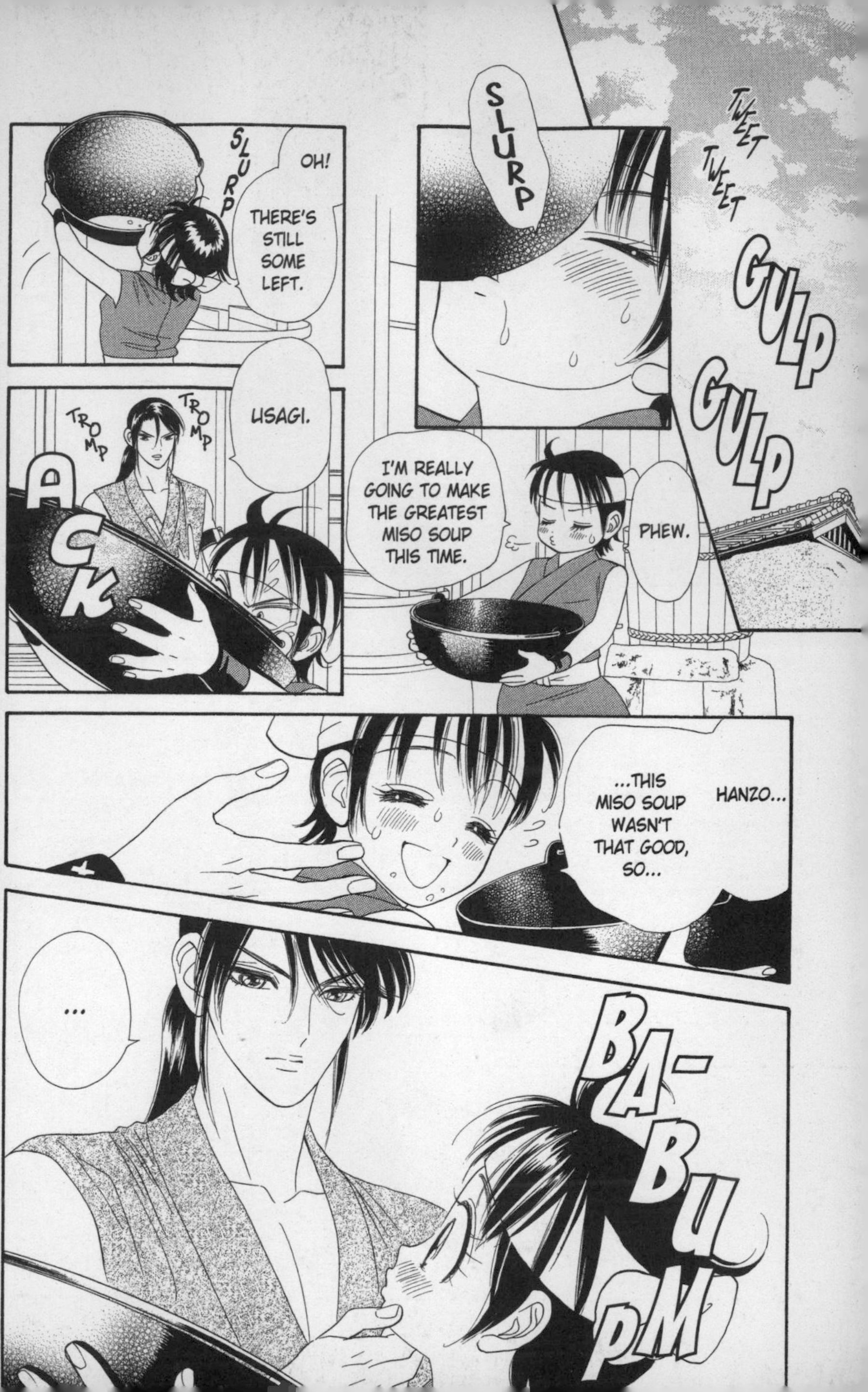
TWEET TWEET
GULP GULP
SLURP
SLURP
OH!
THERE'S STILL SOME LEFT.
PHEW.
I'M REALLY GOING TO MAKE THE GREATEST MISO SOUP THIS TIME.
USAGI.
TROMP TROMP
ACK
HANZO...
...THIS MISO SOUP WASN'T THAT GOOD, SO...
BA-BUMP
...

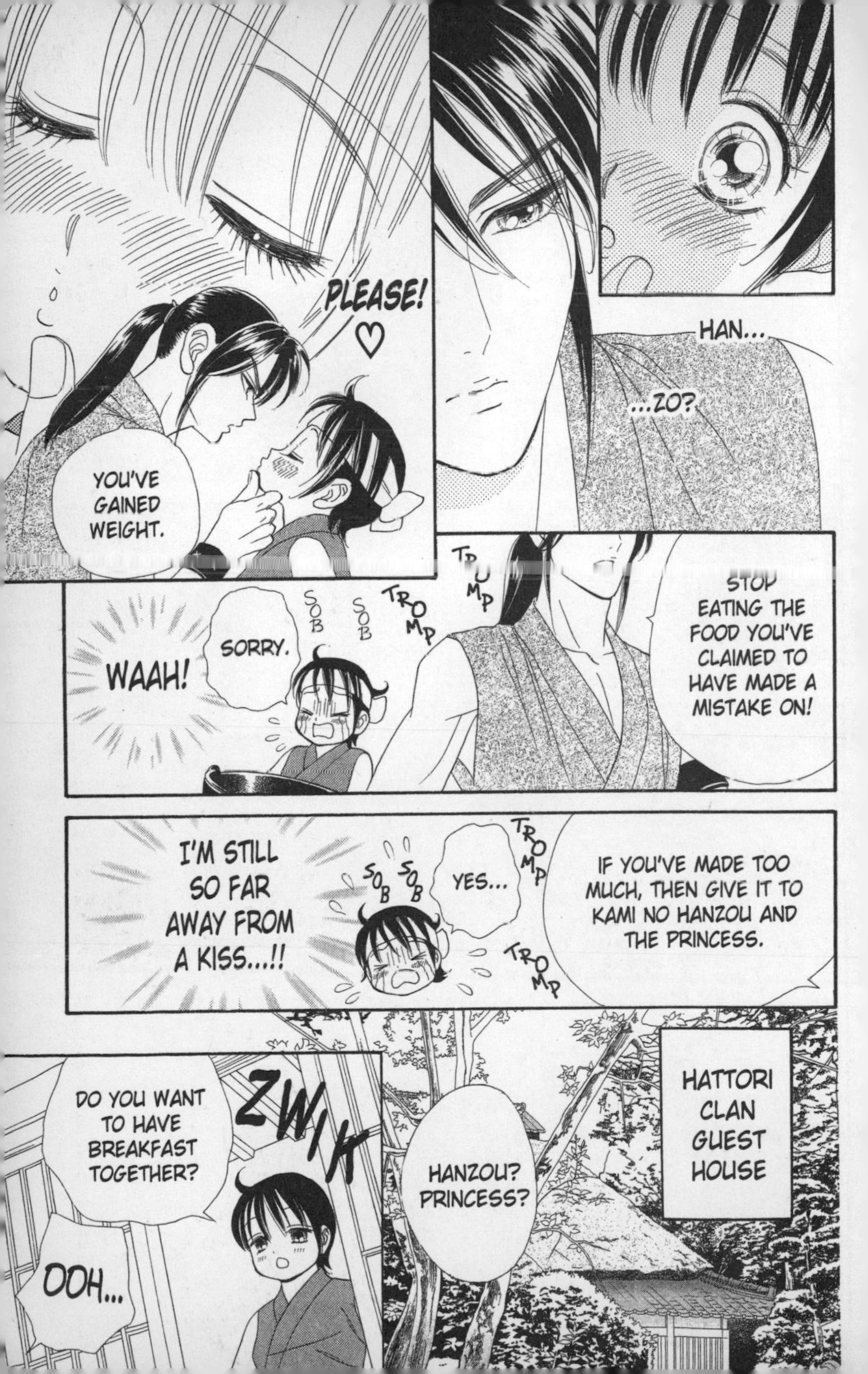
HAN...
...ZO?
PLEASE! ♥
YOU'VE GAINED WEIGHT.
STOP EATING THE FOOD YOU'VE CLAIMED TO HAVE MADE A MISTAKE ON!
TRUMP
TROMP
SOB SOB
SORRY.
WAAH!
IF YOU'VE MADE TOO MUCH, THEN GIVE IT TO KAMI NO HANZOU AND THE PRINCESS.
TROMP
TROMP
YES...
SOB SOB
I'M STILL SO FAR AWAY FROM A KISS...!!
HATTORI CLAN GUEST HOUSE
HANZOU? PRINCESS?
ZWIK
DO YOU WANT TO HAVE BREAKFAST TOGETHER?
OOH...

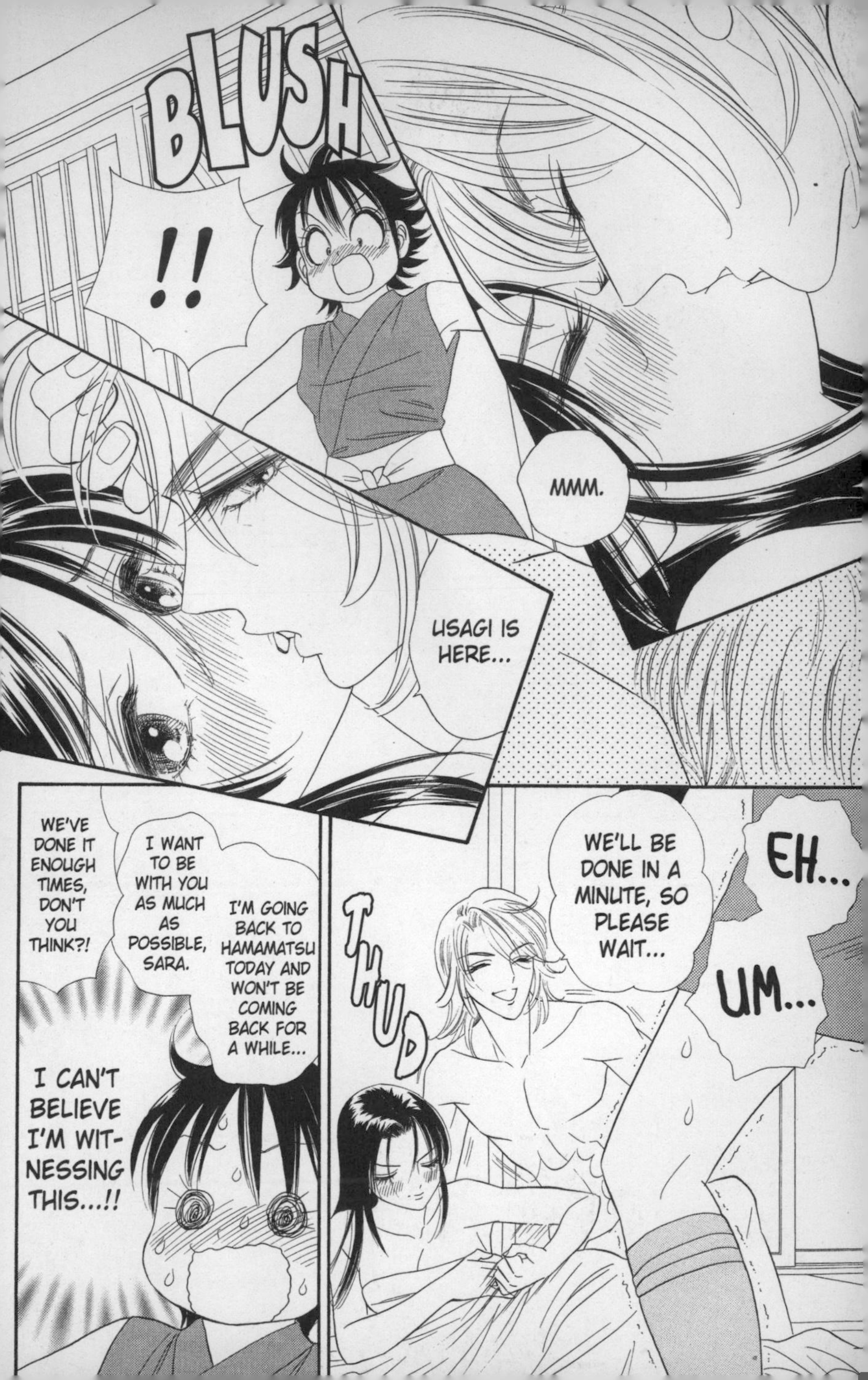
MMM.
BLUSH
!!
USAGI IS HERE...
EH...
UM...
WE'LL BE DONE IN A MINUTE, SO PLEASE WAIT...
THUD
I'M GOING BACK TO HAMAMATSU TODAY AND WON'T BE COMING BACK FOR A WHILE...
I WANT TO BE WITH YOU AS MUCH AS POSSIBLE, SARA.
WE'VE DONE IT ENOUGH TIMES, DON'T YOU THINK?!
I CAN'T BELIEVE I'M WITNESSING THIS...!!

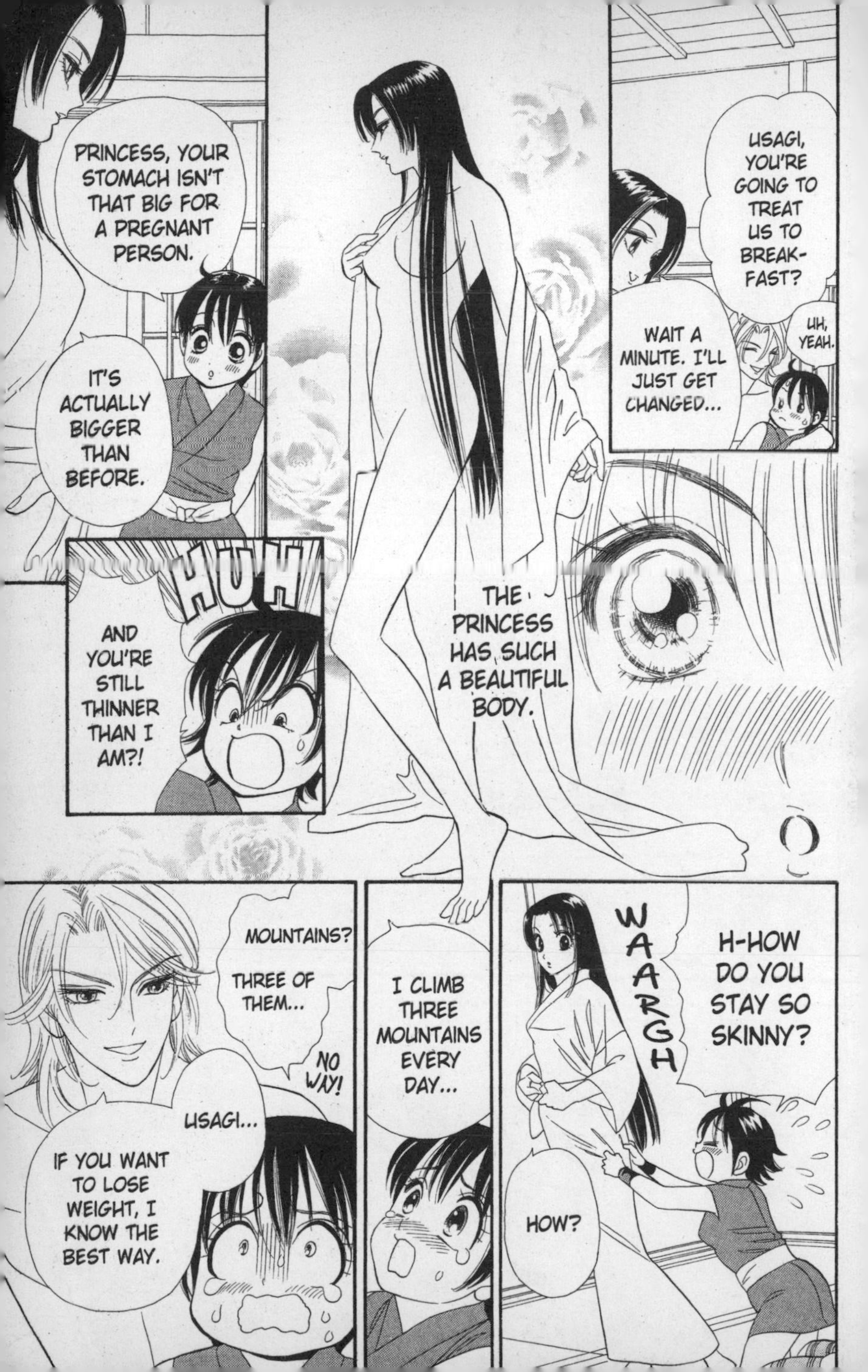
USAGI, YOU'RE GOING TO TREAT US TO BREAK-FAST?
UH, YEAH.
WAIT A MINUTE. I'LL JUST GET CHANGED...
THE PRINCESS HAS SUCH A BEAUTIFUL BODY.
PRINCESS, YOUR STOMACH ISN'T THAT BIG FOR A PREGNANT PERSON.
IT'S ACTUALLY BIGGER THAN BEFORE.
HUH
AND YOU'RE STILL THINNER THAN I AM?!
H-HOW DO YOU STAY SO SKINNY?
WAARGH
HOW?
I CLIMB THREE MOUNTAINS EVERY DAY...
MOUNTAINS?
THREE OF THEM...
NO WAY!
USAGI...
IF YOU WANT TO LOSE WEIGHT, I KNOW THE BEST WAY.

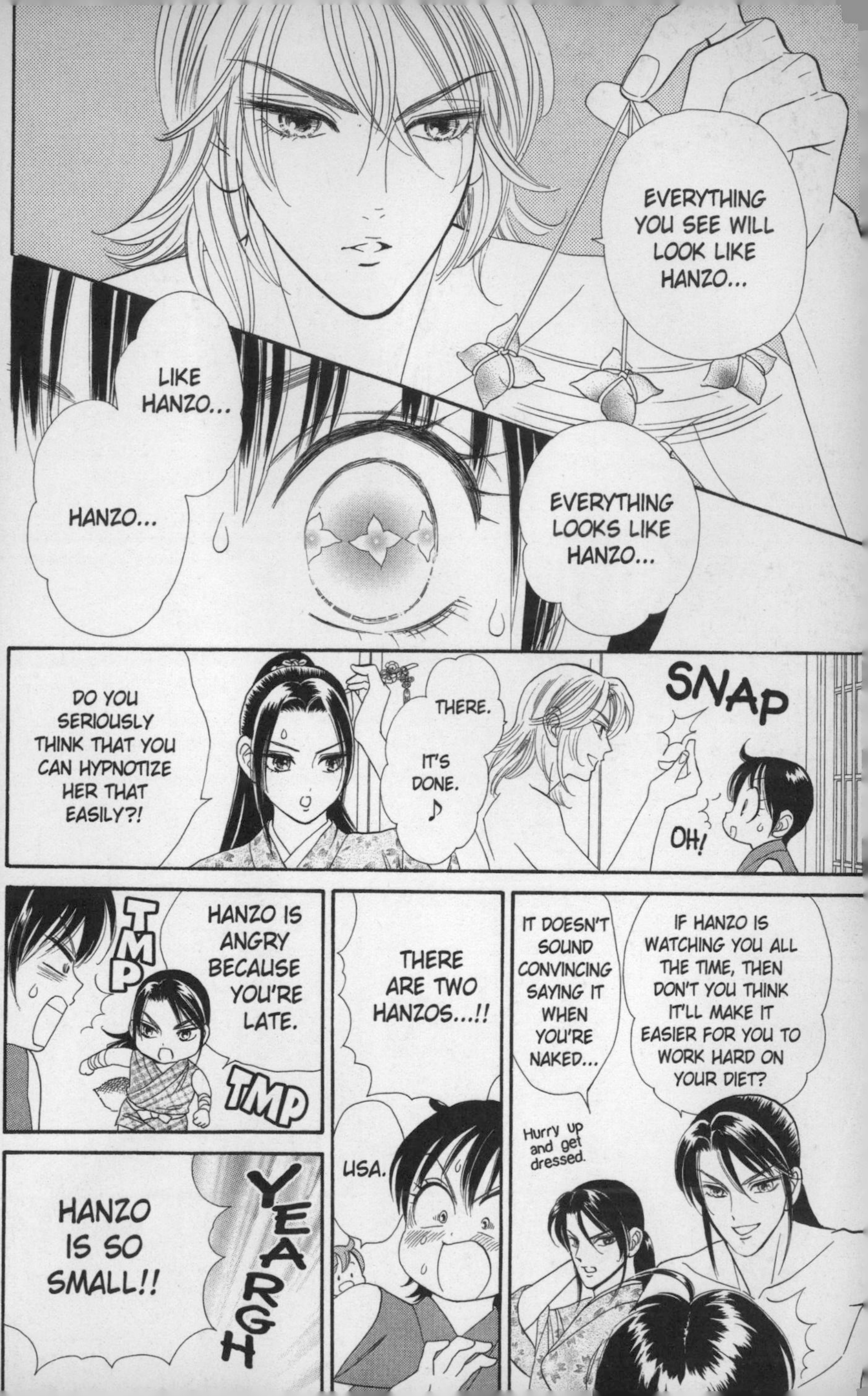
EVERYTHING YOU SEE WILL LOOK LIKE HANZO...
EVERYTHING LOOKS LIKE HANZO...
LIKE HANZO...
HANZO...
SNAP
OH!
THERE.
IT'S DONE. ♪
DO YOU SERIOUSLY THINK THAT YOU CAN HYPNOTIZE HER THAT EASILY?!
IF HANZO IS WATCHING YOU ALL THE TIME, THEN DON'T YOU THINK IT'LL MAKE IT EASIER FOR YOU TO WORK HARD ON YOUR DIET?
IT DOESN'T SOUND CONVINCING SAYING IT WHEN YOU'RE NAKED...
Hurry up and get dressed.
THERE ARE TWO HANZOS...!!
USA.
HANZO IS ANGRY BECAUSE YOU'RE LATE.
TMP
TMP
YEARGH
HANZO IS SO SMALL!!

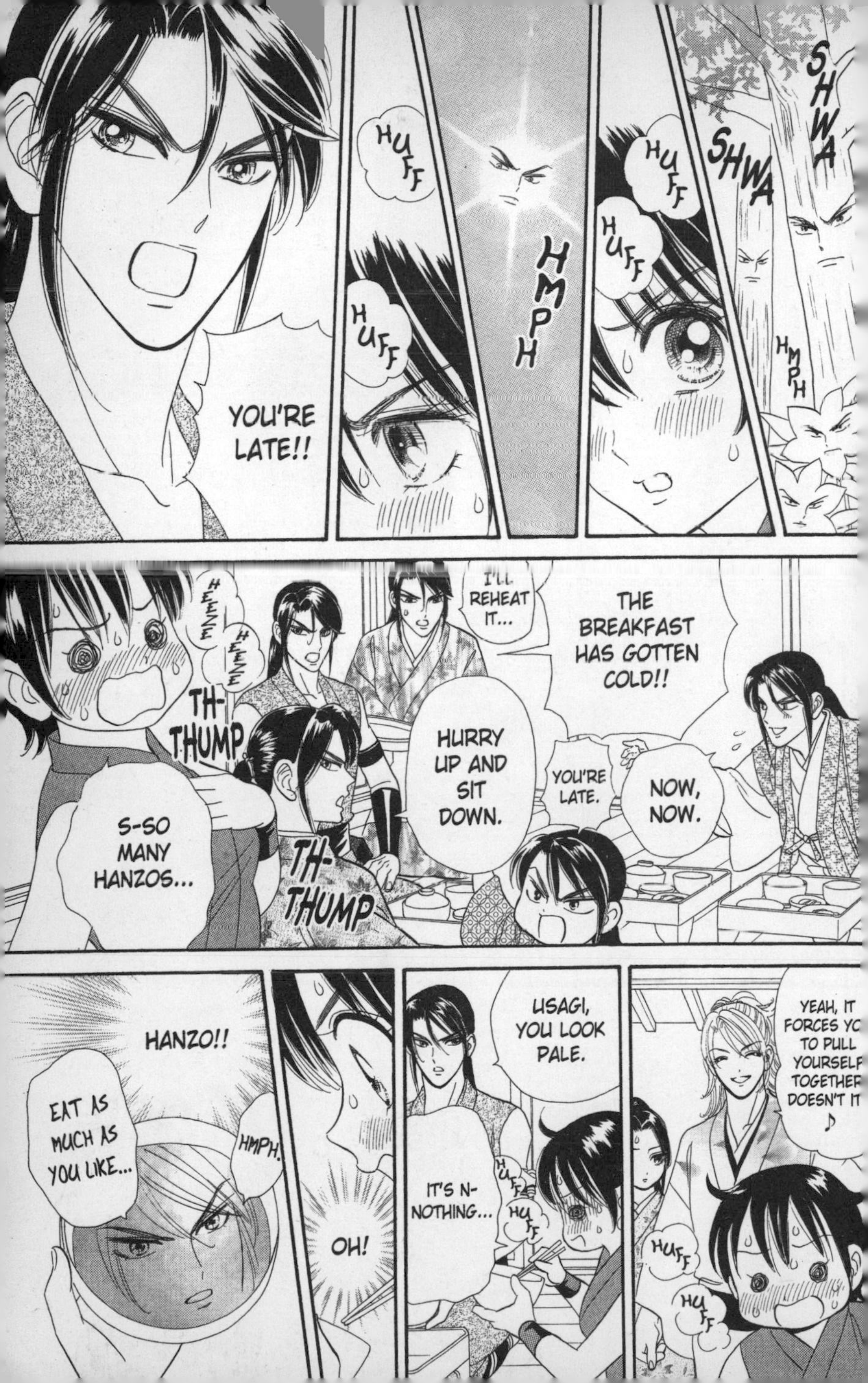
SHWA
SHWA
HMPH
HUFF
HUFF
HMPH
HUFF
HUFF
YOU'RE LATE!!
NOW, NOW.
THE BREAKFAST HAS GOTTEN COLD!!
YOU'RE LATE.
I'LL REHEAT IT...
HURRY UP AND SIT DOWN.
TH-THUMP
HEEZE
HEEZE
TH-THUMP
S-SO MANY HANZOS...
YEAH, IT FORCES YO TO PULL YOURSELF TOGETHER DOESN'T IT ♪
HUFF
HUFF
USAGI, YOU LOOK PALE.
HUFF
HUFF
IT'S N-NOTHING...
OH!
HANZO!!
HMPH.
EAT AS MUCH AS YOU LIKE...

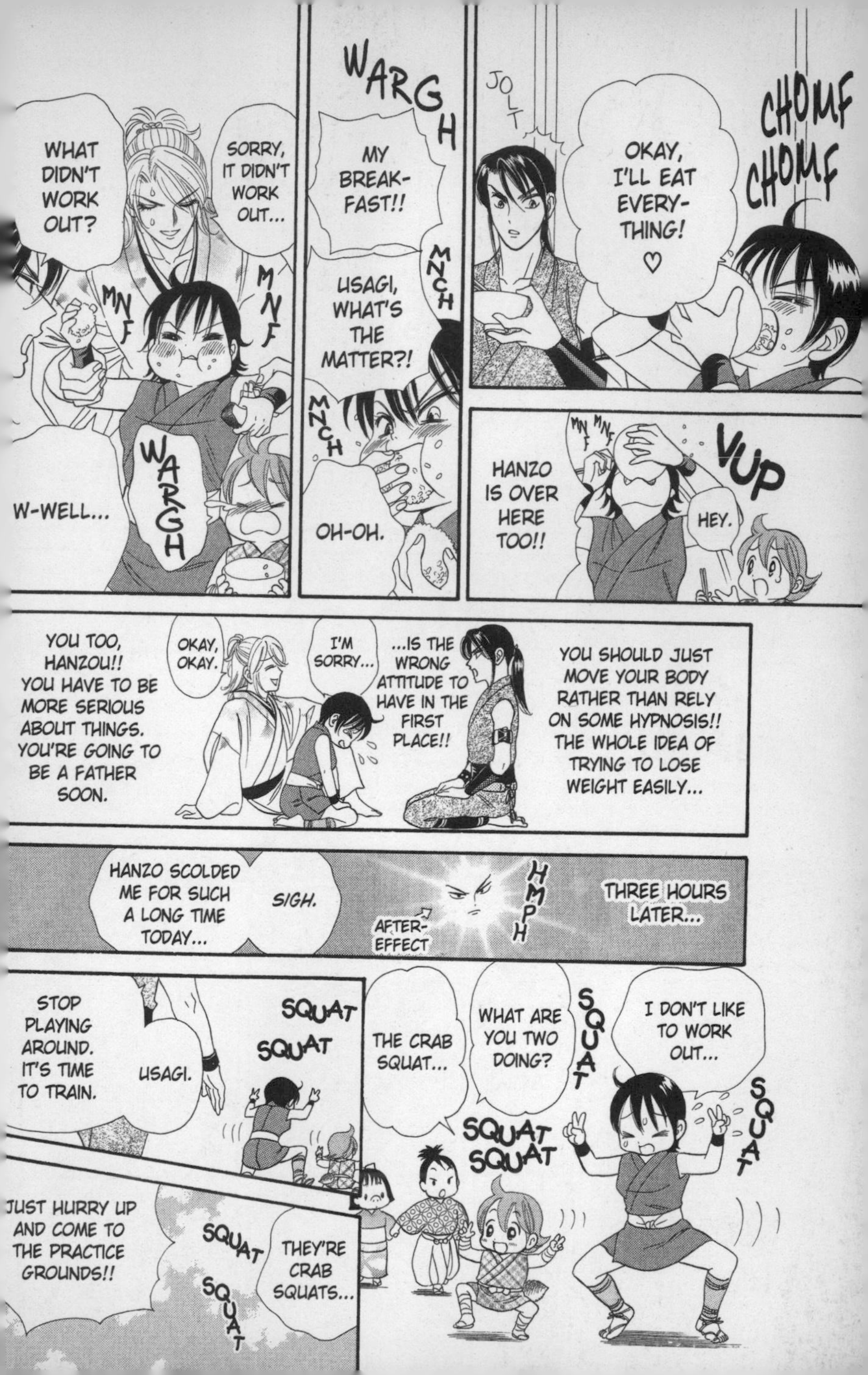
CHOMF CHOMF
JOLT
OKAY, I'LL EAT EVERY-THING! ♡
VUP
HEY.
MNF MNF
HANZO IS OVER HERE TOO!!
WARGH
MY BREAK-FAST!!
MNCH
USAGI, WHAT'S THE MATTER?!
MNCH
OH-OH.
SORRY, IT DIDN'T WORK OUT...
WHAT DIDN'T WORK OUT?
MNF
MNF
WARGH
W-WELL...
YOU SHOULD JUST MOVE YOUR BODY RATHER THAN RELY ON SOME HYPNOSIS!! THE WHOLE IDEA OF TRYING TO LOSE WEIGHT EASILY...
...IS THE WRONG ATTITUDE TO HAVE IN THE FIRST PLACE!!
I'M SORRY...
OKAY, OKAY.
YOU TOO, HANZOU!! YOU HAVE TO BE MORE SERIOUS ABOUT THINGS. YOU'RE GOING TO BE A FATHER SOON.
THREE HOURS LATER...
HMPH
AFTER-EFFECT
SIGH.
HANZO SCOLDED ME FOR SUCH A LONG TIME TODAY...
I DON'T LIKE TO WORK OUT...
SQUAT
SQUAT
WHAT ARE YOU TWO DOING?
SQUAT SQUAT
THE CRAB SQUAT...
THEY'RE CRAB SQUATS...
SQUAT
SQUAT
USAGI.
STOP PLAYING AROUND. IT'S TIME TO TRAIN.
SQUAT
SQUAT
JUST HURRY UP AND COME TO THE PRACTICE GROUNDS!!

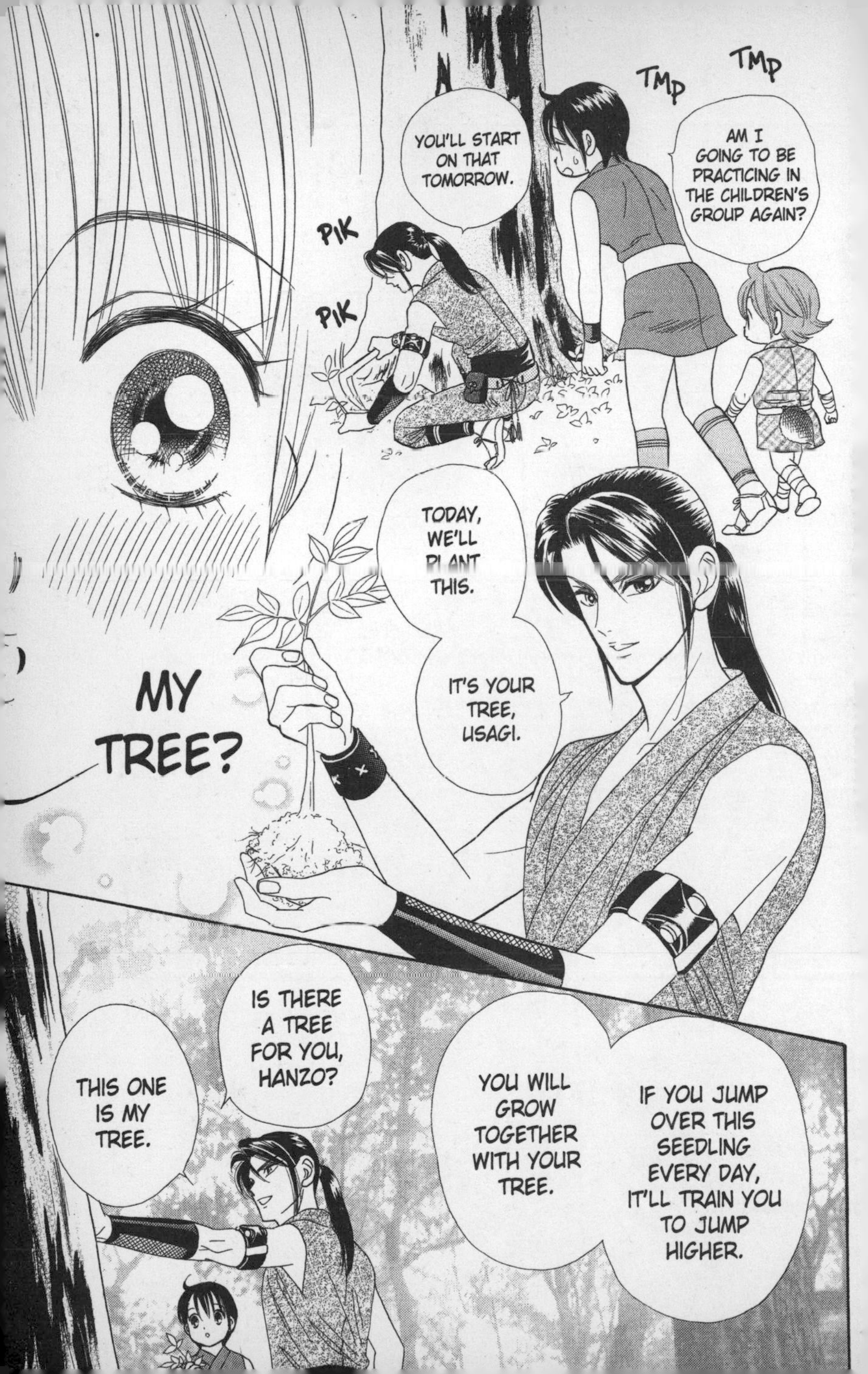
TMP
TMP
AM I GOING TO BE PRACTICING IN THE CHILDREN'S GROUP AGAIN?
YOU'LL START ON THAT TOMORROW.
PIK
PIK
TODAY, WE'LL PLANT THIS.
IT'S YOUR TREE, USAGI.
MY TREE?
IF YOU JUMP OVER THIS SEEDLING EVERY DAY, IT'LL TRAIN YOU TO JUMP HIGHER.
YOU WILL GROW TOGETHER WITH YOUR TREE.
IS THERE A TREE FOR YOU, HANZO?
THIS ONE IS MY TREE.

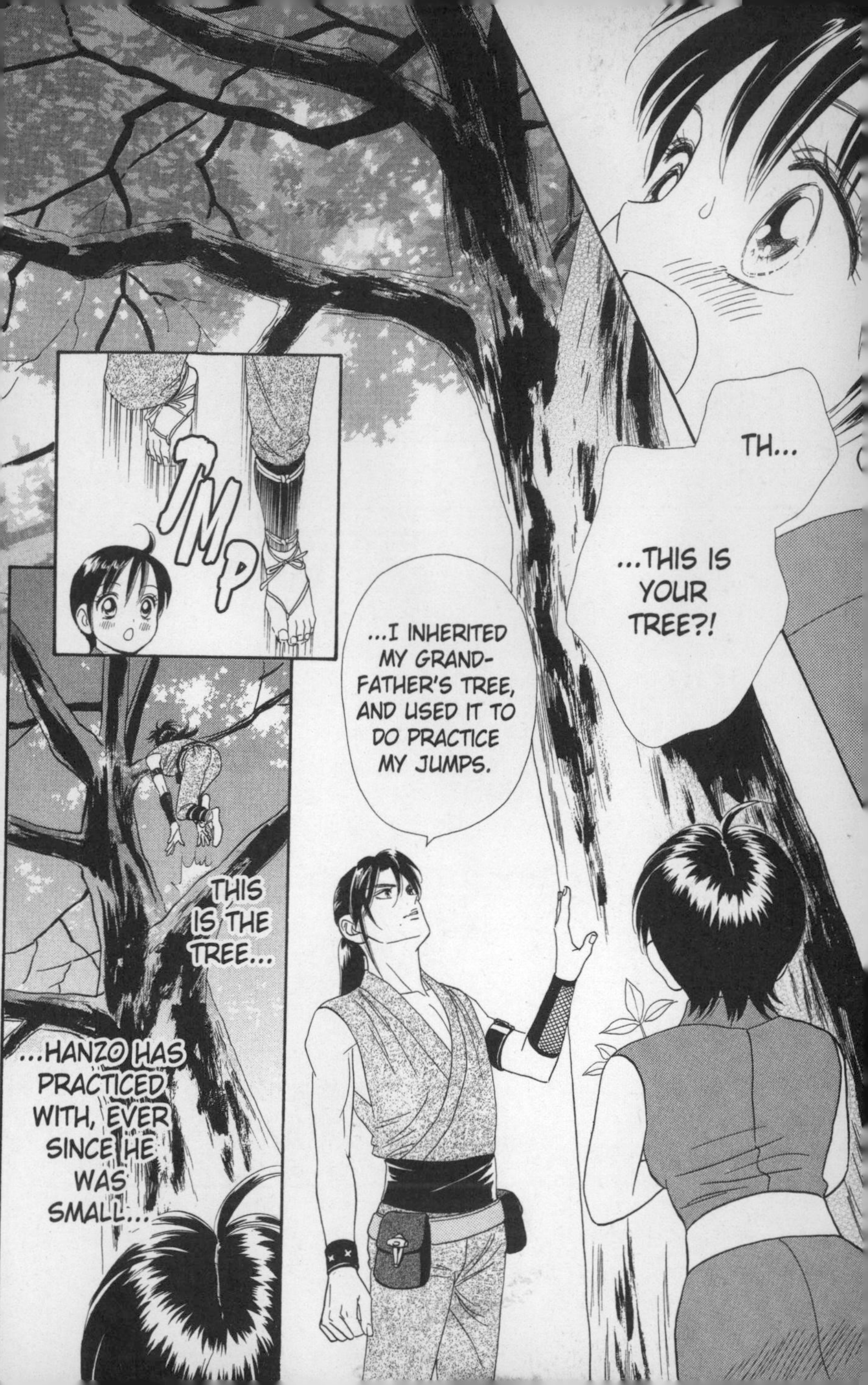
TH...
...THIS IS YOUR TREE?!
TMP
...I INHERITED MY GRAND-FATHER'S TREE, AND USED IT TO DO PRACTICE MY JUMPS.
THIS IS THE TREE...
...HANZO HAS PRACTICED WITH, EVER SINCE HE WAS SMALL...

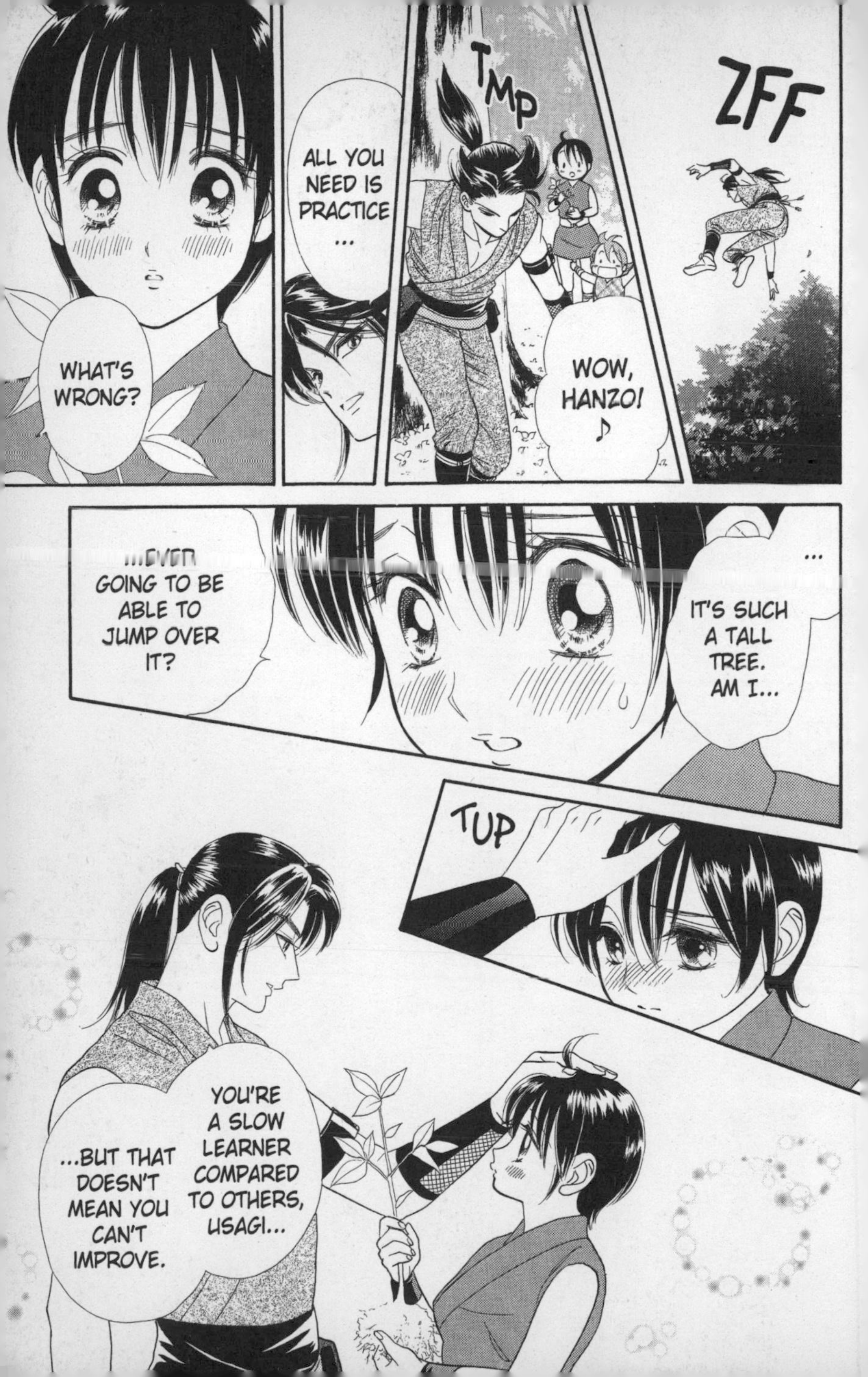
ZFF
TMP
WOW, HANZO! ♪
ALL YOU NEED IS PRACTICE ...
WHAT'S WRONG?
... IT'S SUCH A TALL TREE. AM I...
GOING TO BE ABLE TO JUMP OVER IT?
TUP
YOU'RE A SLOW LEARNER COMPARED TO OTHERS, USAGI...
...BUT THAT DOESN'T MEAN YOU CAN'T IMPROVE.

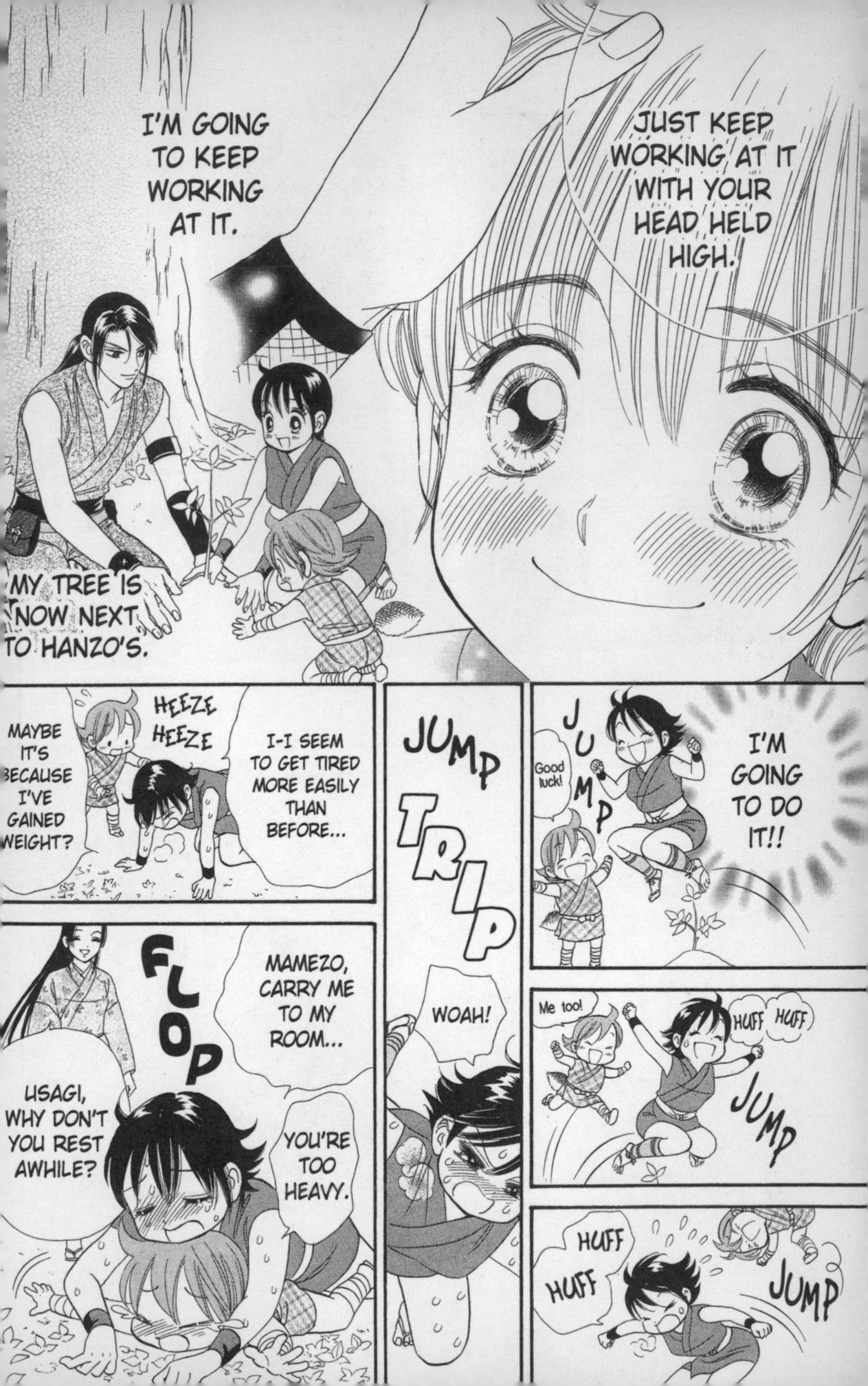
JUST KEEP WORKING AT IT WITH YOUR HEAD HELD HIGH.
I'M GOING TO KEEP WORKING AT IT.
MY TREE IS NOW NEXT TO HANZO'S.
I'M GOING TO DO IT!!
JUMP
Good luck!
HUFF HUFF
Me too!
JUMP
HUFF
HUFF
JUMP
JUMP
TRIP
WOAH!
I-I SEEM TO GET TIRED MORE EASILY THAN BEFORE...
HEEZE HEEZE
MAYBE IT'S BECAUSE I'VE GAINED WEIGHT?
MAMEZO, CARRY ME TO MY ROOM...
FLOP
YOU'RE TOO HEAVY.
USAGI, WHY DON'T YOU REST AWHILE?

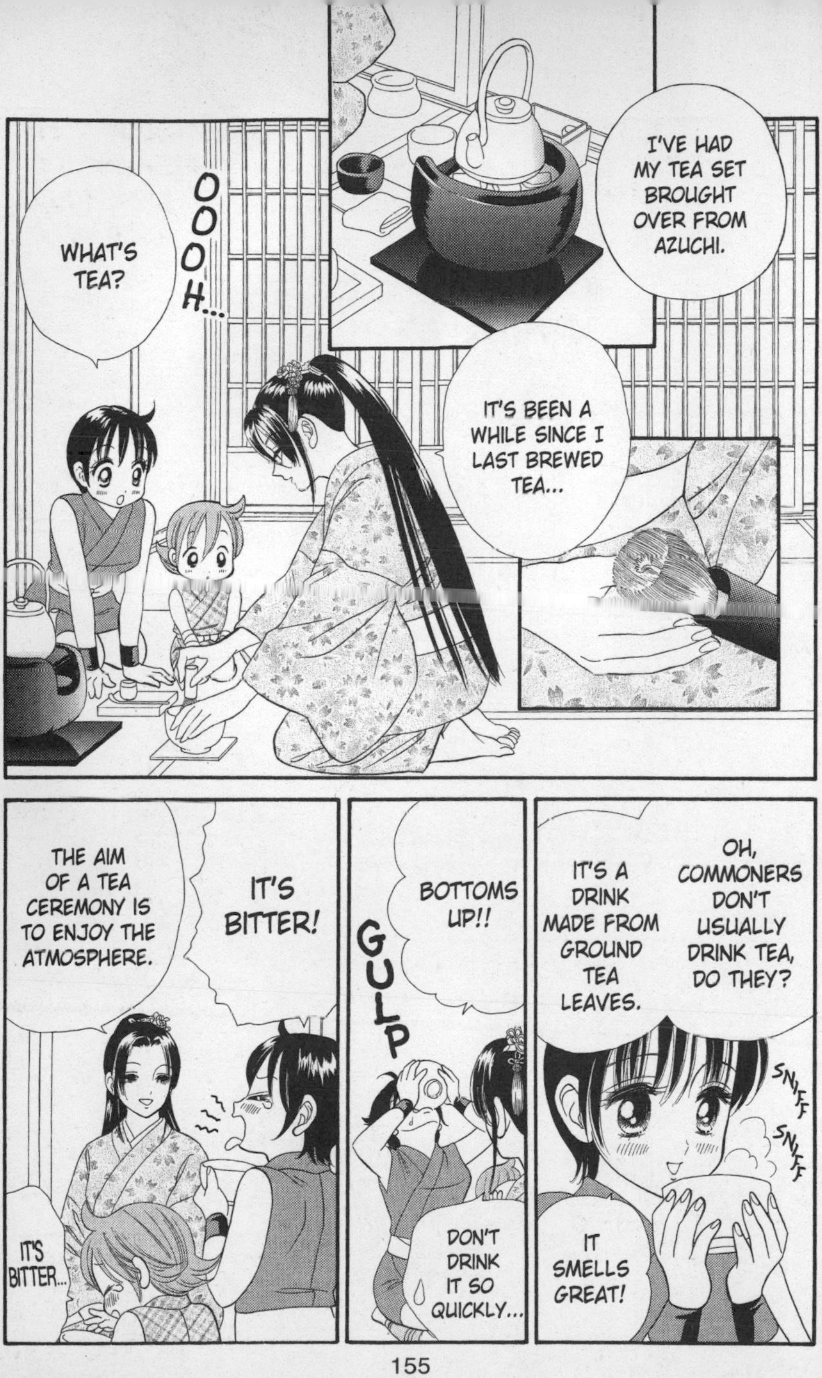
I'VE HAD MY TEA SET BROUGHT OVER FROM AZUCHI.
IT'S BEEN A WHILE SINCE I LAST BREWED TEA...
OOOH...
WHAT'S TEA?
OH, COMMONERS DON'T USUALLY DRINK TEA, DO THEY?
IT'S A DRINK MADE FROM GROUND TEA LEAVES.
SNIFF
SNIFF
IT SMELLS GREAT!
BOTTOMS UP!!
GULP
DON'T DRINK IT SO QUICKLY...
IT'S BITTER!
THE AIM OF A TEA CEREMONY IS TO ENJOY THE ATMOSPHERE.
IT'S BITTER...

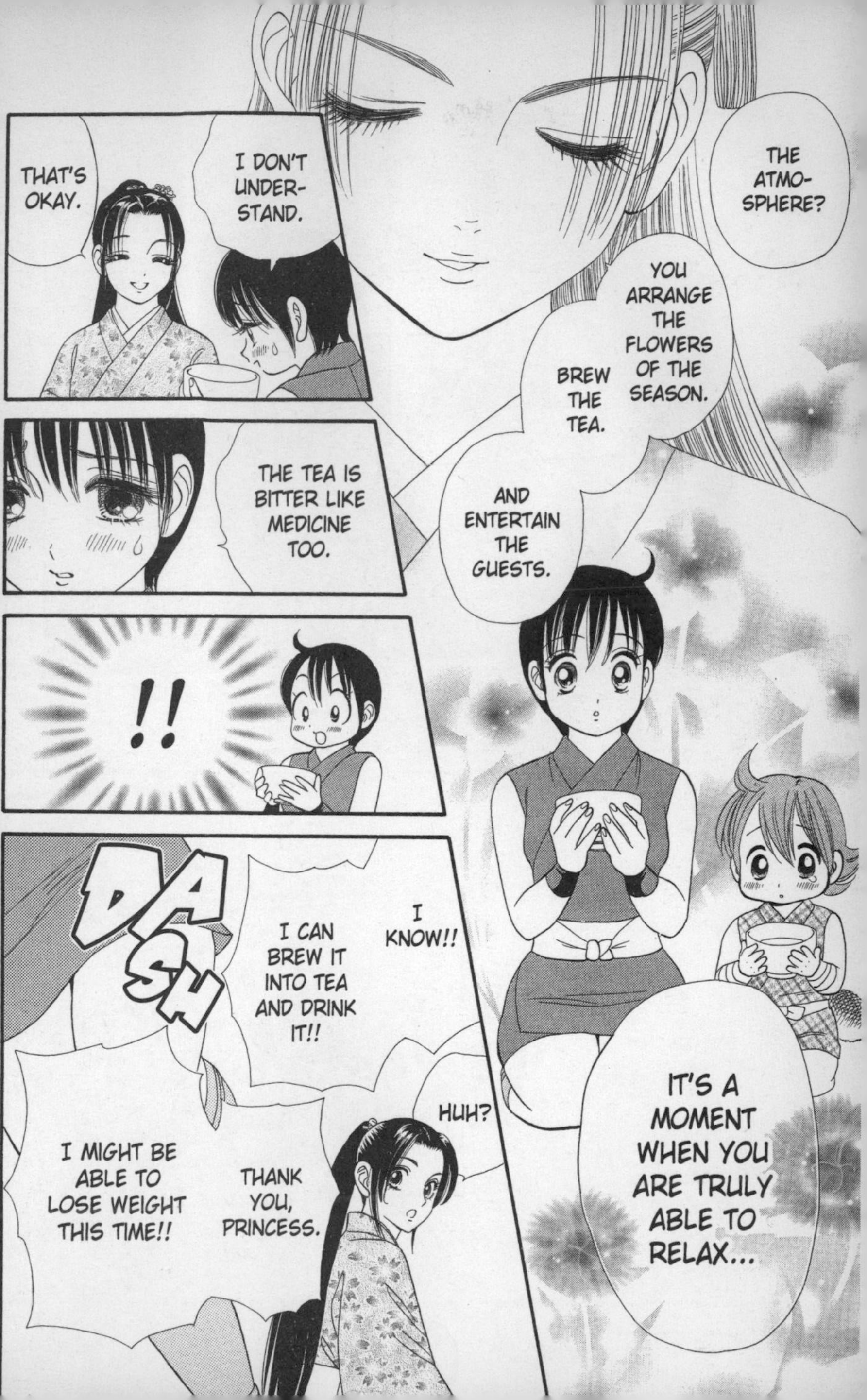
THE ATMO-SPHERE?
YOU ARRANGE THE FLOWERS OF THE SEASON.
BREW THE TEA.
AND ENTERTAIN THE GUESTS.
IT'S A MOMENT WHEN YOU ARE TRULY ABLE TO RELAX...
I DON'T UNDER-STAND.
THAT'S OKAY.
THE TEA IS BITTER LIKE MEDICINE TOO.
!!
I KNOW!!
I CAN BREW IT INTO TEA AND DRINK IT!!
DASH
HUH?
THANK YOU, PRINCESS.
I MIGHT BE ABLE TO LOSE WEIGHT THIS TIME!!

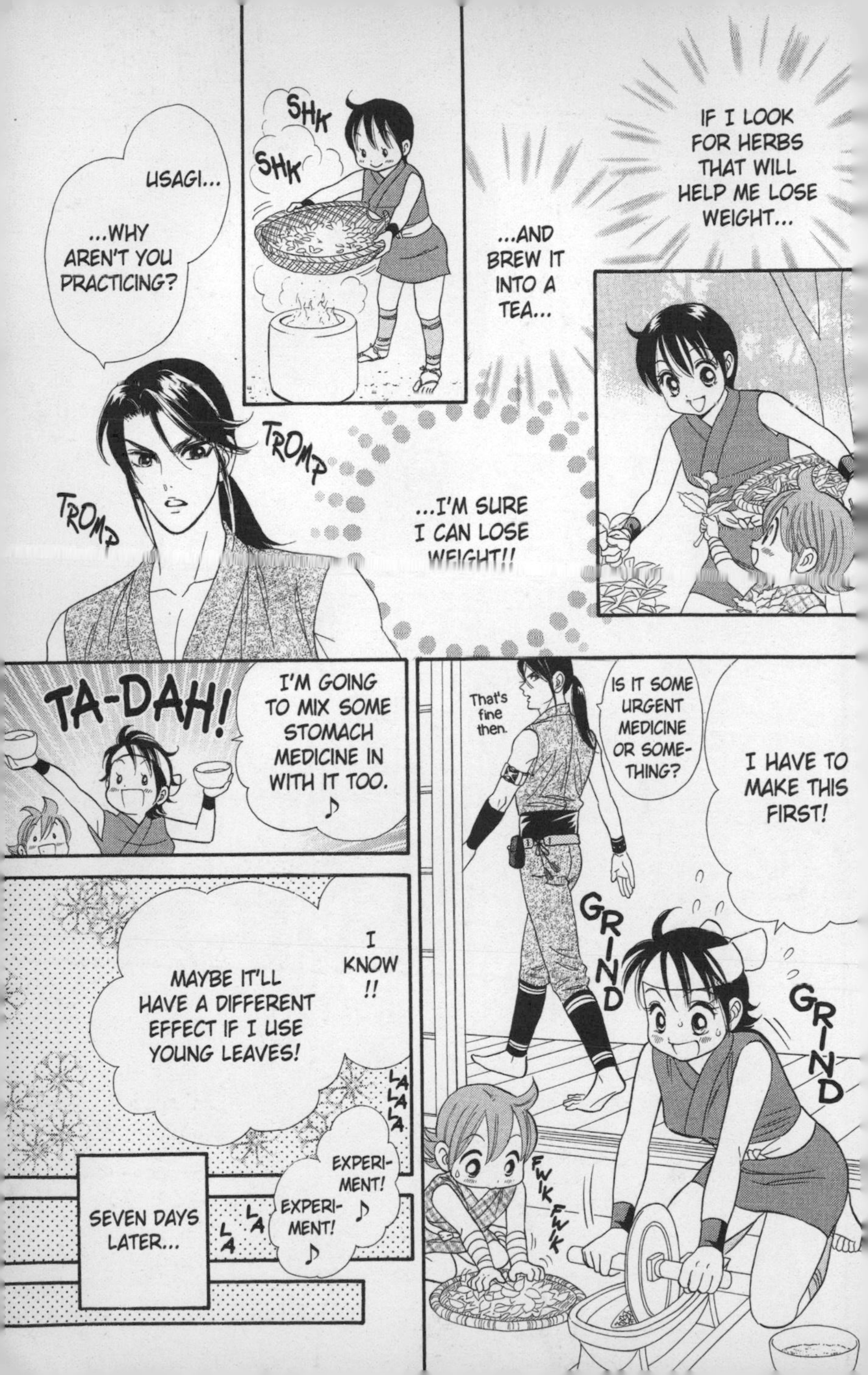
IF I LOOK FOR HERBS THAT WILL HELP ME LOSE WEIGHT...
...AND BREW IT INTO A TEA...
SHK
SHK
...I'M SURE I CAN LOSE WEIGHT!!
TROMP
TROMP
USAGI...
...WHY AREN'T YOU PRACTICING?
I HAVE TO MAKE THIS FIRST!
IS IT SOME URGENT MEDICINE OR SOME-THING?
That's fine then.
GRIND
GRIND
FWIK FWIK
I'M GOING TO MIX SOME STOMACH MEDICINE IN WITH IT TOO. ♪
TA-DAH!
I KNOW!!
MAYBE IT'LL HAVE A DIFFERENT EFFECT IF I USE YOUNG LEAVES!
LA LA LA
EXPERI-MENT! ♪
EXPERI-MENT! ♪
LA LA
SEVEN DAYS LATER...

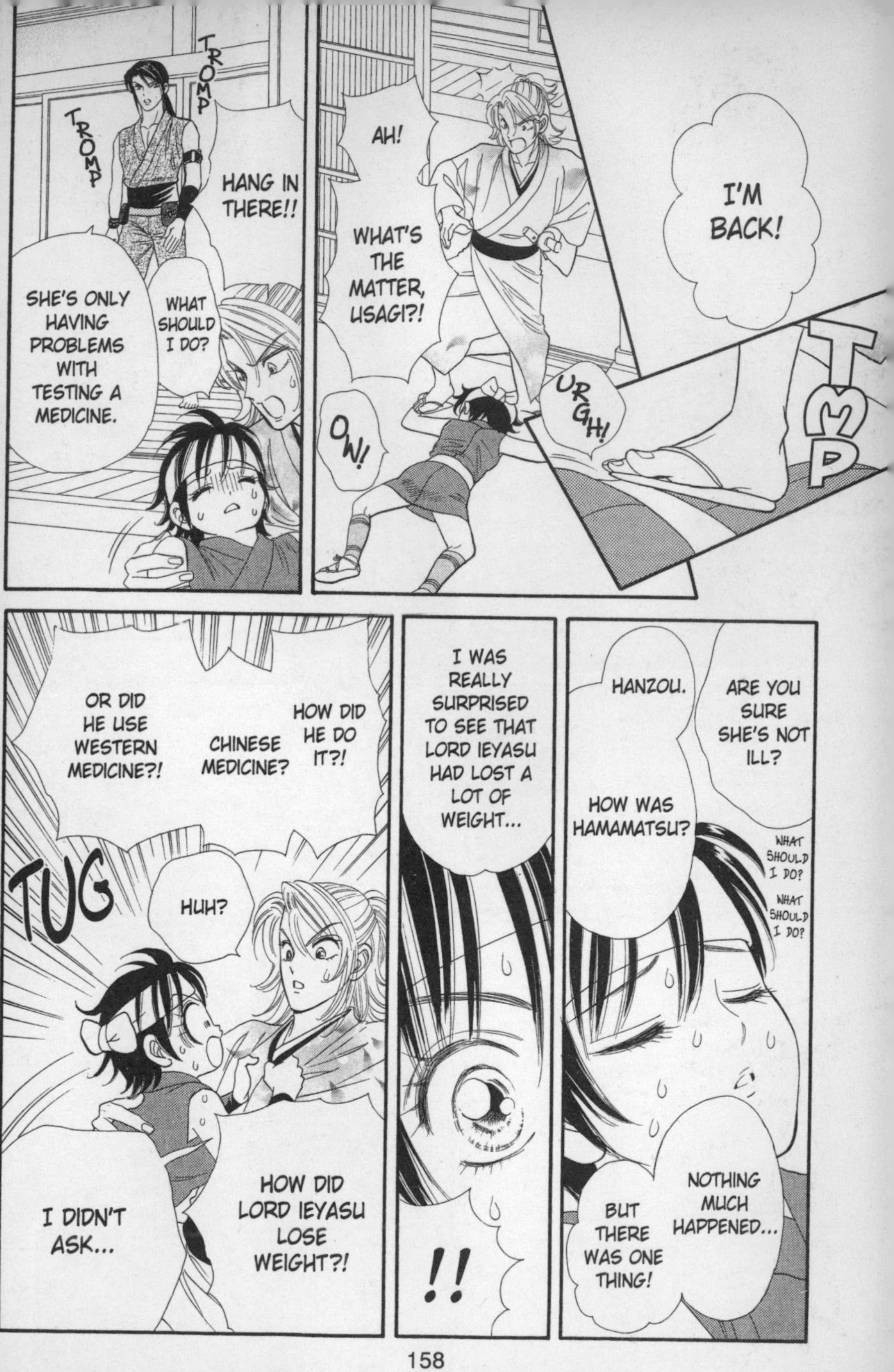
I'M BACK!
TMP
URGH!
AH!
WHAT'S THE MATTER, USAGI?!
OW!
TROMP
TROMP
HANG IN THERE!!
WHAT SHOULD I DO?
SHE'S ONLY HAVING PROBLEMS WITH TESTING A MEDICINE.
ARE YOU SURE SHE'S NOT ILL?
HANZOU.
HOW WAS HAMAMATSU?
WHAT SHOULD I DO?
WHAT SHOULD I DO?
NOTHING MUCH HAPPENED...
BUT THERE WAS ONE THING!
I WAS REALLY SURPRISED TO SEE THAT LORD IEYASU HAD LOST A LOT OF WEIGHT...
!!
HOW DID HE DO IT?!
CHINESE MEDICINE?
OR DID HE USE WESTERN MEDICINE?!
TUG
HUH?
HOW DID LORD IEYASU LOSE WEIGHT?!
I DIDN'T ASK...

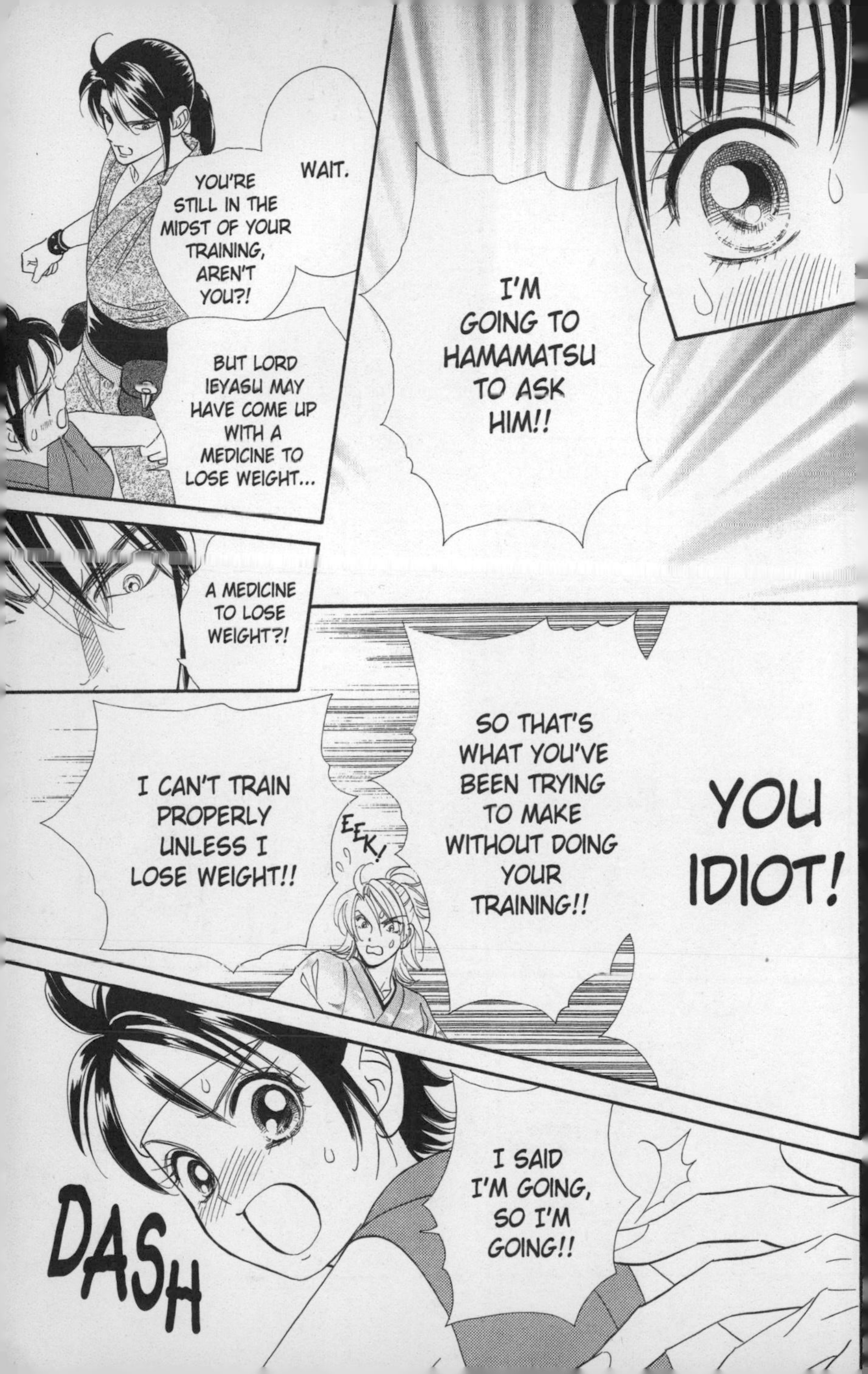
I'M GOING TO HAMAMATSU TO ASK HIM!!
WAIT.
YOU'RE STILL IN THE MIDST OF YOUR TRAINING, AREN'T YOU?!
BUT LORD IEYASU MAY HAVE COME UP WITH A MEDICINE TO LOSE WEIGHT...
A MEDICINE TO LOSE WEIGHT?!
YOU IDIOT!
SO THAT'S WHAT YOU'VE BEEN TRYING TO MAKE WITHOUT DOING YOUR TRAINING!!
EEK!
I CAN'T TRAIN PROPERLY UNLESS I LOSE WEIGHT!!
I SAID I'M GOING, SO I'M GOING!!
DASH

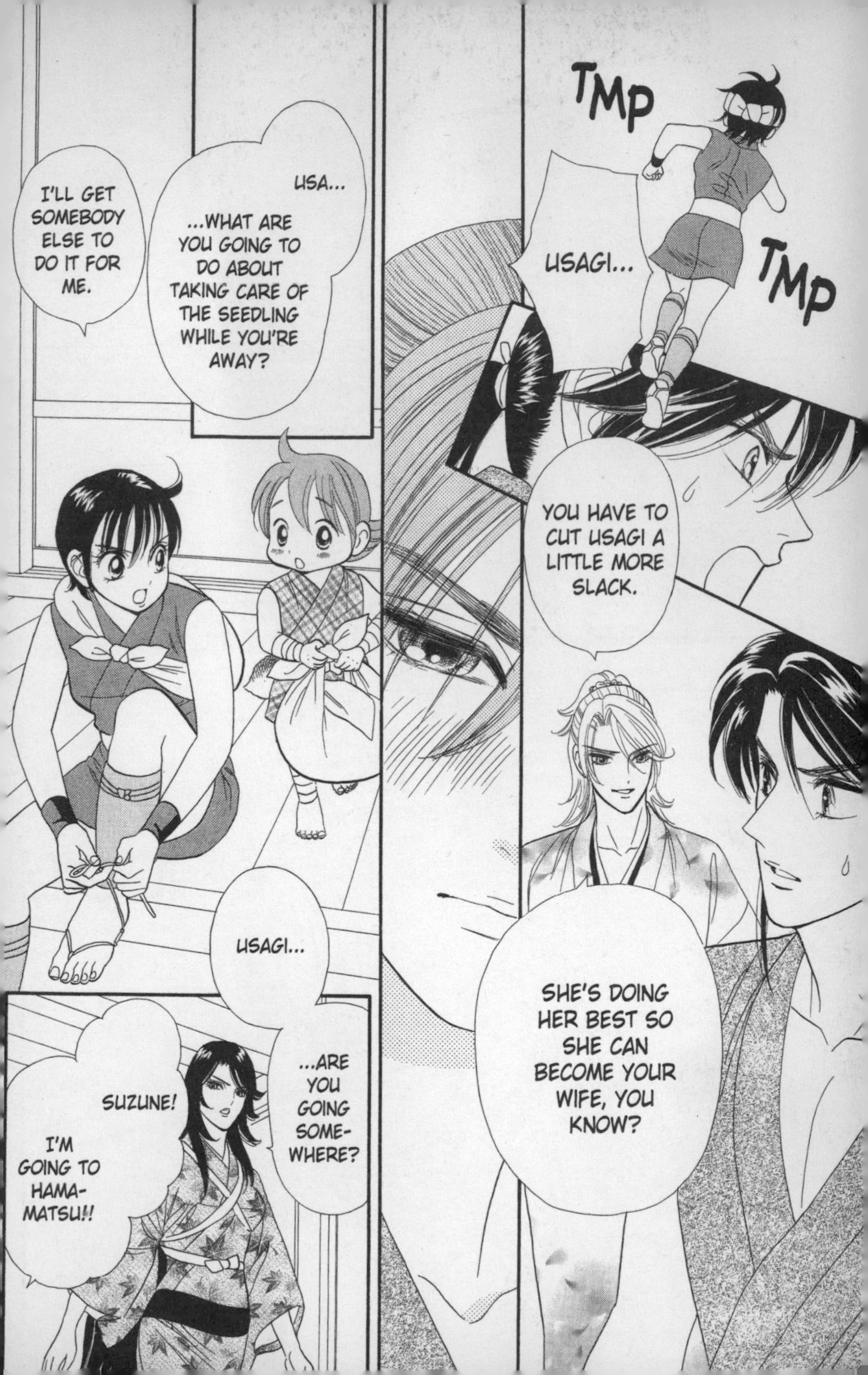
TMP
TMP
USAGI...
YOU HAVE TO CUT USAGI A LITTLE MORE SLACK.
SHE'S DOING HER BEST SO SHE CAN BECOME YOUR WIFE, YOU KNOW?
USA...
...WHAT ARE YOU GOING TO DO ABOUT TAKING CARE OF THE SEEDLING WHILE YOU'RE AWAY?
I'LL GET SOMEBODY ELSE TO DO IT FOR ME.
USAGI...
...ARE YOU GOING SOME-WHERE?
SUZUNE!
I'M GOING TO HAMA-MATSU!!

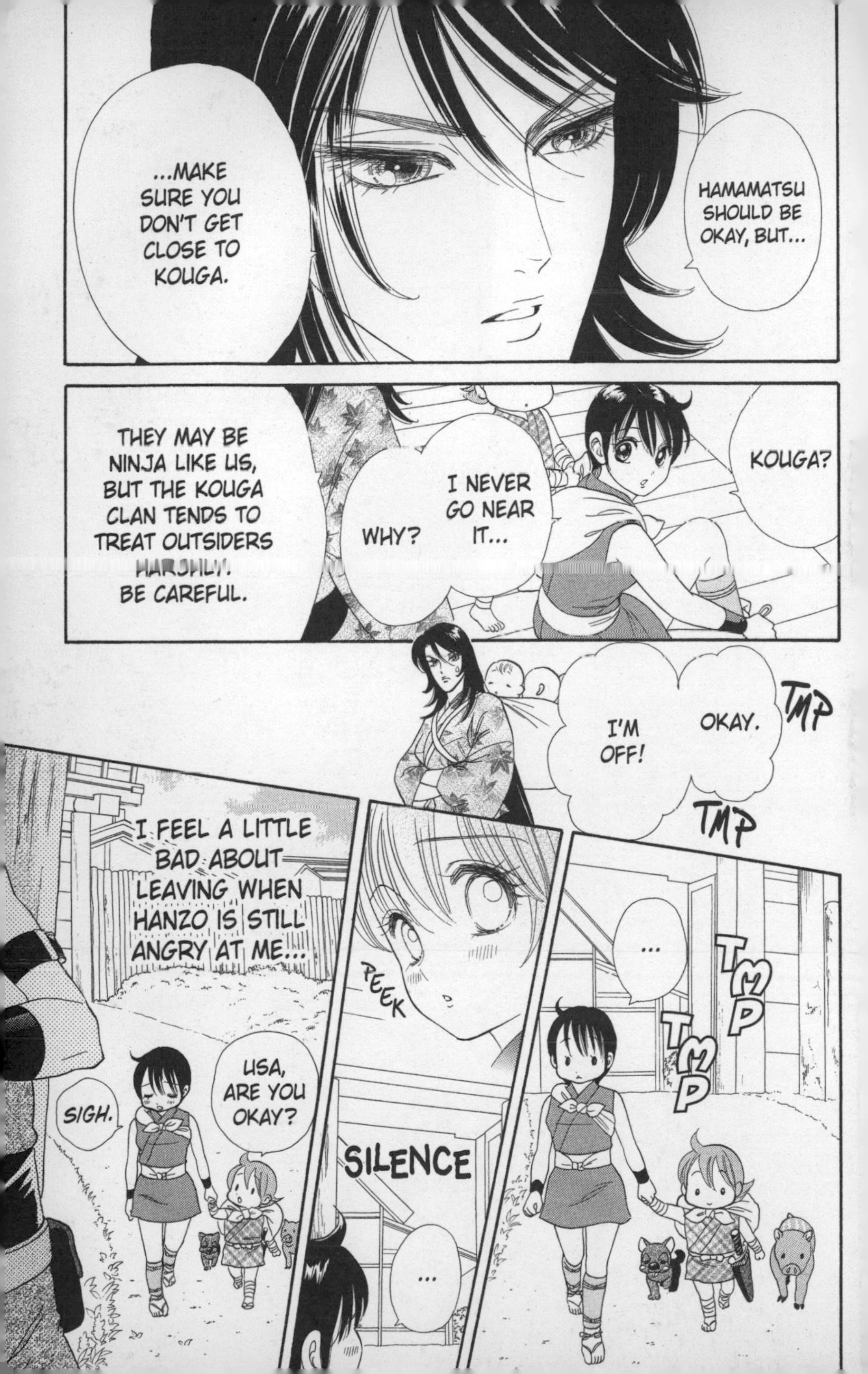
HAMAMATSU SHOULD BE OKAY, BUT...
...MAKE SURE YOU DON'T GET CLOSE TO KOUGA.
KOUGA?
I NEVER GO NEAR IT...
WHY?
THEY MAY BE NINJA LIKE US, BUT THE KOUGA CLAN TENDS TO TREAT OUTSIDERS HARSHLY. BE CAREFUL.
TMP
OKAY.
I'M OFF!
TMP
TMP
TMP
...
PEEK
SILENCE
...
I FEEL A LITTLE BAD ABOUT LEAVING WHEN HANZO IS STILL ANGRY AT ME...
USA, ARE YOU OKAY?
SIGH.

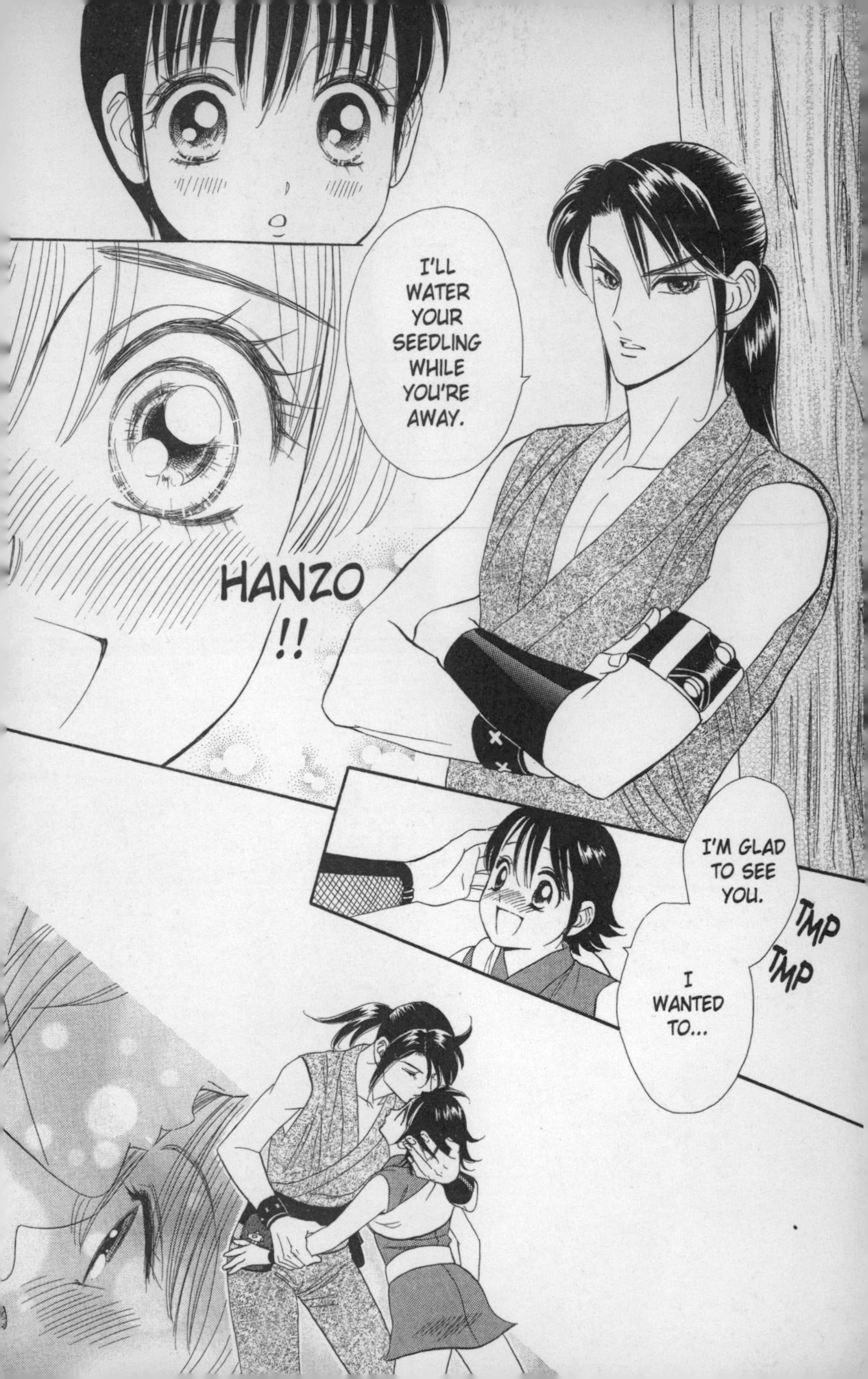
I'LL WATER YOUR SEEDLING WHILE YOU'RE AWAY.
HANZO !!
I'M GLAD TO SEE YOU.
TMP TMP
I WANTED TO...

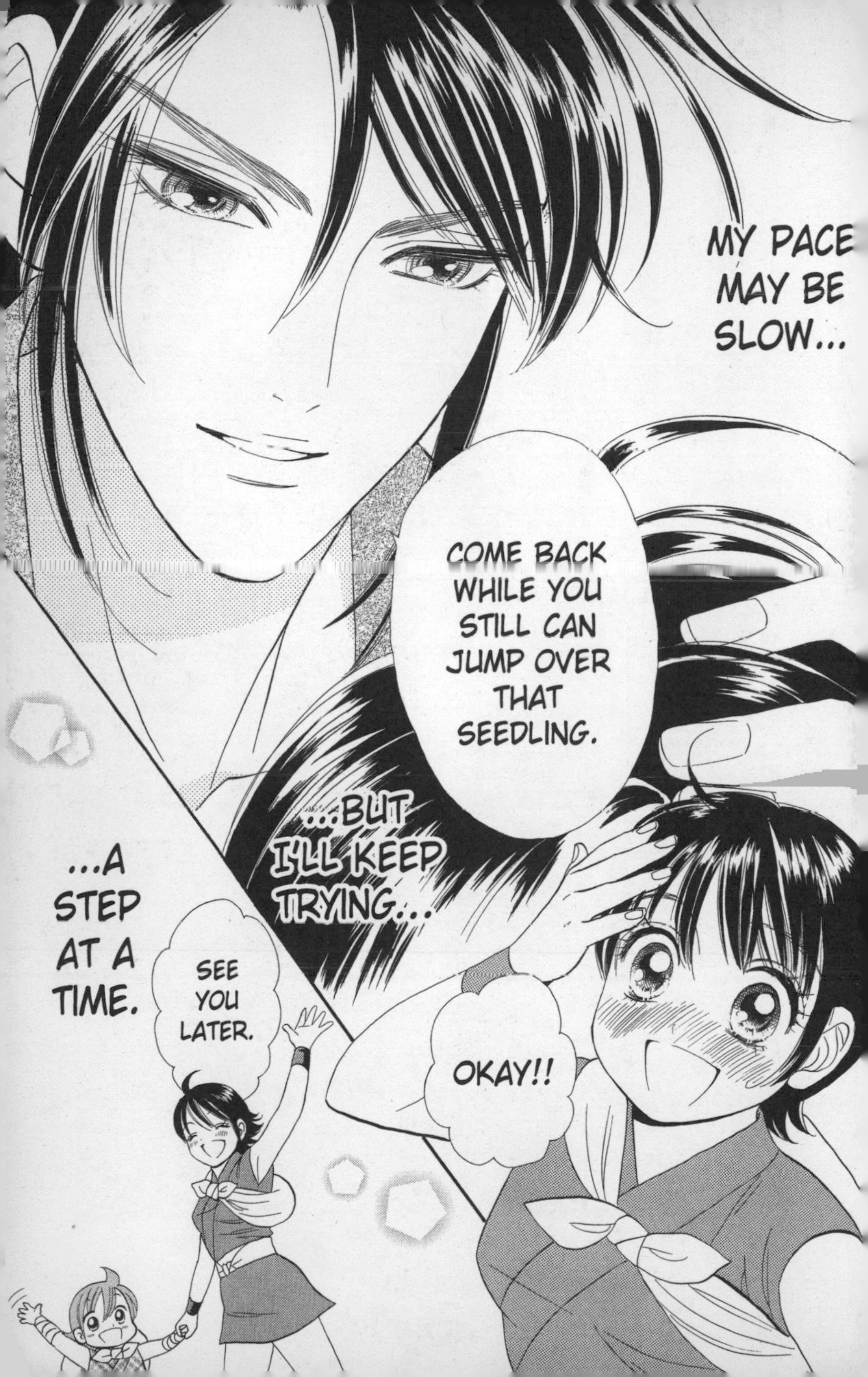
MY PACE MAY BE SLOW...
COME BACK WHILE YOU STILL CAN JUMP OVER THAT SEEDLING.
...BUT I'LL KEEP TRYING...
OKAY!!
...A STEP AT A TIME.
SEE YOU LATER.

TAIL OF THE MOON EXTRA: TODAY'S MISSION

"I WANT TO SEE A HARD-BOILED HANZO!"

-HARURIN-SAN, TOKUSHIMA PREFECTURE

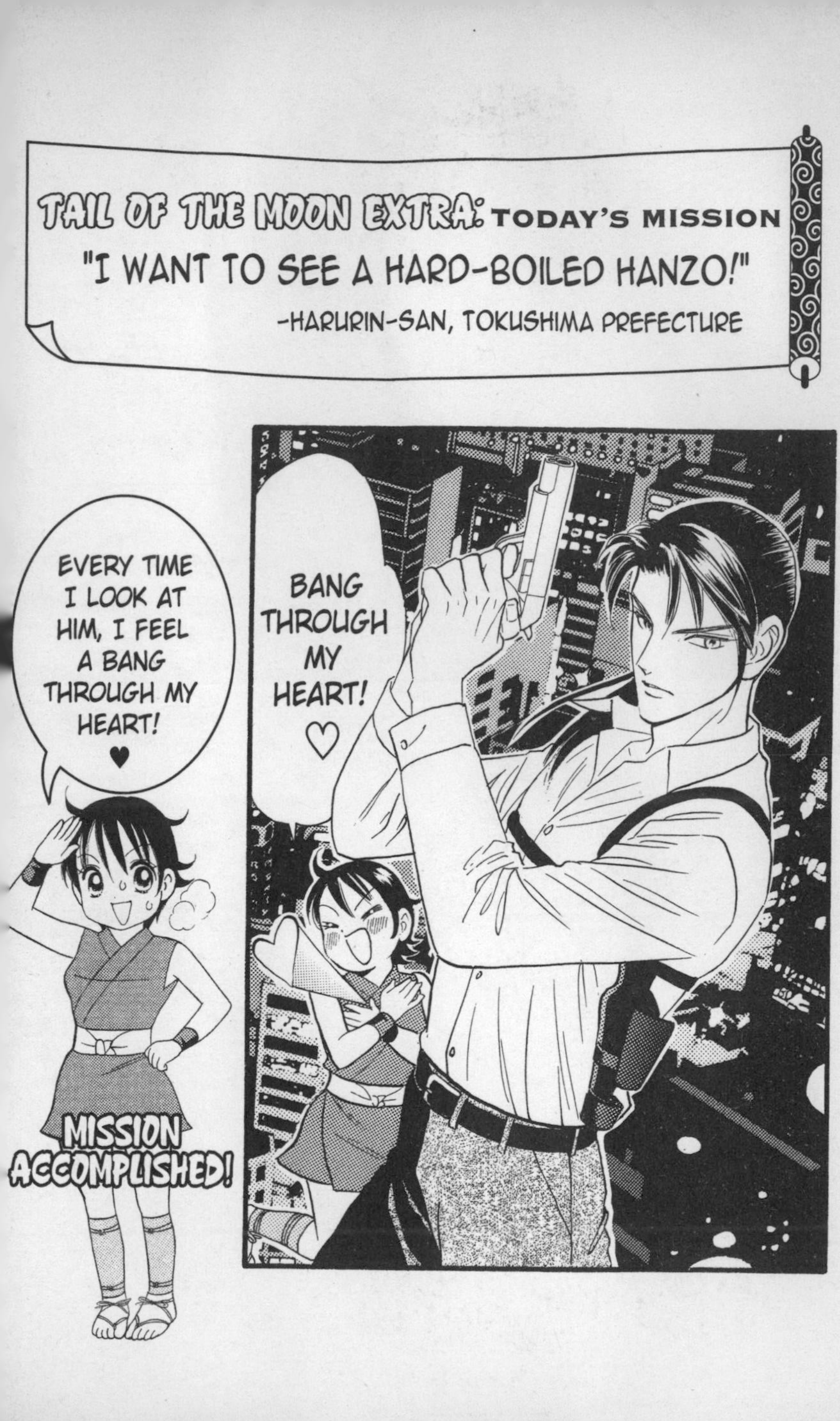
BANG THROUGH MY HEART! ♡
EVERY TIME I LOOK AT HIM, I FEEL A BANG THROUGH MY HEART! ♥
MISSION ACCOMPLISHED!

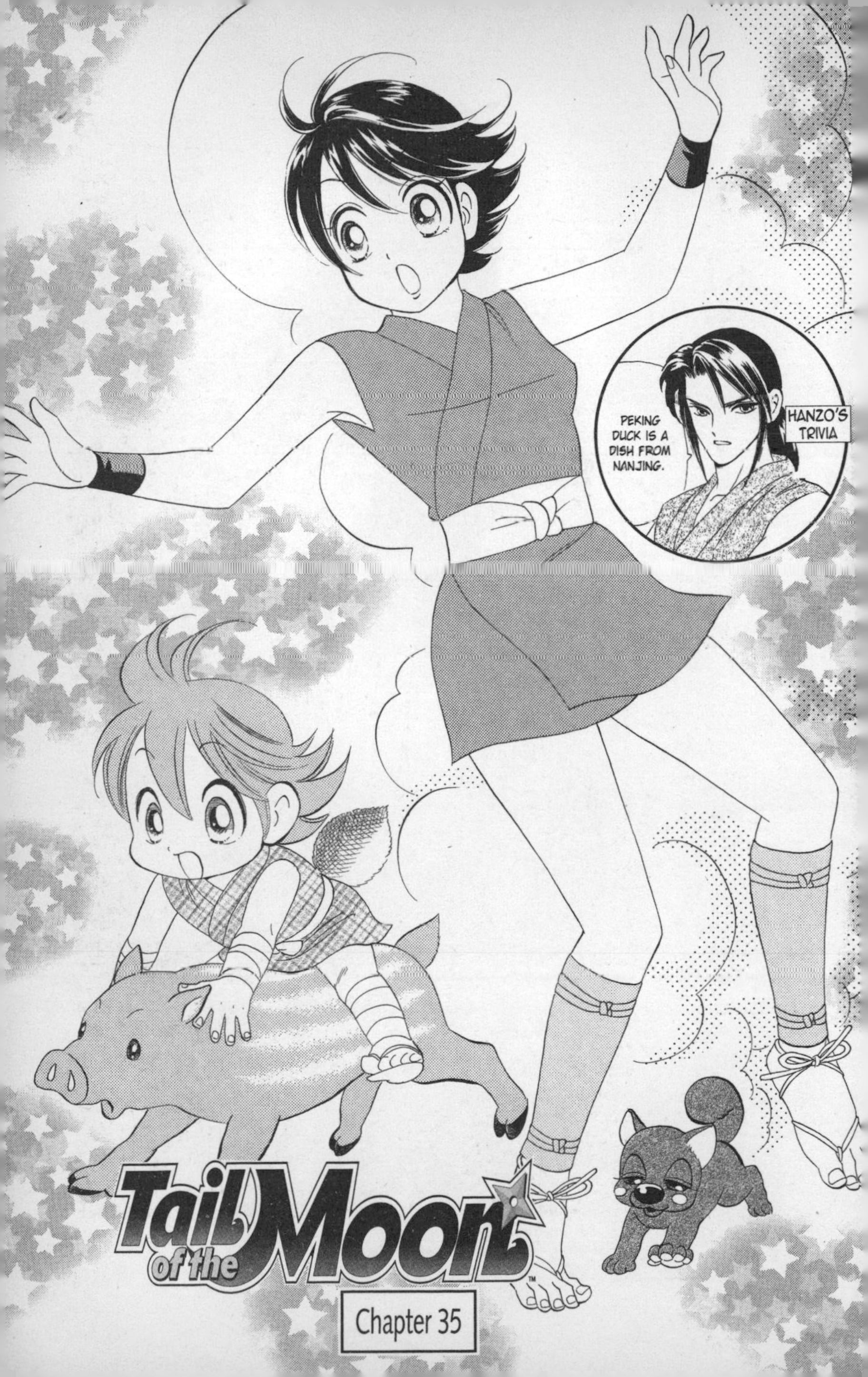
HANZO'S TRIVIA
PEKING DUCK IS A DISH FROM NANJING.
Tail of the Moon™
Chapter 35

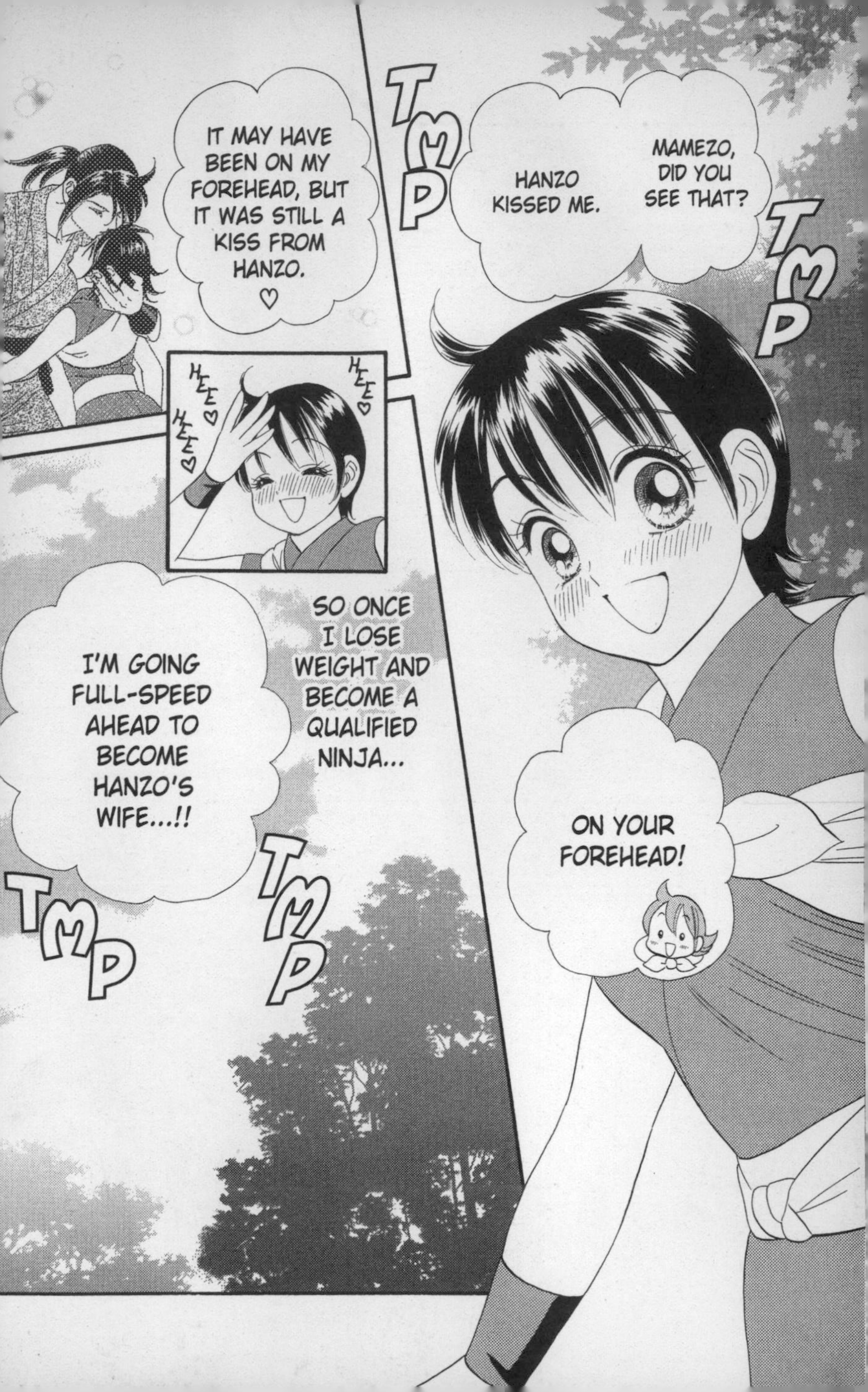
TMP
MAMEZO, DID YOU SEE THAT?
HANZO KISSED ME.
TMP
ON YOUR FOREHEAD!
TMP
IT MAY HAVE BEEN ON MY FOREHEAD, BUT IT WAS STILL A KISS FROM HANZO. ♡
HEE ♡
HEE ♡
HEE ♡
SO ONCE I LOSE WEIGHT AND BECOME A QUALIFIED NINJA...
I'M GOING FULL-SPEED AHEAD TO BECOME HANZO'S WIFE...!!
TMP
TMP

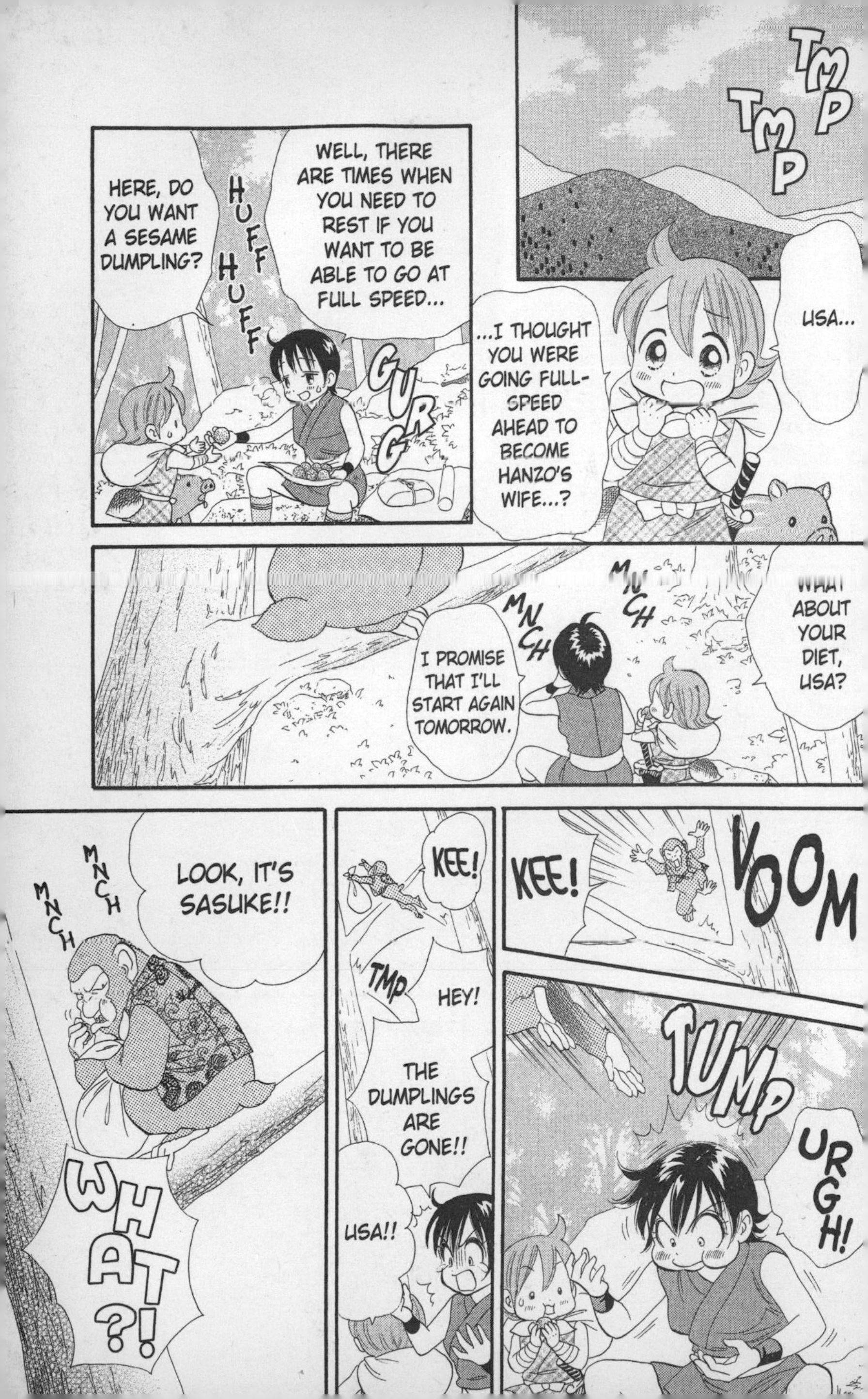
TMP
TMP
USA...
...I THOUGHT YOU WERE GOING FULL-SPEED AHEAD TO BECOME HANZO'S WIFE...?
WELL, THERE ARE TIMES WHEN YOU NEED TO REST IF YOU WANT TO BE ABLE TO GO AT FULL SPEED...
GURG
HUFF
HUFF
HERE, DO YOU WANT A SESAME DUMPLING?
WHAT ABOUT YOUR DIET, USA?
MNCH
MNCH
I PROMISE THAT I'LL START AGAIN TOMORROW.
VOOM
KEE!
TUMP
URGH!
KEE!
TMP
HEY!
THE DUMPLINGS ARE GONE!!
USA!!
LOOK, IT'S SASUKE!!
MNCH
MNCH
WHAT?!

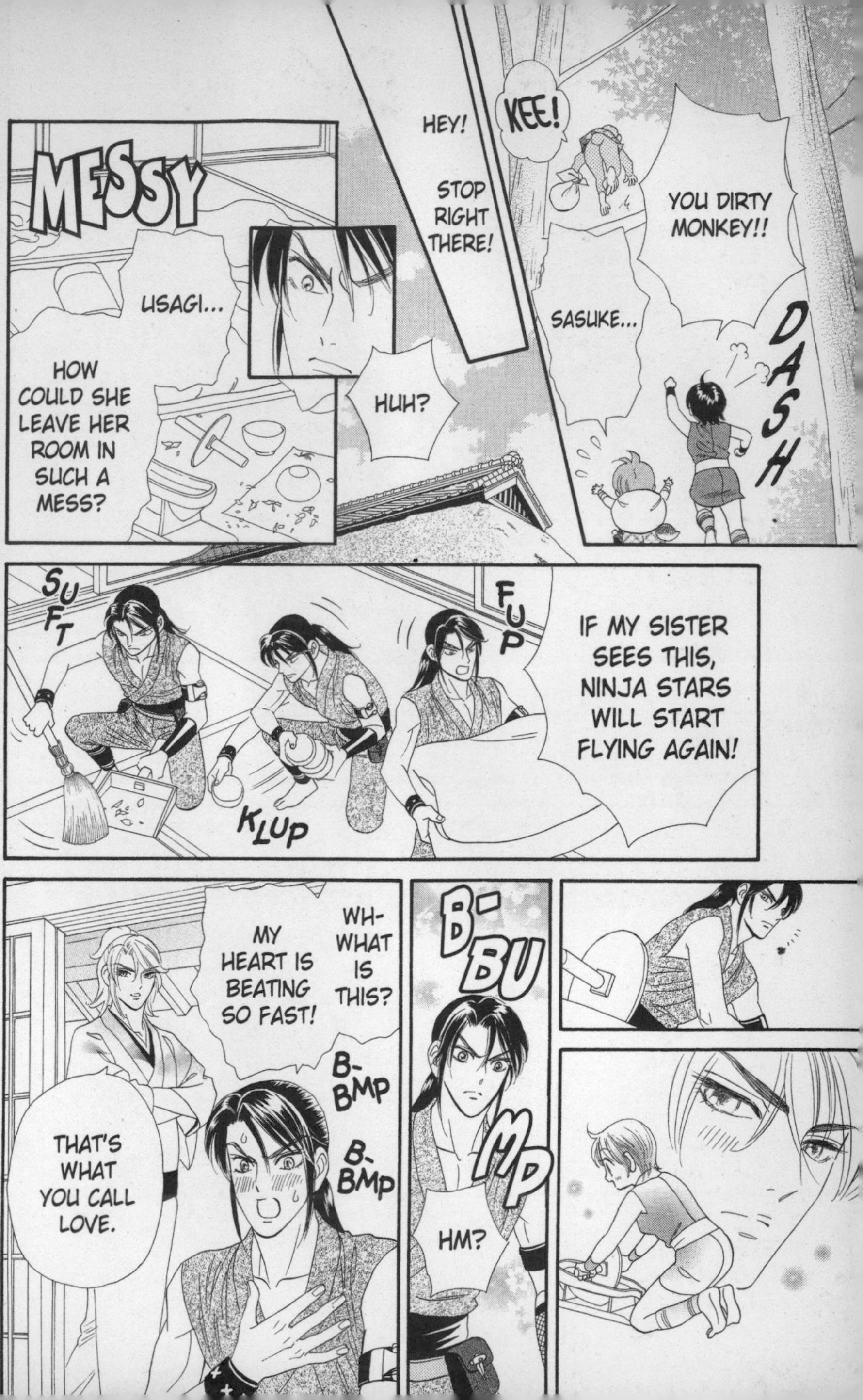
KEE!
YOU DIRTY MONKEY!!
SASUKE...
DASH
HEY!
STOP RIGHT THERE!
HUH?
MESSY
USAGI...
HOW COULD SHE LEAVE HER ROOM IN SUCH A MESS?
IF MY SISTER SEES THIS, NINJA STARS WILL START FLYING AGAIN!
FUP
KLUP
SUFT
B-BUMP
HM?
WH-WHAT IS THIS?
MY HEART IS BEATING SO FAST!
B-BMP
B-BMP
THAT'S WHAT YOU CALL LOVE.

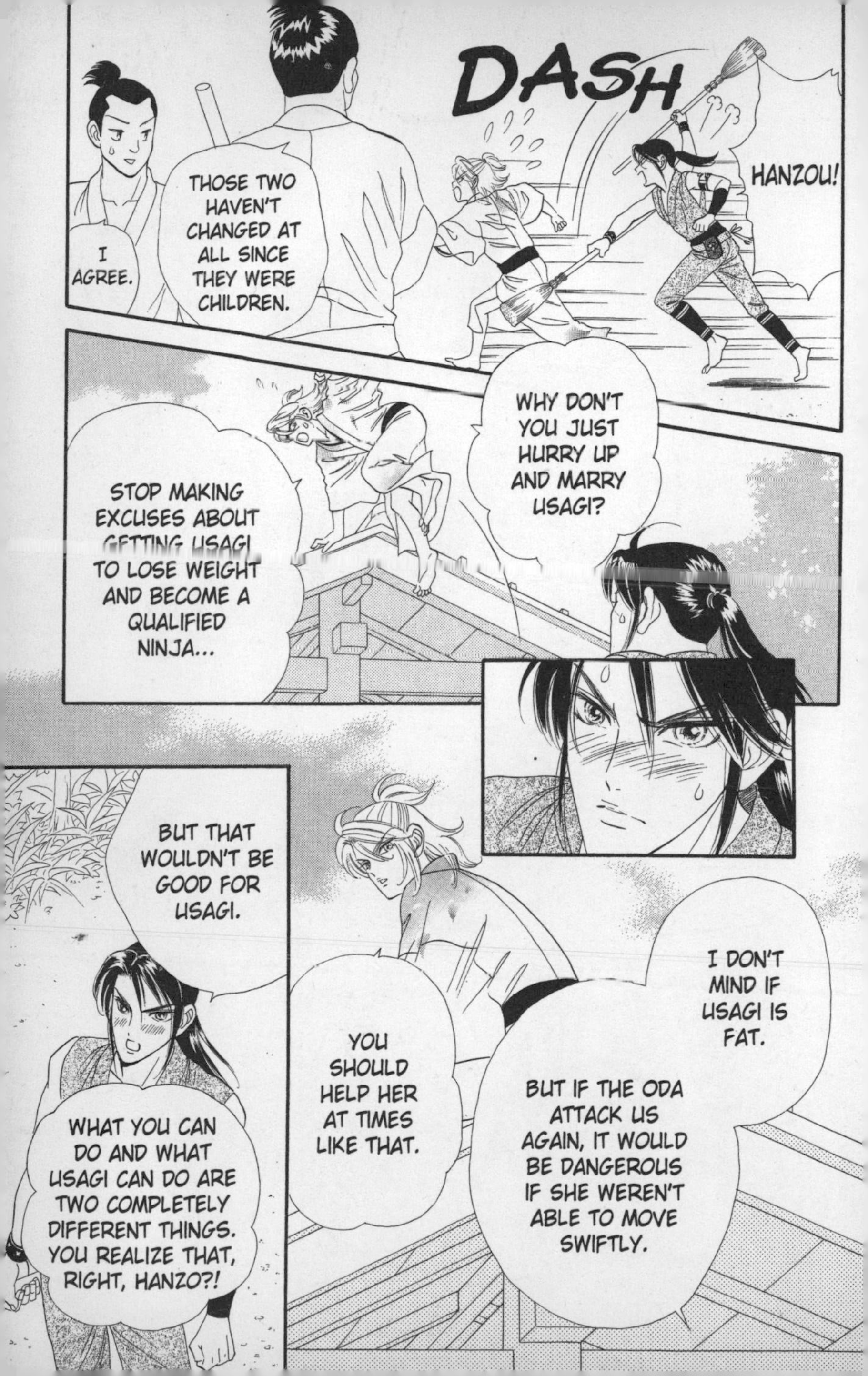
DASH
HANZOU!
THOSE TWO HAVEN'T CHANGED AT ALL SINCE THEY WERE CHILDREN.
I AGREE.
WHY DON'T YOU JUST HURRY UP AND MARRY USAGI?
STOP MAKING EXCUSES ABOUT GETTING USAGI TO LOSE WEIGHT AND BECOME A QUALIFIED NINJA...
I DON'T MIND IF USAGI IS FAT.
BUT IF THE ODA ATTACK US AGAIN, IT WOULD BE DANGEROUS IF SHE WEREN'T ABLE TO MOVE SWIFTLY.
YOU SHOULD HELP HER AT TIMES LIKE THAT.
BUT THAT WOULDN'T BE GOOD FOR USAGI.
WHAT YOU CAN DO AND WHAT USAGI CAN DO ARE TWO COMPLETELY DIFFERENT THINGS. YOU REALIZE THAT, RIGHT, HANZO?!

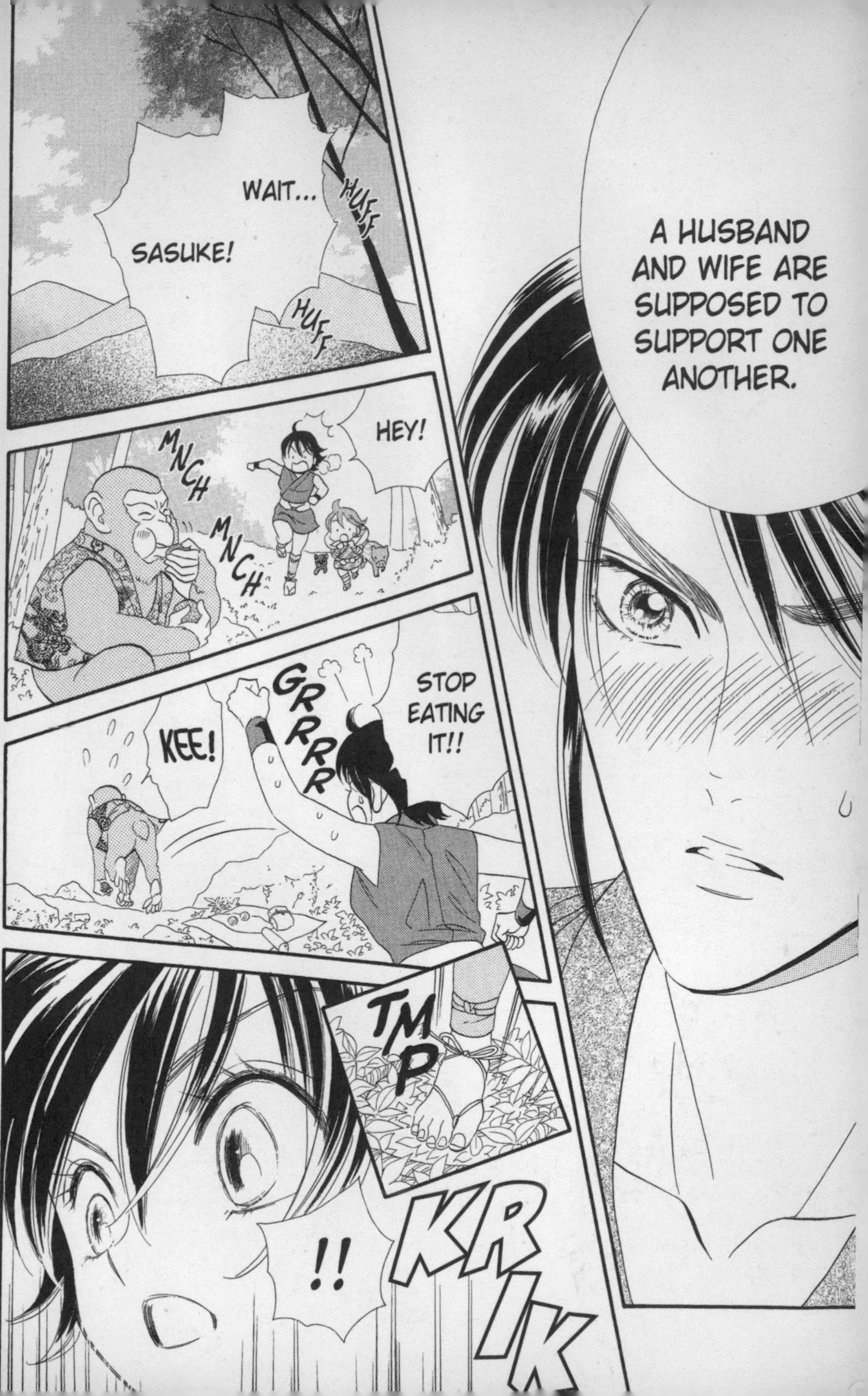
A HUSBAND AND WIFE ARE SUPPOSED TO SUPPORT ONE ANOTHER.
HUFF
WAIT...
SASUKE!
HUFF
HEY!
MNCH
MNCH
STOP EATING IT!!
GRRRR
KEE!
TMP
KRIK
!!

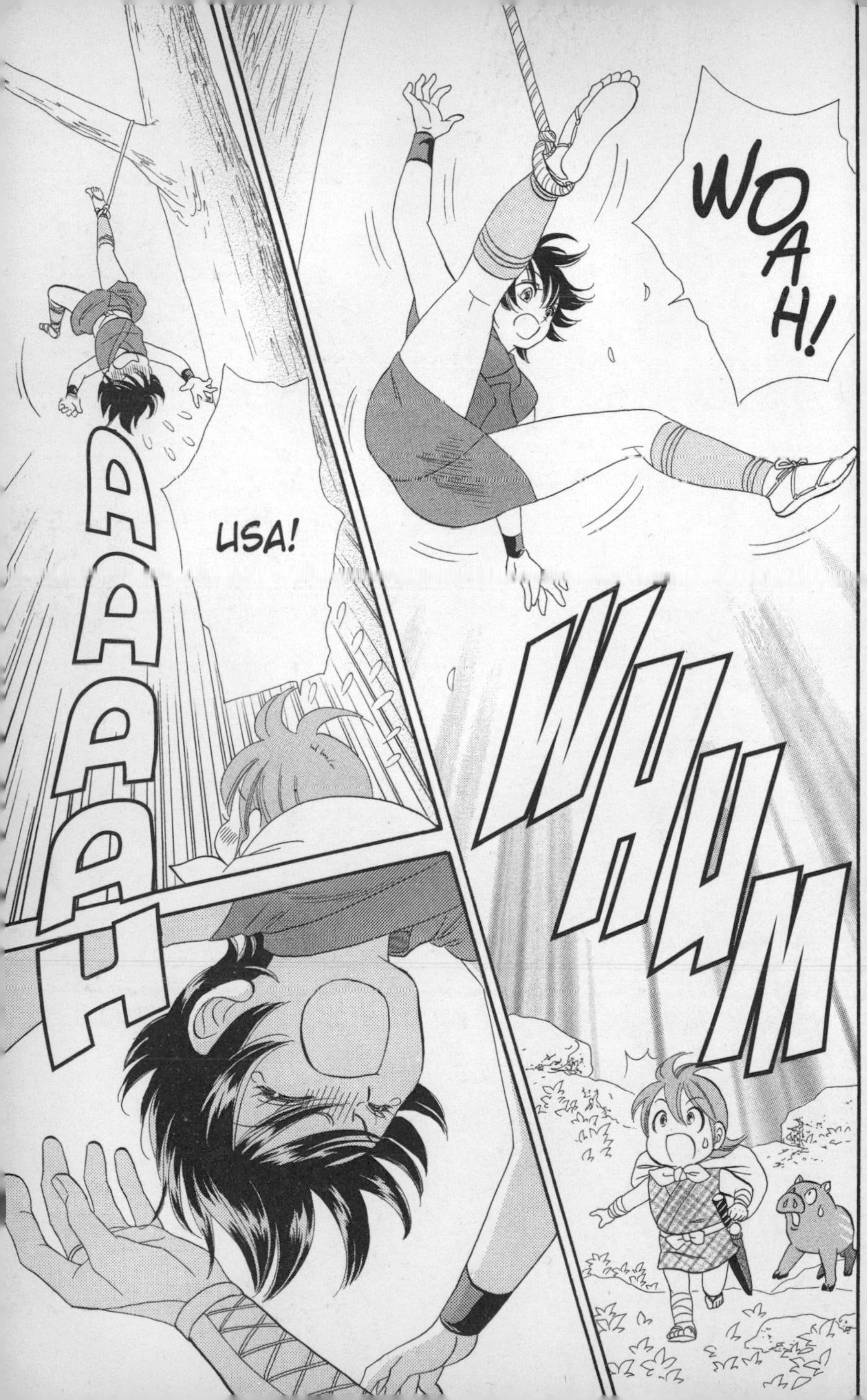
WOAH!
USA!
AAAAH
WHUMM

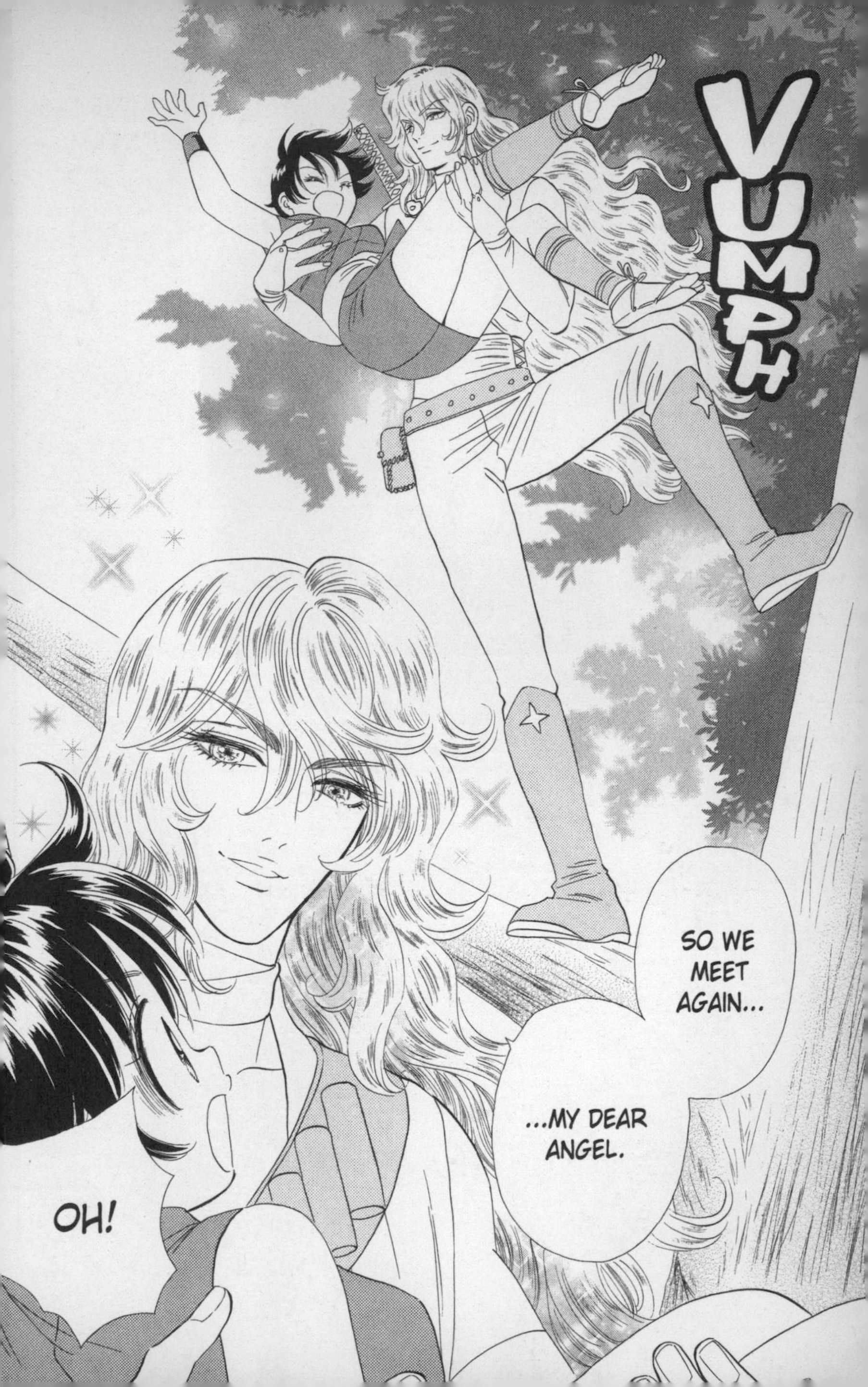
VUMPH
SO WE MEET AGAIN...
...MY DEAR ANGEL.
OH!

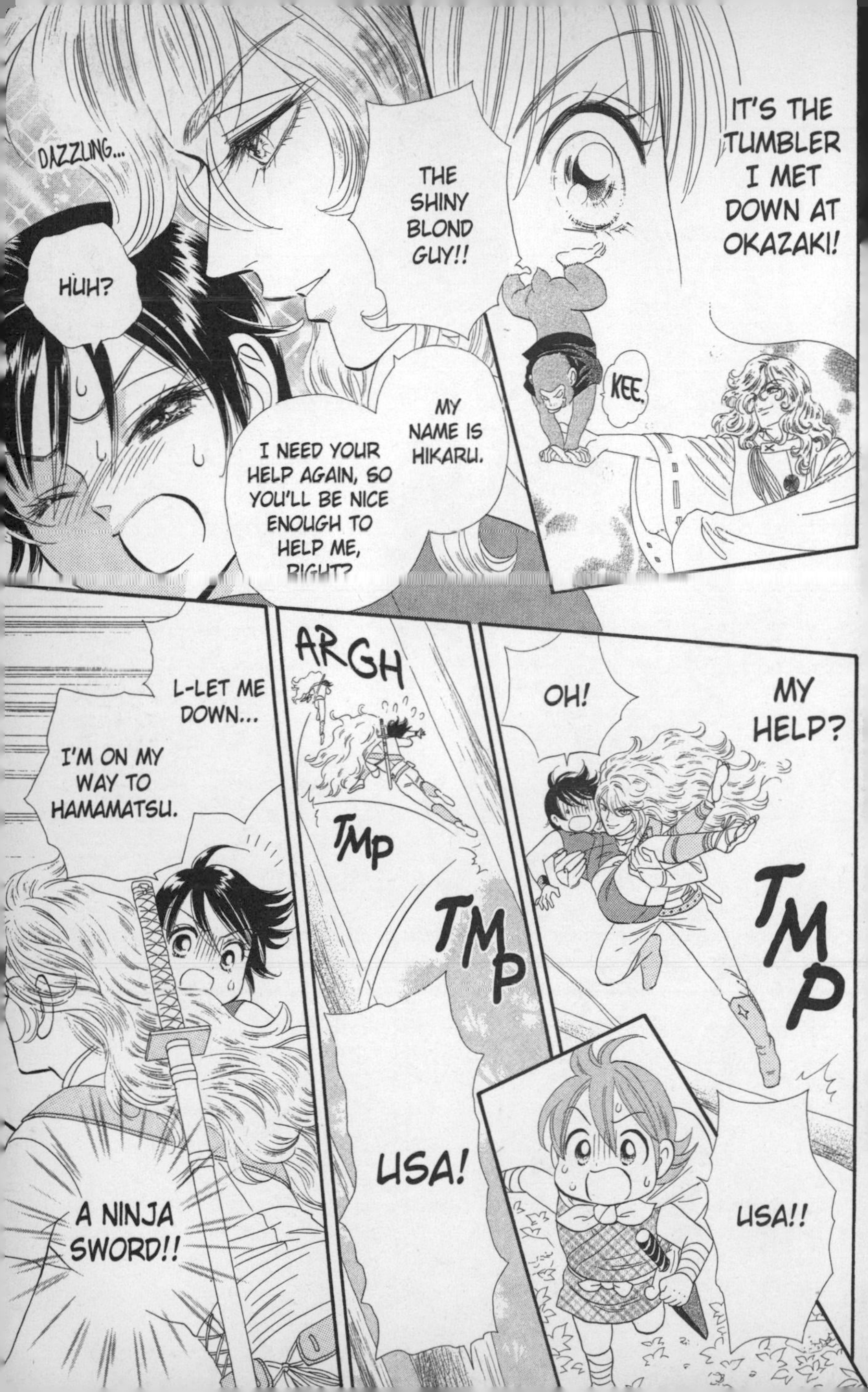
IT'S THE TUMBLER I MET DOWN AT OKAZAKI!
KEE.
THE SHINY BLOND GUY!!
DAZZLING...
HUH?
MY NAME IS HIKARU.
I NEED YOUR HELP AGAIN, SO YOU'LL BE NICE ENOUGH TO HELP ME, RIGHT?
MY HELP?
OH!
TMP
USA!!
ARGH
TMP
TMP
USA!
L-LET ME DOWN...
I'M ON MY WAY TO HAMAMATSU.
A NINJA SWORD!!

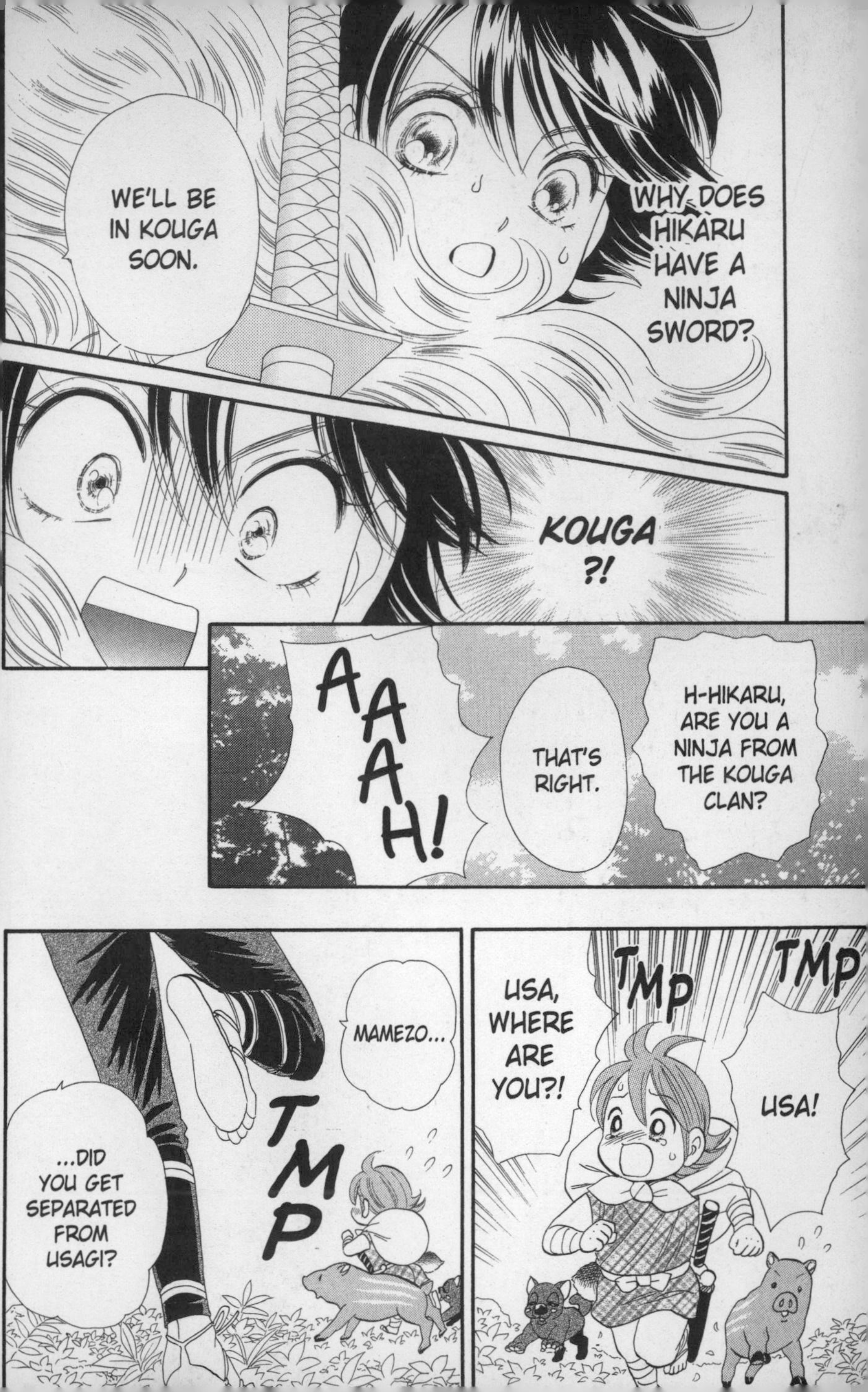
WHY DOES HIKARU HAVE A NINJA SWORD?
WE'LL BE IN KOUGA SOON.
KOUGA ?!
H-HIKARU, ARE YOU A NINJA FROM THE KOUGA CLAN?
THAT'S RIGHT.
AAAAH!
TMP
TMP
USA!
USA, WHERE ARE YOU?!
MAMEZO...
TMP
...DID YOU GET SEPARATED FROM USAGI?

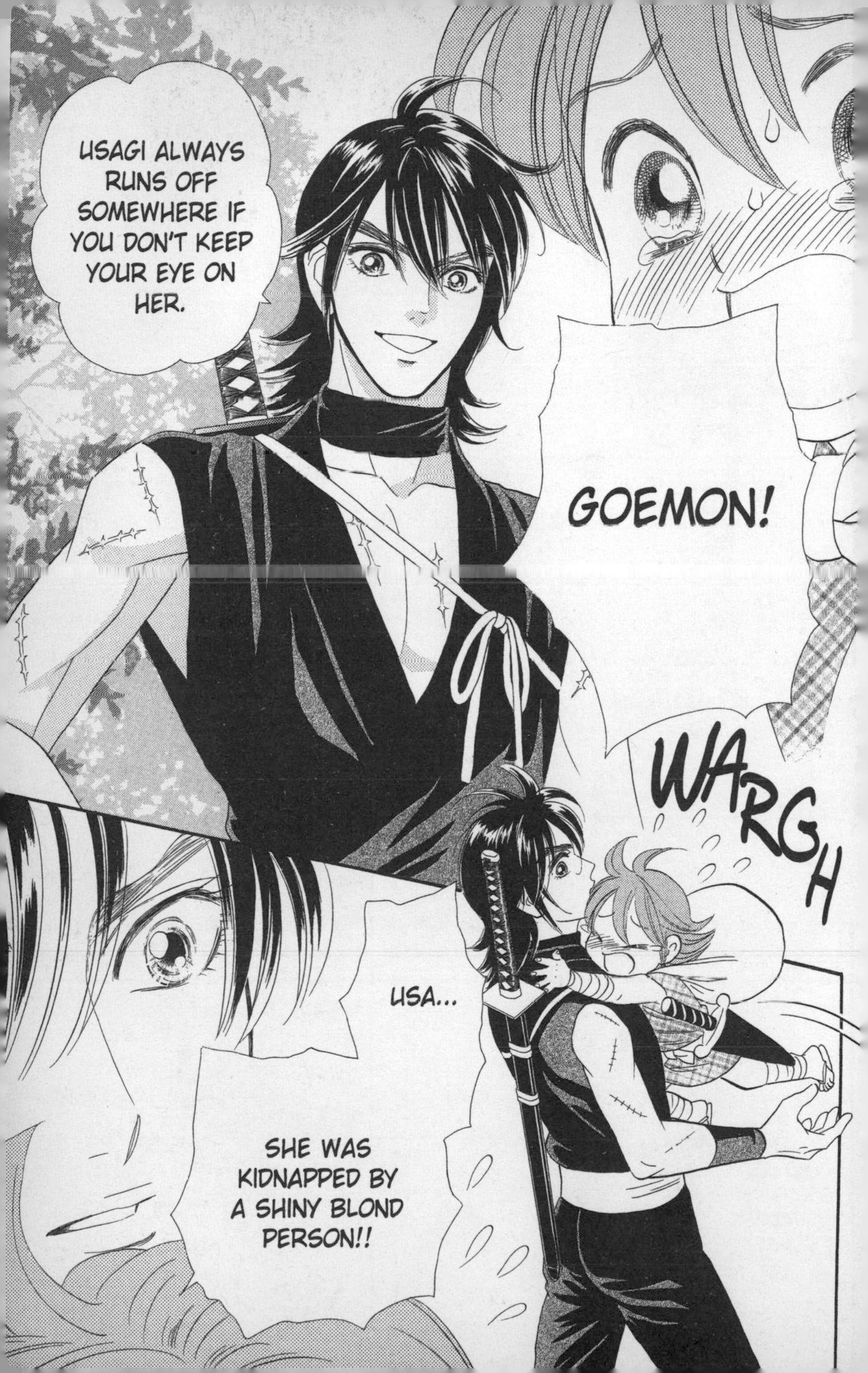
GOEMON!
USAGI ALWAYS RUNS OFF SOMEWHERE IF YOU DON'T KEEP YOUR EYE ON HER.
WARGH
USA...
SHE WAS KIDNAPPED BY A SHINY BLOND PERSON!!

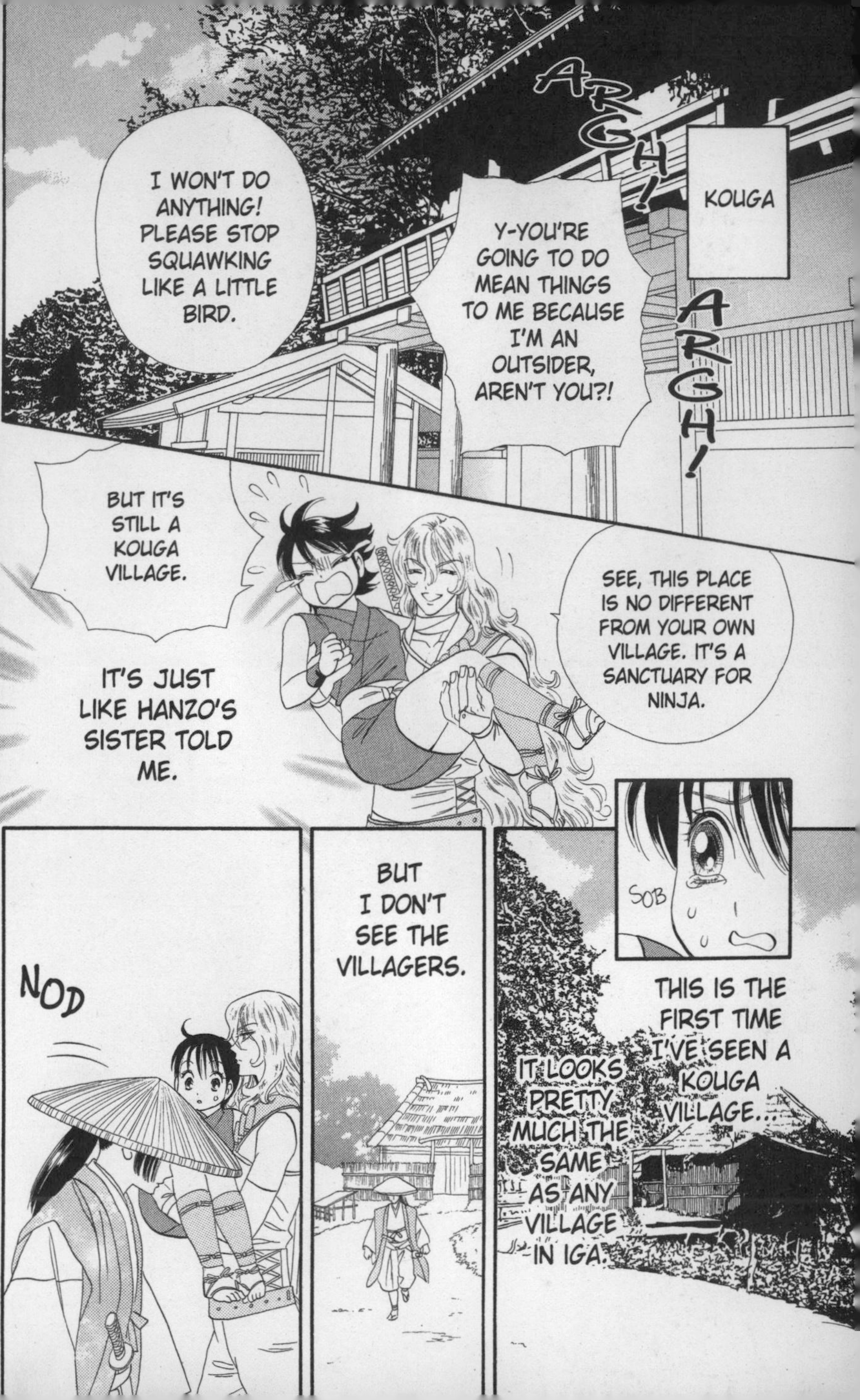
KOUGA
ARGH! ARGH!
Y-YOU'RE GOING TO DO MEAN THINGS TO ME BECAUSE I'M AN OUTSIDER, AREN'T YOU?!
I WON'T DO ANYTHING! PLEASE STOP SQUAWKING LIKE A LITTLE BIRD.
SEE, THIS PLACE IS NO DIFFERENT FROM YOUR OWN VILLAGE. IT'S A SANCTUARY FOR NINJA.
BUT IT'S STILL A KOUGA VILLAGE.
IT'S JUST LIKE HANZO'S SISTER TOLD ME.
SOB
THIS IS THE FIRST TIME I'VE SEEN A KOUGA VILLAGE...
IT LOOKS PRETTY MUCH THE SAME AS ANY VILLAGE IN IGA.
BUT I DON'T SEE THE VILLAGERS.
NOD

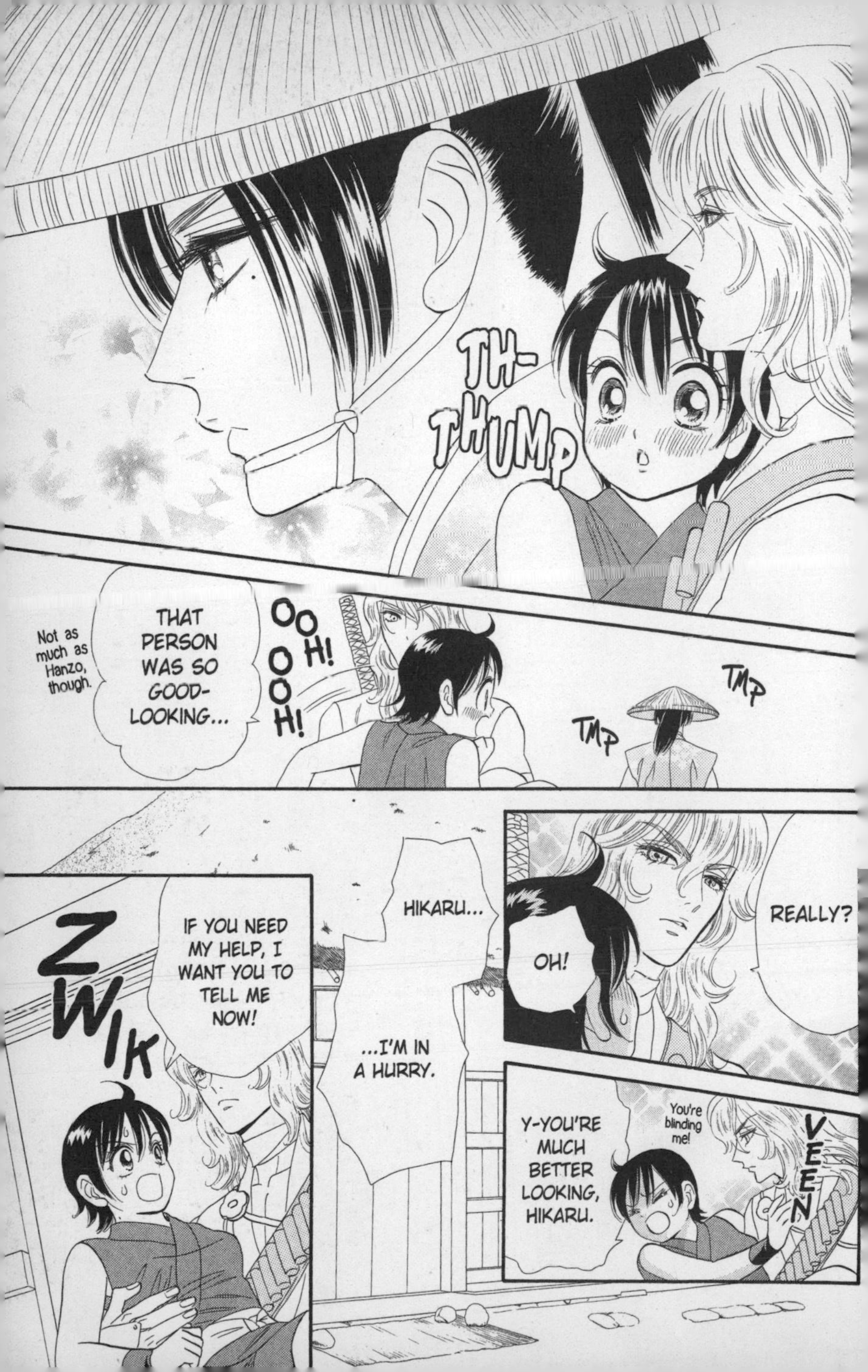
TH-THUMP
TMP
TMP
OOOH!
OOOH!
THAT PERSON WAS SO GOOD-LOOKING...
Not as much as Hanzo, though.
REALLY?
OH!
VEEN
You're blinding me!
Y-YOU'RE MUCH BETTER LOOKING, HIKARU.
HIKARU...
...I'M IN A HURRY.
IF YOU NEED MY HELP, I WANT YOU TO TELL ME NOW!
ZWIK

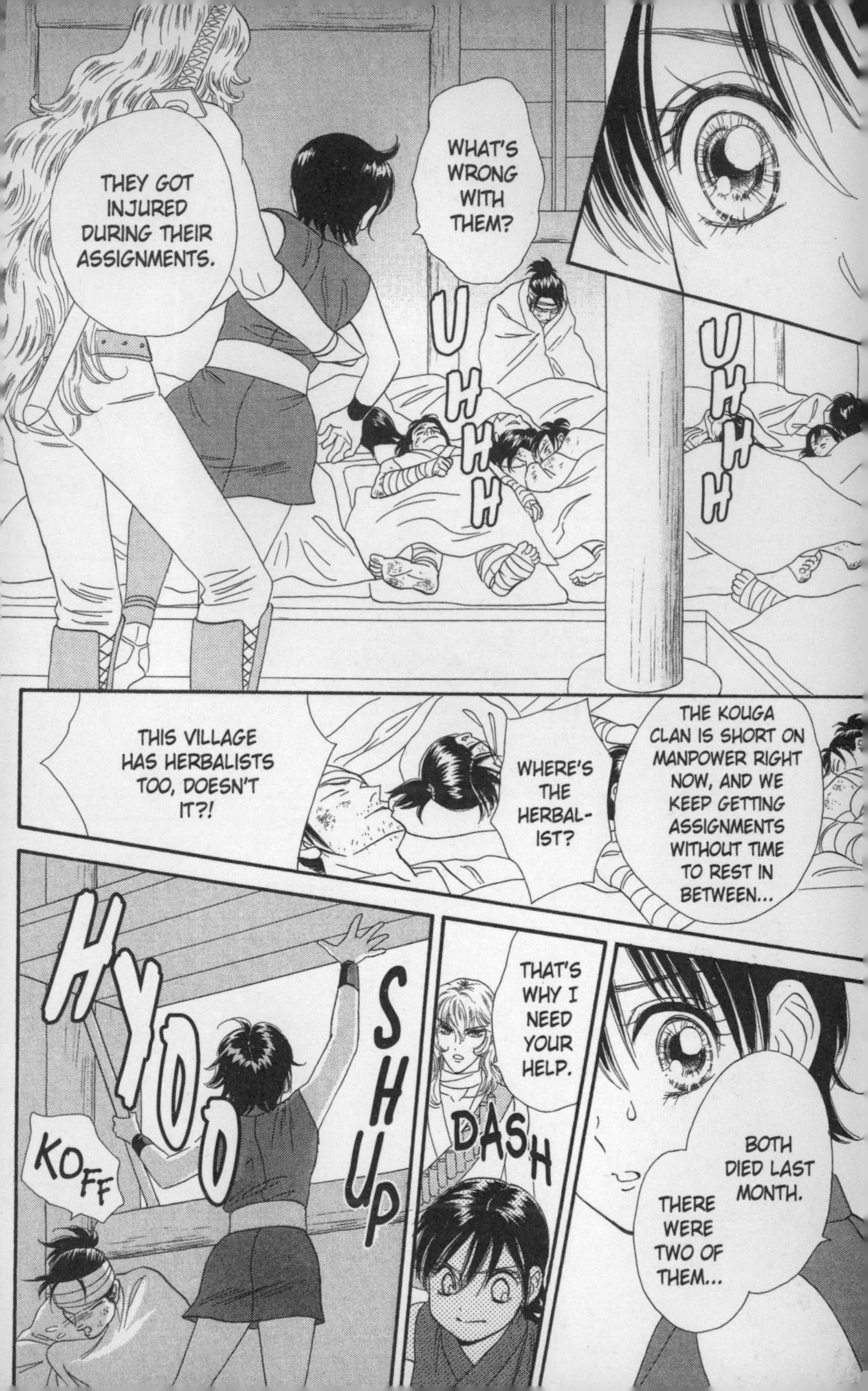
UHHHH
WHAT'S WRONG WITH THEM?
UHHHH
THEY GOT INJURED DURING THEIR ASSIGNMENTS.
THE KOUGA CLAN IS SHORT ON MANPOWER RIGHT NOW, AND WE KEEP GETTING ASSIGNMENTS WITHOUT TIME TO REST IN BETWEEN...
WHERE'S THE HERBALIST?
THIS VILLAGE HAS HERBALISTS TOO, DOESN'T IT?!
THERE WERE TWO OF THEM...
BOTH DIED LAST MONTH.
THAT'S WHY I NEED YOUR HELP.
SHUP
DASH
HYOO
KOFF

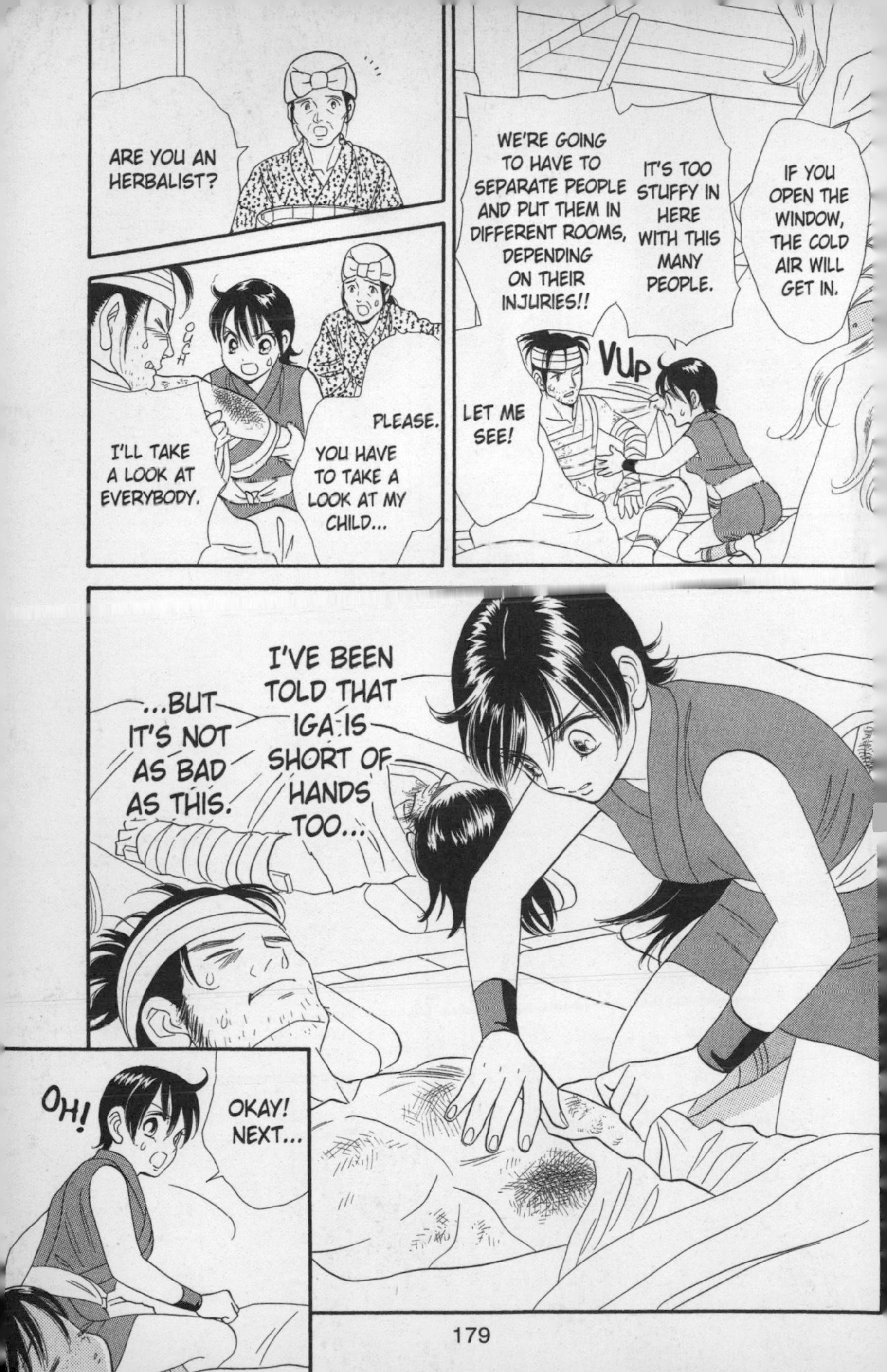
IF YOU OPEN THE WINDOW, THE COLD AIR WILL GET IN.
IT'S TOO STUFFY IN HERE WITH THIS MANY PEOPLE.
WE'RE GOING TO HAVE TO SEPARATE PEOPLE AND PUT THEM IN DIFFERENT ROOMS, DEPENDING ON THEIR INJURIES!!
VUp
LET ME SEE!
ARE YOU AN HERBALIST?
PLEASE.
YOU HAVE TO TAKE A LOOK AT MY CHILD...
OUCH
I'LL TAKE A LOOK AT EVERYBODY.
I'VE BEEN TOLD THAT IGA IS SHORT OF HANDS TOO...
...BUT IT'S NOT AS BAD AS THIS.
OKAY! NEXT...
OH!

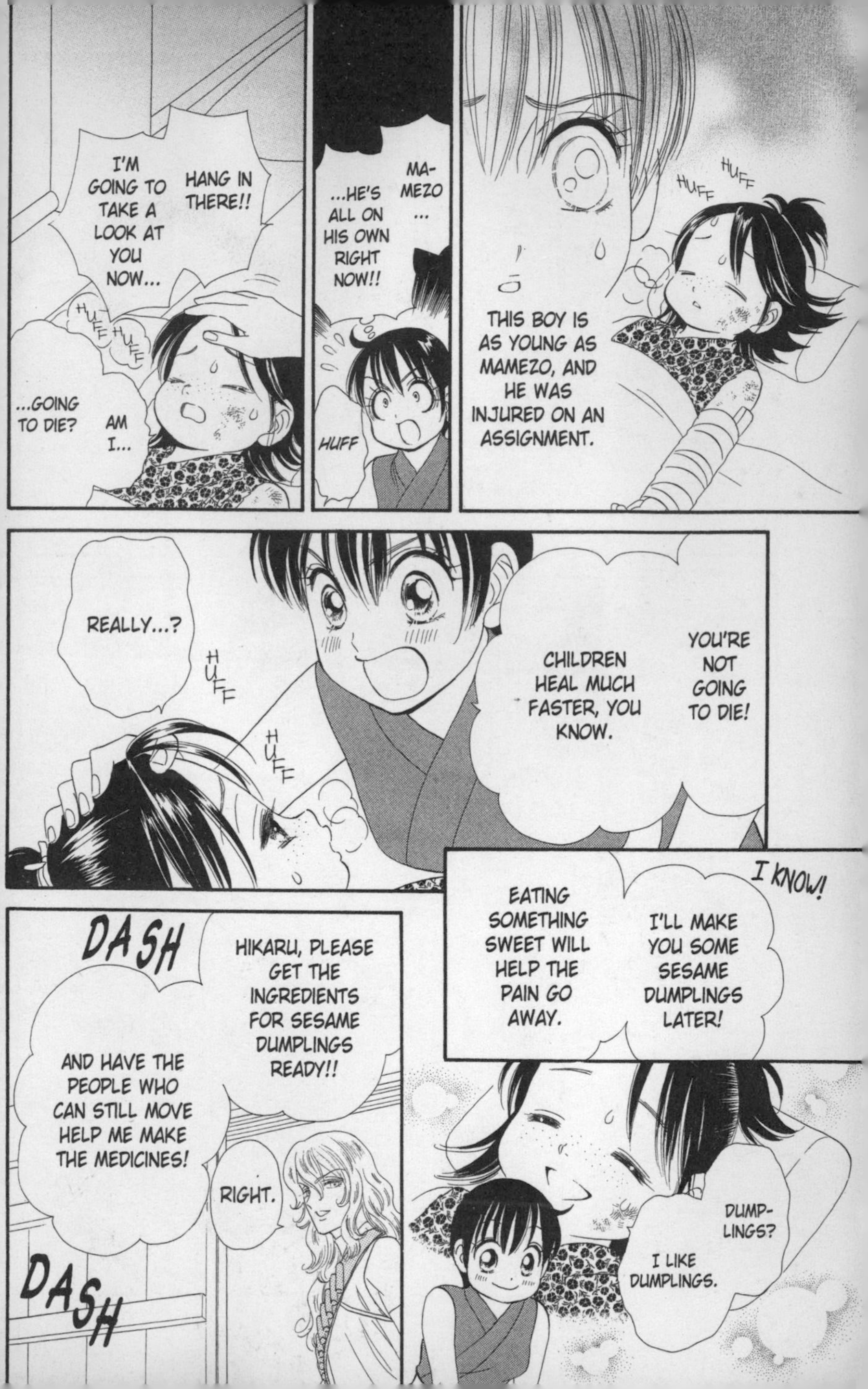
HUFF
HUFF
THIS BOY IS AS YOUNG AS MAMEZO, AND HE WAS INJURED ON AN ASSIGNMENT.
MA-MEZO ...
...HE'S ALL ON HIS OWN RIGHT NOW!!
HUFF
HANG IN THERE!!
I'M GOING TO TAKE A LOOK AT YOU NOW...
HUFF HUFF
AM I...
...GOING TO DIE?
YOU'RE NOT GOING TO DIE!
CHILDREN HEAL MUCH FASTER, YOU KNOW.
HUFF
HUFF
REALLY...?
I KNOW!
I'LL MAKE YOU SOME SESAME DUMPLINGS LATER!
EATING SOMETHING SWEET WILL HELP THE PAIN GO AWAY.
DUMP-LINGS?
I LIKE DUMPLINGS.
DASH
HIKARU, PLEASE GET THE INGREDIENTS FOR SESAME DUMPLINGS READY!!
AND HAVE THE PEOPLE WHO CAN STILL MOVE HELP ME MAKE THE MEDICINES!
RIGHT.
DASH

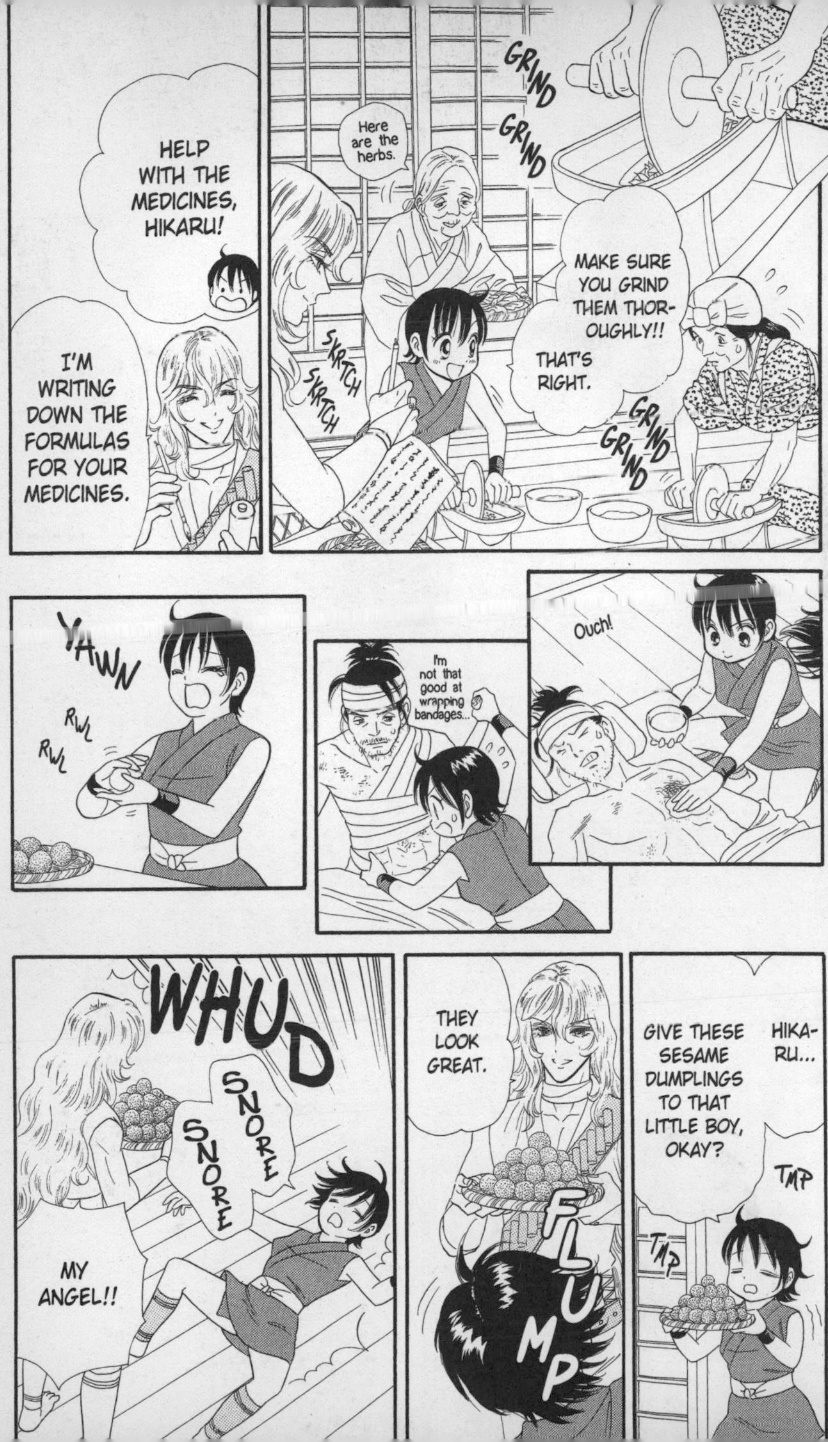
GRIND GRIND
Here are the herbs.
MAKE SURE YOU GRIND THEM THOR-OUGHLY!!
THAT'S RIGHT.
GRIND GRIND
SKRTCH SKRTCH
HELP WITH THE MEDICINES, HIKARU!
I'M WRITING DOWN THE FORMULAS FOR YOUR MEDICINES.
Ouch!
I'm not that good at wrapping bandages...
YAWN
RWL RWL
HIKA-RU...
GIVE THESE SESAME DUMPLINGS TO THAT LITTLE BOY, OKAY?
TMP
TMP
THEY LOOK GREAT.
FLUMP
WHUD
SNORE SNORE
MY ANGEL!!

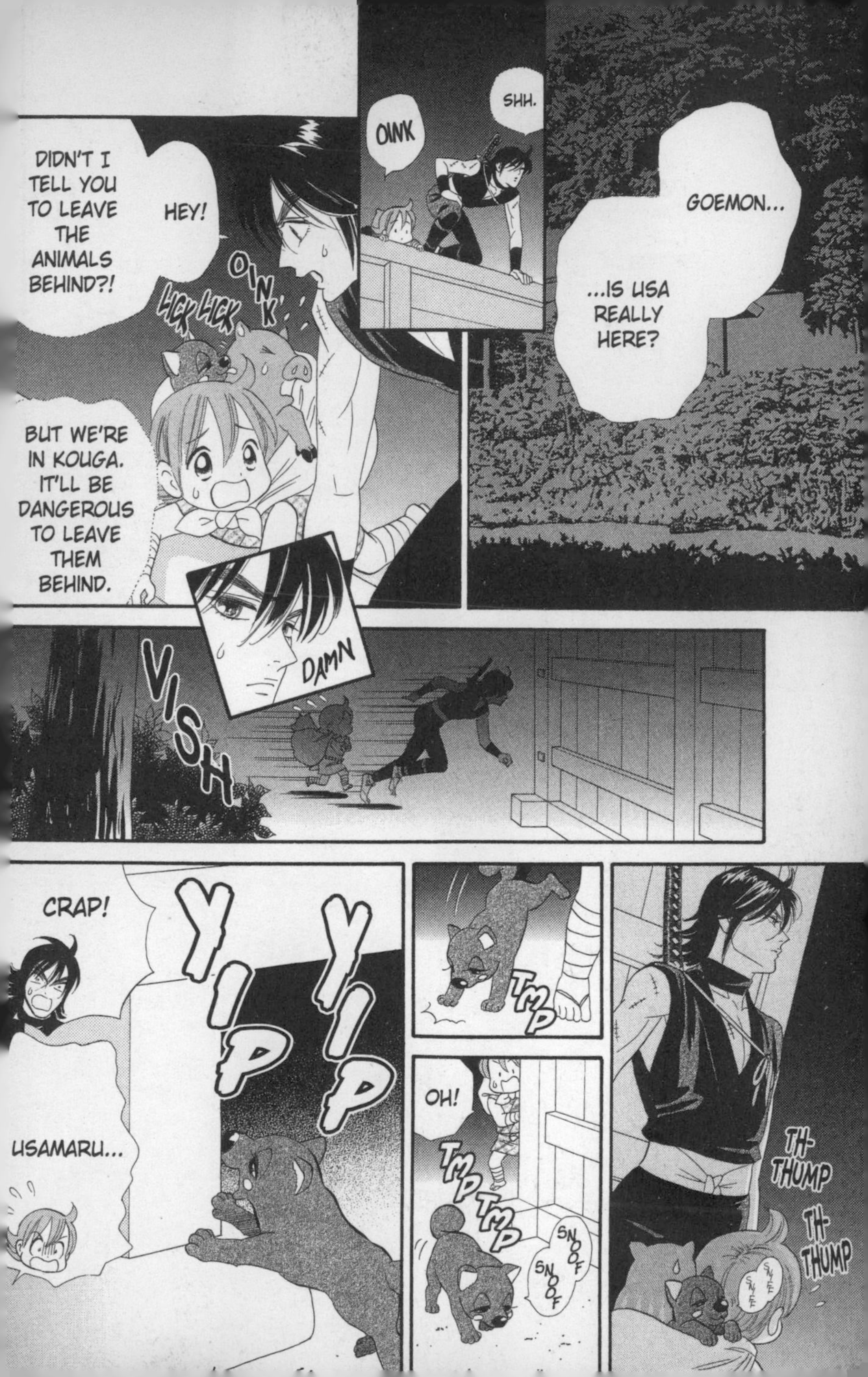
GOEMON...
...IS USA REALLY HERE?
SHH.
OINK
HEY!
DIDN'T I TELL YOU TO LEAVE THE ANIMALS BEHIND?!
OINK
LICK LICK
BUT WE'RE IN KOUGA. IT'LL BE DANGEROUS TO LEAVE THEM BEHIND.
DAMN
VISH
TH-THUMP
TH-THUMP
SNIFF
SNIFF
TMP
OH!
TMP TMP TMP
SNOOF
SNOOF
CRAP!
YIP
YIP
USAMARU...

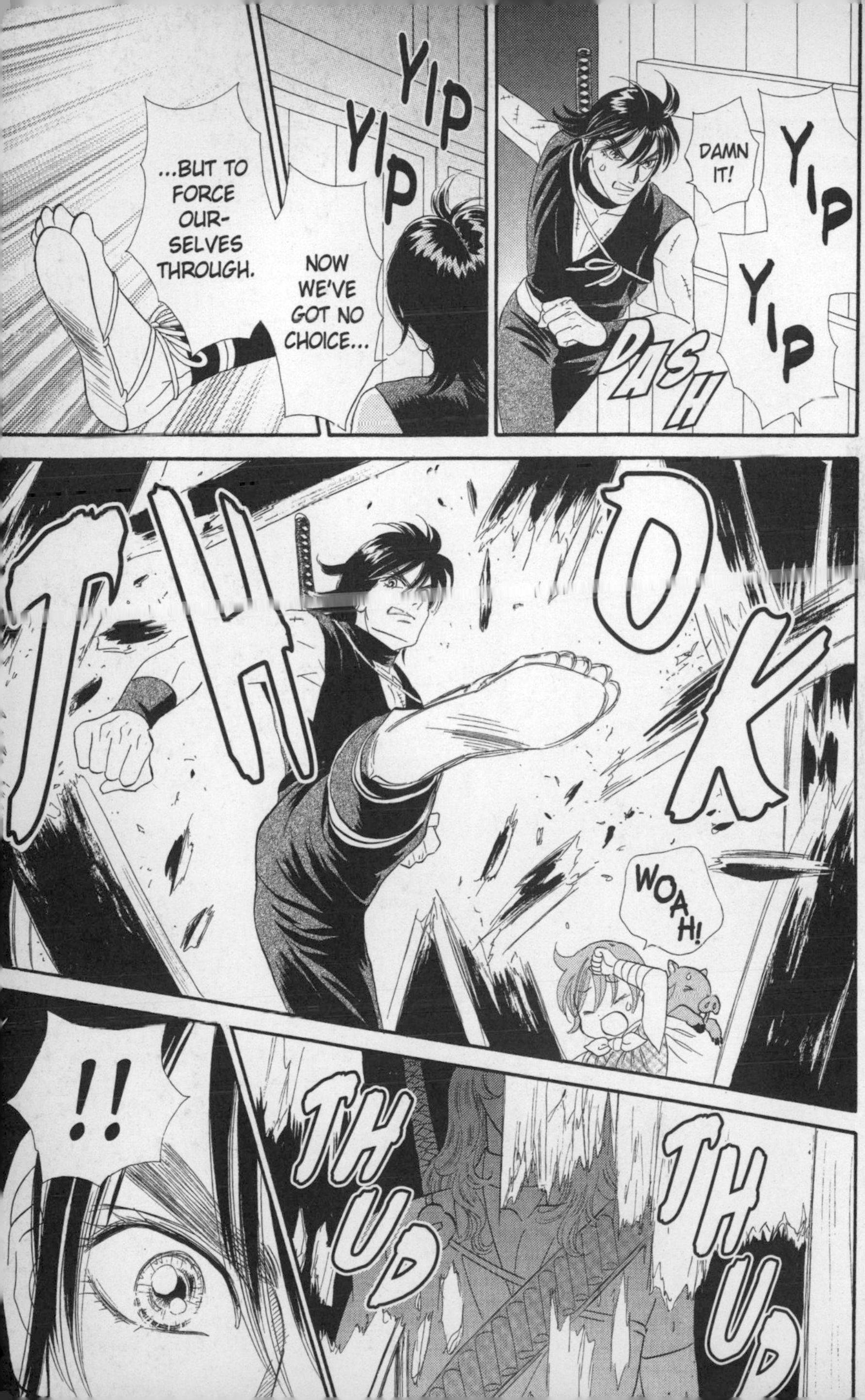
DAMN IT!
YIP YIP
YIP YIP
DASH
YIP YIP
NOW WE'VE GOT NO CHOICE...
...BUT TO FORCE OUR-SELVES THROUGH.
THOK
WOAH!
THUD
THUD
!!

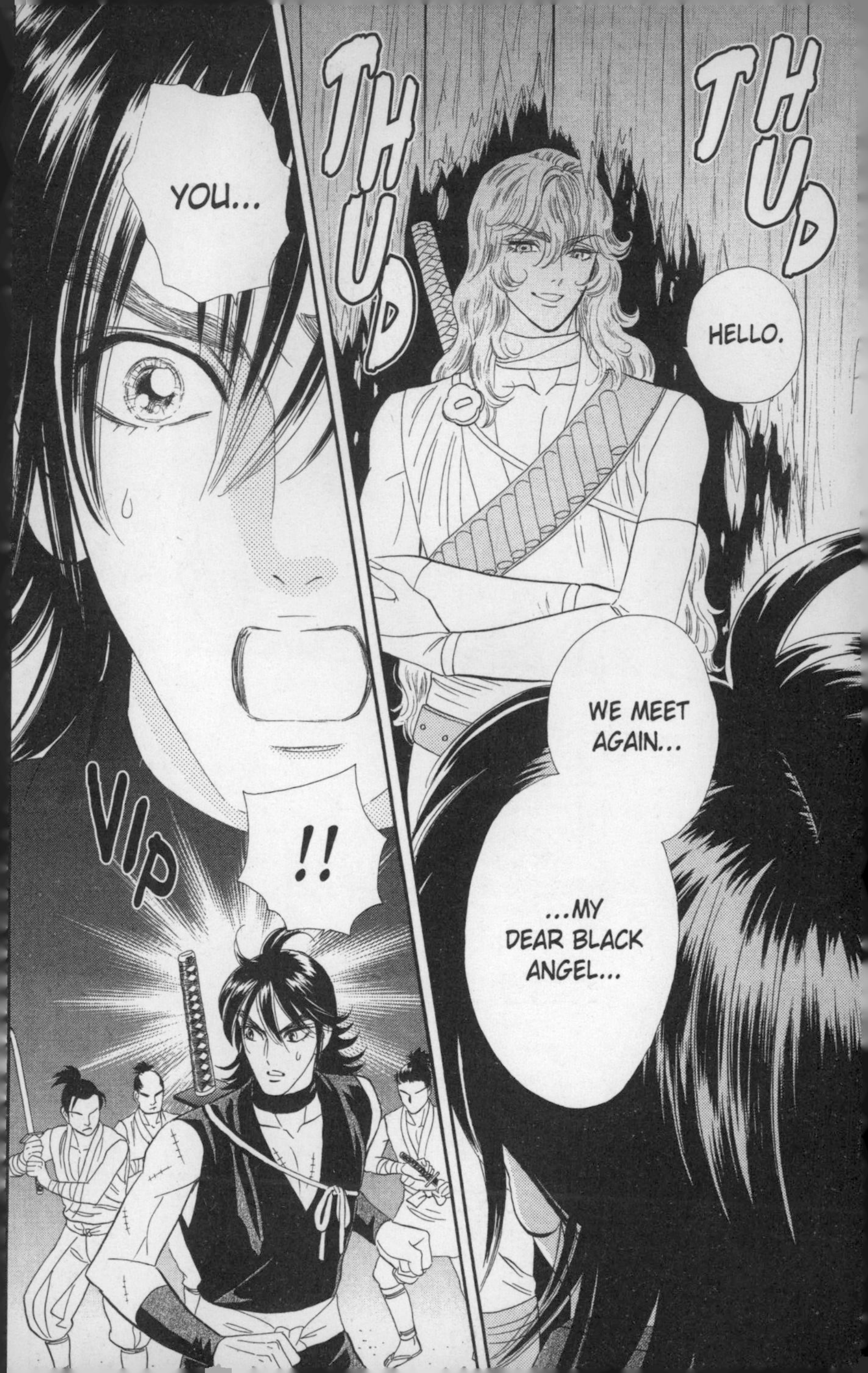
THUD
THUD
HELLO.
WE MEET AGAIN...
...MY DEAR BLACK ANGEL...
YOU...
VIP
!!

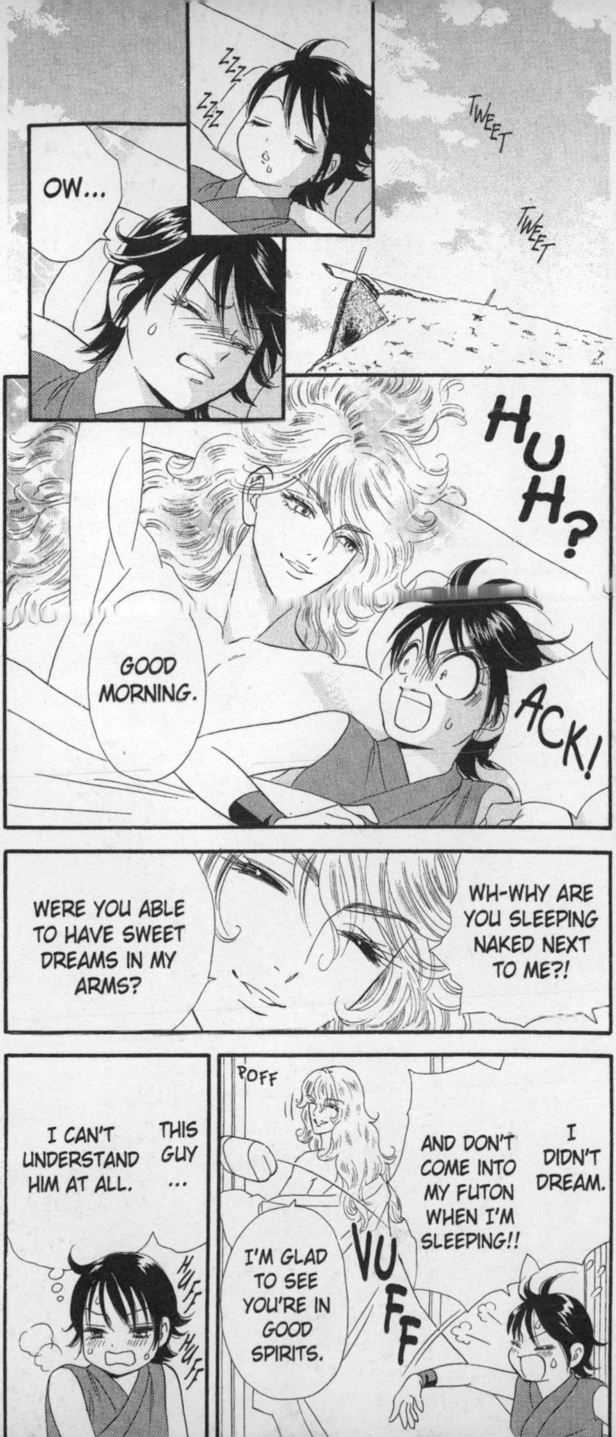
TWEET
TWEET
ZZZ
ZZZ
OW...
HUH?
ACK!
GOOD MORNING.
WH-WHY ARE YOU SLEEPING NAKED NEXT TO ME?!
WERE YOU ABLE TO HAVE SWEET DREAMS IN MY ARMS?
I DIDN'T DREAM.
AND DON'T COME INTO MY FUTON WHEN I'M SLEEPING!!
POFF
VUFF
I'M GLAD TO SEE YOU'RE IN GOOD SPIRITS.
THIS GUY...
I CAN'T UNDERSTAND HIM AT ALL.
HUFF
HUFF

We're waiting for your letters!

- There's still a lot to talk about for my trip to the Kouga-ryu Ninjutsu House, so I'll continue writing about it in the next volume. Please look forward to it!!
- For those who would like to see the characters in a particular room, address your requests to "Tail of the Moon Extra."
- And address fan letters to "Ueda Rinko"!

·····Address······

Tail of the Moon Editor
Viz Media
P.O. Box 77010
San Francisco, CA
94107

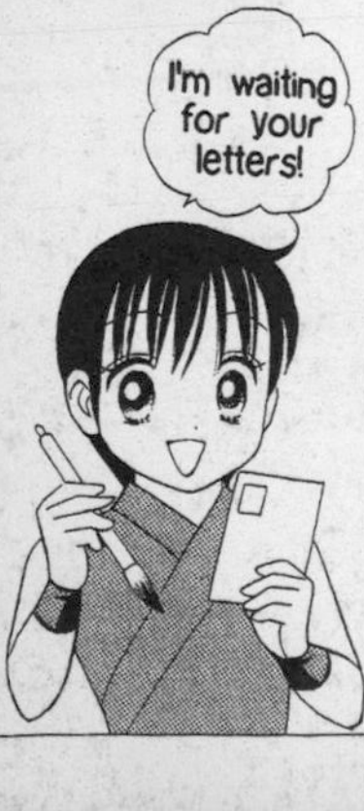
I'm waiting for your letters!

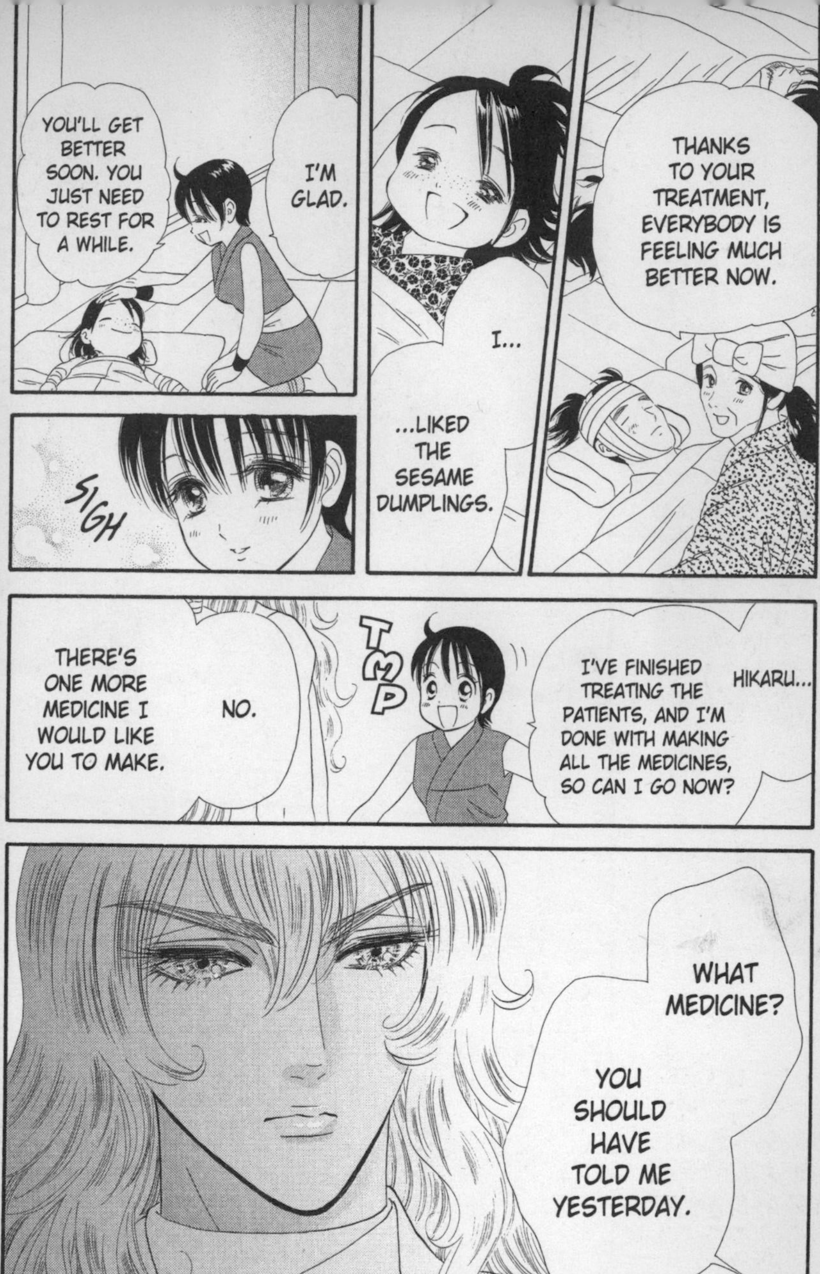
THANKS TO YOUR TREATMENT, EVERYBODY IS FEELING MUCH BETTER NOW.
I...
...LIKED THE SESAME DUMPLINGS.
I'M GLAD.
YOU'LL GET BETTER SOON. YOU JUST NEED TO REST FOR A WHILE.
SIGH
HIKARU...
I'VE FINISHED TREATING THE PATIENTS, AND I'M DONE WITH MAKING ALL THE MEDICINES, SO CAN I GO NOW?
TMP
NO.
THERE'S ONE MORE MEDICINE I WOULD LIKE YOU TO MAKE.
WHAT MEDICINE?
YOU SHOULD HAVE TOLD ME YESTERDAY.

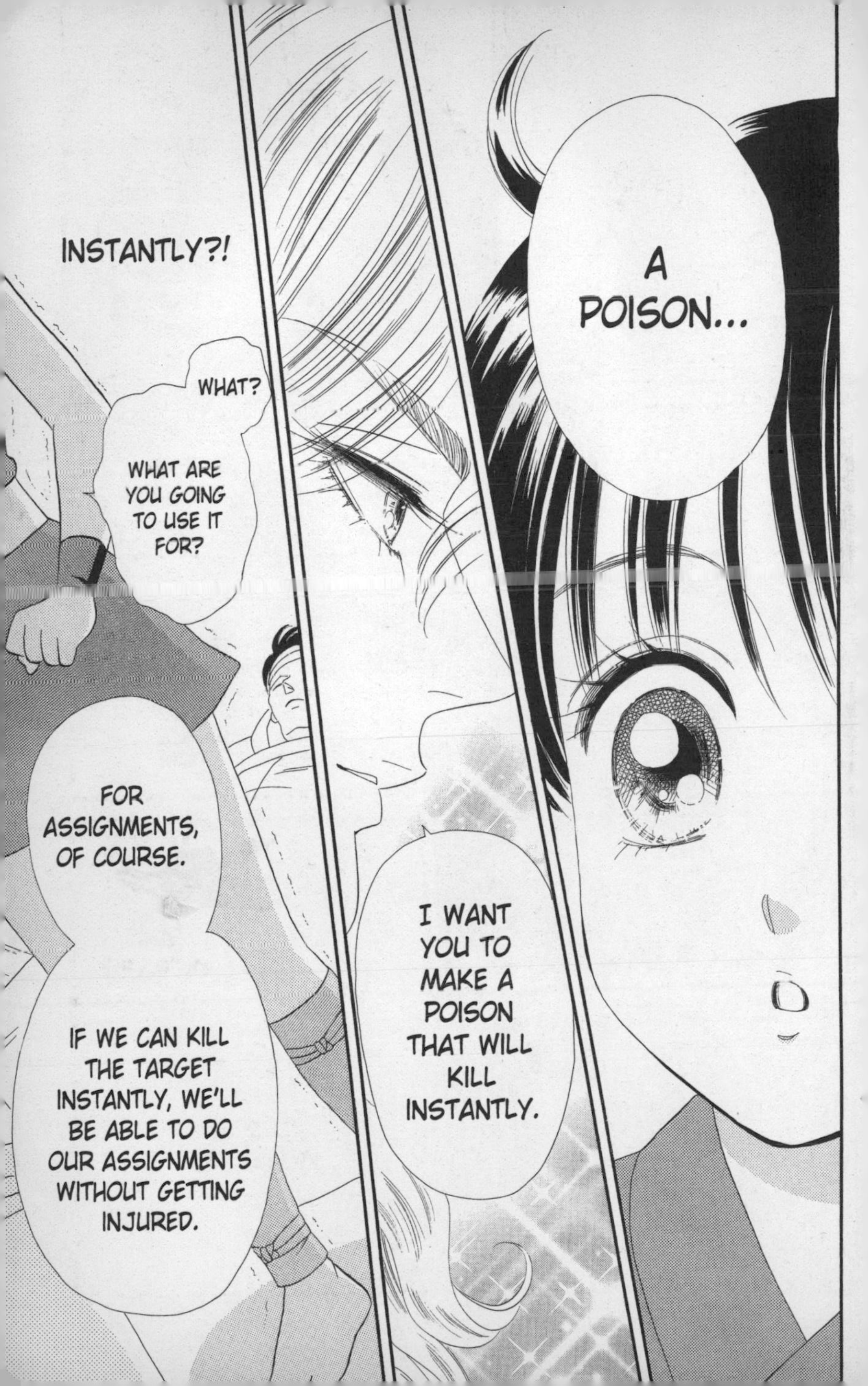
A POISON...
I WANT YOU TO MAKE A POISON THAT WILL KILL INSTANTLY.
INSTANTLY?!
WHAT?
WHAT ARE YOU GOING TO USE IT FOR?
FOR ASSIGNMENTS, OF COURSE.
IF WE CAN KILL THE TARGET INSTANTLY, WE'LL BE ABLE TO DO OUR ASSIGNMENTS WITHOUT GETTING INJURED.

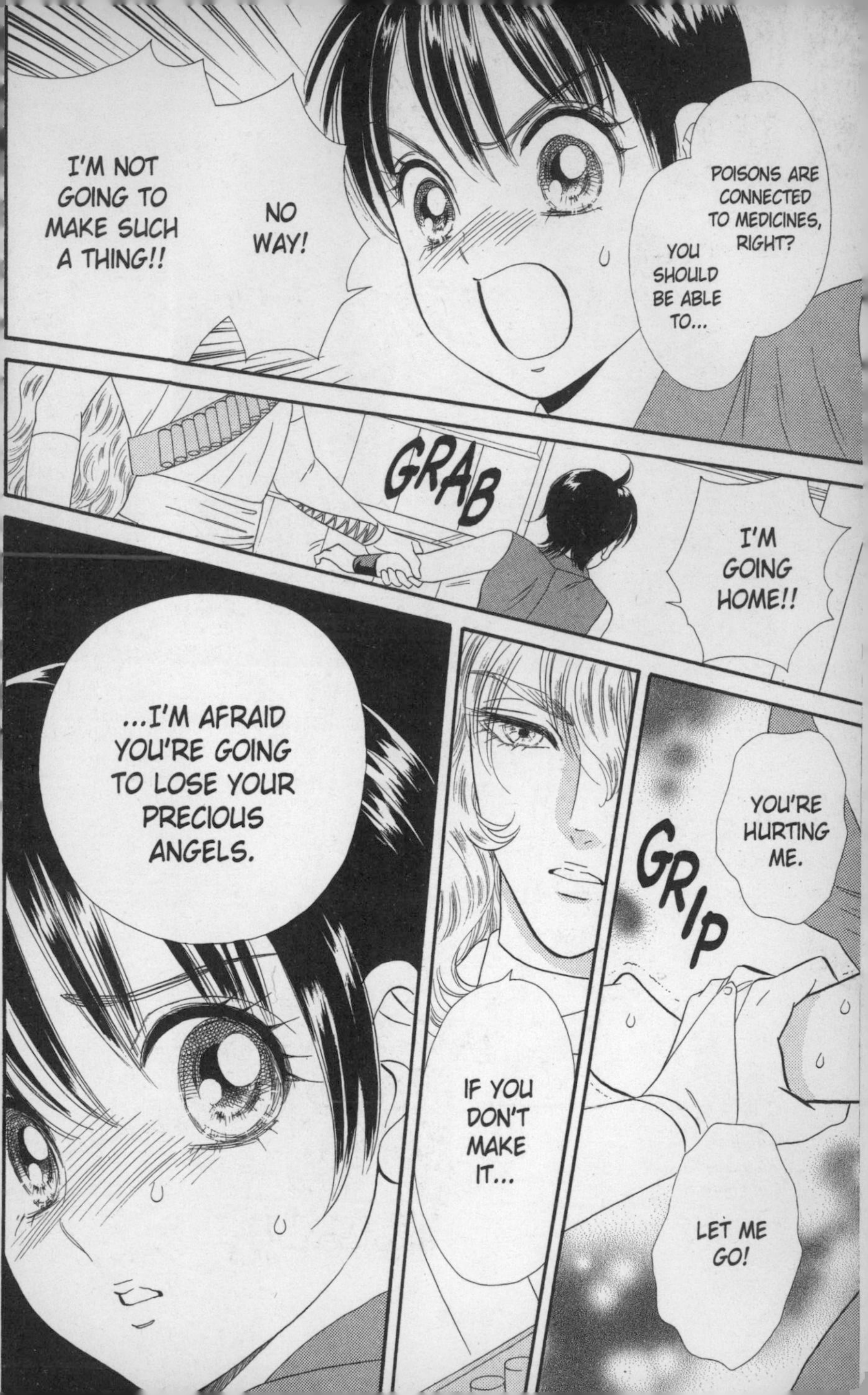
POISONS ARE CONNECTED TO MEDICINES, RIGHT?
YOU SHOULD BE ABLE TO...
NO WAY!
I'M NOT GOING TO MAKE SUCH A THING!!
GRAB
I'M GOING HOME!!
YOU'RE HURTING ME.
GRIP
LET ME GO!
IF YOU DON'T MAKE IT...
...I'M AFRAID YOU'RE GOING TO LOSE YOUR PRECIOUS ANGELS.

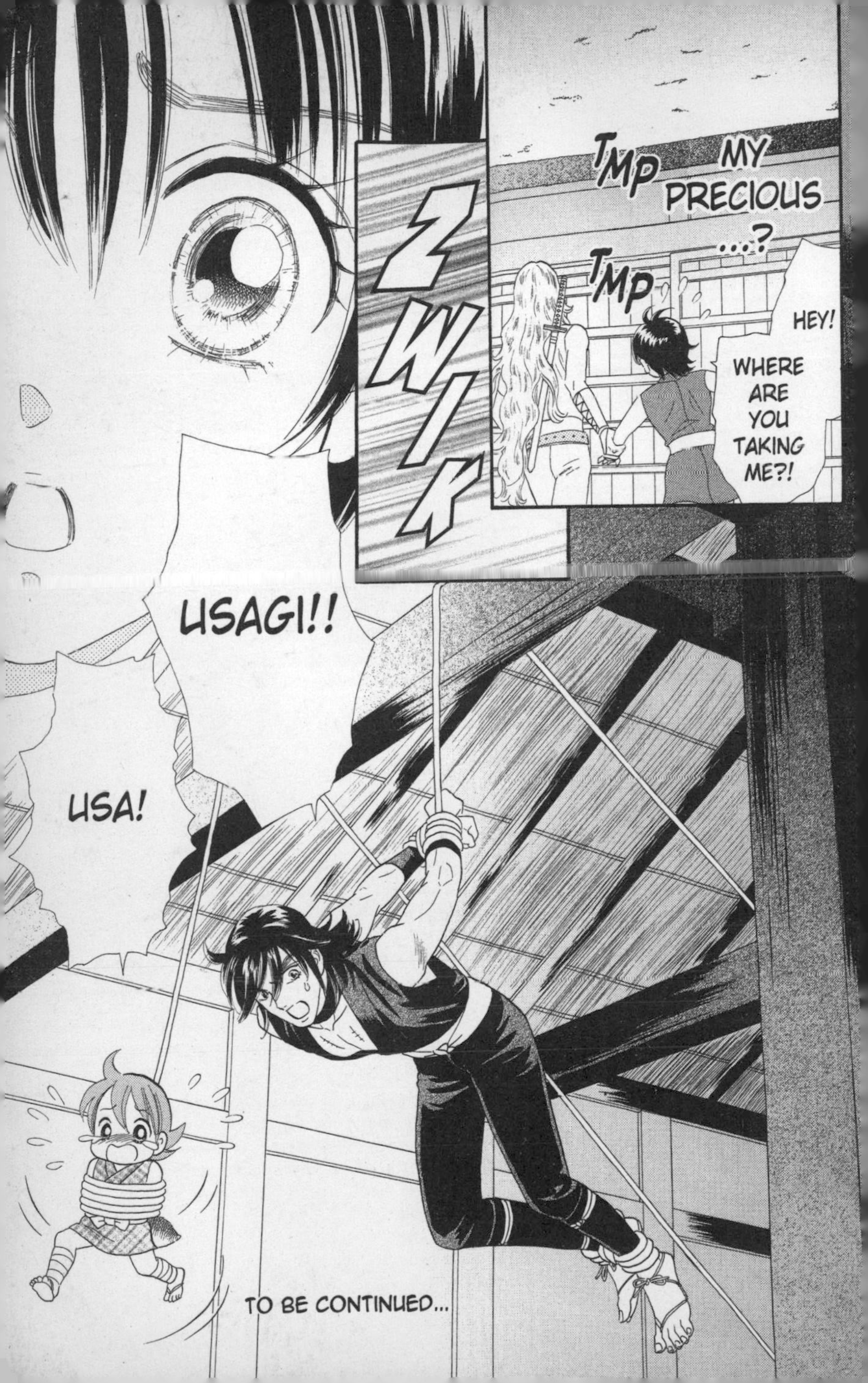
MY PRECIOUS ...?
TMP
TMP
HEY!
WHERE ARE YOU TAKING ME?!
ZWIK
USAGI!!
USA!
TO BE CONTINUED...

> *The ways of the ninja are mysterious indeed, so here is a glossary of terms to help you navigate the intricacies of their world.*

Page 85: Goemon-Buro
Goemon-buro literally translated means "Goemon-bath" or "Goemon-style bath." It is a unique Japanese bath that comes from the legend about a great thief, Ishikawa Goemon, who was boiled to death in a huge iron pot when he was caught. This bathtub is made of iron and is put in a fireplace to heat the water. Since the bottom is burning hot, the person taking the bath must put a wooden plank in the pot and step onto it when bathing.

Page 91: Hatomugi Tea
Hatomugi is a type of grain that Japanese people often eat and use to make tea.

Page 139: Sakura-Nabe and Botan-Nabe
These are traditional Japanese hotpot dishes. *Sakura* means "cherry blossom," but the word is also used to mean "horsemeat." The same is true of *botan*, or "peony," which also can mean "boar meat."

Page 2: Shimo no Hanzo
Shimo no means "the Lower," and in this case refers to Hanzo's geographic location rather than social status.

Page 2: Iga
Iga is a region on the island of Kyushu, and also the name of the famous ninja clan that originated there. Another area famous for its ninja is Kouga, in the Shiga prefecture on Honshu. Many books claim that these two ninja clans were mortal enemies, but in reality inter-ninja relations were not as bad as stories paint them.

Page 18: Ninjutsu
Ninjutsu means the skill or ability of a ninja.

Page 65: Zatoichi
Zatoichi is a famous TV and movie character. He's a blind swordsman who uses his cane as a sword when fighting.

Page 76: Daruma-san ga Koronda
"The Daruma Doll Tripped Over" is a traditional Japanese game that is somewhat similar to "Red Light, Green Light." The person who is "it" will sing a song while looking away, and during the song the other players have to move closer to eventually touch him. *Daruma-san* is a traditional Japanese doll. Its name and shape are based on Bodhidharma, the founder of Zen.

It was tough writing stories about Usagi being tormented and Mamezo being bullied. But now that I read over it again, it is actually very interesting. I've always liked the mother-wife battle in soap operas ever since I was a child, but I never thought I'd be creating a stereotypical story like this myself. The story will probably keep having twists and turns, so please look forward to them.

–Rinko Ueda

Rinko Ueda is from Nara prefecture. She enjoys listening to the radio, drama CDs, and Rakugo comedy performances. Her works include *Ryo*, a series based on the legend of Gojo Bridge, *Home*, a story about love crossing national boundaries, and *Tail of the Moon (Tsuki no Shippo)*, a romantic ninja comedy.

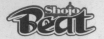

TAIL OF THE MOON

Vol. 5

The Shojo Beat Manga Edition

STORY & ART BY
RINKO UEDA

Translation & Adaptation/Tetsuichiro Miyaki
Touch-up Art & Lettering/Mark McMurray
Design/Izumi Hirayama
Editor/Nancy Thistlethwaite

Managing Editor/Megan Bates
Editorial Director/Elizabeth Kawasaki
Editor in Chief, Books/Alvin Lu
Editor in Chief, Magazines/Marc Weidenbaum
Sr. Director of Acquisitions/Rika Inouye
Sr. VP of Marketing/Liza Coppola
Exec. VP of Sales & Marketing/John Easum
Publisher/Hyoe Narita

Printed in Canada

Published by VIZ Media, LLC
P.O. Box 77064
San Francisco, CA 94107

Shojo Beat Manga Edition
10 9 8 7 6 5 4 3 2 1
First printing, June 2007

www.viz.com

store.viz.com

PARENTAL ADVISORY
TAIL OF THE MOON is rated T+ for Older Teen and is recommended for ages 16 and up. This volume contains brief nudity and ninja violence.

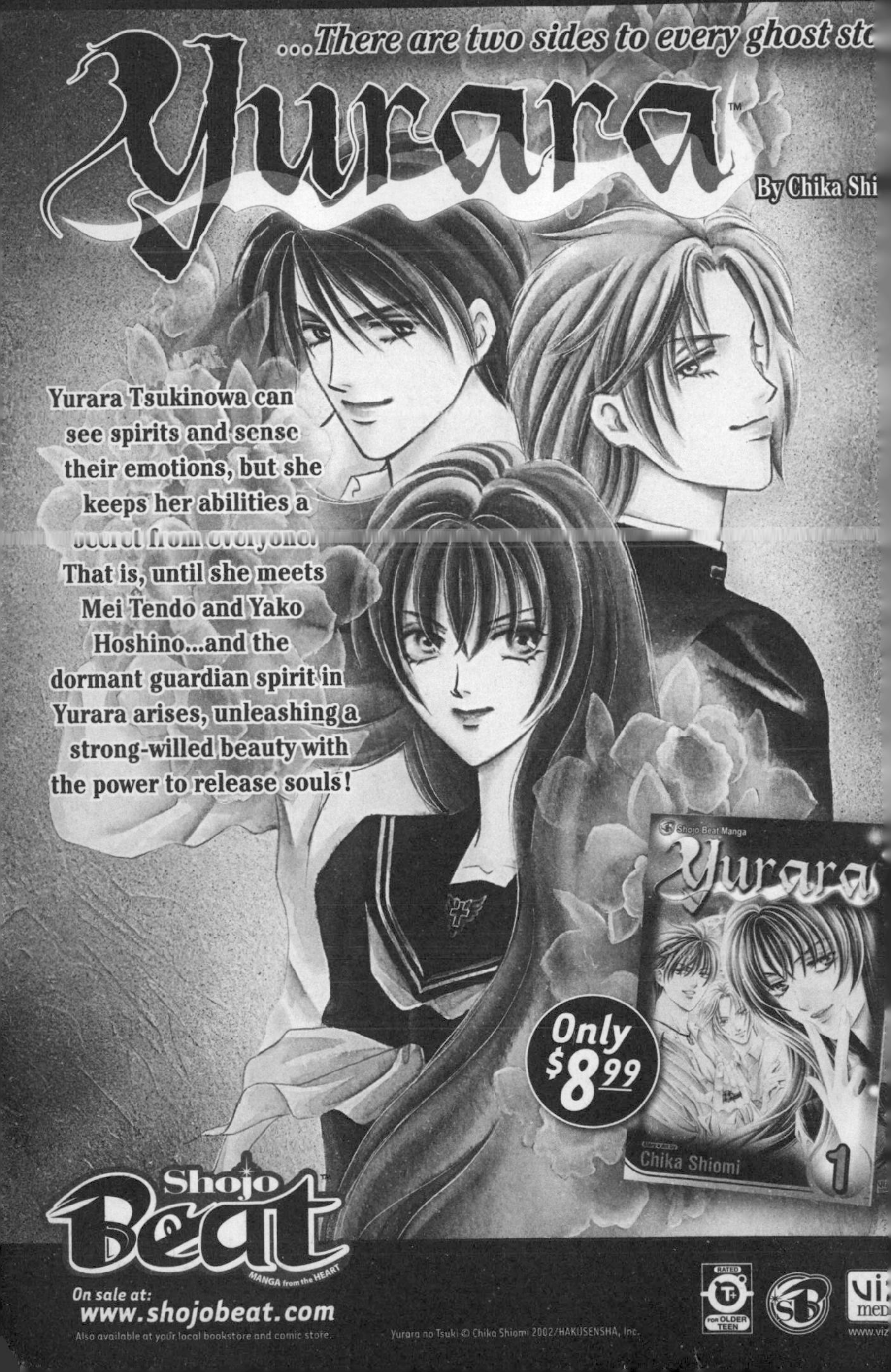

...There are two sides to every ghost sto
Yurara™
By Chika Shi
Yurara Tsukinowa can see spirits and sense their emotions, but she keeps her abilities a
That is, until she meets Mei Tendo and Yako Hoshino...and the dormant guardian spirit in Yurara arises, unleashing a strong-willed beauty with the power to release souls!
Shojo Beat Manga
Yurara
Chika Shiomi
1
Only $8.99
Shojo Beat™
MANGA from the HEART
On sale at:
www.shojobeat.com
Also available at your local bookstore and comic store.
Yurara no Tsuki © Chika Shiomi 2002/HAKUSENSHA, Inc.
RATED T+ FOR OLDER TEEN